Immigration
Made Simple

An Easy-to-Read Guide to the
U.S. Immigration Process

7th Edition

By Barbara Brooks Kimmel
and
Alan M. Lubiner, Esq.

Published by

Next Decade

books that simplify complex subjects

Chester, New Jersey, USA

www.nextdecade.com
info@nextdecade.com

Immigration Made Simple

An Easy-to-Read Guide to the U.S. Immigration Process

by Barbara Brooks Kimmel
and Alan M. Lubiner, Esq.

Copyright ©1990 , 1992 by New Decade Inc.
Copyright ©1996 by Next Decade, Inc.
Copyright ©1998 by Next Decade, Inc.
Copyright ©2000 by Next Decade, Inc.
Copyright ©2003 by Next Decade, Inc.
Copyright ©2006 by Next Decade, Inc.

Printed in the United States of America.

Library of Congress Cataloging-in-Publication Data

Kimmel, Barbara Brooks.
   Immigration made simple : an easy to read guide to the U.S. immigration
process / by Barbara Brooks Kimmel and Alan M. Lubiner.-- 7th ed.
      p. cm.
Includes index.
   ISBN 1-932919-07-4
1. Emigration and immigration law--United States--Popular works. I.
Lubiner, Alan M. II. Title.
   KF4819.6.K56 2006
   342.7308'2--dc22
   2005031202

$22.95 Softcover

Table of Contents

About the Authors

Barbara Kimmel spent over fifteen years employed in the New York area as a relocation consultant to many international corporations and several prominent immigration lawyers. During that time she successfully guided thousands of aliens through the complex immigration process.

In 1990 Barbara began writing and publishing "books that simplify complex subjects". She has written or co-authored seven editions of **Immigration Made Simple**, first published in 1990. Barbara is also the co-author of **Citizenship Made Simple**, first published in 1996. These books have received outstanding professional reviews in ***Library Journal*** and ***Booklist***, and have been Quality Books #1 bestsellers.

Finally, she is the President and Publisher at Next Decade, Inc. in Chester, New Jersey. Barbara's company was named Quality Book's **Publisher of the Year** at the 1997 Book Exposition in Chicago. For more information, visit our web site at www.nextdecade.com.

Ms. Kimmel was awarded a Bachelor of Arts Degree in International Affairs from Lafayette College in Pennsylvania and an MBA from the Bernard M. Baruch Graduate School of Business of the City University of New York.

✳ ✳ ✳

Alan Lubiner has been practicing Immigration Law since 1975. From 1975 until 1981, the Immigration & Naturalization Service employed him in a number of capacities including assisting in the drafting of legislation for the Select Commission on Immigration in Washington, DC. He also spent time in the United States Attorney's Office in the Southern District of Florida where he served as a Special Assistant United States Attorney assigned to special Immigration prosecutions.

In 1981, Mr. Lubiner opened a private law practice, with headquarters in Cranford, New Jersey and specializing in Immigration law. His practice is heavily concentrated in professionals, and he currently represents major corporations, individuals and universities in the scientific field with emphasis on computer science, electrical engineering, chemical engineering, chemistry and pharmaceutical research. He has successfully handled over 1000 cases for foreign students and other individuals.

Mr. Lubiner's credentials include a Bachelor of Science Degree in Finance from New York University and a Juris Doctorate degree from Brooklyn Law School. He is a member of the American Immigration Lawyers Association, an affiliated organization of the American Bar Association, and served on its Board of Governors. He is also a past Chairman of the New Jersey Chapter of the American Immigration Lawyer's Association, and a past chairman of the NJ State Bar Section on Immigration. Mr. Lubiner is a member of the Bar of the States of New Jersey, New York and Pennsylvania and is admitted to practice before the Federal Courts in New Jersey, New York and Pennsylvania, as well as the United States Supreme Court. Finally, he is the co-author of **Immigration Made Simple** and **Citizenship Made Simple**.

*With special thanks to all those who continue to recognize
the importance of this valuable reference book*

✳ ✳ ✳

Disclaimer

The purpose of this book is to provide interested individuals with a basic understanding of the rules and regulations concerning U.S. Immigration procedures. It is sold with the understanding that the publisher and authors are not engaged in rendering legal or other professional services in this book, only in sharing information in regard to the subject matter covered. If legal or other expert assistance is required, the services of a competent professional should be sought.

This book was not written to provide all the information that is available to the authors/and or publisher, but to compliment, amplify and supplement other texts and available information. While every effort has been made to ensure that this book is as complete and accurate as possible, there may be mistakes, either typographical or in content. Therefore, this text should be used as a general guide only, and not as the ultimate source of U.S. Immigration information. Furthermore, this book contains information on U.S. Immigration only up to the printing date. The rules and regulations change frequently.

The authors and Next Decade, Inc. shall not be held liable, nor be responsible to any person or entity with respect to any loss or damage caused, or alleged to be caused, directly or indirectly by the information contained in this book.

If you do not wish to be bound by the above,
you may return this book to the publisher for a full refund.

Preface

The authors have assisted thousands of people from around the world process petitions for temporary and permanent U.S. visas. These individuals included students, trainees, and entry level employees. Others were sophisticated investors and senior executives.

Regardless of their backgrounds, all of the people mentioned above shared one common characteristic. They lacked the necessary knowledge of the U.S. Immigration process. We repeatedly heard the same question. Isn't there a reference book that I can use as a guide in the future, a simple manual that will provide me with a basic understanding of immigration? We could not give them a recommendation that really met those needs, and so in 1990 we published the first edition of **Immigration Made Simple**. Thousands of orders were received from every state in the U.S., and many foreign countries as well, and we were finally able to recommend a book that meets this need!

Over the next several years, many administrative and regulatory changes mandated the publication of several more editions of **Immigration Made Simple**. As we go to press, there are many major areas of our immigration law that are undergoing close scrutiny by our government and various public interest groups.

This revised seventh edition has been updated and covers, in detail, more categories of visas and related matters. **Immigration Made Simple** has, once again, been developed as an easy to use reference for foreign nationals who currently live and work in the United States, and for those wishing to do so in the near future. The book should also continue to be valuable to those who work with foreign students; corporate personnel working with foreign employees; business managers; the legal profession and its support staff; and others who have occasion to work with our U.S. Immigration process.

The order of the subject matter is intended to be useful. We start by defining some frequently used terms. The sections that follow describe the most common categories of temporary and permanent immigration categories, give examples, and explain how to go about obtaining these visas. We have tried to make these sections as easy to understand as possible. This has not been an easy task! The last section of the book will provide the reader with answers to some of the most common immigration questions. At the end of the book, is an updated **Directory of Immigration Lawyers** to assist our readers in locating a qualified attorney. There are also several appendices containing information that we think you will find very helpful.

Keep in mind that this book was not written to give legal advice, recommend solutions to complex immigration problems, or to replace the service of Immigration lawyers. Many topics are not covered, including exclusion and deportation proceedings, political asylum applications and appeal procedures. Our goal in making **Immigration Made Simple** available to you is simply to provide you with a better understanding of the practical side of our immigration system and the options available to you. I hope that the book will serve as a helpful reference guide in the future.

Barbara Brooks Kimmel
Alan M. Lubiner, Attorney

Introduction

The United States has, for generations, been called a "melting pot", a nation of immigrants. For over two hundred years, people from other countries have come to the United States to find safe haven from religious and political persecution, to seek economic opportunity and to reunite with family members. The ethnic and cultural diversity, the brains and talent, as well as the dreams and hopes that immigrants have brought to our country over the years are what have molded our national character and made the United States the super-power that it is today.

In recent years, our immigration policy and our immigrants have come under attack from groups that would have us believe that immigrants are the root of all evil in our society. Major legislation has been proposed with the intention of sealing our borders. Various politicians and special interest groups seek a moratorium on immigration. Over the past several years sweeping changes in our immigration laws have been enacted that severely restrict the ability of our residents and citizens to reunite with their loved ones. Backlogs in quotas and harsh penalties have caused the breakup of families. Husbands are being separated from wives, parents from children, all in the name of "immigration reform".

The reality is that less than one million immigrants arrive in the United States each year. Undocumented immigrants constitute only one percent of the total U.S. population. Most immigrants are coming to join immediate family members, while a relatively small number are coming to jobs where the employer has demonstrated the inability to find U.S. workers.

The extremist groups would have us believe that immigrants take jobs away from Americans. Nothing could be further from the truth. Immigrant entrepreneurial spirit has been the backbone of American industry, and today immigrants are likely to be self-employed and start new businesses.

Politicians, calling for welfare reform and for keeping immigrants off public assistance claim immigrants are a drain on the U.S. economy. Again, rhetoric that has no basis in fact. Immigrants must prove that they have the ability to sustain themselves or they will not be allowed in the U.S. They are barred from any means tested programs for at least two years, and because of recent legislation will be so barred for five years. Their sponsors, who must file an affidavit of support with the U.S. government, are now held to their promise of support by a binding contract.

Immigrants permeate the very fabric of America. They are our parents, grandparents, teachers, friends, doctors, lawyers, sports heroes, actors, cooks, waiters, babysitters, merchants, and yes, even our politicians. They are an integral part of America and what makes the United States the greatest country in the world.

Alan Lubiner
Immigration Attorney and Co-Author

1
Definitions

Citizens of other countries who come to the U.S., and individuals, who have occasion to work with the U.S. visa process, should become familiar with immigration "jargon". You will encounter the following terms frequently, and so it is best to know what they mean before reading further.

- **AC21**—*The American Competitiveness in the 21st Century Act*—Signed into law on October 17, 2000, this law greatly affected the H-1B category, increasing the cap and providing additional benefits to alien workers.

- **ACWIA**—*American Competitiveness and Workforce Improvement Act.*

- **Antiterrorism and Effective Death Penalty Act (AEDPA)**—the Act signed into law by President Clinton on April 24, 1996 included sweeping new reforms, expanding the definition of aggravated felony and severely restricting the ability of an alien to obtain any form of waiver.

- **Alien**—a person who is not a citizen or a national of the U.S. The term refers to all foreign nationals in the U.S., whether they are here temporarily or with permanent resident status. Although the term may seem strange to you, it is frequently used in the immigration field generally and therefore in this book.

- **Asylee**—an alien who is in the U.S., or at a port of entry, who is unable or unwilling to return to his own country because of a well-founded fear of persecution.

- **Beneficiary**—an alien who is the recipient of an application or petition filed on his/her behalf by another individual or organization.

- **Citizen**—a person who owes their loyalty to, either through birth or naturalization, the protection of a given country. A permanent resident of the United States is not a United States citizen.

■ ***CBP***—*Customs and Border Patrol*—one of the three agencies created by the breakup of the former Immigration and Naturalization Service. CBP is responsible for the protection of our borders including the control of goods as well as people. It is an agency within the Department of Homeland Security.

■ ***CSPA***—*Child Status Protection Act*—The Act that gives a benefit to children who otherwise would have failed to qualify for benefits or "aged out" due to the delays in processing by USCIS.

■ ***Dependent***—the spouse, or unmarried dependent children under age 21.

■ ***Employer Sanctions***—the Immigration Reform and Control Act of 1986 prohibits employers from hiring, recruiting, or referring (for a fee) aliens who are known to be unauthorized to work in the U.S.

■ ***Fiscal Year***—the fiscal year for the USCIS covers the twelve-month period from October 1 through September 30.

■ ***Form I-9***—*Employment Eligibility Verification*—an employment form that must be completed by every employer and employee to verify the employee's identity and right to work in the U.S.

■ ***Form I-94***—*Arrival and Departure Record*—a document that is issued to every alien who enters the United States for a temporary stay and who is officially inspected by a U.S. Immigration Officer. This document is stapled in the passport and indicates the amount of time the individual can initially remain in the United States. Form I-94W will be issued to individuals entering the U.S. under the Visa Waiver Pilot Program.

■ ***Green Card***—a slang term for the identity document or alien registration receipt card issued to permanent resident (immigrant) aliens. The card includes the alien's photograph, fingerprint and signature. At one time the Form I-551 identity card was green, which is how it derived its name.

■ ***Illegal Immigration Reform and Immigrant Responsibility Act of 1996 (IIRAIRA)***—the Act signed into law by President Clinton that became effective on April 1, 1997. It made extensive changes to the immigration laws affecting the arrival of aliens, their treatment by the Immigration Court, and available forms of relief.

■ ***Immediate Relatives***—those immigrants who are exempt from the numerical limitations of immigration to the U.S. They are: spouses of U.S. citizens, children (under age 21) of U.S. citizens, and parents of U.S. citizens age 21 or older.

■ ***Immigrant***—an alien who comes to the United States to live permanently.

■ ***Immigration Act of 1990 (IMMACT 90)***—the Act signed into law by President Bush on November 29, 1990. It represents the most extensive change in all areas of immigration in over fifty years.

■ ***ICE***—*Immigration and Customs Enforcement*—one of the three agencies created by the breakup of the former Immigration and Naturalization Service. ICE is responsible for enforcement functions for the Department of Homeland Security.

■ ***INFOPASS***—The system to get an appointment to speak to an officer of the USCIS at one of the District Offices.

■ ***NAFTA***—*North American Free Trade Agreement*, approved by Congress in 1993. The Agreement liberalizes trade between the United States, Canada and Mexico, and contains immigration provisions described in Chapter 6.

■ ***Nationality***—the country of a person's citizenship.

■ ***Naturalization***—a process by which permanent resident aliens can convert their status to U.S. citizenship. Naturalization permits the individual to obtain a U.S. passport and to vote in U.S. elections.

■ ***Nonimmigrant***—an alien who comes to the U.S. for a temporary stay.

■ ***Passport***—a document issued by a government that identifies the holder and his citizenship, and permits that individual to travel abroad.

■ ***PATRIOT ACT***—In the wake of the terrorist attacks on the World Trade Center and the Pentagon on September 11, 2001, Congress passed the Uniting and Strengthening America by Providing Appropriate Tools Required to Intercept and Obstruct Terrorism Act of 2001 (USA PATRIOT Act)-This gives law enforcement broad powers to control and monitor the entry and exit of persons to and from the United States and to investigate and prosecute violators in the name of National Security.

■ ***PERM***—The new permanent foreign labor certification program that went into effect on March 28, 2005.

■ ***Permanent Resident***—a person who has the right to live permanently in the U.S. Individuals are given alien registration cards upon approval of their application for permanent residence and are thereafter called permanent resident aliens. Immigrant is another name for permanent resident alien. A permanent resident is not a U.S. citizen.

■ ***Petitioner***—the employer or individual that is filing a petition on behalf of an alien.

■ ***Port of Entry***—a port or place where an alien may apply for admission into the U.S.

■ ***Preinspection***—immigration inspections of air travel passengers before departing from the foreign country. This alleviates the need for further immigration inspection upon arrival in the U.S.

■ ***Quota Systems***—Established by the U.S. Congress, the system under which a limited number of immigrant visas are issued each year.

■ ***Stateless***—a person who has no nationality.

■ ***United States Embassy or Consulate***—U.S. foreign headquarters of the U.S. Ambassador/Consul, and his or her staff. These offices, which are located in most countries, have many departments, including a visa section that processes temporary and permanent visas for foreigners coming to the U.S.

■ ***USCIS***—*U.S. Citizenship and Immigration Services*—one of the three agencies created by the breakup of the former Immigration and Naturalization Service. USCIS is responsible for adjudication functions within the Department of Homeland Security.

■ ***Visa***—the document needed for entry into the U.S. Individuals planning to travel to the U.S. from many countries as nonimmigrants (for a temporary stay) must apply for entry permission at an American Consulate outside the U.S. A stamp (visa) placed in his or her passport permits that individual to board a carrier to the U.S. The stamp contains the visa category, a visa number, the location and date that it was issued, the number of entries into the United States for which it can be used, and the expiration date.

2

Temporary Visas

The U.S. immigration system is divided into two groups, nonimmigrant and immigrant. Nonimmigrant categories are for individuals who wish to come to the U.S. for a temporary stay, for vacation, to attend school, or for temporary employment. Immigrant categories are for those who wish to live permanently in the U.S.

This chapter covers temporary or nonimmigrant visa categories. It first explains each nonimmigrant classification, then describes processing procedures, and the documents that are required in order to apply for these visas. The reference chart at the end of the chapter lists all of the nonimmigrant visas, and indicates to whom they apply.

CATEGORIES OF TEMPORARY OR NONIMMIGRANT VISAS

Nonimmigrant visas are issued to individuals who wish to enter the United States for a temporary period of time ranging from one day to several years. In most cases, an individual must establish that he or she has a residence in his home country that will not be abandoned. Some people may be eligible for many different types of visas, while others may not qualify at all. There is a long list of reasons why certain individuals cannot be admitted into the U.S. Examples of such reasons are certain mental or physical disorders, criminal convictions, drug or alcohol addiction, prostitution, etc. Waivers are available in some cases. Further information should be obtained from a knowledgeable professional.

A-1, A-2, A-3. Foreign Government Officials

"A" visas are granted to foreign government officials, their families and servants. This includes ambassadors, public ministers, diplomats or consular officers who are assigned to represent their country in the U.S. The processing of these visas is usually handled directly by the sponsoring organization.

B-1. Temporary Business Visitor

B-1 visas are granted to foreign business people coming to the U.S. for their foreign employer. They are also issued to self-employed individuals who need to conduct business, such as attending meetings or conferences, meeting customers, or negotiating contracts. The alien must continue to be paid by the foreign employer, and must maintain a residence abroad that he or she has no intention of abandoning. The B-1 visa holder cannot be employed in the United States or earn money directly from U.S. sources.

In some countries the American Consulate will issue a multiple entry B-1 visa so that the alien may enter the U.S several times using the same visa. In other countries, only a single entry visa will be issued. The validity date of the visa will vary depending upon the country in which the visa is issued. Upon entry into the U.S., the B-1 visitor is usually admitted for the length of time need to complete the purpose of the trip, generally for three months, but not exceeding six months.

The visa application is made to the appropriate American Consulate abroad. It consists of:

1. **DS-156**—*Nonimmigrant Visa Application*

2. **DS-157**—*Supplemental Nonimmigrant Visa Application*—for all male applicants between the ages of 16 and 45 and for all visa applicants, male or female, with travel documents or passports issued by North Korea, Cuba, Syria, Sudan, Iran, Iraq, and Libya.

3. Passport photograph

4. Letter from foreign employer explaining the reason for the visit to the United States

5. Valid passport or travel document

6. $100.00 nonimmigrant visa application fee

7. Visa issuance fee—consult visa reciprocity table which can be found on the internet at: http://travel.state.gov/visa/reciprocity/index.htm

B-2. Temporary Visitor for Pleasure

B-2 visas are issued to people coming to the U.S. to visit friends or relatives, to vacation or to accompany a B-1 visa holder as described above.

In most cases, the American Consulate will require evidence of the nature of the trip, as well as proof that the applicant intends to return to the home country. Sometimes an invitation from a friend or relative in the U.S., proof of residence and employment abroad, and other evidence of permanent ties outside the U.S.

can help to establish the "intention to return". The applicant should also provide a round-trip airline ticket, and proof that he or she has enough money available for the duration of the trip, such as bank statements or credit cards. The B-2 visa can be issued for multiple trips.

Upon entry to the U.S., the alien is generally admitted for six months.

The application must be made at an American Consulate. It consists of:

1. ***DS-156***—*Nonimmigrant Visa Application*
2. ***DS-157***—*Supplemental Nonimmigrant Visa Application*
3. Passport Photograph
4. Valid passport or travel document
5. $100.00 nonimmigrant visa application fee
6. Visa issuance fee—consult visa reciprocity table which can be found on the internet at:
   http://travel.state.gov/visa/reciprocity/index.htm

If the applicant is traveling to the U.S. to obtain medical treatment, they should also present:

1. Medical diagnosis from a local physician, explaining the nature of the ailment and the reason the applicant requires treatment in the United States.
2. Letter from a physician or medical facility in the United States, expressing a willingness to treat this specific ailment and detailing the proposed medical treatment as well as the projected length and cost of treatment (including doctors' fees, hospitalization fees, and all medical-related expenses).
3. Statement of financial responsibility from the individuals or organization which will pay for the patient's transportation, medical and living expenses. The individuals guaranteeing payment of these expenses must provide proof of ability to do so, often in the form of bank or other statements of income/savings or certified copies of income tax returns.

B-2 visas may also be issued to those persons who intend to be bona fide students in the United States but have not yet selected a school. The Consular Officer must be informed of the prospective student's intent and will mark the visa with the notation: ``Prospective Student; school not yet selected.'' Once the student enters the United States and is accepted into a school, he or she can then make an application to change status. However the student cannot start classes until the application for change of status has been approved.

If a visitor can show a good reason for needing to stay in the U.S. beyond the initial six months, the alien can apply for one six month extension. The application is filed with the USCIS Service Center having jurisdiction over the applicant's temporary residence in the U.S. It consists of:

1. *Form I-539—Application to Extend/Change Nonimmigrant Status*

2. Letter of explanation and any documentation in support of the extension request showing why it is requested

3. Copy of return transportation ticket

4. Proof of ability to maintain oneself financially, or an affidavit of support

4. Copy of *Form I-94*

5. Filing fee of $200.00.

Chapter 3 covers the "Visa Waiver Pilot Program", which allows citizens from many countries to travel to the U.S. as business or pleasure visitors without having to apply for a B-1 or B-2 visa at an American Consulate.

C. Transit Visas and Transit Without Visa

"C" visas are transit visas. People use them who are traveling through the U.S. to a final destination outside the U.S. Those admitted in "C" status may remain in the U.S. for a maximum of twenty-nine days. A "transit" alien may not apply for change of status to any other nonimmigrant category except "G", and may not apply for an extension of temporary stay.

Some people who are in transit through the U.S. do not have visas. Transit without visa or TWOV is reserved for those who are applying for admission to the U.S. to travel on to another country. Someone flying into the U.S. who has a confirmed reservation, within a specified time period, to catch a connecting flight to another country will be admitted as TWOV. Aliens in TWOV status are not permitted to leave the airline terminal. Application for TWOV status can only be made at certain designated U.S. ports of entry.

D. Crewmen of Aircraft or Sea Vessels

Aliens who are applying for admission into the U.S. as members of a foreign vessel's crew such as flight attendants on foreign owned airlines or crewmen on foreign owned ships use this visa. Usually the foreign vessel personnel will make the arrangements for "D" visa issuance. Many crewmen have both "C" and "D" visas. They use the "C" visas for the purpose of entering the U.S. to "join" their vessel. There is no derivative classification for the spouse or children of crewmen. They are classified as B-2 visitors if coming solely to the U.S. to accompany the principal alien.

E-1 & E-2. Treaty Trader or Investor

E-1 visas are available to Treaty Traders, while E-2 visas are available to Treaty Investors. Both categories require that the United States maintain treaties of commerce and navigation with the foreign country, allowing for trade and/or investment in the United States. Aliens applying for either type of "E" visa must have the same citizenship of the country that maintains the treaty with the United States. The following is a current list of countries that have such treaties. Countries followed by one asterisk (*) have treaty trader provisions, allowing only for issuance of E-1 visas. Countries followed by two asterisks (**) have treaty investor provisions, allowing only for issuance of E-2 visas. Countries with no asterisk(s) maintain both treaty trader and treaty investor provisions, and issue both types of visas.

Albania **	Costa Rica
Argentina	Czech Republic **
Armenia **	Democratic Republic of Congo
Australia	(Kinshasa)
Austria	Denmark *
Bangladesh **	Ecuador**
Belgium	Egypt **
Bolivia *	Estonia
Brunei * (Borneo)	Ethiopia
Bulgaria **	Finland
Cameroon **	France
Canada	Georgia**
Chile	Germany
China (Taiwan)	Greece *
Colombia	Grenada **
(Republic of)The Congo (Brazzaville) **	Honduras

Iran (may be affected by embargo)	Pakistan
Ireland	Panama**
Israel *	Paraguay
Italy	Philippines
Jamaica**	Poland*
Japan	Romania**
Jordan	Senegal**
Kazakhstan **	Singapore
Korea	Slovak Republic**
Kyrgyzstan**	Suriname
Latvia**	Sweden
Liberia	Switzerland
Lithuania**	Thailand
Luxembourg	Togo
Mexico	Trinidad & Tobago**
Moldova**	Tunisia**
Mongolia**	Turkey
Morocco**	Ukraine**
Netherlands	United Kingdom
Norway	Yugoslavia
Oman	

Bilateral investment treaties will soon authorize E-2 status for nationals of Azerbaijan, Belarus, Croatia, Estonia, Nicaragua, Russia, and Uzbekistan. Once ratified by the U.S. and each country involved, these treaties should take effect about thirty days after the countries exchange instruments of ratification.

1) Treaty Traders

Treaty traders enter the United States for the sole purpose of carrying on substantial trade. Many are self-employed people whose trade with the U.S. accounts for more than 50% of their total volume of trade. The definition of "trade" has been expanded over the years to encompass not only goods and services, but also trade in technology. The treaty trader may also be an employee of a company that qualifies for treaty trader status, but the employment must be in a position that is either executive or supervisory in nature, or one involving essential skills.

2) Treaty Investors

Treaty investors enter the United States to make a substantial investment in a U.S. business, and to direct and develop the business. There is no specific dollar amount needed to qualify for this type of visa. The investment must, however, be substantial in terms of the total investment in the enterprise. The investment must be in a business that generates active income, rather than passive income such as rental property, and the business must be at least 50% owned by nationals of the treaty country, (that being the same country of nationality as the alien investor). Treaty investors may also be employees of a company that qualifies for treaty investor status, but like the treaty trader, the employment must be in a position that is either executive or supervisory, or one that involves essential skills.

Rules involving "E" visas are very complex, and there are ramifications of some treaties, including certain rules under NAFTA (the North American Free Trade Agreement) that affect the procedures for entry into the United States. (See Chapter 6). Those seeking "E" visa status should speak with an experienced immigration practitioner.

F-1. Student

F-1 visas are available to aliens coming temporarily to the United States to attend school. The applicant must plan to pursue a full time program of academic study at an educational institution that is authorized by the USCIS to enroll foreign students. The student must have a home in a foreign country to which he or she will return after completion of studies. In addition, he or she must be proficient in the English language, and have sufficient funds available for his or her support during studies in the U.S.

F-1 status is not available to an alien who seeks to attend a public elementary school or a public adult education program. Entry into the U.S. to attend a public secondary school is also prohibited unless the total period in F-1 status does not exceed one year, and the alien reimburses the school for the costs of providing education. Any alien who violates this provision is barred from admission to the United States for a period of five years.

The visa application consists of:

1. *Form 156—Nonimmigrant Visa Application*

2. *Form 157—Supplemental Nonimmigrant Visa Application*

3. *Form I-20 A-B/I-20ID—Certificate of Eligibility of Nonimmigrant (F-1) Student Status—*for Academic and Language Students-issued by the sponsoring school

4. Passport photographs

list continued on the next page

5. Proof that the applicant has enough money to pay all school related expenses and to support himself or herself during the program, as indicated on Form I-20A-B/I-20ID

6. Proof that the applicant has a home abroad that is not being abandoned, and that the student plans to leave the U.S. when the program is completed

7. Valid passport or travel document.

8. Application fee if required

Note: Students who have not yet made a final decision on the school they wish to attend, and want to come to the U.S. to visit schools in order to make a final selection, may apply for a "B-2" visitor's visa. The applicant must disclose the reason for his/her trip to the American Consul. The Consular Officer will note "prospective student" on the visa. After entry to the U.S., prospective students must apply to the USCIS for a change of visa status when they have made their final school selection, and have been accepted by the school.

Qualified students who wish to enter the U.S. more than ninety days before their school's starting date, can apply for a B-2 visa with the understanding that they will file with the USCIS to change to F-1 status prior to commencing studies.

Note of caution: *In the above instances, after approval of a change of status, the student will not have a student visa, only student status in the U.S. If the student leaves the U.S., he or she must apply for an F-1 visa at an American Consulate before reentering the U.S. as a student.*

The visa is usually granted for the period of time in which the student is pursuing a full time course of study, including engaging in practical training, plus sixty days to prepare for departure from the U.S. This is referred to as "duration of status" or "D/S". The American Consular Official will sometimes write the school's name on the visa. The I-20A-B/I-20ID should be returned to the student, who should subsequently present it to the USCIS official at the point of entry into the U.S. The USCIS officer will then issue Form I-94, write the admission number from Form I-94 on Form I-20, and return the "student part" of Form I-20 (I-20ID). The USCIS will then forward the school's copy of Form I-20 to the USCIS processing center, which will then send it back to the school as evidence of the student's admission in F-1 status.

Under normal conditions, the student is not required to apply for extension of stay in the U.S., as long as he or she is a full time student, and will complete the course of study within the time indicated on Form I-20. Spouses and minor children can be granted F-2 visas, which are not valid for employment.

Students who will remain in one educational level for an extended period of time, or remain in student status for eight consecutive years should check with the Designated School Official (DSO) about extending their stay.

A student who is in F-1 status can leave the U.S. for up to five months and be readmitted in student status as long as he or she has:

1. A current I-20ID endorsed by the Designated School Official (DSO), who is often the Foreign Student Adviser, or

2. A new Form I-20A-B if the student's program is changing (such as a change in major, advancement to a higher level of study, or an intended school transfer)

3. A valid student visa and a passport valid for at least six months.

The Student and Exchange Visitor Information System (SEVIS) was implemented after the September, 2001 terrorist attacks as part of the government's effort to restore integrity to the nation's immigration system. SEVIS is a web-based program that maintains information on international students (F/M visas) and exchange visitors (J visas) and their dependents residing in the United States. It is administered by U.S. Immigration and Customs Enforcement's (ICE) Student Exchange and Visitor Program (SEVP) and used by U.S. Customs and Border Protection (CBP) Officers at ports of entry. SEVIS has simplified what was once a manual process, resulting in more accurate and timely data, faster processing and fewer delays.

Prior to SEVIS, school recordkeeping of students was very haphazard. Schools now adhere strictly to requirements, and USCIS will be notified immediately if a student violates his or her status. Regulations require an approved school to keep records containing the following information and documents relating to each F-1 student attending the school

Name; date and place of birth; country of citizenship; current address; status-full or part time; date of commencement of studies; degree program and field of study; whether the student has been certified for practical training, and the beginning and end dates of certification; termination date and reason, if known;

the documents required for issuance of a certificate of eligibility; the number of credits completed each semester; a photocopy of the student's I-20 ID copy.

An immigration officer may request any, or all, of the above data on any individual student or class of students upon notice. In addition, the DHS (Division of Homeland Security) periodically (but not more frequently than once a term) sends each approved school a list of all F-1 students shown by government records to be attending the school. The DSO (designated school official) must note the status and current addresses of all listed F-1 students, as well as the names, addresses and identifying information in regard to F-1 students not listed by the DHS. If a student does not have an electronic record in SEVIS, the DHS will notify the school if the student enters the United States to attend their institution. If the student fails to register, the school must notify the government no later than 30 days following the deadline for registering for classes.

The government has created two classes of schools under SEVIS, non-SEVIS schools and SEVIS schools. The difference between these classes is beyond the scope of this book and the school will be able to tell the student under which classification they fall.

Students pursuing a full time course of study may transfer from one school to another within the United States without prior USCIS approval, however, the following rules apply:

■ ***Non-SEVIS school to non-SEVIS school***—the student must first notify the school that he or she is currently attending of the intent to transfer, then obtain a Form I-20. Before issuance of any Form I-20, the DSO at the transfer school must verify that the student has been maintaining status. The transfer will be affected only if the student completes the Student Certification portion of the Form I-20 and returns the form to a DSO of the transfer school within 15 days of the program start date listed on Form I-20. Upon receipt of the student's Form I-20 the DSO must note the ``transfer completed" date in the space provided for DSO's remarks. This acknowledges the student's attendance at the transfer school. The DSO must return Form I-20 to the student and submit the school copy of Form I-20 to the DHS within 30 days of receipt from the student. The DSO must then forward a photocopy of the school copy to the school from which the student transferred.

■ ***Non-SEVIS school to SEVIS school***—To transfer from a non-SEVIS school to a SEVIS school, the student must first notify the school he is attending of the intent to transfer, then obtain a SEVIS Form I-20 from the school to which he or she intends to transfer. Before issuance of any Form I-20, the DSO at the transfer school must determine that the student has been maintaining status at his current school and is eligible for transfer to the new school. Once the transfer school has issued the SEVIS Form I-20 to the student indicating a transfer, the transfer school must update and maintain the student's record in SEVIS. The student is then required to notify the DSO at the transfer school within 15 days of the program start date listed on SEVIS Form I-20. Upon notification that the student is enrolled in classes, the DSO of the transfer school must update SEVIS to reflect the student's registration and current address. This acknowledges that the student has completed the transfer process. In the remarks section of the student's SEVIS Form I-20, the DSO must note that the transfer has been completed, including the date, and return the form to the student. The transfer is affected when the transfer school updates SEVIS indicating that the student has registered in classes within 30 days.

■ *SEVIS school to SEVIS school*—The student must first notify his or her current school of the intent to transfer and must indicate the school to which he intends to transfer. Upon notification by the student, the current school will update the student's record in SEVIS as a ``transfer out'' and indicate the school to which the student intends to transfer, and a release date. The current school will retain control over the student's record in SEVIS until the student completes the current term or reaches the release date. At the request of the student, the DSO of the current school may cancel the transfer request at any time before the release date. As of the release date specified by the current DSO, the transfer school will be granted full access to the student's SEVIS record and then becomes responsible for that student. After the release date, the transfer DSO must complete the transfer of the student's record in SEVIS and may issue a SEVIS Form I-20. The student is then required to contact the DSO at the transfer school within 15 days of the program start date listed on the SEVIS Form I-20. Upon notification that the student is enrolled in classes, the DSO of the transfer school must update SEVIS to reflect the student's registration and current address. This acknowledges that the student has completed the transfer process. The DSO must note on Form I-20 that the transfer has been completed, including the date, and return the form to the student. The transfer is affected when the transfer school notifies SEVIS that the student has enrolled in classes within 30 days.

■ *SEVIS school to non-SEVIS school*—The student must first notify his or her current school of the intent to transfer and must indicate the school to which he or she intends to transfer. Upon notification by the student, the current school will update the student's status in SEVIS as "a transfer out", enter a "release" or expected transfer date, and update the transfer school as "non-SEVIS." The student must then notify the school to which the he or she intends to transfer of his or her intent to enroll. After the student has completed his or her current term or session, or has reached the expected transfer date, the DSO at the current school will no longer have full access to the student's SEVIS record. At this point, if the student has notified the transfer school of his or her intent to transfer, and the transfer school has determined that the student has been maintaining status at his or her current school, the transfer school may issue the student a Form I-20. The transfer will be affected only if the student completes the student certification portion of the Form I-20 and returns the form to a DSO of the transfer school within 15 days of the program start date listed on Form I-20. Upon receipt of the student's Form I-20 the DSO must note "transfer completed on (date)" in the space provided for the DSO's remarks. This acknowledges the student's attendance. The DSO must return the Form I-20 to the student and submit the school copy of the Form I-20 to the DHS within 30 days of receipt from the student. The DSO must then forward a photocopy of the school copy to the school from which the student transferred.

Generally, foreign students are not allowed to work in the United States. As noted earlier, one of the requirements for a student visa is that the student proves that enough funds are available to pay for his or her education and support for the duration of studies. However, there are five ways that students can work while in F-1 status. They are:

1. **On campus employment**

2. **Practical training**—includes curricular practical training and optional practical training before or after completion of studies

3. **Off campus employment due to severe economic hardship**

4. **International organization internships**

5. **Special student relief**

1. **On campus employment**—this applies to students who will work in an on-campus establishment such as the cafeteria or bookstore. It may also apply to "off campus" sites which are "affiliated educationally" with the school. The employment must be an "integral part" of the educational program, and cannot exceed twenty hours per week while school is in session. Full time, on campus employment is allowed during summer vacations and holidays when school is not open.

2. Practical training—this is divided into two categories:

A. Curricular Practical Training:

This applies to training as part of an established curriculum during the student's regular course of study. It includes work/study programs, cooperative educational programs, or internships offered by employers through agreements with the school. In order to qualify for curricular practical training, the student must have been lawfully enrolled in school, on a full-time basis, for at least nine consecutive months (exception for students of some graduate study programs who require immediate curricular practical training). The position must be directly related to the student's major field of study.

The application is made as follows:

✓ Student submits Form I-538 and I-20ID to the DSO

✓ DSO certifies the curricular practical training on Form I-538, and on Form I-20ID the DSO certifies the dates and location of the student's curricular practical training

✓ DSO signs and dates the I-20ID and returns it to the student

✓ DSO sends the school certification on Form I-538 to the USCIS data processing center.

Note: Students who have participated in one year or more of full-time curricular practical training may not participate in practical training after completion of their course of study.

B. Optional Practical Training (either before or after completion of studies):

Optional practical training can only be authorized in an occupation that is directly related to the student's major. A student may qualify after he or she has been lawfully enrolled in school, on a full time basis, for at least nine consecutive months. The period of optional practical training, both before and after studies, cannot exceed twelve months. Optional practical training is available during the following four periods:

1. During vacation periods while school is not in session, if the student is currently enrolled and intends to register for the next term

2. While school is in session, not to exceed twenty hours per week

3. After completion of all course requirements

4. After completion of the entire course of study.

All optional practical training must be completed within fourteen months after the completion of study. This application is made as follows:

✓ Student submits Form I-538 and I-20ID to the DSO

✓ DSO certifies on Form I-538 that the employment is directly related to the student's area of study and within his or her educational level

✓ DSO signs and dates the I-20ID to show that the training is recommended, indicates dates of practical training and whether full or part-time, and returns the I-20ID to the student

✓ DSO sends the school certification on Form I-538 to the USCIS data processing center.

The student must then apply to the USCIS office for an employment authorization document (EAD) by submitting the following:

1. Form I-765-Application for Employment Authorization

2. Form I-20ID - endorsed by the DSO

3. Applicable filing fee

4. Copy of Form I-94

5. (Some USCIS offices need a special fingerprint card and photos).

Note: Some USCIS offices require that applications be mailed while others accept in-person applications.

Once the application for optional practical training has been approved, the USCIS will return Form I-20ID and issue an Employment Authorization Document (EAD). The student cannot commence employment until the EAD is received. The USCIS hopes to be able to approve these applications very quickly. Again, training must be completed within fourteen months of finishing studies.

Note: Students in English language training programs are ineligible for practical training.

3) Off-campus employment due to severe economic hardship—A student can apply for part-time (no more than twenty hours per week while school is in session) off-campus employment after having been in good academic standing for at least one year. The request must be based upon severe economic hardship, caused by unforeseen circumstances beyond the student's control. Examples include: loss of financial aid, loss of on-campus employment, substantial fluctuations in the value of currency, inordinate increases in tuition and/or living expenses, unexpected changes in the financial condition of the student's source of support, or unexpected medical bills.

The student must first make a good faith effort to obtain on-campus or off-campus employment under the Pilot Off-Campus Employment Program. The procedure for obtaining work authorization is as follows:

- ✓ Student completes his or her portion of Form I-538 and submits it with the I-20ID to the DSO

- ✓ DSO certifies on Form I-538 that the off-campus employment is warranted and submits Form I-538 to the USCIS data processing center

- ✓ Student submits Form I-765, the I-20ID, Form I-94, a special fingerprint card, two photographs, the required fee, and evidence in support of the application to the USCIS service center having jurisdiction over his place of residence

- ✓ If granted, the Employment Authorization Document will be issued for one-year intervals up to the date the student is expected to complete studies, as long as the student maintains status, and is in good academic standing. The student may not begin work until the EAD has been issued.

4) International Organization Internships—International organizations falling under the International Organizations Immunities Act can employ full-time F-1 students. The procedure is as follows:

- ✓ Student files Form I-765, in-person, with the USCIS office having jurisdiction over the student's place of residence. A filing fee of $100.00 must accompany the application. The application must include an I-20ID endorsed for reentry by the DSO within 30 days preceding the filing of the application, and an I-538 prepared by the DSO. A copy of the I-538 is sent to the USCIS data processing center. The International Organization certifies that the proposed employment is within the scope of the organization's sponsorship.

5) Special Student Relief—In 1998, the USCIS gave itself the authority to suspend its employment authorization requirements in emergencies. The USCIS applied this rule to certain students who were in F-1 status as of June 10, 1998, and whose financial support came from Indonesia, South Korea, Malaysia, Thailand or the Philippines, and who faced severe economic hardship due to rapid currency devaluation. If the economic crises in these countries have caused severe economic hardship, these students can work either on or off-campus.

This "special student relief" program is in effect indefinitely. Eligibility depends on the source of financial support, not the student's citizenship. The regulations apply only to undergraduate and graduate students. F-1 students in non-degree or language programs are not eligible. The twenty-hour per week limit for on-campus employment does not apply. Please note that the USCIS has not yet announced the procedures with which F-1 students must comply, once the relief program is rescinded.

Note: Those who qualify for "special student relief" and plan to travel outside the U.S. may have a problem obtaining a new F-1 visa.

There are two other types of visas for students, the M-1 and the J-1, which are discussed in this chapter. The requirements and regulations are different for each one. Make sure you choose the student status that will offer you the most benefits.

G-1 thru G-5. Representatives to International Organizations

Similar to "A" visas, "G" visas are issued to representatives of international organizations like the United Nations and World Bank, as well as missions. Family members, staff and servants are also eligible for this category. The application is usually handled directly by the sponsoring organization.

H. Temporary Worker

This is a very broad visa category and covers several different types of temporary workers including: aliens in specialty occupations; farm workers and other temporary nonagricultural workers; trainees; and family members of "H" visa holders. The categories will be described in numerical order.

H-1A. Nurses

This visa was previously available to foreign nurses. It became available in December 1989, because of a shortage of qualified nurses in the U.S. In addition to separating nurses into their own "H" category, the Immigration Nursing Relief Act of 1989 (INRA) also provided for certain nurses already in the U.S. to convert to permanent residence. Finally, INRA set up a five-year program, commencing September 1, 1990, where the petitioning health-care facility provided certain documentation to the Department of Labor. This program expired on September 1, 1995. After September 1, 1995 nurses already in H-1A status were permitted to remain in that status and extend their stay to a maximum of six years. Nurses applying after September 1, 1995 are now included in the H-1B category, and must meet all H-1B criteria to be eligible. In addition, all nurses must obtain certification from the Commission on Graduates of Foreign Nursing Schools, the CGFNS, and a Visa Screen Certificate.

H-1B. Aliens in Specialty Occupations

"Aliens in specialty occupations" (professionals) who have a temporary job offer in the U.S. may be eligible for H-1B classification. Note that artists and entertainers were removed from this category under the Immigration Act of 1990. There is a numerical ceiling of 65,000 annual H-1B petitions, although there are some exceptions to this cap.

The maximum period of stay in H-1B status is six years. However, under AC21, certain H-1B status holders reaching the six year limit, who are the beneficiaries of pending or approved Labor Certifications or I-140's (for permanent residence) may receive extensions of H-1B status beyond the six year limit. It is important to consult with an Immigration lawyer well in advance of the expiration of your status to see what options for extension might be available.

The USCIS definition of "specialty occupation" is: "one that requires theoretical and practical application of a body of highly specialized knowledge; and the attainment of a bachelor's degree or higher in the specific specialty as the minimum for entry into the occupation in the U.S."

As indicated above, prospective H-1B employers are required to file Form ETA-9035 "Labor Condition Application for H-1B Nonimmigrants", with the Employment and Training Administration of the U.S. Department of Labor.

The USCIS regulations require the employer to prove the following:

    ✓ That H-1B nonimmigrants and other workers in similar jobs will be paid the actual wage for the occupation at the place of employment, or the prevailing wage level for the occupation in that geographic area, whichever is higher. The employer must use either a State Employment Service (SESA) determination or a wage survey, and indicate the source of the prevailing wage information

✓ That the employment of H-1B workers will not impact adversely on the working conditions of other people similarly employed in that geographic area

✓ That there is no strike, lockout or work stoppage in the occupation at the place of intended employment

✓ That notice of the filing of the H-1B application has been given to workers at the place of intended employment through a bargaining representative, or if not applicable, through a posted notice of the filing at the place of intended employment.

The company that is offering the temporary employment must first file a visa petition with the Regional USCIS Service Center in the U.S. The application consists of:

1. An approved Labor Condition Application from the Department of Labor

2. Form I-129-Petition for a Nonimmigrant Worker

3. Form I-129H and Form I-129W (supplements to Form I-129)

4. Proof of the alien's academic qualifications and professional experience-university degrees, letters of reference, etc.

5. A letter from the company describing the company, the temporary job to be filled, including why it requires at least a bachelor's degree, and why the alien is particularly qualified, as well as a statement that the employer will pay for the alien's return trip abroad if the employment is terminated before the authorized stay expires

6. Filing fee of $190.00

7. ACWIA fee of $1500.00 or $750.00

8. Fraud Fee of $500.00

Note: AC 21 also created an additional fee to fund education, training and scholarship programs for U.S. workers (the American Competitive and Workforce Improvement Act fee- ACWIA). Employers are responsible for paying this fee, and cannot request payment or seek reimbursement from *employees. The ACWIA fee is currently $1500.00 for employers of 25 or more full-time employees and $750.00 for those who employ less than 25. Some petitioners are exempt from the ACWIA fee. There is also a new Fraud Prevention and Detection Fee of $500.00 which must be paid by employers who are seeking a beneficiary's initial grant of H-1B status, or seeking to change a beneficiary's employer. It is best to consult with an experienced Immigration professional to determine the proper fees that must be paid.*

The USCIS will review the application and issue an approval notice to the company. The USCIS should also cable notice of approval to the American Consulate where the alien will apply for the visa. Approval can be granted for an initial period of three years. Extensions of H-1 status can routinely be obtained for an additional three years (maximum stay in H-1 status is six years). The USCIS processing time for H-1 petitions varies, but is usually not more than two to three months.

Note: An employer may request "premium processing" by completing Form I-907 and submitting an additional fee of $1000.00. This insures that the case will be considered within 15 days, although it does not guarantee approval within that time. Because of the heavy demand for H-1B petitions and the annual cap of 65,000, it is highly recommended that all H-1 B petitions be filed under premium processing.

Once the company receives the approval notice, the bottom half should be forwarded to the alien so that visa application can be made at the American Consulate. This consists of:

1. Optional Form 156- Nonimmigrant Visa Application
2. Passport photograph
3. Original H-1B approval notice receipt issued by the USCIS
4. Form DS-157 if applicable.

The alien should obtain a complete copy of the H-1 application prior to applying for the visa. When the application is made, the alien should be able to affirm that he or she will remain in the U.S. temporarily. The visa is normally granted for three years. Spouses and minor children are issued H-4 visas, which are not valid for employment in the U.S.

Note: AC21 also provides for "portability" for those in H-1B status, allowing individuals in H-1B status to immediately change jobs upon filing of a new petition by a new employer, subject to final approval of the petition. If the petition is denied, work authorization ceases. Prior to this, an individual had to have a new petition approved on his behalf before being authorized to start new employment. In order to be eligible for this provision, the individual must have:

1. *Been lawfully admitted to the U.S..*

2. *The new petition must have been filed before the expiration of the person's authorized stay.*

3. *The person must not have accepted unauthorized employment before the petition was filed.*

H-2. Temporary Worker in Field Where U.S. Workers are in Short Supply

This category is divided into two groups:

H-2A. Temporary agricultural service workers

H-2B. Other workers who will be performing temporary services of labor in which U.S. workers are not available, including some seasonal jobs, certain child care situations, and individuals who will be training U.S. workers. The new immigration regulations include a 66,000 annual ceiling on issuance of H-2B visas.

Processing of H-2 applications is complex.

✓ The employer must first file a request with the local office of the State Employment Service (using Form ETA 750, Part A) for a temporary labor certification

✓ The State Employment Service will then issue instructions to the prospective employer regarding attempts to recruit U.S. workers, including advertising the job opening in a newspaper or trade publication, depending on the nature of the job

✓ Assuming approval after complying with the requirements, the Department of Labor will issue a certification.

An application is then filed with the USCIS, consisting of:

1. Department of Labor Certification
2. Form I-129-Petition for Nonimmigrant Worker
3. Form I-129H Supplement
4. A letter from the prospective employer describing the job and including a statement that the employer will pay for the alien's return transportation abroad
5. Evidence of the alien's qualifications
6. Filing fee of $190.00.

Once the application is approved, the process for obtaining the visa is similar to that for the H-1B, and families can be granted H-4 visas. H-2B visas are issued in one-year increments, with maximum duration of three years.

H-3. Temporary Trainee

The H-3 visa is available to individuals employed by a business in the U.S., who will participate in a formal training program that does not involve productive work (productive work can only be incidental to the training). The procedure for applying to the USCIS is similar to the H-1 process described above; however, a Labor Condition Application is not required. The prospective employer's petition to the USCIS must be accompanied by a written description of the formal training program, including details such as: the duration of the different phases of the training including classroom work; the instructors who will provide the training; reading and course work required during the training; why the training is not available in the alien's own country; and the position that the alien will fill abroad at the end of the training in the U.S.

The visa is usually granted for the duration of the training program, or for up to two years. Accompanying family members are issued H-4 visas.

USCIS regulations also allow for an H-3 "Special Education Exchange Visitor Program" for nonimmigrants coming to the U.S. to participate in a special education training program that provides practical training and experience in the education of children with physical, mental or emotional handicaps. Only fifty people per year are eligible, with a limit of stay of eighteen months.

I. Representatives of Information Media

This visa category is reserved for aliens who are coming to the U.S. temporarily to work on behalf of a foreign information media such as a foreign newspaper or television station. "I" visa holders are admitted to the U.S. for the duration of their employment. There are very limited visas issued in this category, so it will not be discussed further in this book.

J-1. Exchange Visitor

J-1 visas are available to aliens who will be participating in an Exchange Visitor Program including experts, foreign students, industrial and business trainees, "international visitors", medical interns and residents, and scholars. Exchange Visitor Programs are approved and administered by the United States Department of State (DOS). Previously, the function was handled by the United States Information Agency (USIA).

The Exchange Visitor Program was developed, in part, to allow aliens to pursue education, training or research, or to teach in the U.S. The types of visitors under the J-1 program may include, but are not limited to: Students, professors and research scholars, short-term scholars, trainees, specialists, foreign medical graduates, international and government visitors, teachers, camp counselors, and au pairs.

Many large companies and educational institutions participate. Foreign medical graduates who wish to study further or train in the U.S. may want to first contact the Educational Commission for Foreign Medical Graduates (ECFMG) located in Philadelphia, Pennsylvania.

Sponsors of J-1 programs can be:
- ❏ An existing U.S. agency or organization
- ❏ A recognized international agency or organization having U.S. membership and offices
- ❏ A reputable organization that is a citizen of the United States.

Citizen of the United States is defined as either:
1. An individual U.S. citizen
2. A partnership of which a majority of the partners are U.S. citizens
3. A corporation or other legal entity, which has its principal place of business in the United States, and either its shares are publicly traded on a U.S. stock exchange or a majority of its officers, directors and shareholders are U.S. citizens.

4. A non-profit legal entity in the U.S. which is qualified as tax-exempt, has its principal place of business in the U.S. and a majority of its officers and directors are U.S. citizens or

5. An accredited college, university or other institution of higher learning created under U.S. law.

Foreign nationals who wish to apply for J-1 visas should proceed with caution, because many aliens must return to their home country for two years after they complete their stay in J-1 status. These include:

1. Individuals who receive any sort of government funding to participate in the J-1 program in the U.S.

2. Aliens receiving graduate medical training in the U.S., such as residents and interns

3. Aliens who are nationals of a country in which a skills list exists.

The skills list indicates occupations for which the foreign country's local workers are in short supply. The Department of State has compiled this list in cooperation with each foreign government. For example, the Brazilian government may have concluded that not enough Brazilians are qualified engineers. Therefore, if a Brazilian citizen comes to the United States with a J-1 visa to pursue a course of study in engineering, he or she is required to return to Brazil for two years after completing the J-1 program in the U.S. This is known as the "two year foreign residence requirement." In some cases this two year requirement can be waived at the end of the program, but it is a difficult procedure, and with no guarantees of approval.

When the alien has been accepted into a J-1 program, the sponsoring organization will issue Form DS-2019- Certificate of Eligibility for Exchange Visitor J-1 Status to the foreign national. The visa application to the American Consulate consists of:

1. Form DS 156- Nonimmigrant Visa Application

2. Passport photograph

3. Form DS-2019

4. Valid passport or travel document

5. Form DS-157 if applicable

The J-1 visa is usually issued to coincide with the length of the J-1 program. Some J-1 visas can be renewed while others are limited to fixed periods of stay. Spouses and minor children are granted J-2 visas. They may accept employment by applying to the USCIS for permission to work on Form I-765. Employment permission can be granted for up to four years, or the duration of the J-1's DS-2019/I-94, whichever is shorter.

SEVIS (see F-1 visa category) also applies to J-1 visitors. J-1 visa holders must be sure to provide their Program sponsors with any change of address within 10 days as Program Sponsors must ensure that the U.S. addresses of all sponsored J program participants that are reported to SEVIS are actual and current. A program sponsor must update address changes within 21 days of the change notification.

The sponsor must also verify within 30 days of a J visitor's start date, that the participant has indeed begun his or her program. In addition, sponsors will continue to submit annual reports to the Department of State.

K. Fiancé or Fiancee of U.S. Citizen

This category is available to aliens who are outside the U.S. and are engaged to be married to a U.S. citizen. The petitioner and the beneficiary must have met in person within the past two years. The U.S. citizen must file the following documents with the USCIS Regional Service Center having jurisdiction over the U.S. citizen's place of residence:

1. Form I-129F-Petition for Alien Fiancé

2. Proof of U.S. citizenship of petitioner

3. Proof of termination of prior marriages for both parties, if applicable

4. Evidence that the two parties have physically met within the past two years

5. Statements from both parties that they plan to marry within 90 days of the alien's admission to the U.S. and evidence as to this intent

6. Two color photos of the U.S. citizen, and two of the fiancé (e) taken within 30 days

7. Filing fee of $170.00.

The USCIS will approve the petition and forward it to the U.S. Consulate where the fiancé(e) will apply for the visa, after complying with the instructions of the Consul. Once the alien is granted the K-1 visa and enters the U.S., the marriage must occur within 90 days. After the marriage, the alien can file Form I-485-Application to Register Permanent Residence with the USCIS to convert from K-1 to conditional residence (See Chapter 8 for procedures on filing Form I-485). Unmarried minor children can accompany the fiancé(e) to the U.S. in "K" status.

K-3 and K-4- Spouses of U.S. citizens and their children

In 2001 a new nonimmigrant classification for the spouses of U.S. citizens and their children was created by the LIFE Act. Previously, spouses of U.S. citizens and their children who were the beneficiaries of pending or approved petitions could enter the United States only with immigrant visas. Following the enactment of LIFE, spouses of U.S. citizens and their children who are the beneficiaries of pending or approved visa petitions can be admitted initially as nonimmigrants in K-3 or K-4 classification and adjust to immigrant status later while in the United States.

The eligibility criteria for the K-3 are as follows:

a) The U.S. citizen (USC) spouse must have filed the I-130 immigrant petition.

b) The USC must have also filed the I-129F petition, and the USCIS must approve it.

c) After arrival in the U.S., the K-3 holder must continue with the permanent immigration process.

The K-4 requirements are:

a) The applicant must be the unmarried child (under 21) of a person who qualifies for the K-3 visa. The K-4 child can be listed on the same I-129F as the K-3 spouse.

b) After arrival in the U.S., the I-130 petition must be filed for the K-4 child, usually together with an I-485 application.

Note that if the K-4 is the stepchild of the USC, the USC cannot file the I-130 petition unless the couple married before the child's 18th birthday. In such case, the K-3 parent will have to file for the child, who will be subject to the long waiting list for relatives of permanent residents. In the meantime, there may also be a status problem and the child may have to wait abroad.

Application Process

The I-129F petition is filed with the new USCIS, PO Box 7218, Chicago, Illinois 60680-7218, which, upon approval, forwards the petition to the National Visa Center (NVC). NVC notifies the consulate by email, sending a scanned version of the I-129F. The consulate will then send a letter to the K-3/K-4 applicants with instructions regarding the medical exam, a list of documents needed, and instructions for notifying the Consulate that all needed documents have been gathered. The Consulate will determine whether applicants will require personal interviews.

The K-3/K-4 visa is issued as a nonimmigrant visa, similar to the K-1. In addition, a packet of documents is given to the K-3/K-4 visa holder, to be presented to the USCIS Inspector at the Port of Entry.

Required Documents

The visa application at the American Consulate consists of:

1. Form DS-156 in duplicate

2. Form DS-157 if applicable

3. Visa application form.

4. Police certificates (as applicable when required for the particular country).

5. Birth certificates for both K-3s and K-4s.

6. Marriage certificate for K-3s as well as proof of termination of prior marriages, if any.

7. Medical exam for K-3's and K-4's, but the vaccination requirement does not apply.

8. Valid passport for each applicant. (minor children can have their own passport, or be included in their parent's passport.

9. Some proof of financial support is needed for the K-3/K-4 visa and the consulate has the discretion to determine the types of documents acceptable for this purpose.

10. Applicable visa fee (check with Consulate).

Consular processing for the K-3 visa will take place in the country where the couple got married.

L-1. Intracompany Transferee

L-1 visas are granted to aliens who have worked for a company abroad, as executives, managers, or in a specialized knowledge capacity, for a total of one year within the immediately preceding three years. The USCIS has very strict definitions of "managerial, executive and specialized knowledge". The alien must be transferred, for a temporary assignment, to a branch office, subsidiary or affiliate company in the U.S. in an executive, managerial or specialized knowledge capacity. The employer in the U.S. must initiate a petition with the USCIS.

The L-1 petition consists of:

1. Form I-129- Petition for A Nonimmigrant Worker and "L" classification supplement

2. A letter describing the alien's current job, held for the past year abroad, and the anticipated job in the U.S. It should include details of the executive, managerial or specialized knowledge features of both positions

3. Proof that the alien has been employed abroad by the foreign company for at least one year

4. Proof that the foreign and U.S. companies are related

5. Filing fee of $185.00

6. Fraud Fee of $500.00

The USCIS will issue a notice of approval to the prospective U.S. employer, usually within thirty days. The visa application process from this point forward is the same as that described for the H-1B.

The initial petition can be approved for up to three years with extensions granted in two-year increments, up to seven years in total for executives and managers. Specialized knowledge L-1 aliens are only eligible for a total of five years in this visa category. Spouses and minor children are granted L-2 visas, which are not valid for work purposes, however a spouse may apply for work permission.

If the U.S. company has just started operating, the application rules are different. The USCIS may ask to see more documents, the petition may only be approved for one year, and the subsequent visa will only be issued for one year. Should the employer need to renew the status of the L-1 alien at the end of the first year, the U.S. company will be required to prove to the USCIS that the new operation is growing. If this proof is available, extensions of stay can also be granted, as described above.

Employers are also entitled to apply to the USCIS for approval of an L-1 "blanket" petition, which eases the application process each time the employer wants to transfer an alien. In order to qualify for this program, the employer must be able to meet certain criteria. Included in these are:

1. That the employer must have had at least ten L-1 approvals within the past twelve months or

2. Have sales of over $25 million or

3. Employ at least 1000 people.

4. Have proof of affiliation between the U.S. and foreign branches of the company and

5. Have proof that the U.S. company has been doing business for at least a year.

The documentation that is required for L-1 blanket approval is extensive but can benefit the employer in saving time on international transfer paperwork.

M-1. Student

M-1 status is similar to F-1 status. This visa category has been in effect since 1982 and is designed for students who wish to pursue vocational or other recognized nonacademic educational programs. This does not include English language programs. The application process is similar to that for F-1 students in that the school issues Form I-20MN to the student. The visa application at the American Consulate consists of:

1. Optional Form 156- Nonimmigrant Visa Application

2. Form DS-157 if applicable

3. Form I-20M-N- Certificate of Eligibility for Nonimmigrant (M-1) Student Status—completed by the student and the DSO

4. Passport photographs

5. Proof that the applicant has enough money to pay school related expenses and to support himself or herself during the program

6. Valid passport or travel document.

The visa may be granted for the length of the course of study shown on Form I-20M. The I-20M-N should be returned to the student by the Consular official. The student should present it to the USCIS official when entering the U.S. The

USCIS officer will return the student's part of the Form and issue Form I-94. The USCIS will also forward Form I-20M-N to the USCIS processing center, which will then send Form I-20N to the sponsoring school. Aliens holding M-1 visas are not permitted to work. Spouses and minor children can be granted M-2 visas, which are not valid for employment. Students can transfer from one school to another within the U.S. after spending six months in valid M-1 status, and assuming he or she is financially able to continue to attend school. The procedure is as follows:

- ✓ Student completes Form I-538- Application by Nonimmigrant Student for Extension of Stay, and attaches Form I-20ID and Forms I-94 for him or herself and all family members

- ✓ Student obtains completed Form I-20M-N from the new sponsoring school and fills out the information required

- ✓ Student submits the application to the USCIS office having jurisdiction over the school the student last attended, consisting of:

1. Form I-538
2. Student's I-20ID
3. Form I-20M-N from the new school
4. Forms I-94 for student and family
5. Applicable filing fee.

The student must wait for sixty days after filing the application for transfer, to start in the new program. If the application is approved it will be retroactive to the date of filing, and the student will be granted an extension of stay. The USCIS will return Form I-20ID and Form I-94. The extension period should coincide with the completion of the new program plus thirty days, or for one year, whichever is less. The USCIS officer will also endorse the name of the new school on the student's I-20N and will forward it with Form I-20M to the USCIS data processing center, which in turn, will record the change and send the form to the new school. If the application for transfer is denied, the student is considered to be out of status.

Students can also qualify for paid practical training upon completion of their program. The alien may only be employed in an occupation or vocation directly related to his or her course of study, as recommended by the DSO. The maximum amount of time for training will be one month for each four months of full time study, but not to exceed six months, plus thirty days to depart the U.S. The application process is as follows:

✓ Student completes his or her portion of Form I-538 and gives this to the DSO with Form I-20ID.

✓ DSO endorses the student's Form I-20ID for practical training and returns it to the student

✓ DSO completes the school's portion of Form I-538 and forwards it to the USCIS data processing center. On Form I-538 the DSO must certify that he or she recommends the proposed employment, that it is related to the student's course of study, and that this type of employment is not available in the student's home country.

The student must them apply to the USCIS service center for an employment authorization document (EAD). The application consists of:

1. Form I-765
2. Copy of Form I-94
3. Special fingerprint card
4. Photos
5. Form I-20ID endorsed for practical training by the DSO
6. Applicable filing fee.

The application must be submitted before the student's authorized stay expires and not more than sixty days before completing the course of study, nor more than thirty days after. The student cannot begin practical training until the USCIS approves the application, endorses the training on Form I-20ID and returns the EAD to the student.

Note: The SEVIS reporting rules that apply to F-1 students also apply to M-1 students.

N. NATO

NATO visas are granted to representatives of countries that are members of the North Atlantic Treaty Organization (NATO). They are primarily under the control of the State Department, with little USCIS involvement, and are therefore, not covered in this book.

O. Extraordinary Aliens

"O" aliens are those who have extraordinary ability in the sciences, arts, education, business or athletics. This includes those in the motion picture or television industries. The alien must have sustained national or international acclaim, or with regard to motion picture and television productions, have a demonstrated record of achievement.

The "O" alien must be entering the United States to continue work in the area of extraordinary ability, or for the purpose of accompanying and assisting in the artistic or athletic performance for a specific event. The alien must be an integral part of the actual performance, and possess skills and experience that cannot be duplicated by other individuals.

In the case of motion picture or television productions, the "O" applicant must have skills and experience that are critical, based on either a preexisting long-standing working relationship with the principal performer, or with respect to the specific production. This must be due to the fact that the significant production will take place both inside and outside the U.S., and the continuing participation of the alien is essential to the successful completion of the production.

Aliens of extraordinary ability, or extraordinary achievement in the motion picture or television industries are designated O-1. Aliens who accompany and assist O-1 aliens are classified O-2. This category is only available, however, for aliens who accompany or assist an O-1 alien in a specific athletic or artistic event. It is not available in the fields of education, science or business.

The spouse and children of O-1 or O-2 aliens are designated O-3. O-1 aliens do not need to have a residence abroad that they have no intention of abandoning, but O-2 aliens do have to maintain a residence abroad.

The standards for this visa category are very high. Television and movie artists must prove that they have a very high level of accomplishment, and that they have been recognized as outstanding, notable or leading. To show extraordinary ability in the sciences, business, education and athletics, applicants must document their recognition, with quality outweighing quantity.

"O" visas require a petition (Form I-129 with appropriate supplement) to be filed with the USCIS Regional Service Center having jurisdiction over the area in which the alien will be employed. The procedure is similar to that in H-1B cases. Established agents may file petitions (in lieu of employers) for an alien who is traditionally self-employed or who plans to arrange short-term employment with numerous employers. There are strict rules that agents must follow. Consult a professional for more information in this area.

The maximum period of validity of an approved "O" petition is three years. A petitioner may seek an extension in one-year increments.

P. Outstanding Athletes, Artists and Entertainers

"P" visas are reserved for athletes, artists and certain entertainers who have achieved national or international recognition as outstanding in their field. The standard is somewhat less than for "O" visas but the scope of eligible services is more limited.

There are three subcategories:

> *P-1. Members of entertainment groups, or individual athletes and members of athletic teams*
>
> *P-2. Artists or entertainers who are part of reciprocal international exchanges*
>
> *P-3. Artists or entertainers coming to perform in programs that are culturally unique.*

Teachers and coaches, as well as performers are now eligible for P-3 status, to encourage them to disseminate their knowledge. Aliens may also now be admitted for commercial or non-commercial performances. It is interesting to note that individual entertainers are not eligible for "P" visas, except for those participating in reciprocal exchanges, or performing in culturally unique shows.

Prior to the Immigration Act of 1990, athletes were admitted as visitors under a variety of situations. Now USCIS regulations grant P-1 status to professional athletes, while amateur athletes may still be granted B-1 status.

Like the "O" category, a petition is required. Family members are eligible for P-4 classification. All "P" nonimmigrants must seek to enter the United States temporarily, and are required to have a residence abroad that they do not intend to abandon. As with "O" petitions, an agent may file the petition. Individual athletes may be admitted for up to five years, and their stay may be extended for up to five years. The total period of stay for an individual athlete may not exceed ten years. All other "P" aliens can be admitted for up to one year, and their stay may be extended in increments of one year.

Q. International Cultural Exchange

This category was created to allow employers like Disney to bring foreigners to the U.S. for temporary periods to work in places such as Epcot in Florida. This visa category applies to aliens coming to the U.S. for no more than fifteen months to participate in an international cultural exchange program. To qualify, the prospective employer must have been conducting business in the U.S. for at least two years, have at least five full-time U.S. workers, and offer working conditions and wages that are the same as those given to local workers.

The "Q" applicant must be at least eighteen years old and be able to communicate about their home country. Application is made on Form I-129.

R. Religious Workers

This category was created for religious workers coming to the U.S. to perform temporary services. The alien must have been a member of a religious organization for at least the immediately preceding two years. Three groups of religious workers can qualify: ministers of religion, professional workers in religious vocations and occupations, and other religious workers who are employed by a religious nonprofit organization, or a related tax exempt entity, under IRS definition. Religious workers can be admitted to the U.S. for an initial period of three years. Total stay is limited to five years. Aliens can apply directly at the American Consulate for the R-1 visa. They must present:

1. Proof that the sponsoring organization is non-profit

2. A letter from the sponsoring organization including the salary for the position; the required two years of membership in the denomination; qualifications as a minister, religious professional, or as an alien in a religious vocation; the affiliation between the religious organization in the U.S. and abroad, and the location where the alien would be working.

The spouse and minor children of religious workers are eligible for R-2 classification, which does not allow for employment.

S. Alien Informants

This classification was created for aliens who assist law enforcement agencies in supplying critical information about criminal enterprises and terrorism. It is not covered in this book.

T. Visas

The "T" classification was created under the Trafficking Victims Protection Act of 2000 (TVPA). This status is designed to assist individuals who are in the U.S.,

American Samoa or the Commonwealth of the Northern Mariana Islands as a result of being victims of severe forms of trafficking in humans, commonly known as slavery. Subject to some limitations, immediate family members of these persons will also benefit from the "T" category.

The T visa is limited to those victims of trafficking who are willing to cooperate with law enforcement actions against human traffickers. An applicant must establish that he or she would suffer extreme hardship involving unusual and severe harm, if removed from the U.S., and that he or she has complied with any reasonable request for assistance in the investigation and prosecution of acts of human trafficking.

A victim files his or her own petition for T status, using Form I-914.

After three years in T status, one is allowed to apply for permanent resident status. Thus, the T visa ultimately provides a long-term solution for the victims of human trafficking.

TN. NAFTA Professionals
This category is covered in Chapter 6.

V. Visas—Spouses and children of lawful permanent residents
The V visa was created in order to provide an interim solution for the spouses and children of lawful permanent residents, who have to wait many years for a visa to become available to them because of the backlogs in quota availability.

In order to qualify, applications for immigration status must have:

been pending for at least three years

OR

if immigration petitions on their behalf have been approved, 3 years or more have elapsed since the filing date and an immigrant visa is not immediately available to the applicant because of a backlog in the quota.

To be eligible for a V visa, the applicant must be the beneficiary of an application for an immediate relative (under the family based second preference category (F2A)) that was filed on or before December 21, 2000. The petition must have been pending for three years at the time the V visa application is made. However, if the petition has been approved, the person can still obtain a V visa, if the petition was filed more than three years ago and there is no immediately available immigrant visa, a pending application for an immigrant visa, or a pending application for adjustment of status.

A person eligible for V visa status may apply for it at a consular office abroad, or if already in the U.S., may apply to the USCIS.

V visa holders may also obtain employment authorization by filing Form I-765, and the appropriate filing fee, with the USCIS.

V visa holders are eligible to apply for adjustment of status when an immigrant visa becomes available, if the applicant was physically present in the U.S. at any time between July 1, 2000 and October 1, 2000. However, if after obtaining the V visa, its holder ever falls out of valid status (other than through no fault of the holder or for technical reasons), they will not be allowed to apply for adjustment of status unless eligible under section 245(i).

Those living in the U.S. who wish to apply for the V visa are required to submit the following documentation:

1. A completed Application to Extend/Change Nonimmigrant Status (Form I-539) along with its Supplement A and required documentation and fees

2. A completed Medical Examination (Form I-693)

3. Fingerprinting fee of $70.00

The USCIS will give V status holders (or applicants that changed to the V status) a maximum 2-year period of admission. The period of the V status may be extended, if the applicant continues to remain eligible for V status.

If an eligible spouse or child has an immigrant visa number available, but has not yet applied for an immigrant visa abroad, or for adjustment of status to lawful permanent residence, the USCIS will grant a one-time 6 month extension of the V status in order to provide them time to file the appropriate application when their V status is expiring.

PREMIUM PROCESSING:

As of June 1, 2001, the USCIS began a program of "premium processing" of certain nonimmigrant visa petitions (Form I-129). Currently, premium processing is available for applicants seeking E-1, E-2, H-1B, H-2A, H-2B, H-3, L-1A, L-1B, O-1, O-2, P-1, P-2, P-3, Q-1, R-1, TN-1 and TN-2. The USCIS will also expedite the forms of dependents seeking extensions of stay or change of status based on the principal alien's form I-129. The request for premium processing must be made on Form I-907 and can either be filed concurrently with the I-129 or subsequently for a pending I-129.

Premium processing guarantees that the USCIS will process the petition within 15 days or it will refund the fee and continue to process the petition on an expedited basis. The premium-processing fee is $1,000.00 and must be paid with a separate check or money order. Please note that premium processing does not guarantee an approval in 15 days, only that USCIS will process the petition. A special address for Premium Processing has been designated for each of the Service Centers:

California Service Center
Email inquiries: CSC.Premium.Processing@dhs.gov
Phone to request information about PENDING applications only: 949-831-9670

Mailing Address
USCIS, California Service Center
P.O. Box 10825
Laguna Niguel, CA 92677

Express Mail Address
USCIS, California Service Center
24000 Avila Road, 2nd Floor, Room 2302
Laguna Niguel, CA 92677

Nebraska Service Center
Email inquiries: NSC.Premium.Processing@dhs.gov
Phone to request information about PENDING applications only: 402-474-5012

Mailing Address
USCIS, Nebraska Service Center
P.O. Box 87103
Lincoln, NE 68501-7103

Express Mail Address
USCIS, Nebraska Service Center
850 S Street
Lincoln, NE 68508

Texas Service Center
Email inquiries: TSC.Premium.Processing@dhs.gov
Phone to request information about PENDING applications only: 214-275-9502

Mailing Address
USCIS, Texas Service Center
P.O. Box 279030
Dallas, TX 75227

Express Mail Address
USUSCIS, Texas Service Center
4141 North St. Augustine Road
Dallas, TX 75227-9030

Vermont Service Center
Email inquiries: VSC.Premium.Processing@dhs.gov
Phone to request information about PENDING applications only: 802-527-4828

Premium Processing
Vermont Service Center
30 Houghton Street
St. Albans, VT 05478-2399

NONIMMIGRANT VISA REFERENCE CHART

A-1, A-2, A-3	Ambassadors, public ministers, diplomats or consular officers assigned to represent their country in the U.S., their immediate families and servants
B-1	Temporary business visitors
B-2	Temporary visitors for pleasure
C-1	Aliens in transit through the U.S. to a third country
D	Crewmen of aircraft or sea vessels
E-1	Treaty trader, spouse and minor children
E-2	Treaty investor, spouse and minor children
F-1	Students pursing academic courses of study
F-2	Spouse and minor children of F-1
G-1 thru 5	Representatives of international organizations like the United Nations and the World Bank, their family, staff and servants
H-1B	Specialty occupations
H-2A	Agricultural temporary workers
H-2B	Non-agricultural temporary workers
H-3	Temporary trainees, special education
H-4	Spouse and minor children of H-1, H- 2 and H-3 visa holders
I	Representatives of foreign information media, and their family
J-1	Exchange visitors
J-2	Spouse and minor children of J-1 visa holders
K-1	Alien fiancé or fiancee of U.S. citizen and minor children
L-1	Temporary intracompany transferees
L-2	Spouse and minor children of L-1 visa holder
M-1	Students enrolled in vocational educational programs
M-2	Spouse and minor children of M-1 visa holders
N-1 thru 7	NATO visa holders
O-1, O-2, O-3	Extraordinary aliens, essential support and family
P-1, P-2, P-3	Artists, Athletes, Entertainers
Q	Cultural exchange
R-1	Religious workers
R-2	Spouse and minor children of religious workers
S-1	Informants relating to criminal enterprises
S-2	Informants related to terrorism
TN	NAFTA Professionals
TD	Dependents of NAFTA Professionals
V	Spouses and children of lawful permanent residents

3
Visa Waiver Pilot Program

Two additional categories of nonimmigrant status exist in which visas are not required for admission into the U.S. The first is the Visa Waiver Pilot Program, covered in this chapter, and the second is the North American Free Trade Agreement, covered in Chapter 6.

On November 6, 1986 the USCIS established a Visa Waiver Pilot Program (VWPP), on an experimental basis, for citizens of certain countries who wished to travel to the U.S. as visitors. It is now a permanent program.

Citizens of the United Kingdom were the first to be granted a benefit under this program. It has now been extended to include citizens of the following countries:

Andorra	Luxembourg
Australia	Monaco
Austria	The Netherlands
Belgium	New Zealand
Brunei	Norway
Denmark	Portugal
Finland	San Marino
France	Singapore
Germany	Slovenia
Iceland	Spain
Ireland	Sweden
Italy	Switzerland
Japan	United Kingdom
Liechtenstein	Uruguay

Citizens of the countries listed above can be admitted to the U.S. for up to ninety days as B-1 or B-2 visitors. Extensions of stay or change of visa status are not permitted. Individuals who wish to participate in the program are required to complete Form I-94W, supplied by the transportation carrier, prior to inspection by a USCIS officer, and the carrier must be one that is participating in the program. The visitor must also:

1. Have a valid passport

2. Have a valid round trip airline ticket that has been signed by a carrier participating in the program, and be arriving on that carrier

3. Have proof of the ability to support himself or herself while in the U.S.

4. Be willing to waive any appeal rights if the immigration officer finds them inadmissible (except for asylum)

5. Be prepared to be screened by the USCIS upon arrival in the U.S.

Individuals taking advantage of this program are also now permitted to enter the U.S. at land border crossing points, such as Canada or Mexico.

4

U.S.-VISIT Program

U.S. Visitor and Immigration Status Indication Technology (U.S.-VISIT) system is designed to keep track of visitors to the United States. It was placed into effect on January 5, 2004 at 115 airports in the U.S., Canada, the Caribbean and Europe, and at 15 seaports in the U.S. and Canada. It is scheduled to become effective at all ports of entry, land, sea and air, by December 31, 2005. The program applies only to foreign nationals entering the U.S. on temporary visas, including those participating in the Visa Waiver Program. It does not screen diplomats, children under 14, and adults over age 79.

The U.S.–Visit Program is, in essence a "check-in" and "check-out" system that allows the Department of Homeland Security to collect biometric identifiers as part of their inspection process. Biometric data (fingerprint and digital photo) is collected on visitors when they check in and out of the United States, and scanned against law enforcement and national security data bases. The Arrival/Departure Information System (ADIS) will electronically show whether they have complied with the departure terms of their admission. Their personal data will also be checked against electronic lookout lists for law enforcement and security purposes. The government will store the images and other information in its data systems for such future use as intelligence, security, criminal investigation, or confirming visa compliance. Therefore, while the data will be used primarily by DHS and DOS (Department of State) officers, it may be made available for law enforcement purposes to other government agencies, U.S. and foreign.

On arrival, individuals will provide two fingerprints on an inkless device, and a digital photograph will be taken. This information, combined with the normal document review, will determine whether the individual will be admitted into the U.S. and issued a Form I-94. When the individual leaves, their travel documents are scanned, the photographs are compared and new fingerprints are taken.

A person who fails to comply with the departure requirements may be found in violation of his admission, parole, or other immigration status. Such failure may also be considered in deciding whether that individual is eligible for a nonimmigrant visa or admission in the future. Failure to comply can also result in a finding of overstay where the visitor has failed to depart when his authorized stay has ended. Thus, the days when government inefficiency failed to keep track of those overstaying their authorized period of stay appear to be over. Overstaying one's period of authorized stay has serious implications for future visits, including the cancellation of one's visa and subjecting the violator to possible long-term bars against re-entry to the United States, even if eligible to immigrate.

5
The INSPASS System

The INS Passenger Accelerated Service System (INSPASS) is an automated inspection system available to eligible travelers to the U.S., at many airports including Los Angeles, Miami, Newark, New York (JFK), San Francisco, Washington–Dulles, and U.S./Canadian preclearance in Toronto and Vancouver.

Eligible travelers to the U.S. must have a special card that is read at INSPASS kiosks, similar to a bank automated teller machine. If the traveler's identity is validated, an I-94 form is printed at the kiosk and the traveler can proceed directly to U.S. Custom's inspection. Those traveling into airports that do not have INSPASS kiosks must proceed through normal immigration inspection.

U.S. citizens, as well as citizens of Canada, Bermuda and Visa Waiver Pilot Program (VWPP) countries who travel to the U.S. on business more than three times a year are eligible. Diplomats, representatives of international organizations, and airline crew from the VWPP countries can also enroll.

Visiting an INSPASS enrollment office and completing Form I-823-Application-Inspections Facilitation Program can complete enrollment. There are offices at most airports that participate in the INSPASS system. You may also obtain forms by calling 800-870-3676.

You must appear in person at an INSPASS enrollment office to complete the application process. All enrollees must have valid passports. At your interview, the USCIS inspector will enter your application into the computer, and complete a digital photograph, fingerprints, hand geometry and other biometrics. You will be interviewed to determine your eligibility. Upon approval, you will be issued a PORTPASS card with instructions.

Currently, INSPASS cards are valid for one year. There is no fee for enrollment.

6

The North American Free Trade Agreement (NAFTA)

In November 1993, Congress approved the North American Free Trade Agreement, commonly known as NAFTA. It became effective on January 1, 1994. NAFTA facilitates trade and investment by liberalizing the rules for entry of temporary business people among the three countries in the agreement: the United States, Mexico and Canada. While NAFTA covers many subjects, this book is concerned only with its immigration aspects.

NAFTA affects four categories of business people; equivalent to the USCIS nonimmigrant categories of B-1, "E", L-1 and H-1B discussed previously. There is no limit to the number of Canadians that can enter the U.S. annually. However, no more than 5,500 citizens of Mexico can be classified as TN (Trade NAFTA) nonimmigrants each year.

1. Business Visitors

This is equivalent to our nonimmigrant B-1 category. It requires the United States, Canada and Mexico to temporarily allow a business person from another NAFTA party into the host country to engage in an occupation or profession from one of several categories of business activities: research and design; growth, manufacture and production; marketing; sales; distribution; after-sales service; and general service.

The business activity must be international in scope, and the business visitor must not be "employed" in the United States, e.g. be seeking to enter the local labor market. The primary source of compensation for the proposed business activity, as well as the actual place where profits are made, must be outside the U.S.

Applicants may apply for admission to the United States at a Port of Entry. Canadian citizens are exempt from visa requirements, but Mexican citizens must still present a valid passport with a B-1 visa, or a border-crossing card. Canadian business people do not need a Form I-94, but may request one to facilitate subsequent entries into the United States. Forms I-94 will be endorsed for "multiple entry". Mexican business people, admitted under NAFTA, will be issued a Form I-94 for a period not to exceed one year.

If an extension is needed, it may be filed with the USCIS on Form I-539 at least fifteen, but not more than sixty days before the expiration of stay. Derivative status for the spouse and minor unmarried children of entrants in this category does not exist, although they may be eligible to enter the U.S. as B-2 visitors.

2. Traders and Investors

This classification is similar to our E-1 and E-2 categories. It is offered to Mexican citizens for the first time. Under NAFTA, the investor category has also been broadened to include entry of Canadians and Mexicans into the U.S to: "establish, develop, administer, or provide advice or key technical services to the operation of an investment to which the business person or the business person's enterprise has committed, or is in the process of committing, a substantial amount of capital". The alien must be entering the United States in a position that is supervisory, executive or involves essential skills. Applicants for this category must obtain a visa. The American Consulates in Canada have a standard "E" visa questionnaire. The American Consulates in Mexico use an "E" visa form for Mexican citizens.

The initial approval period for an "E" visa is at least five years for Canadian citizens and six months for Mexican citizens. The actual initial period of admission into the U.S. is one year for both Canadian and Mexican citizens. Extensions of stay can be filed on Form I-129 with the USCIS Regional Service Center having jurisdiction over the applicant's residence.

If a trader or investor wants to change employers, they may only do so after a written request has been approved by the USCIS office having jurisdiction over their residence in the U.S. After the request is granted, the applicant's Form I-94 will be endorsed on the back "employment by (name of new employer) authorized", date. Extensions may be granted in increments of not more than two years. However, when the "E" visa alien departs the U.S., he or she will only be granted a one-year stay upon reentry. The spouse and minor, unmarried children of traders and investors are entitled to the same classification as the principal applicant, and are admitted into the U.S. for one year.

3. Intracompany Transferees

This category is similar to our L-1 classification for intracompany transferees. Canadian and Mexican managers, executives and people with specialized knowledge can enter the U.S. if they continue to provide services that are managerial, executive or specialized knowledge in nature. They must also be working for the same company, its affiliate or subsidiary. An L-1 petition is required of all applicants, and the applicant must establish at least one year of continuous experience abroad. *See Chapter 2* for complete L-1 petition requirements.

Canadian employers can file the petition at the same time that the alien applies for admission at the U.S.–Canadian border, e.g. at Ports of Entry or PFI (pre-flight inspection stations), located in Canada. If the petition is approved, the USCIS inspector will give the alien a receipt for the fee collected, and send one copy of the petition to the appropriate USCIS Regional Service Center for final action, and issuance of an approval notice, Form I-797. The USCIS inspector will then inspect the alien and issue Form I-94.

Mexican employers must file the petition with an USCIS Regional Service Center having jurisdiction over the alien's prospective place of employment in the U.S., and the applicant must receive an L-1 visa before being allowed entry into the U.S. The visa requirement has been waived for Canadian citizens, but not Mexican citizens.

If an extension is needed, either for Canadian or Mexican citizens, it can be made on Form I-129, with L supplement, to the appropriate USCIS Regional Service Center. The spouse and unmarried minor children of intracompany transferees are entitled to L-2 status. Mexican citizen spouse and children must obtain L-2 visas before they can enter the United States.

4. Professionals

This is similar to our H-1B category. NAFTA established a category for TN (Trade NAFTA) professionals. Canadians are allowed to apply for TN status at the port of entry, without any prior petition or visa approval, but Mexicans are subject to the same requirements as all professionals applying for H-1B status, including LCA and petition requirements. Self-employment in the U.S. is not permitted in TN status. TN status is available to the following listed professionals:

Accountants	Landscape architects
Agriculturists	Lawyers
Agronomists	Librarians
Animal breeders	Management consultants
Animal scientists	Mathematicians
Apiculturists	(including statisticians)
Architects	Medical technologists
Astronomers	Meteorologists
Biochemists	Nutritionists
Biologists	Occupational therapists
Chemists	Pharmacists
College teachers	Pharmacologists
(seminary or university teachers)	Physicians (teaching or research only)
Computer systems analysts	Physicists
Dairy scientists	Physio/Physical therapists

Dentists	Plant breeders
Dietitians	Poultry scientists
Disaster relief insurance claims adjusters	Psychologists
Economists	Range managers
Engineers	Recreational therapists
Entomologists	Registered nurses
Epidemiologists	Research assistants
Foresters	(for post-secondary ed. institution)
Geneticists	Scientific technicians/
Geologists	Technologists
Geochemists	Social workers
Geophysicists	Soil scientists
Graphic designers	Sylviculturists
Horticulturists	Technical publications writers
Hotel managers	Urban planners
Industrial designers	Vocational counselors
Interior designers	Veterinarians
Land surveyors	Zoologists

The various requirements of degrees, credentials in lieu of degrees, and licenses for certain professions are confusing and beyond the scope of this book. If you believe you may be qualified under NAFTA, you should seek the advice of a qualified immigration professional.

Extensions for TN professionals are filed on Form I-129. Applications may be made at the USCIS Nebraska Service Center. Canadians may also apply for readmission at the border. Extensions of stay are granted for up to one year. There is no set limit on the total amount of time one may remain in the U.S. in TN status.

Spouses and unmarried minor children of TN professionals are granted TD status.

7

Change of Nonimmigrant Status and Extension of Temporary Stay

Before concluding our discussion of nonimmigrant visas, two additional types of applications need to be mentioned that apply to aliens who are currently in the U.S.: the application for change of nonimmigrant status and the extension of temporary stay.

Application for Change of Nonimmigrant Status

Aliens who are in the U.S. with certain types of temporary visas, and wish to change to a different visa classification, can file an application for change of nonimmigrant status. Let's take, for example, an alien who is in the U.S. in student (F-1) status. He completes his course of study and is awarded a Master's degree in Chemical Engineering and is then offered a temporary job as a Chemical Engineer with a U.S company. Since the alien seems to be qualified for H-1B classification, the employer could file an H-1B petition with the USCIS as described in Chapter 2. Another example would be that of a spouse who comes to the U.S. in L-2 status and then receives an offer of temporary professional employment. If that person is a professional under the definition of H-1B, he or she could also change status from L-2 to H-1B. The alien must file the application prior to the expiration of Form I-94, have a passport valid for the entire stay, and cannot work in the new visa status while the Application for Change of Nonimmigrant Status is pending with the USCIS.

The approval notice will usually be valid for the same period of time as the approved petition. The alien can remain in the U.S. as long as Form I-94 remains valid. There is no requirement that the alien travel abroad to apply for the temporary visa at an American Consulate. Applications to change status to "E", "H", "L", "O", "P" or "R" are filed on Form I-129. Applications to change status to other nonimmigrant categories are filed on Form I-539.

A change of status application cannot be filed for aliens in certain visa categories, including aliens admitted to the U.S. under the Visa Waiver Pilot Program, "C", "D", "K" and "S" aliens and certain J-1 aliens. Also an M-1 visa holder cannot change to

F-1 status, nor can an M-1 student change to "H" classification, if the "M" training helped to qualify for the "H" position.

Application to Extend Time of Temporary Stay

If an alien is in the United States in B-1 or B-2 status and wants to extend his or her temporary stay, the alien can file an application with the USCIS on Form I-539. If a petition was originally required, as in the case of the "E", "H", "L", "O", "P" and "R", the employer must file for these extensions on Form I-129. For example, if an individual has been in the U.S. in L-1 status for three years and wishes to extend that status for an additional two years, he or she can apply to extend the status. A passport valid for the entire stay is required. The basic application consists of:

1. Form I-129-Petition for a Nonimmigrant Worker (and applicable supplement depending on temporary visa status)

2. Forms I-94 of the employee

3. Letter from the employer explaining reasons for requesting the extension

4. Form I-539 for family members and their Forms I-94

5. Applicable filing fee.

For H-1B extensions an approved labor condition application is required. If the extension is for H-2A or H-2B, a labor certification valid for the new dates must be submitted in most cases.

When the application is approved, the USCIS will issue a new notice of approval. The bottom half will consist of a receipt and a new Form I-94. The application must be filed prior to the expiration of Forms I-94. The alien is permitted to remain in the U.S. during the processing of the extension request, and once the application is approved, he or she can remain in the U.S. for as long as Form I-94 remains valid. Individuals in TN status may also file extension of stay requests in the U.S.

Note: aliens who are attempting to extend B-1 or B-2 status must provide the USCIS with a reasonable explanation as to why they were unable to complete their visit within the time period originally authorized. The alien must also prove that he or she is really still a visitor. It is always a good idea to file a copy of a return trip airline ticket with the application as proof that the stay is, indeed, temporary.

Individuals who are in the U.S. in "C", "D", "K" or "S" status, and those who have entered the U.S. in B-1 or B-2 status under the Visa Waiver Pilot Program described earlier, are not eligible for extensions of temporary stay.

8
Immigrant Visas and Adjustment of Status

The terms "immigrant visa", "permanent resident", "resident alien" and "green card" status all imply the same thing. They represent the right of a foreign national to permanently live and work in the United States. This chapter explains how the U.S. Government uses quotas and a preference system to allocate immigrant visas. Some exceptions, such as the concept of "cross-chargeability" are also discussed. Each of the immigrant visa categories is then explained, including procedures for applying, and the documents required to do so.

If you do not qualify for one of the nonimmigrant categories described in earlier chapters, you may only be able to apply under an immigrant category. The procedure for obtaining an immigrant visa is a lengthy one and can be extremely confusing and frustrating to applicants. One reason for the frustration stems from the inability to predict the actual time it will take to complete the application process.

Timing depends on a variety of factors, such as following the correct filing procedures for each type of application, the extent of processing backlogs in the government offices, which varies from state to state, and the availability of the quota. In some cases, the procedure can be completed in as little as a few months while in other circumstances; applicants from certain countries can wait for ten years or longer! Why is there such a variation in timing for immigrant visa processing?

THE QUOTA

The United States Congress established a very complicated system for issuing immigrant visas. Each month the Department of State in Washington, DC prints a visa bulletin, which lists the availability of visas for every country for that particular month. Only a limited number of immigrant visas are generally issued each year. This limitation is called the "quota" and is based on an alien's country of birth. **A sample visa bulletin is supplied at the end of this chapter.**

An individual born in India, for example, is eligible for one of the visas allocated to that country. If that same Indian citizen has become a citizen of another country, for example Canada, he or she is still subject to the Indian quota. This is because our quota system is based on the alien's country of birth, not the country of citizenship. The country quota under which an applicant must apply for an immigrant visa is commonly referred to as the alien's "chargeability". There are four exceptions to chargeability by place of birth. These exceptions are known as "cross-chargeability".

1. If the alien is married to another alien who is a citizen of a different country, the couple can apply under the more favorable quota. For example, if a woman born in the Philippines is married to a man born in Canada, the application for permanent residence can be made under either the Philippine or Canadian quota. In this case, the Canadian quota would be more favorable than that for the Philippines.

2. If the alien was accidentally born in a different country from the place of birth of his or her parents, and the parents were not firmly settled in the country where the child was born, the alien can be charged to the place of birth of either parent. For example, a Venezuelan couple on vacation in Mexico gives birth to a baby. Subsequently, the family immigrates to the U.S. The baby will be charged to the Venezuelan rather than the Mexican quota.

    If the parents never immigrated to the U.S., but this child later immigrated as an adult, he or she could still be charged to the Venezuelan quota, as long as there was proof that the child's place of birth was, indeed, an accident.

3. Minor children can be charged to either parent's place of birth. For example, a Canadian executive of an international company is sent to work in Taiwan for two years. His British born wife accompanies him. During the couple's stay in Taiwan, the wife gives birth to a child. At the end of the two years, the family is transferred to the U.S. in L-1 status. They subsequently apply for permanent residence. The Taiwan born child could be charged either to the Canadian or British quota.

4. Former U.S. citizens can be charged to their country of last residence or country of citizenship.

Why are these cross-chargeability categories important? Because many countries have more than their maximum allowable number of citizens applying for permanent residence in the U.S. each year. This results in long delays in obtaining green cards. When an applicant benefits from cross-chargeability, the processing time can be significantly shortened.

THE PREFERENCE SYSTEM

Immigrant visas are currently grouped into two general categories:

1.   Family sponsored preferences

2   Employment based preferences.

This is known as the preference system.

Family Based Preferences

The preference categories assigned to relatives of U.S. citizens or permanent residents. The number of visas issued annually in each category are as follows:

■ **Family first preference:** Unmarried sons and daughters (over 21 years of age) of U.S. citizens: 23,400 plus any numbers not used in fourth preference.

■ **Family second preference:** Spouses, children and unmarried sons and daughters of permanent residents: 114,200 plus the number by which the worldwide family preference allocation exceeds 226,000, and any numbers not used in first preference.

Family 2A—Spouses and children (unmarried, under age 21) are granted 77% of the second preference numbers, and 75% of these are exempt from the "per country limitation".

Family 2B—Adult unmarried sons and daughters of permanent residents are entitled to the remaining 23% of the second preference allocation.

■ **Family third preference:** married sons and daughters of U.S. citizens: 23,400 plus any numbers not used in first and second preference.

■ **Family fourth preference:** brothers and sisters of adult U.S. citizens: 65,000 plus any numbers not used in family first, second or third preference.

In each category defined above, the U.S. citizen or permanent resident files a petition with the USCIS. It consists of:

1. Form I-130- Petition for Alien Relative

2. Documentary proof that the petitioner is a U.S. citizen or permanent resident

3. Documentary proof that the petitioner and the alien are related

4. Applicable filing fee.

Note: Second preference spouse cases also require separate photos of petitioner and beneficiary and biographic data forms.

When the USCIS receives the petition, it is date stamped. This date becomes the alien's "priority date" on the waiting list for permanent residence.

As soon as USCIS approves the petition, it forwards the approval notice to the National Visa Center (NVC) which handles the preliminary administration of the visa issuing process for the various Embassies and Consulates. The NVC mails out a "fee bill" to the applicant and after the applicant remits the appropriate fees, the NVC sends out an information packet. Once the applicant completes and returns the information packet and advises that they have all of the documents required for the visa interview, the applicant will be scheduled for a visa interview when the quota becomes available, and when security checks have been completed. The interview will be held at the Embassy or Consulate designated by the NVC based on the applicant's place of residence.

If the immigrant visa application is approved at the interview, the applicant will be given either a sealed envelope to take to the U.S. and present at the port of entry, or a visa will be placed in the applicant's passport. Eventually all applicants will have a visa placed in their passport. The first entry into the United States must be made within four months of visa issuance. With the advent of biometrics processing, the issuance of the permanent resident card or "green card" should be within 90 to 120 days of entry. Under the old system the applicant may have received a "stamp" in his or her passport signifying that the card was in production. Travel while the card production is pending is allowed providing the applicant has some proof that the card is in process.

If the beneficiary is in the U.S., it may be possible to complete the application process in the U.S. When the priority date is reached, the alien files an Application for Adjustment of Status at the following address, regardless of his or her place of residence in the U.S.:

U.S. Citizenship and Immigration Services
PO Box 805887
Chicago, IL 60680-4120

If the applicant is in the United States in legal immigration status, has not accepted unauthorized employment, and has never violated his or her status, the applicant can apply with the following documents:

1. I-130 approval notice

2. Form I-485-Application to Register Permanent Resident or Adjust Status

3. Form G-325A -Biographic Information- for each family member age fourteen or over

4. Photographs for each family member that must meet exact specifications provided by the USCIS

5. $70.00 biometrics fee

6. Copy of Form I-94 for each applicant

7. Copy of any evidence showing continuous lawful status

8. Copy of passport

9. Form I-864 Affidavit of support with supporting documentation for each beneficiary: a letter verifying employment, copies of income tax returns for the past three years,

10. Birth and marriage certificates-see note below

11. Proof of termination of prior marriages if applicable

12. The $325.00 filing fee for each I-485 being submitted

13. Medical examination report (required at time of application in some USCIS offices, but not all).

Note: The USCIS requires that birth certificates be "long form", showing names of parents. All personal documents must be accompanied by certified English translations. In some jurisdictions, the USCIS office routinely requests other documents that are not listed above.

The following groups of aliens were previously able to adjust status under a law that expired on September 30, 1997. This immigration law is known as Section 245(i). However, aliens who are the beneficiaries of visa petitions and labor certification applications filed by April 30, 2001 may be "grandfathered" under certain circumstances. This means that the following groups of aliens will be allowed to continue to adjust status under Section 245(i).

1. Aliens who entered the U.S. illegally

2. Aliens who have remained in the U.S. beyond their authorized stay

3. Aliens who have accepted unauthorized employment.

It is important to consult an immigration professional regarding the grandfathering provision of the law. Applicants under the three categories shown above need to submit all documents shown in the previous box. In addition, a Form I-485A supplement must be filed along with a $1000.00 penalty fee for each applicant. This fee is waived for the following categories of applicants:

1. Children under age seventeen

2. An alien who is the spouse or unmarried child of an individual who was legalized under the Immigration Reform and Control Act of 1986 and who was:

    a. The spouse or unmarried child of the legalized alien as of May 5, 1988;

    b. Entered the United States before May 5, 1988 and resided here on that date;

    c. Applied for family unity benefits under the Immigration Act of 1990.

In addition, under Section 245 (K) of the Immigration & Nationality Act, employment-based visa applicants may adjust status if they are currently maintaining lawful status and have not previously been out status for more than an aggregate of 180 days. This provision is distinct from the grandfathering provision and does not require the applicant to pay a penalty fee.

Although the application forms that need to be filed with the USCIS may differ somewhat from office to office, the events leading up to the final interview are essentially the same as attending a final interview at an American Consulate. At the final interview the applicants must present the following:

1. Valid passports

2. Medical reports (instructions for examination provided by the USCIS)

3. Original birth certificates, marriage certificate and proof of the termination of prior marriages, if applicable

4. Form I-864 Affidavit of Support for the beneficiary and accompanying family members.

5. Letter of employment for petitioner and tax returns for the past three years.

The applicant's passport, and those of accompanying family members, will be stamped with the temporary green card upon approval of the case. The USCIS will then forward the required documents to the Immigration Card Facility in Vermont for processing of the green cards.

Applicants, who are eligible to complete their immigrant visa applications in the United States but choose not to, may complete their applications at an American Consulate abroad. See previous discussion on applying for an immigrant visa at an American Consulate.

Applicants with Permanent Offers of Employment

The Immigration Act of 1990 allows for 140,000 immigrant visas to be issued each year for employment based petitions. The preference categories assigned to applicants who have permanent offers of employment in the U.S., and the number of visas issued in each category are as follows:

∎ ***Employment Based First Preference:*** Priority Workers: 40,000 plus those numbers not used for fourth and fifth preference. Priority workers include aliens of extraordinary ability in the arts, sciences, business, education and athletics; managers and executives of international companies being transferred permanently to the U.S.; and outstanding professors and researchers. Labor certification is not required for employment based first preference (see explanation in Chapter 10). Please note those priority workers of "extraordinary ability" do not require an offer of employment as long as they will continue to work in their area of expertise. This only applies to extraordinary ability.

∎ ***Employment Based Second Preference:*** Members of the professions holding advanced degrees (any degree above a bachelors) and people of exceptional merit and ability in the sciences, arts or business: 40,000 plus those numbers not used in first preference. Labor certification is required.

■ ***Employment Based Third Preference:*** Skilled workers (must be filling a position that requires two years of training and experience), professionals with bachelors degrees and unskilled workers: 40,000 plus those numbers not used in first and second preference. Labor certification is required. Please note that only 10,000 of the 40,000 visas in this category will be allocated to unskilled workers.

■ ***Employment Based Fourth Preference:*** Certain "special" immigrants: 10,000. This category includes juveniles under Court protection; employees of the American Consulate in Hong Kong; and religious workers, such as ministers, who have at least a bachelor's degree. Please note that not more than 5,000 of these visas will be issued to religious workers. (Application to be filed on Form I-360).

■ ***Employment Based Fifth Preference:*** Employment creation (investors): 10,000, with not less than 3000 reserved for investors who invest in a targeted rural or high-unemployment area in the U.S. There is no labor certification requirement in this category, however, there are other strict criteria, which must be met such as the dollar amount of the investment and the number of jobs the investment will create for U.S. workers. See Chapter 11.

Before an application for permanent residence can be made based on an offer of employment in the employment based second and third preference categories, a basis of eligibility for filing the petition must be established. This usually requires that the sponsoring employer file an Application for Alien Employment Certification with the U.S. Department of Labor. This application should eventually result in the issuance of a Labor Certification. Other aliens may establish a basis of eligibility under a category called "Schedule A", and still others, under another employment based category. In these cases, the U.S. Department of Labor has determined that it is not necessary for a sponsoring employer to obtain Labor Certification. The Labor Certification process, Schedule A, and other employment-based categories are discussed in Chapter 10.

Once the alien has established a basis for eligibility, and a visa number becomes available based on the priority date, the procedure for completing the application is similar to the procedure for relatives of U.S. citizens or permanent residents discussed earlier in this chapter. However, the application is made to one of the four Regional Service Centers, depending on where the petition was filed or where the beneficiary resides.

Individuals Not Subject to Quota Limitations

Two common categories of individuals who are not subject to the numerical limitations of the quota described above are:

1) ***Applicants who are Immediate Relatives of U.S. Citizens:*** Citizenship may be on the basis of birth in the U.S. or through naturalization. Immediate relatives include spouses, unmarried sons and daughters under the age of twenty-one, and parents of adult citizens (over the age of 21). This category also includes spouses of deceased U.S. citizens, in certain cases. (This last application is made on Form I-360-Petition for Amerasian, Widow or Special Immigrant.)

   Although the quota system does not apply, the sponsor is still required to file an I-130 petition with the USCIS before the relative can immigrate to America. If the relative is in the U.S. in legal status, the entire application process can be completed within a few months. If the relative applies at an American Consulate overseas, the processing time will vary according to the administrative backlogs at the USCIS and at the Consulate abroad.

   In the case of husbands or wives, an applicant who has been married for less than two years will be granted a conditional green card. After two years, the applicant will be required to file another application with the USCIS on Form I-751 (Petition to Remove the Conditions of Residence). The couple will be required to prove that they entered into the marriage in good faith and are still married to each other. At that point, the conditional status will be removed and the applicant will be issued a permanent green card.

   Note: There are waivers available for battered spouses and in cases of divorce. You should seek the advice of a professional if you fall into either of these categories.

2) ***Refugees:*** Refugees are those who are unwilling to, or cannot, return to their country of origin because they fear persecution based on race, religion, nationality, political views or membership in a particular group. Each year the President of the United States, together with Congress, decides on the number of applicants who will be admitted to the U.S. as refugees or asylees. The refugee application processes are complex and are not covered in this book.

United States Department of State
Bureau of Consular Affairs

VISA BULLETIN
November 2005

IMMIGRANT NUMBERS FOR NOVEMBER 2005

A. STATUTORY NUMBERS

1. This bulletin summarizes the availability of immigrant numbers during November. Consular officers are required to report to the Department of State documentarily qualified applicants for numerically limited visas; the Bureau of Citizenship and Immigration Services in the Department of Homeland Security reports applicants for adjustment of status. Allocations were made, to the extent possible under the numerical limitations, for the demand received by October 11th in the chronological order of the reported priority dates. If the demand could not be satisfied within the statutory or regulatory limits, the category or foreign state in which demand was excessive was deemed oversubscribed. The cut-off date for an oversubscribed category is the priority date of the first applicant who could not be reached within the numerical limits. Only applicants who have a priority date earlier than the cut-off date may be allotted a number. Immediately that it becomes necessary during the monthly allocation process to retrogress a cut-off date, supplemental requests for numbers will be honored only if the priority date falls within the new cut-off date.

2. Section 201 of the Immigration and Nationality Act (INA) sets an annual minimum family-sponsored preference limit of 226,000. The worldwide level for annual employment-based preference immigrants is at least 140,000. Section 202 prescribes that the per-country limit for preference immigrants is set at 7% of the total annual family-sponsored and employment-based preference limits, i.e., 25,620. The dependent area limit is set at 2%, or 7,320.

3. Section 203 of the INA prescribes preference classes for allotment of immigrant visas as follows:

FAMILY-SPONSORED PREFERENCES

First: Unmarried Sons and Daughters of Citizens: 23,400 plus any numbers not required for fourth preference.

Second: Spouses and Children, and Unmarried Sons and Daughters of Permanent Residents: 114,200, plus the number (if any) by which the worldwide family preference level exceeds 226,000, and any unused first preference numbers:

A. Spouses and Children: 77% of the overall second preference limitation, of which 75% are exempt from the per-country limit;

B. Unmarried Sons and Daughters (21 years of age or older): 23% of the overall second preference limitation.

Third: Married Sons and Daughters of Citizens: 23,400, plus any numbers not required by first and second preferences.

Fourth: Brothers and Sisters of Adult Citizens: 65,000, plus any numbers not required by first three preferences

EMPLOYMENT-BASED PREFERENCES
First: Priority Workers: 28.6% of the worldwide employment-based preference level, plus any numbers not required for fourth and fifth preferences.

Second: Members of the Professions Holding Advanced Degrees or Persons of Exceptional Ability: 28.6% of the worldwide employment-based preference level, plus any numbers not required by first preference.

Third: Skilled Workers, Professionals, and Other Workers: 28.6% of the worldwide level, plus any numbers not required by first and second preferences, not more than 10,000 of which to "Other Workers". Schedule A Workers are entitled to up to 50,000 "recaptured" numbers.

Fourth: Certain Special Immigrants: 7.1% of the worldwide level.

Fifth: Employment Creation: 7.1% of the worldwide level, not less than 3,000 of which reserved for investors in a targeted rural or high-unemployment area, and 3,000 set aside for investors in regional centers by Sec. 610 of P.L. 102-395.

4. INA Section 203(e) provides that family-sponsored and employment-based preference visas be issued to eligible immigrants in the order in which a petition in behalf of each has been filed. Section 203(d) provides that spouses and children of preference immigrants are entitled to the same status, and the same order of consideration, if accompanying or following to join the principal. The visa prorating provisions of Section 202(e) apply to allocations for a foreign state or dependent area when visa demand exceeds the per-country limit. These provisions apply at present to the following oversubscribed chargeability areas: CHINA-mainland born, INDIA, MEXICO, and PHILIPPINES.

5. On the chart below, the listing of a date for any class indicates that the class is oversubscribed (see paragraph 1); "C" means current, i.e., numbers are available for all qualified applicants; and "U" means unavailable, i.e., no numbers are available. (NOTE: Numbers are available only for applicants whose priority date is earlier than the cut-off date listed on the following page.)

Priority Dates for Family-Based Immigrant Visas

Family	All Chargeability Except Those Listed	CHINA (Mainland Born)	INDIA	MEXICO	PHILIPPINES
1st	22APR01	22APR01	22APR01	01JAN94	22JUL91
2A*	01DEC01	01DEC01	01DEC01	01NOV98	01DEC01
2B	22MAY96	22MAY96	22MAY96	15JAN92	22MAY96
3rd	08MAY98	08MAY98	08MAY98	08APR94	08JAN91
4th	15MAR94	15MAR94	01OCT93	01AUG91	01JUL83

*NOTE: For November, 2A numbers **EXEMPT from per-country limit** are available to applicants from all countries with priority dates earlier than 01NOV98. 2A numbers **SUBJECT to per-country limit** are available to applicants chargeable to all countries **EXCEPT MEXICO** with priority dates beginning 01NOV98 and earlier than 01DEC01. (All 2A numbers provided for MEXICO are exempt from the per-country limit; there are no 2A numbers for MEXICO subject to per-country limit.)

Priority Dates for Employment-Based Immigrant Visas

	All Chargeability Except Those Listed	CH	IN	ME	PH
Employment-Based					
1st	C	01JAN00	01AUG02	C	C
2nd	C	01MAY00	01NOV99	C	C
3rd	01MAR01	01MAY00	01JAN98	01JAN01	01MAR01
Schedule A Workers	C	C	C	C	C
Other Workers	01OCT00	01OCT00	01OCT00	01OCT00	01OCT00
4th	C	C	C	C	C
Certain Religious Workers	C	C	C	C	C
5th	C	C	C	C	C
Targeted Employment Areas/Regional Centers	C	C	C	C	C

The Department of State has available a recorded message with visa availability information which can be heard at: (area code 202) 663-1541. This recording will be updated in the middle of each month with information on cut-off dates for the following month.

B. DIVERSITY IMMIGRANT (DV) CATEGORY

Section 203(c) of the Immigration and Nationality Act provides a maximum of up to 55,000 immigrant visas each fiscal year to permit immigration opportunities for persons from countries other than the principal sources of current immigration to the United States. The Nicaraguan and Central American Relief Act (NACARA) passed by Congress in November 1997 stipulates that beginning with DV-99, and for as long as necessary, up to 5,000 of the 55,000 annually-allocated diversity visas will be made available for use under the NACARA program. **This reduction has resulted in the DV-2006 annual limit being reduced to 50,000.** DV visas are divided among six geographic regions. No one country can receive more than seven percent of the available diversity visas in any one year.

For **November**, immigrant numbers in the DV category are available to qualified DV-2006 applicants chargeable to all regions/eligible countries as follows. When an allocation cut-off number is shown, visas are available only for applicants with DV regional lottery rank numbers **BELOW** the specified allocation cut-off number:

Region	All DV Chargeability Areas Except Those Listed Separately		
Africa	AF	6,000	Except: Ethiopia 4,600
			Nigeria 3,700
ASIA	AS	1,700	Except: Bangladesh 1,650
EUROPE	EU	3,900	
NORTH AMERICA (BAHAMAS)	NA	S	
OCEANIA	OC	200	
SOUTH AMERICA, and the **CARIBBEAN**	SA	275	

Entitlement to immigrant status in the DV category lasts only through the end of the fiscal (visa) year for which the applicant is selected in the lottery. The year of entitlement for all applicants registered for the DV-2006 program ends as of September 30, 2006. DV visas may not be issued to DV-2006 applicants after that date. Similarly, spouses and children accompanying or following to join DV-2006 principals are only entitled to derivative DV status until September 30, 2006. DV visa availability through the very end of FY-2006 cannot be taken for granted. Numbers could be exhausted prior to September 30.

C. ADVANCE NOTIFICATION OF THE DIVERSITY (DV) IMMIGRANT CATEGORY RANK CUT-OFFS WHICH WILL APPLY IN DECEMBER

For **December**, immigrant numbers in the DV category are available to qualified DV-2006 applicants chargeable to all regions/eligible countries as follows. When an allocation cut-off number is shown, visas are available only for applicants with DV regional lottery rank numbers **BELOW** the specified allocation cut-off number:

Region	All DV Chargeability Areas Except Those Listed Separately		
Africa	AF	7,500	Except: Ethiopia 6,800
			Nigeria 5,400
ASIA	AS	2,500	Except: Bangladesh 2,300
EUROPE	EU	5,500	
NORTH AMERICA (BAHAMAS)	NA	5	
OCEANIA	OC	270	
SOUTH AMERICA, and the **CARIBBEAN**	SA	400	

D. EMPLOYMENT PREFERENCE VISA AVAILABILITY

The backlog reduction efforts of both Citizenship and Immigration Services and the Department of Labor continue to result in very heavy demand for Employment-based numbers. The amount of cases currently being processed is sufficient to use all available numbers in many categories. The level of demand in the Employment categories is expected to be far in excess of the annual limits, and once established, cut-off date movements are likely to be slow.

WHAT CAUSES THE ESTABLISHMENT OF CUT-OFF DATES?

The Visa Office subdivides the annual preference and foreign state limitations specified in the Immigration and Nationality Act (INA) into twelve monthly allotments. The totals of documentarily qualified applicants that have been reported to VO are compared each month with the numbers available for the next regular allotment and numbers are allocated to reported applicants in order of their priority dates, the oldest dates first.

■ If there are sufficient numbers in a particular category to satisfy all reported documentarily qualified demand, the category is considered "Current." For example, if the Employment Third preference monthly target is 5,000 and there are only 3,000 applicants, the category is considered "Current".

■ Whenever the total of documentarily qualified applicants in a category exceeds the supply of numbers available for allotment for the particular month, the category is considered to be "oversubscribed" and a visa availability cut-off date is established. The cut-off date is the priority date of the first documentarily qualified applicant who could not be accommodated for a visa number. For example, if the Employment Third preference monthly target is 5,000 and there are 15,000 applicants, a cut-off date would be established so that only 5,000 numbers would be used, and the cut-off date would be the priority date of the 5,001st applicant.

WILL THERE BE CUT-OFF DATES FOR ANY ADDITIONAL FOREIGN STATES IN THE FIRST AND SECOND PREFERENCE CATEGORIES?

It may be necessary to establish a cut-off date for the "All Chargeability Areas" Second preference category at some point during the second half of the fiscal year. It is too early to estimate whether future demand will warrant such action. As of October 1st, cut-off dates for the First and Second preferences for China and India were established due to heavy demand; cut-off date movement is expected to be limited until a demand pattern has been determined.

WHY ARE THERE CUT-OFF DATES THIS YEAR AS OPPOSED TO PREVIOUS YEARS, WHEN THE CATEGORIES WERE CURRENT?

While the Employment categories had been "Current" for almost four years, several important factors affected the decision to implement cut-offs for FY-2006.

■ Prior to July 2001, demand for Employment numbers was such that cut-off dates were in effect for many categories, and that is the case once again for FY-2006.

The reasons the Employment categories had become current were:

■ The American Competitiveness in the Twenty-First Century Act (AC21) recaptured a "pool" of 131,000 Employment numbers unused in fiscal years 1999 and 2000, and allowed those recaptured numbers to be used by the oversubscribed countries, and

■ The substantial decline in demand for numbers for adjustment of status cases prevented the annual limits from being reached for several years.

In FY-2006, we are faced with continuing heavy demand due to the DHS and DOL backlog reduction efforts, along with an Employment limit which is approximately 40% lower than that of FY-2005. The lower annual Employment limit is a result of the virtual elimination of the "pool" of recaptured AC21 numbers, returning us to the pre-July 2001 situation.

WHAT ABOUT SCHEDULE A NUMBERS?

The 50,000 Schedule A numbers will provide relief to many Employment preference applicants, since any Schedule A applicant whose priority date is beyond the relevant Employment preference cut-off date can be processed and charged against the 50,000 limit. It is expected that Schedule A numbers will be available on a "Current" basis throughout all of FY-2006.

HOW IS THE EMPLOYMENT-BASED PER-COUNTRY LIMIT CALCULATED?

Section 201 of the INA sets an annual minimum Family-sponsored preference limit of 226,000, while the worldwide annual level for Employment-based preference immigrants is at least 140,000. Section 202 sets the per-country limit for preference immigrants at 7% of the total annual Family-sponsored and Employment-based preference limits, i.e. a minimum of 25,620.

- The annual per-country limitation of 7% is a cap, meaning visa issuances to any single country may not exceed this figure. This limitation is not a quota to which any particular country is entitled, however. The per-country limitation serves to avoid monopolization of virtually all the visa numbers by applicants from only a few countries.

- The AC21 removed the per-country limit in any calendar quarter in which overall applicant demand for Employment-based visa numbers is less than the total of such numbers available.

- In recent years, the application of the rules outlined in AC21 has allowed countries such as China—mainland born, India, and the Philippines to utilize large amounts of employment numbers which would have otherwise gone unused.

- During FY-2006, due to anticipated heavy demand, the AC21 provisions are not expected to apply, and the amount of Employment numbers available to any single country will be subject to the 7% cap. It is anticipated that the addition of unused FY-2005 Family numbers and the remaining AC21 numbers to the 140,000 annual minimum will result in an FY-2006 annual Employment limit of 152,000. This will mean an Employment per-country limit for FY-2006 of approximately 10,650.

■ To illustrate the effect of the reduced per-county limitation during FY-2006 on the oversubscribed countries, it should be noted that during FY-2005 India used approximately 47,175 Employment numbers.

E. OBTAINING THE MONTHLY VISA BULLETIN

The Department of State's Bureau of Consular Affairs offers the monthly "Visa Bulletin" on the INTERNET'S WORLDWIDE WEB. The INTERNET Web address to access the Bulletin is:

http://travel.state.gov

From the home page, select the VISA section which contains the Visa Bulletin.

To be placed on the Department of State's E-mail subscription list for the "Visa Bulletin", please send an E-mail to the following E-mail address:

listserv@calist.state.gov

and in the message body type:

**Subscribe Visa-Bulletin First name/Last name
(example: Subscribe Visa-Bulletin Sally Doe)**

To be removed from the Department of State's E-mail subscription list for the "Visa Bulletin", send an e-mail message to the following E-mail address :

listserv@calist.state.gov

and in the message body type:

Signoff Visa-Bulletin

The Department of State also has available a recorded message with visa cut-off dates which can be heard at: (area code 202) 663-1541. The recording is normally updated by the middle of each month with information on cut-off dates for the following month.

Readers may submit questions regarding Visa Bulletin related items by E-mail at the following address:

VISABULLETIN@STATE.GOV

Department of State Publication 9514
CA/VO:October 11, 2005

9
Child Status Protection Act

The Child Status Protection Act (CSPA) was signed into law on August 6, 2002. Prior to the CSPA, if a child was eligible for an immigrant visa or adjustment of status through derivative status, but was not issued the visa or adjustment of status before age 21, the individual lost their eligibility. CSPA finally gives a benefit to children who otherwise would have been "aged out" due to USCIS processing delays.

Children of U.S. Citizens: CSPA accomplishes this for the children of U.S. citizens who seek to qualify as an ``immediate relative'' by freezing their age as of the date that the petition is filed on their behalf.

Family-sponsored second preference: The petition for the child of a lawful permanent resident (FS-2A) is converted to an immediate relative petition when the parent is naturalized. Under the CSPA, the child's age is frozen as of the date of the naturalization. However, to benefit as an immediate relative, the child would need an additional petition filed on his or her behalf by the U.S. citizen parent (because, unlike a derivative relative of a preference petition, a child requires a separate petition to be classified as an immediate relative). But if the child had not yet turned 21 when the naturalization occurred, the immediate relative petition would succeed even if it were filed after her 21st birthday.

Family-sponsored third preference: For a married son or daughter of a U.S. citizen, the petition is converted to an immediate relative petition if the beneficiary's marriage ends and the beneficiary is then under 21, or to the first preference if the beneficiary has by then turned 21. The CSPA preserves the beneficiary's age as of the date of the death, divorce, or other act that terminated the marriage.

The CSPA also offers age-out protection to a child who is the beneficiary of a family-sponsored second-preference or who is a derivative beneficiary under any of the family-sponsored or employment-based (EB) preferences or under the diversity lottery. It does so by preserving the child's age as of the date a visa number becomes available to him or her, less the time the petition was pending. (In the case of a derivative beneficiary, the measuring date is the date a visa number becomes available to the principal beneficiary.) For example, an EB third-preference petition filed on January 2, 2002 and approved a year later (a visa number thereby becoming available to the principal beneficiary). Although the beneficiary's son turned 21 on July 1, 2002, his derivative status as a child is preserved because a year is deducted from the age he reached on January 2, 2003. In the case of a beneficiary whose age, under the calculation, is 21 or more, the petition is converted to the appropriate category, if any, with its original priority date.

To retain the benefit, however, the CSPA requires that the child,whether as a direct beneficiary or derivative, have "sought to acquire the status of lawful permanent residence within one year of such availability . . .", meaning, that they have applied for either adjustment of status or the immigrant visa.

The children of asylum applicants also enjoy aging-out benefits. They may be granted asylum when accompanying or following to join a parent granted asylum. And if they qualified as a "child" when the parent's application was filed, they continue to be eligible for asylum if they are not married when they themselves apply and accompany or follow to join the parent, even if they have meanwhile reached the age of 21. Similarly, the noncitizen who was under the age of 21 when his or her parent applied for refugee status, continues to be classified as a child for purposes of accompanying or following to join the parent granted refugee status even if he or she turned 21 while the application was pending.

CSPA is not only prospective but also covers any petition approved before its enactment, if there was no final decision on the beneficiary's application for adjustment of status or for an immigrant visa.

10
Labor Certification, Schedule A and Other Exemptions

As explained in Chapter 8, aliens who are offered permanent employment in the U.S. must establish a basis of eligibility for filing an employment based preference petition, either through:

1. Labor certification (employment based preference Category 2 and 3),

2. Exemption from labor certification (employment based Categories 1, 4 and 5) or

3. Under a Schedule A category.

This chapter describes the various stages involved in obtaining general labor certification for employment based preference Categories 2 and 3, and exemptions from labor certification.

The Labor Certification Process-Perm

Aliens who have been offered permanent employment in the U.S., and who do not meet the criteria for exemption from labor certification, must obtain Alien Employment Certification, commonly referred to as labor certification from the U.S. Department of Labor (DOL). The DOL must be satisfied that there are no qualified U.S. workers available to fill the permanent job offered to the alien, and that the working conditions and wages offered for the position will not have an adverse effect on the U.S. labor market. Once the labor certification is approved, it serves as the basis for filing an employment based 2nd or 3rd preference petition with the USCIS. (Appendix C contains Regional Department of Labor office addresses, and the jurisdictions that they cover.)

To obtain labor certification, the employer must demonstrate that he or she has followed a precise program of recruitment that tests the local labor market for qualified and available U.S. workers in the geographic area where the job will be filled.

The PERM process requires that all recruitment be conducted prior to filing the application and recruitment must be conducted within 6 months of filing. Each filing requires the following recruitment:

1. a job order must be placed with the State Workforce Agency serving the area of intended employment

2. ads on two different Sundays in a newspaper of general circulation (if the job requires experience and an advanced degree, a professional journal may be substituted for one of the Sunday newspaper ads).

3. three forms of additional recruitment must be conducted out of the following list of ten: (a) job fairs (b) employer's web site (c) job search web site other than employers (d) on-campus recruiting (e) trade or professional organizations (f) private employment firms (g) employee referral program with incentives (h) campus placement offices (i) local and ethnic newspapers (j) radio and tv ads. In addition, there must be an internal posting for 10 consecutive business days, as was previously done for regular or RIR labor certification applications.

The application can be filed either electronically or by mail on Form ETA 9089, describing the job in detail, indicating the salary offered and describing the minimum qualifications for the position, including minimum education and experience and any special requirements. The Labor Department will either approve the application or select the application for audit. The routine processing time for non-audited cases is expected to be about 60 days.

Once the case is certified by the Labor Department, the applicant's employer can file an I-140 petition with the USCIS and if the applicant is eligible to adjust status, the applicant can simultaneously file an application for adjustment of status. Employment based petitions are filed at one of the four Regional Service Centers.

Note: The American Competitiveness in the 21st Century Act of 2000 also provided, for the first time, some flexibility in the ability to change jobs or employers, for those whose adjustment of status applications had been pending for more than 180 days. The new job must be in the same or similar occupational classification as the one for which the petition was originally filed.

Previously, one had to remain with the same employer, and in the same position, until the application for adjustment of status had been approved.

Schedule A Categories

In some cases, known as Schedule A, the U.S. Department of Labor has determined that the sponsoring employer need not obtain labor certification. There are presently two Schedule A categories:

■ ***Schedule A Group I:*** Applies to professional nurses and physical therapists. In each case, the alien must have very specific credentials, including licenses, and must have passed certain exams required by each state to practice their vocation in the United States. Labor certifications are not available to professional nurses and physical therapists, even if their Schedule A Group I applications are denied.

Note: A nurse or physical therapist must provide a CGFNS (Commission on Graduates of Foreign Nursing Schools) Certificate dated after October 1, 1998 in order to obtain permanent residence.

■ ***Schedule A Group II:*** Applies to aliens who have exceptional ability in the arts and sciences and may not qualify under employment based first preference. This category is primarily reserved for individuals who have received widespread international acclaim in their specific field, such as scientists, professors, and authors. Aliens of exceptional ability in the performing arts may also qualify under certain circumstances. The USCIS has very stringent documentary requirements for Schedule A Group II classification, including testimonial letters from experts in the alien's field of endeavor, published works by or about the alien, invitations extended to the alien to speak at international conferences, and awards.

Schedule A applications are filed directly with the USCIS Regional Service Center. Once the application is approved, and the priority date becomes current, the permanent residence application can be completed through adjustment of status, or by visa processing at an American Consulate. The procedures are the same as for aliens who have approved labor certifications, described above.

National Interest Waiver

An alien may seek a waiver of the offer of employment by establishing that his admission to permanent residence would be in the "national interest". There is no hard and fast rule, nor any statutory standards as to what will qualify an alien for a National Interest Waiver. The USCIS considers each case on an individual basis. The procedure is to file Form I-140 together with evidence to establish that the alien's admission to the United States for permanent residence would be in the national interest. Factors that have been considered in successful cases include:

■ The alien's admission will improve the U.S. economy.

■ The alien's admission will improve wages and working conditions of U.S. workers.

■ The alien's admission will improve educational and training programs for U.S. children and underqualified workers.

■ The alien's admission will provide more affordable housing for young, aged, or poor U.S. residents.

■ The alien's admission will improve the U.S. environment and lead to more productive use of the national resources.

■ The alien's admission is requested by an interested U.S. government agency.

Many of the cases in which national interest waivers have been approved were supported by affidavits from well-known, established and influential people or organizations. For example, an application being submitted for a scientist should contain affidavits from leading scientists, representatives of scientific institutions, and from other organizations associated with the type of research to be pursued. Documenting past achievements, as well as proof that the alien has already created jobs, turned around a business or created an increase in exports or other economic improvements should prove instrumental in gaining approval.

Other Employment-based Categories

Aliens applying for permanent residence in employment-based preference Categories 1, 4 and 5 do not require labor certification. Aliens in employment-based preference categories 2 & 3, who can establish that their admission is in the "National Interest", also do not require labor certification. Application is made directly to the USCIS on Form I-140—Immigrant Petition for Alien Worker in employment-based preference Categories 1, 2 & 3, on Form I-360—Petition for Amerasian, Widow or Special Immigrant in employment-based preference Category 4, and on Form I-526—Immigrant Petition by Alien Entrepreneur in employment-based preference Category 5. Supporting documentation varies depending on the category in which the alien is applying.

11

Immigrant Visas for Alien Investors

The Immigration Act of 1990 created a new preference category for immigrants who are able to invest at least $1 million in the United States.

Immigrant visas are available, subject to quota limitations (approximately 10,000 annually), for immigrants seeking to enter the United States to engage in a new commercial enterprise. This new business must benefit the U.S. economy and create at least ten full-time jobs for U.S. citizens or permanent residents, other than the applicant or his or her immediate family.

The minimum amount of the investment is $1 million, although the USCIS may consider less if the investment is in a "targeted employment" area, i.e., and one where the unemployment rate is 150% of the national average. The investment must have been made after November 29, 1990.

Under this category, the term "investment" generally means that the alien must place his or her capital at risk for the purpose of generating a profit. The company must have been formed for the "ongoing conduct of lawful business". The investment must be in a commercial enterprise that generates active income. Apartment buildings, for example, would not qualify, since the income they generate is considered passive. The term "capital" is defined as "cash, equipment, inventory, tangible property, cash equivalents and indebtedness secured by the investor's assets, provided he or she is personally liable".

The enterprise may be a sole proprietorship, a partnership, a holding company, a joint venture, a corporation or other entity publicly or privately owned. The investment does not have to be completed, but the investor must be "in the process" of investing, showing an actual commitment of funds.

Generally, the investment must be in either:

- A newly created business
- The purchase of an existing business and simultaneous or subsequent restructuring or reorganization such that a new commercial enterprise results

■ The expansion of an existing business so long as there is a substantial change of at least 140% in either net worth or in the number of employees of the company.

Debt can be used to secure capital, provided that the alien is personally and primarily liable, and the debt is not secured against the assets of the enterprise. Capital may come from abroad, but ownership of the capital must be established.

The investor will also have to show that he will be actively engaged in the management of the enterprise. Any assets or capital derived from illegal means or criminal activity will not be considered.

Generally, the documents for the immigrant investor are those that would establish the investment, that is, proof of the capital invested, proof of the creation of new jobs, proof of the alien's management position and evidence of the nature of the enterprise. Form I-526—Immigrant Petition by Alien Entrepreneur, is also required.

The legal definitions and rules for alien investors are complex, and you should seek the advice of a professional if you intend to pursue this category.

12
Immigrant Visas for Foreign Born Orphans

The Immigration and Nationality Act allows for U.S. citizens to apply for immigrant visas for foreign born children who are orphans, and have not yet reached the age of 16.

Two categories of U.S. citizens can file an orphan petition:

1. A married U.S. citizen and spouse (no age requirement). The spouse does not have to be a U.S. citizen, but must be here legally, if living in the U.S.

2. An unmarried U.S. citizen who is at least 25 years old.

A child is an orphan if he or she does not have any parents due to death or disappearance, desertion or abandonment, or separation or loss from both parents. A child can also qualify if a sole surviving parent cannot take proper care of the child, and has issued a written and irrevocable release of the child for adoption and emigration.

Application can be made for advance processing before the U.S. citizen actually locates an orphan to adopt. This allows USCIS to process the part of the application that proves the U.S. citizen's ability to provide a proper home and your suitability as a parent. It is recommended that all prospective adoptive parents do advance processing. The advance processing application is filed with the USCIS office having jurisdiction over where the petitioner lives and consists of:

1. Form I-600A-Application for Advance Processing of Orphan Petition

2. Proof of U.S. citizenship

3. Proof of spouse's U.S. citizenship or lawful immigration status, if living in the U.S.

4. Proof of marriage, and termination of prior marriages

5. Complete home study

6. Proof of compliance with the pre-adoption requirements of the state where you will live with the adopted child

7. Fingerprints for each adult household member

8. Filing fee of $545.00.

Note: The USCIS publishes Document M-249N-The Immigration of Adopted and Prospective Adoptive Children that contains more detailed information.

Approval of the Application for Advance Processing will facilitate the filing of Form I-600-Petition to Classify Orphan as an Immediate Relative. This second application can be processed at an overseas USCIS office or American Embassy or Consulate, once an orphan is located for adoption. The complete application consists of:

1. Form I-600-Petition to Classify Orphan as an Immediate Relative

2. The child's birth certificate or evidence of the child's age and identity

3. Proof that the child is an orphan, as defined above

4. A final adoption decree, if applicable

5. Proof of legal custody of the child for adoption and emigration, if applicable.

6. Proof of compliance with pre-adoption requirements, if applicable

7. Filing fee of $545.00.

The adoption of a foreign born child by a U.S. citizen does not guarantee the child's right to immigrate to the U.S. If the orphan petition is approved, the child becomes an immediate relative of a U.S. citizen, and can apply for an immigrant visa. However, just like any other foreign-born person, the child must qualify for the immigrant visa. Assuming the visa is approved, the orphan will enter the U.S. as a lawful permanent resident, not a U.S. citizen.

A subsequent application for U.S. citizenship must be filed (Form N-643-Application for Certificate of Citizenship on Behalf of an Adopted Child), before the child is 18 years old. If the application is not completed before the child reaches the age of 18, the child will have to apply for citizenship on their own.

13

The ANNUAL Visa Lottery Program

In 1995, the Immigration and Nationality Act established an annual visa lottery. Natives of certain countries, selected by a mathematical formula, are able to compete for visas in this category. The numerical limit on these types of visas is 50,000 per year for people from countries with low rates of immigration to the U.S. The applicant can apply either from within the U.S. or from outside the U.S.

In 1995 the program was known as the DV-1 lottery. In subsequent years the identifying symbol will be "DV" followed by the fiscal year. For example, the 2007 lottery is known as DV-2007. (The government fiscal year begins on October 1 and ends on September 30.) The registration period for DV-2007 began October 5, 2005 and ended on December 4, 2005.

For DV-2007,natives of the following countries were excluded from the lottery: Canada, China (mainland-born), Colombia, Dominican Republic, El Salvador, Haiti, India, Jamaica, Mexico, Pakistan, Philippines, Poland, Russia, South Korea, United Kingdom (except Northern Ireland), and Vietnam. People born in Hong Kong SAR, Macau SAR and Taiwan were eligible.

Special requirements for the DV lottery are as follows:

1. Each applicant must have a high school education or its equivalent
   or

2. Within the past five years, have had two years of work experience in an occupation requiring at least two years of training or experience.

Currently, the Department of State will only accept completed applications submitted electronically at www.dvlottery.state.gov during the registration period. The Department of State has tripled the number of servers hosting the registration website this year in response to demand. In addition, those who submit entries to the 2007 lottery will receive a receipt containing their name, date of birth, county of chargeability, and a time/date stamp when information has been properly registered.

1. Only one application per person may be submitted. Multiple applications disqualify an applicant from registration.

2. Successfully registered entries will result in a computer confirmation screen which should be printed and saved.

3. Paper entries will not be accepted.

4. The application will be disqualified if the required digital photos are not submitted.

After the end of the application period, a computer will randomly select cases from among all the applicants from each geographic region. If you are selected, you will receive a letter from the Kentucky Consular Center (for DV 2007 between May and July 2006) with instructions on how to complete the process. Once you get this letter it is imperative that you complete all applications, follow the instructions and file the necessary documents immediately. Those not selected, will not be notified. DV-2007 visas will be issued between October 1, 2006 and September 30, 2007. Successful applicants may either apply for an immigrant visa at the American Consulate in their country of residence or, if they are in the United States and are eligible to adjust status, apply at the USCIS office having jurisdiction over their place of residence.

The formal visa application made at the American Consulate consists of:

1. Form DS- 230 I & II- Special Lottery Form

2. Police certificates where applicable

3. Birth certificates

4. Marriage certificate or proof of termination of prior marriages

5. Proof of high school education or equivalent, or required work experience

6. Photographs

7. Completed medical examination

8. Proof of support or job offer for permanent employment.

The application for adjustment of status filed at the USCIS is similar to the application for adjustment of status described in Chapter 8. In addition, the applicant must provide:

1. Copy of the notification letter from the Kentucky Consular Center

2. Proof of high school education or equivalent, or required work experience

3. Proof of support or job offer.

List of Countries by Region Whose Natives Qualify

The lists below show the countries whose natives are QUALIFIED within each geographic region for this diversity program. The determination of countries within each region is based on information provided by the Geographer of the Department of State. The countries whose natives do not qualify for the DV-2006 program were identified by the U.S. Citizenship and Immigration Services (USCIS) according to the formula in Section 203(c) of the Immigration and Nationality Act. Dependent areas overseas are included within the region of the governing country. The countries whose natives do NOT qualify for this diversity program (because they are the principal source countries of Family-Sponsored and Employment-Based immigration, or "high admission" countries) are noted after the respective regional lists.

AFRICA

Algeria	Libya
Angola	Madagascar
Benin	Malawi
Botswana	Mali
Burkina Faso	Mauritania
Burundi	Mauritius
Cameroon	Morocco
Cape Verde	Mozambique
Central African Republic	Namibia
Chad	Niger
Comoros	Nigeria
Congo	Rwanda
Congo, Democratic Republic of the	Sao Tome and Principe
Cote D'Ivoire (Ivory Coast)	Senegal
Djibouti	Seychelles
Egypt	Sierra Leone
Equatorial Guinea	Somalia
Eritrea	South Africa
Ethiopia	Sudan
Gabon	Swaziland
Gambia, The	Tanzania

Ghana
Guinea
Guinea-Bissau
Kenya
Lesotho
Liberia

Togo
Tunisia
Uganda
Zambia
Zimbabwe

ASIA

Afghanistan
Bahrain
Bangladesh
Bhutan
Brunei
Burma
Cambodia
East Timor
Hong Kong Special Administrative Region
Indonesia
Iran
Iraq
Israel
Japan
Jordan
Kuwait
Laos

Lebanon
Malaysia
Maldives
Mongolia
Nepal
North Korea
Oman
Qatar
Saudi Arabia
Singapore
Sri Lanka
Syria
Taiwan
Thailand
United Arab Emirates
Yemen

Natives of the following Asian countries do not qualify for this year's diversity program: China [mainland-born], India, Pakistan, South Korea, Philippines, and Vietnam. The Hong Kong S.A.R and Taiwan do qualify and are listed above. Macau S.A.R. also qualifies and is listed below.

EUROPE

Albania
Andorra
Armenia
Austria
Azerbaijan
Belarus
Belgium
Bosnia and Herzegovina
Bulgaria

Croatia
Cyprus
Czech Republic
Denmark (including components and
    dependent areas overseas)
Estonia
Finland
France (including components and
    dependent areas overseas)

Georgia	Ireland
Germany	Italy
Greece	Kazakhstan
Hungary	Kyrgyzstan
Iceland	Latvia

Natives of the following European countries do not qualify for this year's diversity program: Great Britain, Poland and Russia. Great Britain (United Kingdom) includes the following dependent areas: Anguilla, Bermuda, British Virgin Islands, Cayman Islands, Falkland Islands, Gibraltar, Montserrat, Pitcairn, St. Helena, Turks and Caicos Islands. Note that for purposes of the diversity program only, Northern Ireland is treated separately; Northern Ireland does qualify and is listed among the qualifying areas.

NORTH AMERICA

Countries in this region whose natives do not qualify for this year's diversity program: Colombia, Dominican Republic, El Salvador, Haiti, Jamaica, and Mexico.

The Bahamas
In North America, natives of Canada
   and Mexico do not qualify for this
   year's diversity program.

OCEANIA

Australia (including components and dependent areas overseas)	Palau
	Papua New Guinea
Fiji	Solomon Islands
Kiribati	Tonga
Marshall Islands	Tuvalu
Micronesia, Federated States of	Vanuatu
Nauru	Samoa
New Zealand (including components and dependent areas overseas)	

SOUTH AMERICA, CENTRAL AMERICA, AND THE CARIBBEAN

Antigua and Barbuda	Costa Rica
Argentina	Cuba
Barbados	Dominica
Belize	Ecuador
Bolivia	Grenada
Brazil	Guatemala
Chile	Guyana

Honduras	Saint Lucia
Nicaragua	Saint Vincent and the Grenadines
Panama	Suriname
Paraguay	Trinidad and Tobago
Peru	Uruguay
Saint Kitts and Nevis	Venezuela

Countries in this region whose natives do not qualify for this year's diversity program: Colombia, Dominican Republic, El Salvador, Haiti, Jamaica, and Mexico.

14
Renewal of Expiring Green Cards

Since 1989, the USCIS has been issuing Green Cards with a ten-year expiration date on the front of the card. This allowed the agency to update photo identification and implement new card technologies to increase the card's resistance to counterfeiting and tampering.

Procedures are now in place to accommodate Green Card renewal applicants. Application can be made up to six months in advance of the expiration.

Applicants should complete Form I-90 (Application to Replace a Permanent Resident Card). The application can be obtained by calling the toll-free forms request line (1-800-870-3676) or on line at http://uscis.gov/graphics/formsfee/forms/index.htm. The form can be completed on line as well.

Renewal applicants should mail their applications to:

USCIS Citizenship and Immigration Services
PO Box 54870
Los Angeles, CA 90054-0870

Or may send them by courier to:

U.S. Citizenship and Immigration Services
Attention I-90
16420 Valley View Avenue
La Mirada, CA 90638

The application consists of:

> 1. Form I-90-Application to Replace a Permanent Resident Card
> 2. Check or money order for $190.00 payable to USCIS
> 3. $70.00 Biometrics fee

After you apply, USCIS will schedule your biometrics appointment to have your biometrics taken at a USCIS Application Support Center (ASC). You will be receiving a biometrics appointment notice with a specific date, time, and place where you will have your fingerprints and/or photos taken. You MUST wait for your biometrics appointment notice to arrive in the mail prior to going to the ASC for biometrics processing.

Bring the following to your biometrics appointment:

- Biometrics appointment notice.
- Photo identification. Acceptable kinds of photo identifications are:
    - Passport or national photo identification issued by your country, or
    - Driver's license, or
    - Military photo identification, or
    - State-issued photo identification card.
- Required initial evidence, including:
    - Your prior card, or
    - Other evidence of permanent residence or commuter status
- Supporting documentation, which may include but is not limited to:
    - Court ordered name change,
    - Marriage certificate,
    - Birth certificate, or
    - Police report for a stolen or lost card.

If you fail to renew your expiring card, you may have difficulties in obtaining employment, benefits and reentry into the U.S. from abroad.

If your Green Card has already expired, you should apply for a renewal as soon as possible, since you are required by law to carry evidence of your status/registration. You will not be penalized.

15

Infopass and the USCIS Website

InfoPass is a free and convenient internet-based system. It eliminates the need to go in person to make an appointment, obtain forms, general information or even specific information about a case pending at one of the Service Centers. The USCIS website is a wonderful resource for immigration information, for obtaining forms and for checking the status of your case filed at a Service Center. The USCIS website can be found at: http://uscis.gov/graphics/index.htm

INFOPASS eliminates the need to stand in line at a USCIS District Office. It is accessible by computer at: http://infopass.uscis.gov/. If you do not have a computer available, the District Offices have kiosks set up and an information officer available to help you. With INFOPASS you can schedule an appointment at a local office by entering your zip code, then choosing one of the following options:

1. You need an immigration form

2. You need to replace your Alien Registration Card

3. You need to file an application for yourself or someone else

4. You have a question about your case

5. You have received an approval letter or Form I-797C from the Service Center or local office instructing you to come into the office for alien identification card processing/passport stamp

6. It has been more than 90 days since you filed an I-765 and you did not receive an Employment Authorization Card

7. You wish to speak to an immigration officer.

Interviews are scheduled two weeks in advance. The best time to access the site is after 5 pm.

The information provided on the following page should help with routine inquiries.

YOU NEED A FORM: All immigration forms are free and can be downloaded from www.uscis.gov or by calling the National Customer Service Center (NCSC) at 1-800-375-5283.

YOU WANT TO CHECK THE STATUS OF A CASE: Go to www.uscis.gov and select "Case Status & Processing Dates" under "Hot Topics" on the right side of the home page. You must have your Service Center receipt number.

YOU WANT TO RENEW OR REPLACE A GREEN CARD: You need to file Form I-90 "Application for Replacement of Green Card". Go to www.uscis.gov and select "E-filing" under "Hot Topics" on the right side of the home page.

YOU NEED EMPLOYMENT AUTHORIZATION: To apply or renew employment authorization, you will need Form I-765 "Application for Employment Authorization". This form can be filed online by going to www.uscis.gov and selecting "E-filing" under "Hot Topics" on the right side of the home page.

YOU NEED GENERAL INFORMATION: Before planning a trip to the USCIS, call the NCSC at 1-800-375-5283 to see if they can help you over the phone.

16
Naturalization

Aliens elect to become citizens of the United States in order to reap the benefits, such as the right to vote, the right to obtain a U.S. passport, and the ability to sponsor relatives for permanent residence. This chapter describes the rules and procedures for applying for citizenship or naturalization.

Permanent residents are eligible for naturalization five years after permanent residence is granted. The applicant must have physically resided in the U.S. for at least two and one half years out of the five years and have been a resident of the state where the application for naturalization is filed for at least three months. If the applicant spent more than one full year during the five-year qualifying period outside the U.S., he or she is not eligible for citizenship under the same guidelines.

If the applicant was granted permanent residence based on marriage to a U.S. citizen, he or she can apply for naturalization after three years.

However, the following conditions must be met:

- The spouse must have been a citizen for three years, and
- The couple must have been married for at least three years.
- The applicant must have lived in the U.S. for at least eighteen months out of the three years, and
- The applicant must have been a resident of the state for at least three months.

The application is filed with the USCIS at the Regional Service Center having jurisdiction over the alien's place of residence. It can be filed up to three months in advance of actual eligibility. It consists of:

1. Form N-400-Application for Naturalization
2. Check for $70.00 for fingerprint fee
3. Photographs
4. Copy of front and back of your green card
5. Filing fee of $330.00.

The applicant will then be called for an interview at the USCIS. It may take up to eight months to receive the notice. At the interview, the applicant will be asked a series of questions to determine good moral character, the ability to read, write and speak elementary English and the intention to reside in the U.S. permanently. (Aliens over the age of fifty-five who have been living in the U.S. as permanent residents for at least fifteen years can have the English language requirement waived. Aliens who are over the age of fifty and have been permanent residents for at least twenty years can also have this requirement waived.) The applicant will also be tested for a basic understanding of U.S. history and the U.S. government, including their belief in the U.S. constitution. The exam can also be taken as part of a course of study given by an independent organization approved by the USCIS. If the applicant passes, he or she will be given a certificate, valid for one year. The USCIS will accept the certificate in lieu of the written exam.

People who are certified by a physician to have physical or developmental disabilities or mental impairments are exempt from the literacy and government/history knowledge requirements.

The application must be approved or denied within four months of the interview. Assuming it is approved, the final swearing-in ceremony will be held the same day, or at a later date, depending on the current procedure at your local USCIS office. At the time of the swearing-in ceremony, the applicant is required to take the following oath of allegiance to the United States of America, and sign this oath.

*I hereby declare, on oath, that I absolutely and entirely renounce and abjure all allegiance and fidelity to any foreign prince, potentate, state or sovereignty of whom or which I have heretofore been a subject or citizen; that I will support and defend the Constitution and laws of the United States of America against all enemies, foreign and domestic; that I will bear true faith and allegiance to the same; * that I will bear arms on behalf of the United States when required by law; * that I will perform noncombatant service in the Armed Forces of the United States when required by law; that I will perform work of national importance under civilian direction when required by law; and that I take this obligation freely without any mental reservation or purpose of evasion; so help me God.*

 * In some cases, the USCIS will allow these clauses to be omitted.

At the end of the ceremony the applicant is granted a Certificate of Naturalization. This can then be presented at a U.S. Passport Agency office to obtain a U.S. passport. During the naturalization process, the applicant retains his or her U.S. permanent resident status.

For more information, please obtain a copy of our book *Citizenship Made Simple, an easy to read guide to the U.S. citizenship process*. This book can be ordered through your local bookstore, by using the order form provided in the back of this book, or at our web site: www.nextdecade.com.

17

IRCA Employer Obligations and Verification of Employment

In 1986, the Immigration Reform and Control Act (IRCA) was established in the U.S. It was developed, in part, to control the number of illegal aliens coming to the U.S. to work. Since the enactment of the program, there have been many controversial issues and regulatory changes. The Immigration Act of 1990 brought about even further changes.

IRCA requires that employers check the identity and the right to work of all new hires (including U.S. citizens), and complete Form I-9- Employment Eligibility Verification for every employee, regardless of their nationality. These regulations also state that the employer cannot discriminate against potential hires on the basis of their origin or citizenship. Form I-9 must be completed for all employees hired after November 6, 1986. Processing and record keeping of Forms I-9 are as follows:

- The employee completes Section 1 of the form when he or she starts to work.

- The employer reviews the documents that establish the employee's right to work and his or her identity, and completes Section 2 within three business days of hire. (Lists of documents that the employer can accept to prove identity and the right to work are given later in this chapter.) If the employee cannot produce the documents, but can produce an application receipt for them, this should be recorded, and the employee has 90 days to present the actual document. Section 2 of Form I-9 should be amended at that time. Note that special rules apply to the completion of Form I-9 for minors (under age 18) and handicapped employees.

- The employer keeps all Forms I-9 for three years after the employee starts to work or one year after the employee leaves the employer, whichever is later.

- Employers must again verify employment authorization for those employees who initially produced documents with an expiration date, and complete Section 3 on Form I-9. If updated proof of work authorization cannot be provided, the employer cannot continue to employ that individual.

■ The employer must have all Forms I-9 available to be inspected by an USCIS officer, or related official. Three days notice should be given.

An employer cannot require that the employee present different documents, or more documents, or refuse to accept documents that appear to be genuine. Forms I-9 can be photocopied, or the employer can order several copies from: Superintendent of Documents, U.S. Government Printing Office, Washington, DC 20402. Following are lists of acceptable documents:

List A: Employment Eligibility and Identity

1. U.S. passport (even if it has expired)

2. Certificate of U.S. citizenship (Form N-560 or N-561)

3. Certificate of Naturalization (Form N-550 or N-570)

4. Valid foreign passport with a valid I-551 stamp or Form I-94 indicating valid employment authorization

5. Alien Registration Receipt Card (Form I-151 or I-551), which contains a photo of the alien—(i.e. green card)

6. Unexpired Temporary Resident Card (Form I-688)

7. Unexpired Employment Authorization Card (USCIS Form I-688A)

8. Unexpired Reentry Permit (Form I-327)

9. Unexpired Refugee Travel Document (Form I-571)

10. Unexpired Employment Authorization Document issued by the USCIS with photo (Form I-688B).

These ten documents establish both employment eligibility and identity. If the employee can produce one of these documents, they have satisfied both the identity and employment eligibility requirement to complete Form I-9:

List B: Identity

1. Driver's license or identification card issued by a state or possession of the U.S., which contains a photo or personal information such as name, birth date, eye color

2. Identification card issued by a Federal, State or Local government agency, which contains a photo or personal information as indicated above (includes U.S. Citizen ID Card—USCIS Form I-197 and ID Card for use of Resident Citizen in the U.S.—USCIS Form I-179

3. School identification card with a photo

4. Voter registration card

5. U.S. military card or draft records

6. Military dependent's identification card

7. U.S. Coast Guard Merchant Marine Card

8. Native American Tribal Document

9. Driver's license issued by the Canadian government

10. Non-driver's ID Card issued by a state.

The previous ten documents establish only identity for employees over the age of eighteen. If the employee can produce one of these documents and one document from List C, he or she has satisfied the identity and employment eligibility requirement for completing Form I-9:

List C: Employment Eligibility

1. U.S. Social Security Card (if it states that it is "not valid for employment", it cannot be accepted)

2. Certification of Birth Abroad that is issued by the U.S. Department of State on Form FS-545 or Form DS-1350

3. Original or certified copy of a birth certificate issued by the U.S. and bearing an official seal

4. Native American Tribal Document

5. U.S. Citizen identification card (Form I-197)

6. Identification card for use of Resident Citizen in the U.S. (Form I-179)

7. Valid employment authorization document, issued by the USCIS (other than those in List A).

8. Form I-797: The USCIS form issued when a petition is approved for nonimmigrant "H","L","O","P","Q" and "R" status and for change of status to "E". Aliens in these categories are only authorized to work for the employers who petitioned for them. The bottom half of this form, together with Form I-94, can be accepted as an employment document under List C.

9. Form I-20ID Copy: This document consists of pages 3 and 4 of the Form I-20, (the certificate of eligibility issued by a school to permit a foreign student to attend that school). Some foreign students may have their work authorization endorsed on this form. Form I-20ID together with Form I-94, showing that a student was admitted for D/S, can be accepted as an employment authorization document under List C.

10. Form DS-2019: Some J-1 exchange visitors have permission to work. Their Form DS-2019 will show this. Form IAP-66, together with Form I-94, is considered an employment authorization document under List C.

The ten documents listed above establish employment eligibility only. As indicated above, one document from List C must be produced with one document from List B.

Note: Certain documents including the U.S. Citizen ID card, Resident Citizen ID card and Native American Tribal Document appear on both List B and List C. These documents can be presented to establish both identity and employment eligibility and should be recorded in both spaces on Form I-9. They are not included in List A, only because Congress has not designated them in the law.

The USCIS has proposed changes to the List of I-9 documents, but as of this publication the rule has not been finalized. Those proposed changes are:

Eliminate from List A:

Employment authorization card Form I-688A

Reentry permit

Refugee travel document

Eliminate from List B:

School ID card

Voter's registration card

U.S. military card or draft record

Military dependent's ID card

U.S. Coast Guard Merchant Mariner card

Identity documents for persons under age 18

Eliminate from List C:

Birth certification issued by the Department of State

U.S. citizen ID card

Hiring or continuing to hire aliens who do not have work authorization; failure to complete I-9 forms; and/or unlawful discrimination can result in severe penalties including escalating monetary fines, and in some cases imprisonment.

18
Questions and Answers

Over the years, we have been asked many questions about various aspects of processing visas and related matters involving international relocation. We thought that it would be helpful to include some of these questions so that you may benefit from the answers as well.

Q. Do I need to retain an attorney to assist me in processing my immigration papers and how can I find one to help me?

A. In most cases, you will need an attorney. The U.S. immigration process is extremely complex, and recent changes make it even more so. There are always administrative changes taking place at the USCIS offices. If papers are not prepared and filed properly, the odds for a successful outcome are greatly diminished.

Most aliens have friends who have sought immigration counsel in the past and may be able to provide you with the name of a qualified attorney. The Directory of Immigration Lawyers is in this book to assist you, as well. The local office of the state Bar Association can also be a helpful source of referral, as can the Legal Aid Society. Many attorneys also advertise their services in the Yellow Pages of the Telephone Directory.

One fact to keep in mind is that not every attorney is as qualified as the next to give you advice on immigration matters. Consult with at least two attorneys and choose the one with whom you feel most comfortable. Make sure to find out, before retaining the lawyer, what his or her legal fee will be and exactly what the fee will include —e.g., filing fees, miscellaneous expenses such as copy charges and postage. These disbursements can add up quickly! Ask the attorney about the billing schedule so that you can allocate your money through the various stages of your immigration case.

Never retain the services of a lawyer who promises or guarantees you anything, or who gives you time frames that seem unrealistic. Do not hesitate to change from one lawyer to another during your case, if you are unhappy with the services being provided. Make sure to obtain your complete file to ensure an easy transition from one lawyer to the next.

Q. Will the USCIS be a good source of information on processing my immigration case?

A. In most situations, calling or visiting the USCIS will not be very helpful. The USCIS employees are very busy and usually do not have the time to plan individual immigration strategies. You may also be putting yourself in jeopardy if you are in the U.S. illegally. However, you should visit the USCIS web site (http://uscis.gov/graphics/index.htm)that has quite a bit of valuable information.

Q. What is the difference between a visa and an arrival-departure record?

A. A visa is a permit to enter the U.S. that is normally obtained at an American Consulate outside the U.S. The USCIS creates an arrival-departure record (Form I-94) when the traveler arrives in the U.S. The fact that an individual has a visa does not guarantee their entry into the U.S., nor the amount of time they can remain in the U.S.

Q. Why is my green card case taking so long compared to my friend's?

A. Do not compare your case with those of friends or relatives. In most situations, the facts are not the same, even though they may appear to be. In addition, there are a variety of reasons why identical cases may vary in time frames. Your attorney is interested in completing your case as quickly as possible.

Q. Where can I obtain immigration forms without visiting the USCIS?

A. The easiest way to obtain forms is to call 1-800-870-FORMS. If you have a computer, you can download forms from the USCIS web site at http://uscis.gov/graphics/formsfee/forms/index.htm

Q. What if I do not have all of the personal documents that are required to complete my case?

A. The USCIS and the Consular officials are very strict in this matter. It is almost always possible to obtain duplicate originals of any document that was lost or destroyed. Ask your attorney how to do so. For example, some countries do not issue birth certificates. In these cases, the authorities will accept secondary evidence of birth in the form of affidavits from close relatives. However, the USCIS and Consular officials maintain books that list which documents are available from each country. If you go to a visa interview without all of the required documents, there is a good chance that your case will be delayed or denied.

Q. What if a visa appointment is scheduled for me at the USCIS or at the Consular office and I cannot keep it?

A. It is very difficult to reschedule appointments because of the heavy volume of cases that these offices must process, and delays of several months can result if requests for rescheduling are made. Do not attempt to change appointment dates unless you absolutely must. In addition, never ignore a notice to appear for an interview at the USCIS.

Q. If I have filed an Application for Adjustment of Status from a temporary visa to permanent residence through an Immigration office in the U.S., can I travel while the application is pending?

A. Once you have filed for permanent residence, your temporary visa should not be used for travel purposes, with the exception of H & L visas. If you need to travel outside the U.S. during this process for critical business or personal reasons such as a family emergency abroad, you can apply to the USCIS for a travel document known as an Advance Parole. Use Form I-131—Application for Travel Document. This document allows you to leave and reenter the U.S. within a given period of time. You must, however, be prepared to provide the USCIS with ample evidence of the need to travel.

Q. How can I check the status of my case?

A. If you filed your case at an USCIS Service Center you can follow up in two ways:

Online at: https://egov.immigration.gov/cris/jsps/index.jsp

By calling the NCSC at 1-800-375-5283.

If you filed at a local USCIS office, you will need to make an InfoPass appointment.

Q. If I obtain my green card through labor certification, must I always work for the same employer?

A. No. At the time that you are granted permanent residence, the sponsoring employer must intend to have you work for them and you must plan to do so. If the employment relationship does not work out after you have started the job, you can seek other employment.

Q. How can I obtain a work permit?

A. Work permits are only issued if you are eligible under one of the categories authorized by the law, and described in this book.

Q. How can I get a Social Security Number?

A. If you are in the U.S. legally, and have a working visa, Form I-94, or other document authorizing employment in the U.S., you can obtain a number. You must apply in person at the nearest Social Security Administration Office. Bring your passport; Form I-94 and proof of work authorization. You will be asked to complete an application form (Form SS-5). The Social Security Card will be mailed to you within several weeks.

If you are in the U.S. and do not have work authorization, you cannot obtain a Social Security Number. However, if you need an identification number, for example, to open a brokerage account or to purchase investment property in the U.S., you should request Form W-7 from the Internal Revenue Service and apply for a Taxpayer Identification Number.

Q. If I have a Social Security number can I work in the U.S.?

A. The Social Security number is not a work permit. You must also have a visa, Form I-94, or other document that proves you have employment authorization.

Q. Am I eligible to collect Social Security?

A. The following classes of individuals are included in those who may be eligible for Social Security benefits: naturalized citizens; permanent resident aliens; temporary residents through a variety of programs including amnesty; refugees and asylees. This list is not all-inclusive.

Q. Am I eligible for unemployment benefits?

A. If you are a naturalized U.S. citizen or have permanent work authorization, you may be eligible for unemployment benefits.

Q. How can I obtain a U.S. driver's license?

A. In most states you need proof that you are in the U.S. in legal status. If you are in the U.S. illegally, it is very difficult to obtain a driver's license. It is also difficult to obtain a driver's license if you are in the U.S. as a visitor.

Q. If I give birth to a baby in the U.S., what is the baby's status and can the baby grant me an immigration benefit?

A. The baby is a U.S. citizen by having been born in the U.S. A child cannot pass on an immigration benefit to a parent until the child reaches the age of twenty-one.

Q. Should I marry a U.S. citizen solely to obtain a green card?

A. No. Doing so may be illegal. The USCIS continues to tighten its policy regarding marriages strictly for immigration purposes, and the penalties can be severe. In fact, you should not get involved in any arrangement that is meant to defraud the USCIS. Remember that the USCIS is a branch of the U.S. Government and should be treated with respect.

Q. What if I am in the United States illegally, can I still adjust my status in the United States?

A. Under certain circumstances you may be allowed to adjust your status. There have been recent changes in the law, however, that may affect your application. Consult a professional before you file any applications.

Q. What do I do if I complete my permanent residence application but do not receive my green card in the mail?

A. This is a common occurrence. If you do not receive your card within ninety days of approval of your application, you should follow up with the NCSC at 1-800-375-5283.

Q. What happens if I lose my green card or if it is stolen?

A. A lost or stolen green card can be replaced. When you first receive your card, record your alien registration number and keep it in a safe place. If your green card is lost and you are in the U.S., you must process an application with USCIS to replace the card. The application consists of Form I-90—Application to Replace Alien Registration Card, photographs and the applicable filing fee. You will need to make an InfoPass appointment. If your green card is stolen, USCIS may ask that you obtain a police report from your local police station. In either event, once the I-90 is filed, USCIS will stamp a new temporary green card in your passport so that you can travel. They will then forward the I-90 application to the Immigration Card Facility for processing of a new card.

If you are outside the U.S. and your card is lost or stolen, go to the nearest American Embassy or Consulate. Your permanent residence will be verified with the Department of State in Washington, DC and you will be issued a document to allow you to return to the U.S. This can sometimes take several days. Once you are back in the U.S., you will need to file an I-90 application as described above.

Q. If I received my green card as a young child do I need to update it?

A. Yes. If your card was issued before the age of fourteen it must be updated to include fingerprints. You will need an InfoPass appointment to file Form I-90 as described above. The USCIS should stamp a temporary green card in your passport so that you can travel outside the U.S. while you are waiting for the new card.

Q. Can I keep my green card if I am not living in the U.S.?

A. If you are temporarily residing outside the U.S. but continue to consider the U.S. your permanent home, and plan to return permanently, it is possible to keep your green card. However, you must comply with several USCIS rules. These rules are complex and you should consult a professional for advice. You can also apply to the USCIS for a Permit to Reenter the United States using Form I-131—Application for Travel Document. The granting of this permit allows you to remain outside the U.S. for up to two years without jeopardizing your permanent resident status. Your absence from the U.S. for more than one year however, can still affect your ability to apply for U.S. citizenship.

Q. Does my green card need to be renewed or does it remain valid forever?

A. In 1989 the Alien Registration Card regulations were revised by the USCIS. The card used to be valid as long as the alien remained a permanent resident. Now the card expires ten years after the date it was issued. The alien will then be required to obtain a new card. In addition, all Alien Registration Cards issued before 1978 must be replaced with new cards. See Chapter 13—Renewal of Expiring Green Cards.

19
Sample Forms

The following pages contain sample forms that you will need to process applications through the USCIS and the Department of Labor. The forms are updated from time to time. However, the ones we have included in the book are current up until the time of printing. The most recent version of each form can be obtained by calling the USCIS office at 1-800-870-FORMS, or download them from the USCIS website. Forms "ETA" can be obtained from the Department of Labor.

Department of Homeland Security
U.S. Citizenship and Immigration Services

OMB No. 1615-0008

G-325A, Biographic Information

(Family Name)	(First Name)	(Middle Name)	☐ Male ☐ Female	Birthdate (mm/dd/yyyy)	Citizenship/Nationality	File Number A

All Other Names Used (Including names by previous marriages)	City and Country of Birth	U.S. Social Security #*(f any)*

	Family Name	First Name	Date, City and Country of Birth (If known)	City and Country of Residence
Father				
Mother (Maiden name)				

Husband (If none, so state.) or Wife	Family Name (For wife, give maiden name)	First Name	Birthdate	City and Country of Birth	Date of Marriage	Place of Marriage

Former Husbands or Wives (if none, so state.) Family Name (For wife, give maiden name.)	First Name	Birthdate	Date and Place of Marriage	Date and Place of Termination of Marriage

Applicant's residence last five years. List present address first.				From		To	
Street and Number	City	Province or State	Country	Month	Year	Month	Year
						Present Time	

Applicant's last address outside the United States of more than one year.				From		To	
Street and Number	City	Province or State	Country	Month	Year	Month	Year

Applicant's employment last five years. (If none, so state.) List present employment first.		From		To	
Full Name and Address of Employer	Occupation (Specify)	Month	Year	Month	Year
				Present Time	

Show below last occupation abroad if not listed above. (Include all information requested above.)

This form is submitted in connection with application for: ☐ Naturalization ☐ Status as Permanent Resident ☐ Other (Specify):	Signature of Applicant	Date

Submit all copies of this form. | If your native alphabet is in other than Roman letters, write your name in your native alphabet below:

Penalties: Severe penalties are provided by law for Knowingly and willfully falsifying or concealing a material fact.

Applicant: Be sure to put your name and Alien Registration Number in the box outlined by heavy border below.

Complete This Box (Family Name)	(Given Name)	(Middle Name)	(Alien Registration Number)

(1) Ident.

Form G-325A (Rev. 05/31/05)N (Prior editions may be used until 12/31/05)

Department of Homeland Security
U.S. Citizenship and Immigration Services

OMB No. 1615-0047; Expires 03/31/07

Employment Eligibility Verification

INSTRUCTIONS
PLEASE READ ALL INSTRUCTIONS CAREFULLY BEFORE COMPLETING THIS FORM.

Anti-Discrimination Notice. It is illegal to discriminate against any individual (other than an alien not authorized to work in the U.S.) in hiring, discharging, or recruiting or referring for a fee because of that individual's national origin or citizenship status. It is illegal to discriminate against work eligible individuals. Employers **CANNOT** specify which document(s) they will accept from an employee. The refusal to hire an individual because of a future expiration date may also constitute illegal discrimination.

Section 1- Employee.
All employees, citizens and noncitizens, hired after November 6, 1986, must complete Section 1 of this form at the time of hire, which is the actual beginning of employment. **The employer is responsible for ensuring that Section 1 is timely and properly completed.**

Preparer/Translator Certification. The Preparer/Translator Certification must be completed if Section 1 is prepared by a person other than the employee. A preparer/translator may be used only when the employee is unable to complete Section 1 on his/her own. However, the employee must still sign Section 1 personally.

Section 2 - Employer.
For the purpose of completing this form, the term "employer" includes those recruiters and referrers for a fee who are agricultural associations, agricultural employers or farm labor contractors.

Employers must complete Section 2 by examining evidence of identity and employment eligibility within three (3) business days of the date employment begins. If employees are authorized to work, but are unable to present the required document(s) within three business days, they must present a receipt for the application of the document(s) within three business days and the actual document(s) within ninety (90) days. However, if employers hire individuals for a duration of less than three business days, Section 2 must be completed at the time employment begins. **Employers must record: 1)** document title; **2)** issuing authority; **3)** document number; **4)** expiration date, if any; and **5)** the date employment begins. Employers must sign and date the certification. Employees must present original documents. Employers may, but are not required to, photocopy the document(s) presented. These photocopies may only be used for the verification process and must be retained with the I-9. **However, employers are still responsible for completing the I-9.**

Section 3 - Updating and Reverification.
Employers must complete Section 3 when updating and/or reverifying the I-9. Employers must reverify employment eligibility of their employees on or before the expiration date recorded in Section 1. Employers **CANNOT** specify which document(s) they will accept from an employee.

- If an employee's name has changed at the time this form is being updated/reverified, complete Block A.

- If an employee is rehired within three (3) years of the date this form was originally completed and the employee is still eligible to be employed on the same basis as previously indicated on this form (updating), complete Block B and the signature block.

- If an employee is rehired within three (3) years of the date this form was originally completed and the employee's work authorization has expired **or** if a current employee's work authorization is about to expire (reverification), complete Block B and:

- examine any document that reflects that the employee is authorized to work in the U.S. (see List A **or** C),

- record the document title, document number and expiration date (if any) in Block C, and

- complete the signature block.

Photocopying and Retaining Form I-9. A blank I-9 may be reproduced, provided both sides are copied. The Instructions must be available to all employees completing this form. Employers must retain completed I-9s for three (3) years after the date of hire or one (1) year after the date employment ends, whichever is later.

For more detailed information, you may refer to the Department of Homeland Security (DHS) Handbook for Employers, (Form M-274). You may obtain the handbook at your local U.S. Citizenship and Immigration Services (USCIS) office.

Privacy Act Notice. The authority for collecting this information is the Immigration Reform and Control Act of 1986, Pub. L. 99-603 (8 USC 1324a).

This information is for employers to verify the eligibility of individuals for employment to preclude the unlawful hiring, or recruiting or referring for a fee, of aliens who are not authorized to work in the United States.

This information will be used by employers as a record of their basis for determining eligibility of an employee to work in the United States. The form will be kept by the employer and made available for inspection by officials of the U.S. Immigration and Customs Enforcement, Department of Labor and Office of Special Counsel for Immigration Related Unfair Employment Practices.

Submission of the information required in this form is voluntary. However, an individual may not begin employment unless this form is completed, since employers are subject to civil or criminal penalties if they do not comply with the Immigration Reform and Control Act of 1986.

Reporting Burden. We try to create forms and instructions that are accurate, can be easily understood and which impose the least possible burden on you to provide us with information. Often this is difficult because some immigration laws are very complex. Accordingly, the reporting burden for this collection of information is computed as follows: **1)** learning about this form, 5 minutes; **2)** completing the form, 5 minutes; and **3)** assembling and filing (recordkeeping) the form, 5 minutes, for an average of 15 minutes per response. If you have comments regarding the accuracy of this burden estimate, or suggestions for making this form simpler, you can write to U.S. Citizenship and Immigration Services, Regulatory Management Division, 111 Massachuetts Avenue, N.W., Washington, DC 20529. OMB No. 1615-0047.

NOTE: This is the 1991 edition of the Form I-9 that has been rebranded with a current printing date to reflect the recent transition from the INS to DHS and its components.

EMPLOYERS MUST RETAIN COMPLETED FORM I-9
PLEASE DO NOT MAIL COMPLETED FORM I-9 TO ICE OR USCIS

Form I-9 (Rev. 05/31/05)Y

Department of Homeland Security
U.S. Citizenship and Immigration Services

OMB No. 1615-0047; Expires 03/31/07

Employment Eligibility Verification

Please read instructions carefully before completing this form. The instructions must be available during completion of this form. **ANTI-DISCRIMINATION NOTICE:** It is illegal to discriminate against work eligible individuals. Employers CANNOT specify which document(s) they will accept from an employee. The refusal to hire an individual because of a future expiration date may also constitute illegal discrimination.

Section 1. Employee Information and Verification. To be completed and signed by employee at the time employment begins.

Print Name: Last	First	Middle Initial	Maiden Name
Address *(Street Name and Number)*		Apt. #	Date of Birth *(month/day/year)*
City	State	Zip Code	Social Security #

I am aware that federal law provides for imprisonment and/or fines for false statements or use of false documents in connection with the completion of this form.

I attest, under penalty of perjury, that I am (check one of the following):
☐ A citizen or national of the United States
☐ A Lawful Permanent Resident (Alien #) A _____
☐ An alien authorized to work until _____
(Alien # or Admission #) _____

Employee's Signature	Date *(month/day/year)*

Preparer and/or Translator Certification. *(To be completed and signed if Section 1 is prepared by a person other than the employee.)* I attest, under penalty of perjury, that I have assisted in the completion of this form and that to the best of my knowledge the information is true and correct.

Preparer's/Translator's Signature	Print Name
Address *(Street Name and Number, City, State, Zip Code)*	Date *(month/day/year)*

Section 2. Employer Review and Verification. To be completed and signed by employer. Examine one document from List A OR examine one document from List B and one from List C, as listed on the reverse of this form, and record the title, number and expiration date, if any, of the document(s).

List A	OR	List B	AND	List C
Document title: _____		_____		_____
Issuing authority: _____		_____		_____
Document #: _____		_____		_____
Expiration Date *(if any)*: _____		_____		_____
Document #: _____				
Expiration Date *(if any)*: _____				

CERTIFICATION - I attest, under penalty of perjury, that I have examined the document(s) presented by the above-named employee, that the above-listed document(s) appear to be genuine and to relate to the employee named, that the employee began employment on *(month/day/year)* _____ **and that to the best of my knowledge the employee is eligible to work in the United States. (State employment agencies may omit the date the employee began employment.)**

Signature of Employer or Authorized Representative	Print Name	Title
Business or Organization Name	Address *(Street Name and Number, City, State, Zip Code)*	Date *(month/day/year)*

Section 3. Updating and Reverification. To be completed and signed by employer.

A. New Name *(if applicable)*	B. Date of rehire *(month/day/year) (if applicable)*

C. If employee's previous grant of work authorization has expired, provide the information below for the document that establishes current employment eligibility.

Document Title: _____ Document #: _____ Expiration Date (if any): _____

I attest, under penalty of perjury, that to the best of my knowledge, this employee is eligible to work in the United States, and if the employee presented document(s), the document(s) I have examined appear to be genuine and to relate to the individual.

Signature of Employer or Authorized Representative	Date *(month/day/year)*

NOTE: This is the 1991 edition of the Form I-9 that has been rebranded with a current printing date to reflect the recent transition from the INS to DHS and its components.

Form I-9 (Rev. 05/31/05)Y Page 2

LISTS OF ACCEPTABLE DOCUMENTS

LIST A		LIST B		LIST C
Documents that Establish Both Identity and Employment Eligibility	**OR**	**Documents that Establish Identity**	**AND**	**Documents that Establish Employment Eligibility**

LIST A — Documents that Establish Both Identity and Employment Eligibility

1. U.S. Passport (unexpired or expired)

2. Certificate of U.S. Citizenship *(Form N-560 or N-561)*

3. Certificate of Naturalization *(Form N-550 or N-570)*

4. Unexpired foreign passport, with *I-551 stamp or* attached *Form I-94* indicating unexpired employment authorization

5. Permanent Resident Card or Alien Registration Receipt Card with photograph *(Form I-151 or I-551)*

6. Unexpired Temporary Resident Card *(Form I-688)*

7. Unexpired Employment Authorization Card *(Form I-688A)*

8. Unexpired Reentry Permit *(Form I-327)*

9. Unexpired Refugee Travel Document *(Form I-571)*

10. Unexpired Employment Authorization Document issued by DHS that contains a photograph *(Form I-688B)*

LIST B — Documents that Establish Identity

1. Driver's license or ID card issued by a state or outlying possession of the United States provided it contains a photograph or information such as name, date of birth, gender, height, eye color and address

2. ID card issued by federal, state or local government agencies or entities, provided it contains a photograph or information such as name, date of birth, gender, height, eye color and address

3. School ID card with a photograph

4. Voter's registration card

5. U.S. Military card or draft record

6. Military dependent's ID card

7. U.S. Coast Guard Merchant Mariner Card

8. Native American tribal document

9. Driver's license issued by a Canadian government authority

For persons under age 18 who are unable to present a document listed above:

10. School record or report card

11. Clinic, doctor or hospital record

12. Day-care or nursery school record

LIST C — Documents that Establish Employment Eligibility

1. U.S. social security card issued by the Social Security Administration *(other than a card stating it is not valid for employment)*

2. Certification of Birth Abroad issued by the Department of State *(Form FS-545 or Form DS-1350)*

3. Original or certified copy of a birth certificate issued by a state, county, municipal authority or outlying possession of the United States bearing an official seal

4. Native American tribal document

5. U.S. Citizen ID Card *(Form I-197)*

6. ID Card for use of Resident Citizen in the United States *(Form I-179)*

7. Unexpired employment authorization document issued by DHS *(other than those listed under List A)*

Illustrations of many of these documents appear in Part 8 of the Handbook for Employers (M-274)

U.S. Department of Justice
Immigration and Naturalization Service
Please Read Instructions on Page 2

**Certificate of Eligibility for Nonimmigrant (F-1) Student
Status - For Academic and Language Students**

OMB No. 1115-0051

Page 1

This page must be completed and signed in the U.S. by a designated school official.

1. Family Name (surname)

   First (given) name (do not enter middle name)

Country of birth	Date of birth (mo./day/year)

Country of citizenship	Admission number (Complete if known)

   For Immigration Official Use

Visa issuing post	Date Visa issued

2. School (school district) name

   School official to be notified of student's arrival in U.S. (Name and Title)

   Reinstated, extension granted to:

   School address (include zip code)

   School code (including 3-digit suffix, if any) and approval date

   _____ 214F_____ approved on _____

3. This certificate is issued to the student named above for:
   (Check and fill out as appropriate)

   a. ☐ Initial attendance at this school

   b. ☐ Continued attendance at this school

   c. ☐ School transfer.
      Transferred from _____

   d. ☐ Use by dependents for entering the United States.

   e. ☐ Other _____

4. Level of education the student is pursuing or will pursue in the United States:
   (check only one)

   a. ☐ Primary   e. ☐ Master's

   b. ☐ Secondary   f. ☐ Doctorate

   c. ☐ Associate   g. ☐ Language training

   d. ☐ Bachelor's   h. ☐ Other

5. The student named above has been accepted for a full course of study at
   this school, majoring in_____

   The student is expected to report to the school no later than (date)
   _____ and complete studies not later than (date)_____

   The normal length of study is _____

6. ☐ English proficiency is required:

   ☐ The student has the required English proficiency

   ☐ The student is not yet proficient, English instructions will be given at
      the school.

   ☐ English proficiency is not required because_____

7. This school estimates the student's average costs for an academic term of
   _____ (up to 12) months to be:

   a. Tuition and fees $ _____

   b. Living expenses $ _____

   c. Expenses of dependents $ _____

   d. Other (specify): $ _____

      Total $ _____

8. This school has information showing the following as the students means of
   support, estimated for an academic term of _____ months (Use the same
   number of months given in item 7).

   a. Student's personal funds $_____

   b. Funds from this school $_____
      (specify type)   _____

   c. Funds from another source $_____
      (specify type and source)   _____

   d. On-campus employment (if any) $_____

      Total $_____

9. Remarks: _____

   _____

   _____

   _____

   _____

10. School Certification: I certify under penalty of perjury that all information provided above in items 1 through 8 was completed before I signed this form and is true and correct; I executed this form in the United States after review and evaluation in the United States by me or other officials of the school of the student's application, transcripts or other records of courses taken and proof of financial responsibility, which were received at the school prior to the execution of this form; the school has determined that the above named student's qualifications meet all standards for admission to the school; the student will be required to pursue a full course of study as defined by 8 CFR 214.2(f)(6); I am a designated official of the above named school and I am authorized to issue this form.

Signature of designated school official	Name of school official (print or type)	Title	Date issued	Place issued (city and state)

11. Student Certification: I have read and agreed to comply with the terms and conditions of my admission and those of any extension of stay as specified on page 2. I certify that all information provided on this form refers specifically to me and is true and correct to the best of my knowledge. I certify that I seek to enter or remain in the United States temporarily, and solely for the purpose of pursuing a full course of study at the school named on page 1 of this form. I also authorize the named school to release any information from my records which is needed by the INS pursuant to 8 CFR 214.3(g) to determine my nonimmigrant status.

Signature of student	Name of student	Date

Signature of parent or guardian if student is under 18	Name of parent/guardian (Print or type)	Address(city)	(State or province)	(Country)	(Date)

Form I20 A-B/I20ID(Rev 04-27-88)N

For official use only
Microfilm Index Number

Authority for collecting the information on this and related student forms is contained in 8 U.S.C. 1101 and 1184. The information solicited will be used by the Department of State and the Immigration and Naturalization Service to determine eligibility for the benefits requested.

INSTRUCTIONS TO DESIGNATED SCHOOL OFFICIALS

1. The law provides severe penalties for knowingly and willfully falsifying or concealing a material fact or using any false document in the submission of this form. Designated school officials should consult regulations pertaining to the issuance of Form I-20 A-B at 8 CFR 214.3 (K) before completing this form. Failure to comply with these regulations may result in the withdrawal of the school approval for attendance by foreign students by the Immigration and Naturalization Service (8 CFR 214.4).

2. ISSUANCE OF FORM I-20 A-B. Designated school officials may issue a Form I-20 A-B to a student who fits into one of the following categories, if the student has been accepted for full-time attendance at the institution: a) a prospective F-1 nonimmigrant student; b) an F-1 transfer student; c) an F-1 student advancing to a higher educational level at the same institution; d) an out of status student seeking reinstatement. The form may also be issued to the dependent spouse or child of an F-1 student for securing entry into the United States.

When issuing a Form I-20 A-B, designated school officials should complete the student's admission number whenever possible to ensure proper data entry and record keeping.

3. ENDORSEMENT OF PAGE 4 FOR REENTRY. Designated school officials may endorse page 4 of the Form I-20 A-B for reentry if the student and/or the F-2 dependents is to leave the United States temporarily. This should be done only when the information on the Form I-20 remains unchanged. If there have been substantial changes in item 4, 5, 7, or 8, a new Form I-20 A-B should be issued.

4. REPORTING REQUIREMENT. Designated school official should always forward the top page of the form I-20 A-B to the INS data processing center at P.O. Box 140, London, Kentucky 40741 for data entry except when the form is issued to an F-1 student for initial entry or reentry into the United States, or for reinstatement to student status. (Requests for reinstatement should be sent to the Immigration and Naturalization Service district office having jurisdiction over the student's temporary residence in this country.)

The INS data processing center will return this top page to the issuing school for disposal after data entry and microfilming.

5. CERTIFICATION. Designated school officials should certify on the bottom part of page 1 of this form that the Form I-20 A-B is completed and issued in accordance with the pertinent regulations. The designated school official should remove the carbon sheet from the completed and signed Form I-20 A-B before forwarding it to the student.

6. ADMISSION RECORDS. Since the Immigration and Naturalization Service may request information concerning the student's immigration status for various reasons, designated school officials should retain all evidence which shows the scholastic ability and financial status on which admission was based, until the school has reported the student's termination of studies to the Immigration and Naturalization Service.

INSTRUCTIONS TO STUDENTS

1. Student Certification. You should read everything on this page carefully and be sure that you understand the terms and conditions concerning your admission and stay in the United States as a nonimmigrant student before you sign the student certification on the bottom part of page **1. The law provides severe penalties for knowingly and willfully falsifying or concealing a material fact, or using any false document in the submission of this form.**

2. ADMISSION. A nonimmigrant student may be admitted for duration of status. This means that you are authorized to stay in the United States for the entire length of time during which you are enrolled as a full-time stu-

dent in an educational program and any period of authorized practical training plus sixty days. While in the United States, you must maintain a valid foreign passport unless you are exempt from passport requirements.

You may continue from one educational level to another, such as progressing from high school to a bachelor's program or a bachelor's program to a master's program, etc., simply by invoking the procedures for school transfers.

3. SCHOOL. For initial admission, you must attend the school specified on your visa. If you have a Form I-20 A-B from more than one school, it is important to have the name of the school you intend to attend specified on your visa by presenting a Form I-20 A-B from that school to the visa issuing consular officer. Failure to attend the specified school will result in the loss of your student status and subject you to deportation.

4. REENTRY. A nonimmigrant student may be readmitted after a temporary absence of five months or less from the United States, if the student is otherwise admissible. You may be readmitted by presenting a valid foreign passport, a valid visa, and either a new Form I-20 A-B or a page 4 of the Form I-20 A-B (the I-20 ID Copy) properly endorsed for reentry if the information on the I-20 form is current.

5. TRANSFER. A nonimmigrant student is permitted to transfer to a different school provided the transfer procedure is followed. To transfer school, you should first notify the school you are attending of the intent to transfer, then obtain a Form I-20 A-B from the school you intend to attend. Transfer will be effected only if you return the Form I-20 A-B to the designated school official within 15 days of beginning attendance at the new school. The designated school official will then report the transfer to the Immigration and Naturalization Service.

6. EXTENSION OF STAY. If you cannot complete the educational program after having been in student status for longer than the anticipated length of the program plus a grace period in a single educational level, or for more than eight consecutive years, you must apply for extension of stay. An application for extension of stay on a Form I-538 should be filed with the Immigration and Naturalization Service district office having jurisdiction over your school at least 15 days but no more than 60 days before the expiration of your authorized stay.

7. EMPLOYMENT. As an F-1 student, you are not permitted to work off campus or to engage in business without specific employment authorization. After your first year in F-1 student status, you may apply for employment authorization on Form I-538 based on financial needs arising after receiving student status, or the need to obtain practical training.

8. Notice of Address. If you move, you must submit a notice within 10 days of the change of address to the Immigration and Naturalization Service. (Form AR-11 is available at any INS office.)

9. Arrival/Departure. When you leave the United States, you must surrender your Form I-94 Departure Record. Please see back side of Form I-94 for detailed instructions. You do not have to turn in the I-94 if you are visiting Canada, Mexico, or adjacent islands other than Cuba for less than 30 days.

10. Financial Support. You must demonstrate that you are financially able to support yourself for the entire period of stay in the United States while pursuing a full course of study. You are required to attach documentary evidence of means of support.

11. Authorization to Release Information by School. To comply with requests from the United States Immigration & Naturalization Service for information concerning your immigration status, you are required to give authorization to the named school to release such information from your records. The school will provide the Service your name, country of birth, current address, and any other information on a regular basis or upon request.

12. Penalty. To maintain your nonimmigrant student status, you must be enrolled as a full-time student at the school you are authorized to attend. You may engage in employment only when you have received permission to work. Failure to comply with these regulations will result in the loss of your student status and subject you to deportation.

Public Reporting Burden. Reporting burden for this collection of information is estimated to average 30 minutes per response. If you have comments regarding the accuracy of this estimate, or suggestions for simplifying this form, you can write to both the U.S. Department of Justice, Immigration and Naturalization Service (Room 5304), Washington, D.C., 20536; and to the Office of Management and Budget, Paperwork Reduction Project: OMB No. 1115-0051; Washington, D.C. 20503.

U.S. Department of Justice
Immigration and Naturalization Service
Please Read Instructions on Page 2

Certificate of Eligibility for Nonimmigrant (F-1) Student Status - For Academic and Language Students

OMB No. 1115-0051

Page 3

This page must be completed and signed in the U.S. by a designated school official.

1. Family Name (surname)

   First (given) name (do not enter middle name)

Country of birth	Date of birth (mo./day/year)

Country of citizenship	Admission number (Complete if known)

   For Immigration Official Use

Visa issuing post	Date Visa issued

   Reinstated, extension granted to:

2. School (school district) name

   School official to be notified of student's arrival in U.S. (Name and Title)

   School address (include zip code)

   School code (including 3-digit suffix, if any) and approval date

   _____ 214F_____ approved on _____

3. This certificate is issued to the student named above for:
   (Check and fill out as appropriate)

   a. ☐ Initial attendance at this school

   b. ☐ Continued attendance at this school

   c. ☐ School transfer.
   Transferred from _____

   d. ☐ Use by dependents for entering the United States.

   e. ☐ Other _____

4. Level of education the student is pursuing or will pursue in the United States:
   (check only one)

   a. ☐ Primary   e. ☐ Master's

   b. ☐ Secondary   f. ☐ Doctorate

   c. ☐ Associate   g. ☐ Language training

   d. ☐ Bachelor's   h. ☐ Other

5. The student named above has been accepted for a full course of study at this school, majoring in_____

   The student is expected to report to the school no later than (date) _____ and complete studies not later than (date)_____

   The normal length of study is _____

6. ☐ English proficiency is required:

   ☐ The student has the required English proficiency

   ☐ The student is not yet proficient, English instructions will be given at the school.

   ☐ English proficiency is not required because_____

7. This school estimates the student's average costs for an academic term of _____ (up to 12) months to be:

   a. Tuition and fees $ _____

   b. Living expenses $ _____

   c. Expenses of dependents $ _____

   d. Other(specify): $ _____

   Total $ _____

8. This school has information showing the following as the students means of support, estimated for an academic term of _____ months (Use the same number of months given in item 7).

   a. Student's personal funds $_____

   b. Funds from this school $_____
   (specify type)   _____

   c. Funds from another source $_____
   (specify type and source)   _____

   d. On-campus employment (if any) $_____

   Total $_____

9. Remarks: _____

10. School Certification: I certify under penalty of perjury that all information provided above in items 1 through 8 was completed before I signed this form and is true and correct; I executed this form in the United States after review and evaluation in the United States by me or other officials of the school of the student's application, transcripts or other records of courses taken and proof of financial responsibility, which were received at the school prior to the execution of this form; the school has determined that the above named student's qualifications meet all standards for admission to the school; the student will be required to pursue a full course of study as defined by 8 CFR 214.2(f)(6); I am a designated official of the above named school and I am authorized to issue this form.

Signature of designated school official	Name of school official (print or type)	Title	Date issued	Place issued (city and state)

11. Student Certification: I have read and agreed to comply with the terms and conditions of my admission and those of any extension of stay as specified on page 2. I certify that all information provided on this form refers specifically to me and is true and correct to the best of my knowledge. I certify that I seek to enter or remain in the United States temporarily, and solely for the purpose of pursuing a full course of study at the school named on page 1 of this form. I also authorize the named school to release any information from my records which is needed by the INS pursuant to 8 CFR 214.3(g) to determine my nonimmigrant status.

Signature of student	Name of student	Date

Signature of parent or guardian if student is under 18	Name of parent/guardian (Print or type)	Address(city)	(State or province)	(Country)	(Date)

Form I20 A-B/I20ID(Rev 04-27-88)N

For official use only
Microfilm Index Number

IF YOU NEED MORE INFORMATION CONCERNING YOUR F-1 NONIMMIGRANT STUDENT STATUS AND THE RELATING IMMIGRATION PROCEDURES, PLEASE CONTACT EITHER YOUR FOREIGN STUDENT ADVISOR ON CAMPUS OR A NEARBY IMMIGRATION AND NATURALIZATION SERVICE OFFICE.

THIS PAGE, WHEN PROPERLY ENDORSED, MAY BE USED FOR ENTRY OF THE SPOUSE AND CHILDREN OF AN F-1 STUDENT FOLLOWING TO JOIN THE STUDENT IN THE UNITED STATES OR FOR REENTRY OF THE STUDENT TO ATTEND THE SAME SCHOOL AFTER A TEMPORARY ABSENCE FROM THE UNITED STATES.

For reentry of the student and/or the F-2 dependents (EACH CERTIFICATION SIGNATURE IS VALID FOR ONLY ONE YEAR.)

Signature of Designated School Official	Name of School Official(print or type)	Title	Date

Dependent spouse and children of the F-1 student who are seeking entry/reentry to the U.S.

Name family (caps) first	Date of birth	Country of birth	Relationship to the F-1 student

Student Employment Authorization and other Records

For sale by the Superintendent of Documents, U.S. Government Printing Office, Washington, D.C. 20402

OMB No. 1615-0082; Expires 04/30/06

Department of Homeland Security
U.S. Citizenship and Immigration Services

I-90, Application to Replace
Permanent Resident Card

Instructions

NOTE: You may file Form I-90 electronically. Go to our internet website at **www.uscis.gov** and follow the instructions on e-filing.

What Is the Purpose of This Form?

This form is for permanent residents and conditional residents to apply to the U.S. Citizenship and Immigration Services (USCIS) for replacement of permanent resident cards. USCIS is comprised of offices of the former Immigration and Naturalization Service (INS).

NOTE: Do not use this Form I-90 if you are a conditional resident and your status is expiring. You must apply accordingly to remove the conditions:

● If you became a conditional resident through marriage to a U.S. citizen or permanent resident, submit Form I-751, Petition to Remove Conditions on Residence; or

● If you became a conditional resident based on a financial investment in a U.S. business, submit Form I-829, Petition by Entrepreneur to Remove Conditions.

Who May File This Application?

If you are a permanent resident or conditional resident, file this application:

● To replace a lost, stolen or destroyed card; or

● To update a card after change of name or other biographic data; or

● To replace a card that is mutilated; or

● To replace a card that is incorrect on account of USCIS error; or

● To replace a card that was never received.

If you are a permanent resident, you must also file this application:

● To replace a card that is expiring; or

● Within 30 days of your 14th birthday, to replace a card issued before your 14th birthday; or

● If you have been a lawful permanent resident in the United States and are now taking up Commuter status while actually residing outside the United States; or

● If you have been in resident Commuter status and are now taking up actual residence in the United States; or

● If your status has been automatically converted to permanent resident; or

● When you have an older edition of the card and must replace it with the current type of card.

Where Should You File the Application?

You have the option of filing this paper form at the Los Angeles, California, Lockbox facility (see address below), or you may file it electronically by using the internet.

NOTE: If you are filing this application to replace a card that **was never received or to replace a card that is incorrect on account of a USCIS error**, you must mail your application to the service center or National Benefits Center that processed your previously filed Form I-90 application. Please refer to **www.uscis.gov** for special mailing instructions and the appropriate mailing address for each service center and the National Benefits Center.

To file electronically, visit our website at **www.uscis.gov** and follow the instructions on how to properly complete and submit the form.

NOTE: While many of our customers are eligible to e-file, there are restrictions for some applicants. Please check our website for a list of who is eligible to e-file this form.

If you choose to file this paper application, you must submit your application with the appropriate fees. If you are submitting this paper version of the form, you must include a check or money order with the application to pay the fees.

After filing your application, USCIS will inform you in writing when to go to your local USCIS Application Support Center (ASC) for your biometrics appointment.

NOTE: Do not include your initial evidence and supporting documents when submitting your application. You must submit all required initial evidence, including your prior permanent resident card or other evidence of identity, and any supporting documentation at the time of your in person appearance at your local ASC.

File this application with appropriate fees directly at the following Lockbox address:

U.S. Citizenship and Immigration Services
P.O. Box 54870
Los Angeles, CA 90054-0870

Or, for non-U. S. Postal Service deliveries:

U.S. Citizenship and Immigration Services
Attention I-90
16420 Valley View Avenue
La Mirada, CA 90638

What Are the General Filing Instructions?

Please answer all questions by typing or clearly printing in black ink. If an answer is "none," write "none."

Form I-90 Instructions (Rev. 10/26/05)Y

If you need extra space to answer any item, attach a separate sheet(s) of paper with your name and your Alien Registration Number (A#), and indicate the number of the item to which the answer refers.

Every application must be properly signed and accompanied by the appropriate fee. (See "**What Is the Fee**" on **Page 2** of these Instructions.) A photocopy of a signed application is not acceptable.

If you are under 14 years of age, your parent or guardian may sign the application on your behalf.

Translations. Any foreign language document must be accompanied by a full English translation that the translator has certified as complete and correct, and by the translator's certification that he or she is competent to translate the foreign language into English.

Copies. If these instructions state that a copy of a document must be filed with this application and you choose to send us the original, we may keep that original for our records. All copies must be clear and legible.

What Initial Evidence Is Required?

You must submit all required initial evidence as well as all supporting documentation at the time of your in person appearance at your local ASC. This includes:

- **Your Prior Card or Other Evidence of Identity.**

  Renewing Expiring or Expired Card. If your card has already expired or will expire in the next six months, you will be required to submit your card at the time of your in person appearance at your local ASC.

  Replacing Lost or Damaged Card. If your card has been lost, stolen, damaged or you never received it, bring a copy of your card, if you have one, to your in person appearance at your local ASC. If you do not have a copy and are at least 18 years old, you must bring an identity document, such as a driver's license, passport or a copy of another document containing your name, date of birth, photograph and signature to your in person appearance at your local ASC.

  If you have been automatically converted to permanent residence status, you are considered to be replacing your card. In such case, you must bring your original temporary status document, with you at the time of your in person appearance at your local ASC.

- **Correction or Change in Biographic Data.**

  All supporting documentation must be submitted at the time of your in person appearance at your local ASC. If you are applying to replace a card because of a name change, you must bring the original court order or a certified copy of your marriage certificate reflecting the new name to your in person appearance at the ASC. To replace a card because of a change of any other biographic data, you must bring copies of documentation to prove that the new data is correct. A replacement application based on a USCIS administrative error must also include an explanation.

Biometrics Services.

Applicants will now have their photograph, fingerprints and signature taken by USCIS. You no longer need to submit photographs with the Form I-90. When you file your Form I-90, USCIS will notify you in writing of the time and location where you must go for the required biometrics services. Failure to appear for the biometrics services may result in a denial of your application.

NOTE: Because USCIS is now taking photographs of applicants, you no longer need to submit photos with your application.

What Is the Fee?

The fee for this application is **$190.00**.

The fee for biometrics services is **$70.00**.

You may submit one check or money order for both the application and biometrics fees, for a total of **$260.00**.

Exceptions. There are three exceptions to having to pay the **$190.00** application filing fee.

- If you are filing only because when your card was issued it was incorrect due to a USCIS administrative error.

- If you are filing only because you never received your card.

- If you are filing only to register at age 14 years, and your existing card will not expire before your 16th birthday.

NOTE: All applicants, regardless of age, **except those filing to replace a card that was never received or to replace a card that is incorrect on account of a USCIS error**, are required to submit the **$70.00** biometrics services fee.

Fee Payment. If you are submitting this paper version of Form I-90, include a check or money order with your application.

Fees must be submitted in the exact amount. Fees cannot be refunded. **Do not mail cash.**

All checks and money orders must be drawn on a bank or other financial institution located in the United States and must be payable in United States currency. The check or money order should be made payable to the **U.S. Department of Homeland Security, unless:**

- If you reside in Guam, make your check or money order payable to the "Treasurer, Guam."

- If you reside in the U.S. Virgin Islands, make your check or money order payable to the "Commissioner of Finance of the Virgin Islands."

Checks are accepted subject to collection. An uncollected check in payment of an application fee will render the application and any document issued invalid. A charge of $30.00 will be imposed if a check in payment of a fee is not honored by the bank on which it is drawn.

Notice to Applicants Making Payment by Check. If you send us a check, it will be converted into an electronic funds transfer (EFT). This means we will copy your check and use the account information on it to electronically debit your account for the amount of the check. The debit from your account will usually occur within 24 hours, and will be shown on your regular account statement.

You will not receive your original check back. We will destroy your original check, but we will keep a copy of it. If the EFT cannot be processed for technical reason, you authorize us to process the copy in place of your original check. If the EFT cannot be completed because of insufficient funds, we may try to make the transfer up to two times.

How To Check If the Fee Is Correct.

The fee on this form is current as of the edition date appearing in the lower right hand corner of this page. However, because USCIS fees change periodically, you can verify if the fee is correct by following one of the steps below:

- Visit our website at **www.uscis.gov** and scroll down to "Forms and E-Filing" to check the appropriate fee, or

- Review the Fee Schedule included in your form package, if you called us to request the form, or

- Telephone our National Customer Service Center at **1-800-375-5283** and ask for the fee information.

What Is Evidence of Registration?

A pending application for a replacement permanent resident card is temporary evidence of registration.

What Is the Processing Information?

Acceptance. An application is not considered properly filed until it is accepted by USCIS.

Initial Processing. Once the application has been accepted, it will be checked for completeness. If you do not completely fill out the form, you will not establish a basis for eligibility and we may deny your application.

Requests for More Information or Interview. We may request more information or evidence or we may request that you appear at a USCIS office for an interview. We may also request that you provide the originals of any copies you submit. We will return these originals when they are no longer required.

Decision. If your application is approved, your Permanent Resident Card will be manufactured and mailed to you. If your application is denied, we will mail you a notice explaining why we made such decision.

What If You Change Your Address?

If you change your address after filing for a new card, you must fill out a Form AR-11, Alien's Change of Address Card. Enclose the AR-11 in an envelope and mail it to the USCIS address listed on that form.

NOTE: USCIS mail is not forwarded by the U.S. Postal Service. It is returned to our mailing office as undeliverable. USCIS will destroy undeliverable cards if not claimed by the applicant within one year.

Do You Need Forms and Information?

To order USCIS forms, call our toll-free forms line at **1-800-870-3676.** You can also order USCIS forms and obtain information on immigration laws, regulations and procedures by telephoning our **National Customer Service Center** toll-free at **1-800-375-5283** or visiting our internet website at **www.uscis.gov.**

What Are the Penalties for Fraud?

If you knowingly and willfully falsify or conceal a material fact or submit a false document with this request, we will deny the benefit you are seeking and may deny any other immigration benefit. In addition, you will face severe penalties provided by law and may be subject to criminal prosecution.

Privacy Act Notice.

We ask for the information on this form and associated evidence to determine if you have established eligibility for the immigration benefit you are seeking. Our legal right to ask for this information is in 8 USC 1302 and 1304. We may provide this information to other government agencies. Failure to provide this information and any requested evidence may delay a final decision or result in denial of your request.

Paperwork Reduction Act Notice.

A person is not required to respond to a collection of information unless it displays a currently valid OMB control number.

We try to create forms and instructions that are accurate, can be easily understood and that impose the least possible burden on you to provide us with information. Often this is difficult because some immigration laws are very complex.

The estimated average time to complete and submit this application is computed as follows: (1) 10 minutes to learn about the law and form; (2) 10 minutes to complete the form; and (3) 35 minutes to assemble and submit the application, including the required submission of this application; for a total estimated average of 55 minutes per application.

If you have comments regarding the accuracy of this estimate or suggestions for making this form simpler, you may write to the U.S. Citizenship and Immigration Services, Regulatory Management Division, 111 Massachusetts Avenue, N.W., Washington, DC 20529; OMB No. 1516-0082.

NOTE: Do not mail your completed application to the Washington, D.C. address listed above. That office does not accept applications. Mail your application to the USCIS Lockbox facility listed on Page 1 of these Instructions.

OMB No. 1615-0082; Expires 04/30/06

| Department of Homeland Security
U.S. Citizenship and Immigration Services | **I-90, Application to Replace
Permanent Resident Card** |

| **START HERE - Please type or print in black ink.** | **FOR USCIS USE ONLY** |

Part 1. Information about you.

Family Name	Given Name	Middle Initial

U.S. Mailing Address - C/O

Street Number and Name	Apt. #

City

State	ZIP Code

Date of Birth (Month/Day/Year)	Country of Birth
Social Security #	A #

FOR USCIS USE ONLY

Returned	Receipt
_____	
_____	
Resubmitted	
_____	
_____	
Reloc Sent	
_____	
_____	
Reloc Rec'd	
_____	
_____	
☐ Applicant Interviewed	

| Status as _____ Verified by _____ |
| Class _____ Initials _____ |
| FD-258 forwarded on _____ |
| I-89 forwarded on _____ |
| I-551 seen and returned _____ |
| (Initials) |
| Photocopy of I-551 verified _____ |
| (Initials) |
| _____ |
| Name   Date |
| Sticker # _____ |
| (ten-digit number) |

Part 2. Application type.

1. My status is: (check one)

    a. ☐ Permanent Resident - (Not a Commuter)

    b. ☐ Permanent Resident - (Commuter)

    c. ☐ Conditional Permanent Resident

2. Reason for application: (check one)

    I am a Permanent Resident or Conditional Permanent Resident and:

    a. ☐ My card was lost, stolen or destroyed.

    b. ☐ My authorized card was never received.

    c. ☐ My card is mutilated.

    d. ☐ My card was issued with incorrect information because of a USCIS administrative error.

    e. ☐ My name or other biographic information has changed since the card was issued.

    I am a Permanent Resident and:

    f. ☐ My present card has an expiration date and it is expiring.

    g. ☐ I have reached my 14th birthday since my card was issued.

    h. 1. ☐ I have taken up Commuter status.

    h. 2. ☐ I was a Commuter and am now taking up residence in the U.S.

    i. ☐ My status has been automatically converted to permanent resident.

    j. ☐ I have an old edition of the card.

Action Block

Part 3. Processing information.

Mother's First Name	Father's First Name
City of Residence where you applied for an Immigrant Visa or Adjustment of Status	Consulate where Immigrant Visa was issued or USCIS office where status was Adjusted
City/Town/Village of Birth	Date of Admission as an immigrant or Adjustment of Status

**To Be Completed by
Attorney or Representative, if any**

☐ Fill in box if G-28 is attached to
represent the applicant

VOLAG#

ATTY State License #

f

Form I-90 (Rev. 10/26/05)Y

Part 3. Processing information (continued):

If you entered the U.S. with an Immigrant Visa, also complete the following:

Destination in U.S. at time of Admission	Port of Entry where Admitted to U.S.

Are you in removal/deportation or recission proceedings? ☐ No ☐ Yes

Since you were granted permanent residence, have you ever filed Form I-407, Abandonment by Alien of Status as Lawful Permanent Resident, or otherwise been judged to have abandoned your status? ☐ No ☐ Yes

If you answer yes to any of the above questions, explain in detail on a separate piece of paper.

Part 4. Signature. *(Read the information on penalties in the instructions before completing this section. You must file this application while in the United States.)*

I certify, under penalty of perjury under the laws of the United States of America, that this application and the evidence submitted with it is all true and correct. I authorize the release of any information from my records that U.S. Citizenship and Immigration Services needs to determine eligibility for the benefit I am seeking.

Signature	Date	Daytime Phone Number

Please Note: If you do not completely fill out this form or fail to submit required documents listed in the instructions, you cannot be found eligible for the requested document and this application may be denied.

Part 5. Signature of person preparing form, if other than above. *(Sign below)*

I declare that I prepared this application at the request of the above person and it is based on all information of which I have knowledge.

Signature	Print Your Name	Date	Daytime Phone Number

Name and Address of Business/Organization (if applicable)

SAMPLE

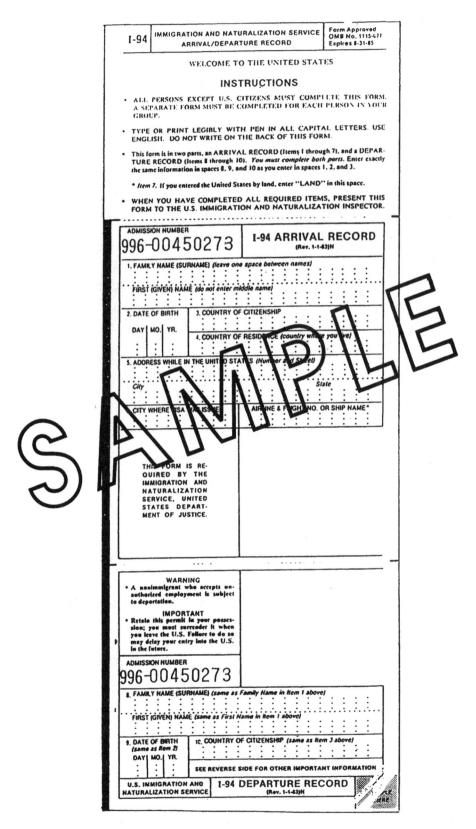

OMB No.1615-0009; Expires 05/31/08

Department of Homeland Security
U.S. Citizenship and Immigration Services

I-129, Petition for a
Nonimmigrant Worker

START HERE - Please type or print in black ink.

For USCIS Use Only

Part 1. Information about the employer filing this petition. *If the employer is an individual, complete* **Number 1.** *Organizations should complete* **Number 2.**

1. Family Name *(Last Name)*   Given Name *(First Name)*

Full Middle Name   Telephone No. w/Area Code
(   )

2. Company or Organization Name   Telephone No. w/Area Code
(   )

Mailing Address: *(Street Number and Name)*   Suite #

C/O: *(In Care Of)*

City   State/Province

Country   Zip/Postal Code   E-Mail Address *(If Any)*

Federal Employer Identification #   U.S. Social Security #   Individual Tax #

Part 2. Information about this petition. *(See instructions for fee information.)*

1. Requested Nonimmigrant Classification. *(Write classification symbol):*

2. Basis for Classification *(Check one):*

   a. ☐ New employment (including new employer filing H-1B extension).

   b. ☐ Continuation of previously approved employment without change with the same employer.

   c. ☐ Change in previously approved employment.

   d. ☐ New concurrent employment.

   e. ☐ Change of employer.

   f. ☐ Amended petition

3. If you checked **Box 2b, 2c, 2d, 2e,** or **2f,** give the petition receipt number.

4. Prior Petition. If the beneficiary is in the U.S. as a nonimmigrant and is applying to change and/or extend his or her status, give the prior petition or application receipt #:

5. Requested Action *(Check one):*

   a. ☐ Notify the office in **Part 4** so the person(s) can obtain a visa or be admitted. (**NOTE:** *a petition is not required for an E-1, E-2 or R visa*).

   b. ☐ Change the person(s)' status and extend their stay since the person(s) are all now in the U.S. in another status *(see instructions for limitations)*. This is available only where you check "New Employment" in **Item 2,** above.

   c. ☐ Extend the stay of the person(s) since they now hold this status.

   d. ☐ Amend the stay of the person(s) since they now hold this status.

   e. ☐ Extend the status of a nonimmigrant classification based on a Free Trade Agreement. *(See Free Trade Supplement for TN and H1B1 to Form I-129).*

   f. ☐ Change status to a nonimmigrant classification based on a Free Trade Agreement. *(See Free Trade Supplement for TN and H1B1 to Form I-129).*

6. Total number of workers in petition *(See instructions relating to when more than one worker can be included):*

Returned

Date

Date

Resubmitted

Date

Date

Reloc Sent

Date

Date

Reloc Rec'd

Date

Date

☐ Petitioner Interviewed on

☐ Beneficiary Interviewed on

Receipt

Class: _____
# of Workers: _____
Priority Number: _____
Validity Dates: _____
   From: _____
   To: _____

☐ **Classification Approved**
  ☐ Consulate/POE/PFI Notified
    At _____
  ☐ Extension Granted
  ☐ COS/Extension Granted

Partial Approval *(explain)*

Action Block

To Be Completed by
Attorney or Representative, if any.
☐ Fill in box if G-28 is attached to represent the applicant.

ATTY State License #

SAMPLE

Form I-129 (Rev. 10/26/05)Y

Part 3. Information about the person(s) you are filing for. *Complete the blocks below. Use the continuation sheet to name each person included in this petition.*

1. If an Entertainment Group, Give the Group Name

Family Name *(Last Name)*	Given Name *(First Name)*	Full Middle Name

All Other Names Used *(include maiden name and names from all previous marriages)*

Date of Birth *(mm/dd/yyyy)*	U.S. Social Security # *(if any)*	A # *(if any)*

Country of Birth	Province of Birth	Country of Citizenship

2. If in the United States, Complete the Following:

Date of Last Arrival *(mm/dd/yyyy)*	I-94 # *(Arrival/Departure Document)*	Current Nonimmigrant Status

Date Status Expires *(mm/dd/yyyy)* Passport Number	Date Passport Issued *(mm/dd/yyyy)*	Date Passport Expires *(mm/dd/yyyy)*

Current U.S. Address

Part 4. Processing Information.

1. If the person named in **Part 3** is outside the United States or a requested extension of stay or change of status cannot be granted, give the U.S. consulate or inspection facility you want notified if this petition is approved.

Type of Office *(Check one)*: ☐ Consulate   ☐ Pre-flight inspection   ☐ Port of Entry

Office Address *(City)*	U.S. State or Foreign Country

Person's Foreign Address

2. Does each person in this petition have a valid passport?

☐ Not required to have passport   ☐ No - explain on separate paper   ☐ Yes

3. Are you filing any other petitions with this one?   ☐ No   ☐ Yes - How many? [____]

4. Are applications for replacement/initial I-94s being filed with this petition?   ☐ No   ☐ Yes - How many? [____]

5. Are applications by dependents being filed with this petition?   ☐ No   ☐ Yes - How many? [____]

6. Is any person in this petition in removal proceedings?   ☐ No   ☐ Yes - explain on separate paper

Form I-129 (Rev. 10/26/05)Y Page 2

Part 4. Processing Information. *(Continued)*

7. Have you ever filed an immigrant petition for any person in this petition?   ☐ No   ☐ Yes - explain on separate paper

8. If you indicated you were filing a new petition in **Part 2**, within the past seven years has any person in this petition:

    a. Ever been given the classification you are now requesting?   ☐ No   ☐ Yes - explain on separate paper

    b. Ever been denied the classification you are now requesting?   ☐ No   ☐ Yes - explain on separate paper

9. Have you ever previously filed a petition for this person?   ☐ No   ☐ Yes - explain on separate paper

10. If you are filing for an entertainment group, has any person in this petition not been with the group for at least one year?   ☐ No   ☐ Yes - explain on separate paper

Part 5. Basic information about the proposed employment and employer. *Attach the supplement relating to the classification you are requesting.*

1. Job Title

2. Nontechnical Job Description

3. LCA Case Number

4. NAICS Code

5. Address where the person(s) will work if different from address in **Part 1**. *(Street number and name, city/town, state, zip code)*

6. Is this a full-time position?

    ☐ No - Hours per week: ☐ Yes - Wages per week or per year:

7. Other Compensation *(Explain)*

8. Dates of intended employment *(mm/dd/yyyy)*:

    From: To:

9. Type of Petitioner - *Check one*:

    ☐ U.S. citizen or permanent resident   ☐ Organization   ☐ Other - explain on separate paper

10. Type of Business

11. Year Established

12. Current Number of Employees

13. Gross Annual Income

14. Net Annual Income

Form I-129 (Rev. 10/26/05)Y Page 3

Part 6. Signature. *Read the information on penalties in the instructions before completing this section.*

I certify, under penalty of perjury under the laws of the United States of America, that this petition and the evidence submitted with it is all true and correct. If filing this on behalf of an organization, I certify that I am empowered to do so by that organization. If this petition is to extend a prior petition, I certify that the proposed employment is under the same terms and conditions as stated in the prior approved petition. I authorize the release of any information from my records, or from the petitioning organization's records that the U.S. Citizenship and Immigration Services needs to determine eligibility for the benefit being sought.

Signature

Daytime Phone Number *(Area/Country Code)*

( )

Print Name

Date *(mm/dd/yyyy)*

NOTE: If you do not completely fill out this form and the required supplement, or fail to submit required documents listed in the instructions, the person(s) filed for may not be found eligible for the requested benefit and this petition may be denied.

Part 7. Signature of person preparing form, if other than above.

I declare that I prepared this petition at the request of the above person and it is based on all information of which I have any knowledge.

Signature

Daytime Phone Number *(Area/Country Code)*

( )

Print Name

Date *(mm/dd/yyyy)*

Firm Name and Address

OMB No.1615-0009; Expires 05/31/08

Department of Homeland Security
U.S. Citizenship and Immigration Services

E Classification Supplement
to Form I-129

1. Name of person or organization filing petition:

2. Name of person you are filing for:

3. Classification sought *(Check one)*:

☐ E-1 Treaty trader   ☐ E-2 Treaty investor

4. Name of country signatory to treaty with U.S.:

Section 1.   Information about the employer outside the United States (if any)

Employer's Name

Total Number of Employees

Employer's Address *(Street number and name, city/town, state/province, zip/postal code)*

Principal Product, Merchandise or Service

Employee's Position - Title, duties and number of years employed

Section 2.   Additional information about the U.S. Employer

1. The U.S. company is to the company outside the United States *(Check one)*:

☐ Parent   ☐ Branch   ☐ Subsidiary   ☐ Affiliate   ☐ Joint Venture

2. Date and Place of Incorporation or Establishment in the United States

3. Nationality of Ownership *(Individual or Corporate)*

Name *(First/Middle/Last)*	Nationality	Immigration Status	% Ownership

4. Assets

5. Net Worth

6. Total Annual Income

7. Staff in the United States

   a. How many executive and/or managerial employees does petitioner have who are nationals of the treaty country in either E or L status?

   b. How many specialized qualifications or knowledge persons does the petitioner have who are nationals of the treaty country in either E or L status?

   c. Provide the total number of employees in executive or managerial positions in the United States.

   d. Provide the total number of specialized qualifications or knowledge persons positions in the United States.

8. Total number of employees the alien would supervise; or describe the nature of the specialized skills essential to the U.S. company.

Section 3.   Complete if filing for an E-1 Treaty Trader

1. Total Annual Gross Trade/Business of the U.S. company

2. For Year Ending *(yyyy)*

3. Percent of total gross trade between the United States and the country of which the treaty trader organization is a national.

Section 4.   Complete if filing for an E-2 Treaty Investor

Total Investment:

Cash	Equipment	Other

Inventory	Premises	Total

OMB No.1615-0009; Expires 05/31/08

Department of Homeland Security
U.S. Citizenship and Immigration Services

Nonimmigrant Classification Based on Free Trade Agreement Supplement to Form I-129

1. Name of person or organization filing petition:

2. Name of person you are filing for:

3. Employer is a *(Check one)*:

☐ U.S. Employer   ☐ Foreign Employer

4. If Foreign Employer, name the foreign country.

Section 1. Information about requested extension or change *(See instructions attached to this form.)*

1. This is a request for an extension of Free Trade status based on *(Check one)*:   **Or**

2. This is a request for a change of nonimmigrant status to *(Check one)*:

a. ☐ Free Trade, Canada (TN)

b. ☐ Free Trade, Chile (H1B1)

c. ☐ Free Trade, Mexico (TN)

d. ☐ Free Trade, Singapore (H1B1)

e. ☐ Free Trade, Other

f. ☐ I am an H-1B1 Free Trade Nonimmigrant from Chile or Singapore and this is my sixth consecutive request for an extension.

a. ☐ Free Trade, Canada (TN)

b. ☐ Free Trade, Chile (H1B1)

c. ☐ Free Trade, Mexico (TN)

d. ☐ Free Trade, Singapore (H1B1)

e. ☐ Free Trade, Other

f. ☐ I am an H-1B1 Free Trade Nonimmigrant from Chile or Singapore and this is my first request for a change of status to H-1B1 within the past six years.

Part 2. Signature. *Read the information on penalties in the instructions before completing this section.*

I certify, under penalty of perjury under the laws of the United States of America, that this petition and the evidence submitted with it is all true and correct. If filing this on behalf of an organization, I certify that I am empowered to do so by that organization. If this petition is to extend a prior petition, I certify that the proposed employment is under the same terms and conditions as stated in the prior approved petition. I authorize the release of any information from my records, or from the petitioning organization's records, that the U.S. Citizenship and Immigration Services needs to determine eligibility for the benefit being sought.

Signature

Daytime Phone Number *(Area/Country Code)*

( )

Print Name

Date *(mm/dd/yyyy)*

NOTE: If you do not completely fill out this form and the required supplement, or fail to submit required documents listed in the instructions, the person(s) filed for may not be found eligible for the requested benefit and this petition may be denied.

Part 3. Signature of person preparing form, if other than above.

I declare that I prepared this petition at the request of the above person and it is based on all information of which I have any knowledge.

Signature

Daytime Phone Number *(Area/Country Code)*

( )

Print Name

Date *(mm/dd/yyyy)*

Firm Name and Address

Form I-129 Supplement FT (Rev. 10/26/05)Y Page 6

OMB No.1615-0009; Expires 05/31/08

**H Classification Supplement
to Form I-129**

Department of Homeland Security
U.S. Citizenship and Immigration Services

1. Name of person or organization filing
petition:

2. Name of person or total number of workers or trainees you
are filing for:

3. List the alien's and any dependent family member's prior periods of stay in H classification in the United States for the last six years.
Be sure to list only those periods in which the alien and/or family members were actually in the United States in an H classification.
NOTE: Submit photocopies of Forms I-94, I-797 and/or other USCIS issued documents noting these periods of stay in the H
classification. If more space is needed, attach an additional sheet(s). (If applying for H-2A/H-2B classification skip this item.)

Subject's Name	Period of Stay *(mm/dd/yyyy)*		Subject's Name	Period of Stay *(mm/dd/yyyy)*	
	From:	To:		From:	To:
	From:	To:		From:	To:

4. Classification sought *(Check one)*:

☐ H-1B1   Specialty occupation

☐ H-1B2   Exceptional services relating to a cooperative
research and development project administered by
the U.S. Department of Defense (DOD)

☐ H-1B3   Fashion model of national or international acclaim

☐ H-2A   Agricultural worker

☐ H-2B   Non-agricultural worker

☐ H-3   Trainee

☐ H-3   Special education exchange visitor program

Section 1. Complete this section if filing for H-1B classification.

1. Describe the proposed duties

2. Alien's present occupation and summary of prior work experience

---

Statement for H-1B specialty occupations only:

By filing this petition, I agree to the terms of the labor condition application for the duration of the alien's authorized period of stay
for H-1B employment.

Petitioner's Signature	**Print or Type Name**	**Date** *(mm/dd/yyyy)*

Statement for H-1B specialty occupations and U.S. Department of Defense projects:

As an authorized official of the employer, I certify that the employer will be liable for the reasonable costs of return transportation
of the alien abroad if the alien is dismissed from employment by the employer before the end of the period of authorized stay.

Signature of Authorized Official of Employer	**Print or Type Name**	**Date** *(mm/dd/yyyy)*

Statement for H-1B U.S. Department of Defense projects only:

I certify that the alien will be working on a cooperative research and development project or a co-production project under a
reciprocal government-to-government agreement administered by the U.S. Department of Defense.

DOD Project Manager's Signature	**Print or Type Name**	**Date** *(mm/dd/yyyy)*

Section 2. Complete this section if filing for H-2A or H-2B classification.

1. Employment is: *(Check one)*   **2.** Temporary need is: *(Check one)*

a. ☐ Seasonal   **c.** ☐ Intermittent   **a.** ☐ Unpredictable   **c.** ☐ Recurrent annually

b. ☐ Peakload   **d.** ☐ One-time occurence   **b.** ☐ Periodic

3. Explain your temporary need for the alien's services *(attach a separate sheet(s) paper if additional space is needed)*.

```



```

Section 3. Complete this section if filing for H-2A classification.

The petitioner and each employer consent to allow government access to the site where the labor is being performed for the purpose of determining compliance with H-2A requirements. The petitioner further agrees to notify USCIS in the manner and within the time frame specified if an H-2A worker absconds, or if the authorized employment ends more than five days before the relating certification document expires, and pay liquidated damages of ten dollars ($10.00) for each instance where it cannot demonstrate compliance with this notification requirement. The petitioner agrees also to pay liquidated damages of two hundred dollars ($200.00) for each instance where it cannot be demonstrated that the H-2A worker either departed the United States or obtained authorized status during the period of admission or within five days of early termination, whichever comes first.

The petitioner must execute **Part A**. If the petitioner is the employer's agent, the employer must execute **Part B**. If there are joint employers, they must each execute **Part C**.

Part A. Petitioner:

By filing this petition, I agree to the conditions of H-2A employment and agree to the notice requirements and limited liabilities defined in 8 CFR 214.2(h)(3)(vi).

Petitioner's Signature	Print or Type Name	Date *(mm/dd/yyyy)*

Part B. Employer who is not the petitioner:

I certify that I have authorized the party filing this petition to act as my agent in this regard. I assume full responsibility for all representations made by this agent on my behalf and agree to the conditions of H-2A eligibility.

Employer's Signature	Print or Type Name	Date *(mm/dd/yyyy)*

Form I-129 Supplement H (Rev. 10/26/05)Y Page 8

Part C. Joint Employers:

I agree to the conditions of H-2A eligibility.

Joint Employer's Signature(s)	Print or Type Name	Date *(mm/dd/yyyy)*

Joint Employer's Signature(s)	Print or Type Name	Date *(mm/dd/yyyy)*

Joint Employer's Signature(s)	Print or Type Name	Date *(mm/dd/yyyy)*

Joint Employer's Signature(s)	Print or Type Name	Date *(mm/dd/yyyy)*

Section 4. Complete this section if filing for H-3 classification.

1. If you answer "yes" to any of the following questions, attach a full explanation.

   a. Is the training you intend to provide, or similar training, available in the alien's country? ☐ No ☐ Yes

   b. Will the training benefit the alien in pursuing a career abroad? ☐ No ☐ Yes

   c. Does the training involve productive employment incidental to training? ☐ No ☐ Yes

   d. Does the alien already have skills related to the training? ☐ No ☐ Yes

   e. Is this training an effort to overcome a labor shortage? ☐ No ☐ Yes

   f. Do you intend to employ the alien abroad at the end of this training? ☐ No ☐ Yes

2. If you do not intend to employ this person abroad at the end of this training, explain why you wish to incur the cost of providing this training and your expected return from this training.

Form I-129 Supplement H (Rev. 10/26/05)Y Page 9

OMB No.1615-0009; Expires 05/31/08

Department of Homeland Security
U.S. Citizenship and Immigration Services

H-1B Data Collection and
Filing Fee Exemption Supplement

Petitioner's Name [   ]

Part A.   General Information.

1. **Employer Information** - *(check all items that apply)*

   a. Is the petitioner a dependent employer?   ☐ No   ☐ Yes

   b. Has the petitioner ever been found to be a willful violator?   ☐ No   ☐ Yes

   c. Is the beneficiary an exempt H-1B nonimmigrant?   ☐ No   ☐ Yes

      1. If yes, is it because the beneficiary's annual rate of pay is equal to at least $60,000?   ☐ No   ☐ Yes

      2. Or is it because the beneficiary has a master's or higher degree in a speciality related to the employment?   ☐ No   ☐ Yes

2. Beneficiary's Last Name   First Name   Middle Name
   [   ]   [   ]   [   ]

   Attention To or In Care Of   Current Residential Address - Street   Apt. #
   [   ]   [   ]   [   ]

   City   State   Zip/Postal Code
   [   ]   [   ]   [   ]

   U.S. Social Security # *(If Any)*   I-94 # *(Arrival/Departure Document)*   Previous Receipt # *(If Any)*
   [   ]   [   ]   [   ]

3. **Beneficiary's Highest Level of Education.** Please check one box below.

   ☐ NO DIPLOMA   ☐ Associate's degree *(for example: AA, AS)*
   ☐ HIGH SCHOOL GRADUATE - high school   ☐ Bachelor's degree *(for example: BA, AB, BS)*
      DIPLOMA or the equivalent (example: GED)   ☐ Master's degree *(for example: MA, MS, MEng, MEd, MSW, MBA)*
   ☐ Some college credit, but less than one year   ☐ Professional degree *(for example: MD, DDS, DVM, LLB, JD)*
   ☐ One or more years of college, no degree   ☐ Doctorate degree *(for example: PhD, EdD)*

4. Major/Primary Field of Study.
   [ ]

5. Has the beneficiary of this petition earned a master's or higher degree from a U.S. institution of higher education as defined in 20 U.S.C. section 1001(a)?

   ☐ No   ☐ Yes (If "Yes" provide the following information):

   Name of the U.S. institution of higher education   Date Degree Awarded   Type of U.S. Degree
   [   ]   [   ]   [   ]

   Address of the U.S. institution of higher education
   [   ]

6. Rate of Pay Per Year.   7. LCA Code.   8. NAICS Code.
   [   ]   [ ][ ][ ][ ]   [ ][ ][ ][ ][ ][ ]

Part B.   Fee Exemption and/or Determination

In order for USCIS to determine if you must pay the additional $1,500 or $750 fee, please answer all of the following questions:

1.   ☐ Yes   ☐ No   Are you an institution of higher education as defined in the Higher Education Act of 1965, section 101 (a), 20 U.S.C. section 1001(a)?

2.   ☐ Yes   ☐ No   Are you a nonprofit organization or entity related to or affiliated with an institution of higher education, as such institutions of higher education are defined in the Higher Education Act of 1965, section 101 (a), 20 U.S.C. section 1001(a)?

3. ☐ Yes ☐ No Are you a nonprofit research organization or a governmental research organization, as defined in 8 CFR 214.2(h)(19)(iii)(C)?

4. ☐ Yes ☐ No Is this the second or subsequent request for an extension of stay that you have filed for this alien?

5. ☐ Yes ☐ No Is this an amended petition that does not contain any request for extensions of stay?

6. ☐ Yes ☐ No Are you filing this petition in order to correct a USCIS error?

7. ☐ Yes ☐ No Is the petitioner a primary or secondary education institution?

8. ☐ Yes ☐ No Is the petitioner a non-profit entity that engages in an established curriculum-related clinical training of students registered at such an institution?

If you answered "Yes" to any of the questions above, you are ONLY required to submit the fee for your H-1B Form I-129 petition, which is $190. If you answered "No" to all questions, please answer Question 9.

9. ☐ Yes ☐ No Do you currently employ a total of no more than 25 full-time equivalent employees in the United States, including any affiliate or subsidiary of your company?

If you answered "Yes" to Question 9 above, then you are required to pay an additional fee of $750. If you answered "No", then you are required to pay an additional fee of $1,500.

NOTE: On or after March 8, 2005, a U.S. employer seeking initial approval of H-1B or L nonimmigrant status for a beneficiary, or seeking approval to employ an H-1B or L nonimmigrant currently working for another U.S. employer, must submit an additional $500 fee. This additional $500 Fraud Prevention and Detection fee was mandated by the provisions of the H-1B Visa Reform Act of 2004. **There is no exemption from this fee.**

Part C.   Numerical Limitation Exemption Information.

1. ☐ Yes ☐ No Are you an institution of higher education as defined in the Higher Education Act of 1965, section 101 (a), 20 U.S.C. section 1001(a)?

2. ☐ Yes ☐ No Are you a nonprofit organization or entity related to or affiliated with an institution of higher education, as such institutions of higher education are defined in the Higher Education Act of 1965, section 101 (a), 20 U.S.C. section 1001(a)?

3. ☐ Yes ☐ No Are you a nonprofit research organization or a governmental research organization, as defined in 8 CFR 214.2(h)(19)(iii)(C)?

4. ☐ Yes ☐ No Is the beneficiary of this petition a J-1 nonimmigrant alien who received a waiver of the 2-year foreign residency requirement described in section 214 (l)(1)(B) or (C) of the Act?

5. ☐ Yes ☐ No Has the beneficiary of this petition been previously granted status as an H-1B nonimmigrant in the past 6 years and not left the United States for more than one year after attaining such status?

6. ☐ Yes ☐ No If the petition is to request a change of employer, did the beneficiary previously work as an H-1B for an institution of higher education, an entity related to or affiliated with an institution of higher education, or a nonprofit research organization or governmental research institution defined in questions 1, 2 and 3 of Part C of this form?

7. ☐ Yes ☐ No Has the beneficiary of this petition earned a master's or higher degree from a U.S. institution of higher education, as defined in the Higher Education Act of 1965, section 101(a), 20 U.S.C. section 1001(a)?

I certify under penalty of perjury, under the laws of the United States of America, that this attachment and the evidence submitted with it is true and correct. If filing this on behalf of an organization or entity, I certify that I am empowered to do so by that organization or entity. I authorize the release of any information from my records, or from the petitioning organization or entity's records, that the U.S. Citizenship and Immigration Services may need to determine eligibility for the exemption being sought.

Certification.

Signature	**Print Name**

Title	**Date** *(mm/dd/yyyy)*

OMB No.1615-0009; Expires 05/31/08

Department of Homeland Security
U.S. Citizenship and Immigration Services

L Classification Supplement
to Form I-129

1. Name of person or organization filing petition:

2. Name of person you are filing for:

3. This petition is *(Check one)*:

    a. ☐ An individual petition   **b.** ☐ A blanket petition

Section 1.   Complete this section if filing for an individual petition.

1. Classification sought *(Check one)*:

    a. ☐ L-1A manager or executive   **b.** ☐ L-1B specialized knowledge

2. List the alien's and any dependent family member's prior periods of stay in an H or L classification in the United States for the last seven years. Be sure to list only those periods in which the alien and/or family members were actually in the U.S. in an H or L classification. **NOTE:** Submit photocopies of Forms I-94, I-797 and/or other USCIS issued documents noting these periods of stay in the H or L classification. If more space is needed, attach an additional sheet(s).

Subject's Name	Period of Stay *(mm/dd/yyyy)*	
	From:	To:
	From:	To:
	From:	To:
	From:	To:
	From:	To:

3. Name of employer abroad

4. Address of employer abroad *(Street number and name, city/town, state/province, zip/postal code)*

5. Dates of alien's employment with this employer. Explain any interruptions in employment.

Dates of Employment *(mm/dd/yyyy)*	Explanation of Interruptions
From: To:	
From: To:	
From: To:	

6. Description of the alien's duties for the past three years.

7. Description of the alien's proposed duties in the United States.

8. Summary of the alien's education and work experience.

Form I-129 Supplement L (Rev. 10/26/05)Y Page 12

1. Name of person or organization filing petition:

2. Name of person you are filing for:

Section 1.   Complete this section if filing for an individual petition.   *(Continued)*

9. The U.S. company is to the company abroad: *(Check one)*

    a. ☐ Parent   **b.** ☐ Branch   **c.** ☐ Subsidiary   **d.** ☐ Affiliate   **e.** ☐ Joint Venture

10. Describe the stock ownership and managerial control of each company. Provide the U.S. Tax Code Number for each company.

Company stock ownership and managerial control of each company	U.S. Tax Code Number

11. Do the companies currently have the same qualifying relationship as they did during the one-year period of the alien's employment with the company abroad?   ☐ Yes   ☐ No *(Attach explanation)*

12. Is the alien coming to the United States to open a new office?   ☐ Yes *(Attach explanation)*   ☐ No

13. If you are seeking L-1B specialized knowledge status for an individual, answer the following question:

    Will the beneficiary be stationed primarily offsite (at the worksite of an employer other than the petitioner or its affiliate, subsidiary, or parent)?   ☐ Yes   ☐ No

    If you answered "Yes" to the preceding question, describe how and by whom the beneficiary's work will be controlled and supervised. Include a description of the amount of time each supervisor is expected to control and supervise the work. Use an attachment if needed.

    If you answered "Yes" to the preceding question, also describe the reasons why placement at another worksite outside the petitioner, subsidiary or parent is needed. Include a description of how the beneficiary's duties at another worksite relate to the need for the specialized knowledge he or she possesses. Use an attachment if needed.

Section 2.   Complete this section if filing a blanket petition.

List all U.S. and foreign parent, branches, subsidiaries and affiliates included in this petition. *(Attach a separate sheet(s) of paper if additional space is needed.)*

Name and Address	Relationship

Section 3.   Fraud Prevention and Detection Fee.

Beginning on **March 8, 2005**, a U.S. employer seeking initial approval of L nonimmigrant status for a beneficiary, or seeking approval to employ an L nonimmigrant currently working for another U.S. employer, must submit an additional **$500.00** fee. This additional **$500.00** Fraud Prevention and Detection fee was mandated by the provisions of the H-1B Visa Reform Act of 2004. **There is no exemption from this fee.** You must include payment of this **$500.00** fee with your submission of this form. Failure to submit the fee when required will result in rejection or denial of your submission.

Form I-129 (Rev. 10/26/05)Y Page 13

OMB No.1615-0009; Expires 05/31/08

Department of Homeland Security
U.S. Citizenship and Immigration Services

O and P Classifications
Supplement to Form I-129

1. **Name of person or organization filing petition:**

2. **Name of person or group or total number of workers you are filing for:**

3. **Classification sought** *(Check one)*:

   a. ☐ O-1A Alien of extraordinary ability in sciences, education, business or athletics (not including the arts, motion picture or television industry.)

   b. ☐ O-1B Alien of extraordinary ability in the arts or extraordinary achievement in the motion picture or television industry.

   c. ☐ O-2 Accompanying alien who is coming to the U.S. to assist in the performance of the O-1.

   d. ☐ P-1 Athletic/Entertainment group.

   e. ☐ P-1S Essential Support Personnel for P-1.

   f. ☐ P-2 Artist or entertainer for reciprocal exchange program.

   g. ☐ P-2S Essential Support Personnel for P-2.

   h. ☐ P-3 Artist/Entertainer coming to the United States to perform, teach or coach under a program that is culturally unique.

   i. ☐ P-3S Essential Support Personnel for P-3.

4. Explain the nature of the event

5. Describe the duties to be performed

6. If filing for an O-2 or P support alien, list dates of the alien's prior experience with the O-1 or P alien.

7. Have you obtained the required written consultation(s)? ☐ Yes - Attached   ☐ No - Copy of request attached

   If not, give the following information about the organization(s) to which you have sent a duplicate of this petition.

   O-1 Extraordinary Ability

Name of Recognized Peer Group	Daytime Telephone # *(Area/Country Code)* ( )
Complete Address	Date Sent *(mm/dd/yyyy)*

   O-1 Extraordinary achievement in motion pictures or television

Name of Labor Organization	Daytime Telephone # *(Area/Country Code)* ( )
Complete Address	Date Sent *(mm/dd/yyyy)*
Name of Management Organization	Daytime Telephone # *(Area/Country Code)* ( )
Complete Address	Date sent *(mm/dd/yyyy)*

   O-2 or P alien

Name of Labor Organization	Daytime Telephone # *(Area/Country Code)* ( )
Complete Address	Date Sent *(mm/dd/yyyy)*

SAMPLE

OMB No.1615-0009; Expires 05/31/08

Q-1 and R-1 Classifications
Supplement to Form I-129

Department of Homeland Security
U.S. Citizenship and Immigration Services

1. Name of person or organization filing petition:

2. Name of person you are filing for:

Section 1. Complete this section if you are filing for a Q-1 international cultural exchange alien.

I hereby certify that the participant(s) in the international cultural exchange program:

- Is at least 18 years of age,
- Is qualified to perform the service or labor or receive the type of training stated in the petition,
- Has the ability to communicate effectively about the cultural attributes of his or her country of nationality to the American public, and
- Has resided and been physically present outside the United States for the immediate prior year, if he or she was previously admitted as a Q-1.

I also certify that I will offer the alien(s) the same wages and working conditions comparable to those accorded local domestic workers similarly employed.

Petitioner's signature

Date *(mm/dd/yyyy)*

Section 2. Complete this section if you are filing for an R-1 religious worker.

1. List the alien's and any dependent family member's prior periods of stay in R classification in the United States for the last six years. Be sure to list only those periods in which the alien and/or family members were actually in the United States in an R classification. **NOTE:** Submit photocopies of Forms I-94, I-797 and/or other USCIS issued documents noting these periods of stay in the R classification. If more space is needed, attach an additional sheet(s).

Subject's Name	Period of Stay *(mm/dd/yyyy)*		Subject's Name	Period of Stay *(mm/dd/yyyy)*
	From:	To:		From: To:
	From:	To:		From: To:
	From:	To:		From: To:

2. Describe the alien's proposed duties in the United States.

3. Describe the alien's qualifications for the vocation or occupation.

4. Description of the relationship between the religious organization in the United States and the organization abroad of which the alien was a member.

Attachment - 1

Attach to Form I-129 when more than one person is included in the petition. *(List each person separately. Do not include the person you named on the form).*

Family Name *(Last Name)*	Given Name *(First Name)*	Full Middle Name	Date of Birth *mm/dd/yyyy*

Country of Birth	Country of Citizenship	U.S. Social Security # *(if any)*	A # *(if any)*

IF IN THE U.S.

Date of Arrival *(mm/dd/yyyy)*	I-94 # (Arrival/Departure Document)	Current Nonimmigrant Status	Date Status Expires *(mm/dd/yyyy)*

Country Where Passport Issued	Date Passport Expires *(mm/dd/yyyy)*	Date Started With Group *(mm/dd/yyyy)*

Family Name *(Last Name)*	Given Name *(First Name)*	Full Middle Name	Date of Birth *mm/dd/yyyy*

Country of Birth	Country of Citizenship	U.S. Social Security # *(if any)*	A # *(if any)*

IF IN THE U.S.

Date of Arrival *(mm/dd/yyyy)*	I-94 # (Arrival/Departure Document)	Current Nonimmigrant Status	Date Status Expires *(mm/dd/yyyy)*

Country Where Passport Issued	Date Passport Expires *(mm/dd/yyyy)*	Date Started With Group *(mm/dd/yyyy)*

Family Name *(Last Name)*	Given Name *(First Name)*	Full Middle Name	Date of Birth *mm/dd/yyyy*

Country of Birth	Country of Citizenship	U.S. Social Security # *(if any)*	A # *(if any)*

IF IN THE U.S.

Date of Arrival *(mm/dd/yyyy)*	I-94 # (Arrival/Departure Document)	Current Nonimmigrant Status	Date Status Expires *(mm/dd/yyyy)*

Country Where Passport Issued	Date Passport Expires *(mm/dd/yyyy)*	Date Started With Group *(mm/dd/yyyy)*

Family Name *(Last Name)*	Given Name *(First Name)*	Full Middle Name	Date of Birth *mm/dd/yyyy*

Country of Birth	Country of Citizenship	U.S. Social Security # *(if any)*	A # *(if any)*

IF IN THE U.S.

Date of Arrival *(mm/dd/yyyy)*	I-94 # (Arrival/Departure Document)	Current Nonimmigrant Status	Date Status Expires *(mm/dd/yyyy)*

Country Where Passport Issued	Date Passport Expires *(mm/dd/yyyy)*	Date Started With Group *(mm/dd/yyyy)*

Form I-129 Attachment - 1 (Rev. 10/26/05)Y Page 16

Attachment - 1

Attach to Form I-129 when more than one person is included in the petition. *(List each person separately. Do not include the person you named on the form).*

Family Name *(Last Name)*	Given Name *(First Name)*	Full Middle Name	Date of Birth *mm/dd/yyyy*

Country of Birth	Country of Citizenship	U.S. Social Security # *(if any)*	A # *(if any)*

IF IN THE U.S.

Date of Arrival *(mm/dd/yyyy)*	I-94 # (Arrival/Departure Document)	Current Nonimmigrant Status	Date Status Expires *(mm/dd/yyyy)*

Country Where Passport Issued	Date Passport Expires *(mm/dd/yyyy)*	Date Started With Group *(mm/dd/yyyy)*

Family Name *(Last Name)*	Given Name *(First Name)*	Full Middle Name	Date of Birth *mm/dd/yyyy*

Country of Birth	Country of Citizenship	U.S. Social Security # *(if any)*	A # *(if any)*

IF IN THE U.S.

Date of Arrival *(mm/dd/yyyy)*	I-94 # (Arrival/Departure Document)	Current Nonimmigrant Status	Date Status Expires *(mm/dd/yyyy)*

Country Where Passport Issued	Date Passport Expires *(mm/dd/yyyy)*	Date Started With Group *(mm/dd/yyyy)*

Family Name *(Last Name)*	Given Name *(First Name)*	Full Middle Name	Date of Birth *mm/dd/yyyy*

Country of Birth	Country of Citizenship	U.S. Social Security # *(if any)*	A # *(if any)*

IF IN THE U.S.

Date of Arrival *(mm/dd/yyyy)*	I-94 # (Arrival/Departure Document)	Current Nonimmigrant Status	Date Status Expires *(mm/dd/yyyy)*

Country Where Passport Issued	Date Passport Expires *(mm/dd/yyyy)*	Date Started With Group *(mm/dd/yyyy)*

Family Name *(Last Name)*	Given Name *(First Name)*	Full Middle Name	Date of Birth *mm/dd/yyyy*

Country of Birth	Country of Citizenship	U.S. Social Security # *(if any)*	A # *(if any)*

IF IN THE U.S.

Date of Arrival *(mm/dd/yyyy)*	I-94 # (Arrival/Departure Document)	Current Nonimmigrant Status	Date Status Expires *(mm/dd/yyyy)*

Country Where Passport Issued	Date Passport Expires *(mm/dd/yyyy)*	Date Started With Group *(mm/dd/yyyy)*

Form I-129 Attachment - 1 (Rev. 10/26/05)Y Page 17

U.S. Department of Homeland Security
Bureau of Citizenship and Immigration Services

OMB No. 1615-0001: Expires 11/30/04

I-129F, Petition for Alien Fiancé(e)

Read the instructions carefully. If you do not follow the instructions, we may have to return your petition, which may delay final action.

---

1. Who May File?

A. You are a U.S. citizen, and

B. You and your fiancé(e) intend to marry within 90 days of your fiancé(e) entering the United States, and are both free to marry, and have met in person within two years before your filing of this petition unless:

   l) The requirement to meet your fiancé(e) in person would violate strict and long-established customs of your or your fiancé(e)'s foreign culture or social practice; or

   2) It is established that the requirement to personally meet your fiancé(e) would result in extreme hardship to you.

   OR

C. You wish to have your alien spouse or child enter as a nonimmigrant. See Question 12.

   NOTE: Unmarried children of your fiancé(e) or spouse who are under 21 years of age and listed on this form will be eligible to apply to accompany your fiancé(e) or spouse.

2. General Filing Instructions.

A. Type or print legibly in black ink.

B. If extra space is needed to complete any item, attach a continuation sheet, indicate the item number, and date and sign each sheet.

C. Answer all questions fully and accurately. State that an item is not applicable with "N/A." If the answer is "none," write none.

D. *Translations*. Any foreign language document must be accompanied by a full English translation, that the translator has certified as complete and correct, and by the translator's certification that he or she is competent to translate the foreign language into English.

E. *Copies*. If these instructions state that a copy of a document may be filed with this petition and you choose to send us the original, the Bureau of Citizenship and Immigration Services (CIS) will keep that original for our records. If the CIS requires the original, we will request it.

   NOTE: The CIS is comprised of offices of the former Immigration and Naturalization Service (INS).

3. What Documents Do You Need to Show That You Are a United States Citizen?

A. If you were born in the United States, give the CIS a copy, front and back, of your birth certificate.

B. If you were naturalized, give the CIS a copy, front and back, of your original Certificate of Naturalization.

C. If you were born outside the United States, and you are a U.S. citizen through your parents, give the CIS:

   1) Your original Certificate of Citizenship, or

   2) Your Form FS-240 (Report of Birth Abroad of a United States Citizen).

D. In place of any of the above, you may give the CIS a copy of your valid, unexpired U.S. passport that was issued for at least five years. You must submit copies of all pages in the passport.

E. If you do not have any of the above and were born in the United States, see instruction under Number 4 below, "What If a Document Is Not Available?".

4. What If a Document Is Not Available?

If the documents needed above are not available, you can give CIS the following instead. However, the CIS may request in writing that you obtain a statement from the appropriate civil authority certifying that the needed document is not available. Any evidence submitted must contain enough information, such as a birth date, to establish the event you are trying to prove.

A. *Baptismal certificate*. A copy, front and back, of the certificate under the seal of the church, synagogue or other religious entity showing where the baptism, dedication or comparable rite occurred, as well as the date and place of the child's birth, date of baptism and names of the child's parents. The baptism must have occurred within two months after the birth of the child.

B. *School record*. A letter from the school authority (preferably from the first school attended), showing the date of admission to the school, child's date or age at that time, place of birth, and the names of the parents.

C. *Census record*. State or Federal census record showing the name(s), date(s) and place(s) of birth or age(s) of the person(s) listed.

D. *Affidavits*. Written statements sworn to, or affirmed by, two persons who were living at the time and who have personal knowledge of the event. For example, a birth, marriage or death. These persons may be relatives and do not have to be citizens of the United States. Each affidavit should contain the person's full name and address, date and place of birth, and relationship to you and must fully describe the event and explain how he or she acquired knowledge of the event.

Form I-129F Instructions (Rev. 04/16/04)Y

5. What Documents Do You Need to Prove That You Can Legally Marry?

A. Provide copies of evidence that you and your fiancé(e) have personally met within the last two years, or if you have never met within the last two years, provide a detailed explanation and evidence of the extreme hardship or customary, cultural or social practices that have prohibited your meeting; and

B. Provide original statements from you and your fiancé(e) whom you plan to marry within 90 days of his or her admission, and copies of any evidence you wish to submit to establish your mutual intent; and

C. If either of you is of an age that requires special consent or permission for you to marry in the jurisdiction where your marriage will occur, give proof of that consent or permission; and

D. If either you or your fiancé(e) were married before, give copies of documents showing that each prior marriage was legally terminated.

6. What Other Documents Do You Need?

A. Give the CIS one color photo of you and one of your fiancé(e), taken within 30 days of the date of this petition. These photos must have a white background. The photos must be glossy, un-retouched and not mounted. The dimension of the facial image should be about one inch from your chin to the top of your hair in 3/4 frontal view, showing the right side of your face with your right ear visible. Using a pencil or felt pen, lightly print the name (and Alien Registration Number, if known) on the back of each photograph.

B. Submit separate completed and signed Forms G-325A (Biographic Information) for you and your fiancé(e). Except for name and signature, you do not have to repeat on the Biographic Information forms the information given on your Form I-129F.

C. If either you or the person you are filing for is using a name other than that shown on the relevant documents, you must give the CIS copies of the legal documents that made the change, such as a marriage certificate, adoption decree or court order.

7. Where Should You File This Form?

A. If you are filing for your fiancé(e), submit this application according to your place of residence, as listed below:

- If you live in Connecticut, Delaware, District of Columbia, Maine, Maryland, Massachusetts, New Hampshire, New Jersey, New York, Pennsylvania, Puerto Rico, Rhode Island, Vermont, U.S. Virgin Islands, Virginia or West Virginia, mail this petition to: **USCIS Vermont Service Center, 75 Lower Welden Street, St. Albans, VT 05479-0001**

- If you live in Alabama, Arkansas, Florida, Georgia, Kentucky, Louisiana, Mississippi, New Mexico, North Carolina, Oklahoma, South Carolina, Tennessee or Texas, mail this petition to: **USCIS Texas Service Center, P.O. Box 850965, Mesquite, TX 75185-0965.**

- If you live in Arizona, California, Guam, Hawaii or Nevada, mail this petition to: **USCIS California Service Center, P.O. Box 10130, Laguna Niguel, CA 92607-1013.**

- If you live in Alaska, Colorado, Idaho, Illinois, Indiana, Iowa, Kansas, Michigan, Minnesota, Missouri, Montana, Nebraska, North Dakota, Ohio, Oregon, South Dakota, Utah, Washington, Wisconsin or Wyoming, mail the petition to: **USCIS Nebraska Service Center, P.O. Box 87130, Lincoln, NE 68501-7130.**

- If you live outside the United States, mail your petition to the CIS Service Center listed above that has jurisdiction over the last place you lived in the United States. **NOTE:** Your petition cannot be adjudicated at a CIS office abroad.

B. If you are filing for your spouse under the K nonimmigrant visa program, mail your application to: **USCIS, P.O. Box 7218, Chicago, IL 60680-7218.**

8. What Is the Fee?

You must pay **$165.00** to file this form. **The fee will not be refunded, whether the petition is approved or not. Do not mail cash.** All checks or money orders, whether U.S. or foreign, must be payable in U.S. currency at a financial institution in the United States. When a check is drawn on the account of a person other than yourself, write your name on the face of the check.   If the check is not honored, the CIS will charge you $30.00.

Pay by check or money in the exact amount. Make the check or money order payable to **U.S. Department of Homeland Security,** unless:

A. If you live in Guam and are filing your petition in Guam, make the check or money order payable to "Treasurer, Guam" or

B. If you live in the U.S. Virgin Island and are filing your petition in the U.S. Virgin Islands, make the check or money order payable to "Commissioner of Finance of the Virgin Islands."

9. How Does Your Alien Fiancé(e) Obtain Permanent Resident Status?

Your alien fiancé(e) may apply for conditional permanent resident status after you have entered into a valid marriage to each other within 90 days of your fiancé(e)'s entry into the United States. Your alien spouse should then apply promptly to the BCIS for adjustment of status to conditional permanent resident, using Form I-485, Application to Register or Adjust Status.

10. How Does Your Conditional Permanent Resident Spouse Become a Lawful Permanent Resident Without Conditions?

Both you and your conditional permanent resident spouse are required to file a petition, Form I-751, Petition to Remove the Conditions on Residence, during the 90-day period immediately before the second anniversary of the date your alien spouse was granted conditional permanent residence. Children who were admitted as conditional permanent residents with your spouse may be included in the joint petition to remove the conditions.

The rights, privileges, responsibilities and duties that apply to all other permanent residents apply equally to a conditional permanent resident to file petitions on behalf of qualifying relatives, or to reside permanently in the United States as an immigrant in accordance with the immigration laws.

NOTICE
Failure to file Form I-751, Petition to Remove the Conditions on Residence, will result in termination of permanent residence status and initiation of removal proceedings.

---

11. How Do You Use This Form for Your Spouse or Child Seeking Entry Using a K-3/K-4 visa?

This form may be used to obtain a K-3/K-4 visa for your alien spouse or child. Fill out the form as directed, except assume that "fiancé" or "fiancé(e)" means "spouse." In addition, omit Questions **B.18** and **B.19** by entering "N/A." Note that this form is only necessary to facilitate the entry of your spouse or child as a **nonimmigrant**.

You must submit the documents required in Questions **3**, **4** and **6** of the instructions, but may omit the documents required in Question **5**. In addition, citizens petitioning for K-3 visas for their alien spouses must also include evidence that they have filed Form I-130 on behalf of the alien spouse listed on this form, and a marriage certificate evidencing the legal marriage between the citizen and alien.

The LIFE Act requires applicants to apply for a K-3/K-4 visa in the country where their marriage to the U.S. citizen petitioner took place. Petitioners should make sure to identify the appropriate consulate, in the same country where they married the alien for whom they are petitioning, in block **20** to avoid lengthy delays. In the event the petitioner and alien were married in the United States, they should list the country of the alien's current residence. See U.S. State Department regulations at 21 CFR 41.81.

12. Processing Information.

Any petition that is not signed or accompanied by the correct fee will be rejected with a notice that it is deficient. You may correct the deficiency and resubmit the petition. However, a petition is not considered properly filed until accepted by the CIS. Once the petition has been accepted, it will be checked for completeness, including submission of the required evidence. If you do not completely fill out the form or file it without required initial evidence, you will not establish a basis for eligibility and we may deny your petition.

We may request more information or evidence or we may request that you appear at a CIS office for an interview.

13. What Are the Penalties for Committing Marriage Fraud or Submitting False Information or Both?

Title 18, United States Code, Section 100 states that whoever willfully and knowingly falsifies a material fact, makes a false statement, or makes use of a false document will be fined up to $10,000 or imprisoned up to five years, or both.

Title 8, United States Code, Section 1325 states that any individual who knowingly enters into a marriage contract for the purpose of evading any provision of the immigration laws shall be imprisoned for not more than five years, or fined not more than $250,000, or both.

14. Information and CIS Forms.

For information on immigration laws, regulations and procedures and to order CIS forms, call our National Customer Service Center toll-free at **1-800-375-5283** or visit our internet website at **www.uscis.gov**.

15. What Is Our Authority for Collecting This Information?

We request the information on this form to carry out the immigration laws contained in Title 8, United States Code 1184(d). We need this information to determine whether a person is eligible for immigration benefits. The information you provide may also be disclosed to other federal, state, local and foreign law enforcement and regulatory agencies during the course of the investigation required by the CIS. You do not have to give this information. However, if you refuse to give some or all of it, your petition may be denied.

16. What Is the Reporting Burden?

Under the Paperwork Reduction Act, a person is not required to respond to a collection of information unless it displays a currently valid OMB control number. We try to create forms and instructions that are accurate, can be easily understood and that impose the least possible burden on you to provide us with information. Often this is difficult because some immigration laws are very complex. The estimated time to file this application is 30 minutes per application.

If you have any comments regarding the accuracy of this estimate, or suggestions for making this form simpler, you can write to the Bureau of Citizenship and Immigration Services, HQRFS, 425 I Street, N.W., Room 4034, Washington, DC 20529, OMB No. 1115-0071. **Do not mail your completed application to this address.**

U.S. Department of Homeland Security
Bureau of Citizenship and Immigration Services

OMB No. 1615-0001: Expires 11/30/04

I-129F, Petition for Alien Fiancé(e)

DO NOT WRITE IN THIS BLOCK		FOR CIS USE ONLY
Case ID #	**Action Block**	**Fee Stamp**
A #		
G-28 #		
The petition is approved for status under Section 101(a)(5)(k). It is valid for four months from the date of action.		**AMCON:** _____ ☐ Personal Interview ☐ Previously Forwarded ☐ Document Check ☐ Field Investigation
Remarks:		

Part A. Information about you.	**Part B. Information about your alien fiancé(e).**
1. **Name** *(Family name in CAPS)* *(First)* *(Middle)*	1. **Name** *(Family name in CAPS)* *(First)* *(Middle)*
2. **Address** *(Number and Street)* Apt. #	2. **Address** *(Number and Street)* Apt. #
(Town or City) (State or Country) (Zip/Postal Code)	(Town or City) (State or Country) (Zip/Postal Code)
3. **Place of Birth** *(Town or City)* (State/Country)	3. **Place of Birth** *(Town or City)* (State/Country)
4. **Date of Birth** *(mmdd/yyyy)* 5. **Gender** ☐ Male ☐ Female	4. **Date of Birth** *(mmdd/yyyy)* 5. **Gender** ☐ Male ☐ Female
6. **Marital Status** ☐ Married ☐ Single ☐ Widowed ☐ Divorced	6. **Marital Status** ☐ Married ☐ Single ☐ Widowed ☐ Divorced
7. **Other Names Used** *(including maiden name)*	7. **Other Names Used** *(including maiden name)*
8. **Social Security Number**	8. **U.S. Social Security #** 9. **A#** *(if any)*
9. **Names of Prior Spouses** **Date(s) Marriage(s) Ended**	10. **Names of Prior Spouses** **Date(s) Marriage(s) Ended**
12. **My citizenship was acquired through** *(check one)* ☐ Birth in the U.S. ☐ Naturalization Give number of certificate, date and place it was issued. ☐ Parents Have you obtained a certificate of citizenship in your name? ☐ Yes ☐ No If "Yes," give certificate number, date and place it was issued.	11. **Has your fiané(e) ever been in the U.S.?** ☐ Yes ☐ No 12. **If your fiancé(e) is currently in the U.S., complete the following:** **He or she last arrived as a:** *(visitor, student, exchange alien, crewman, stowaway, temporary worker, without inspection, etc.)*
13. **Have you ever filed for this or any other alien fiancé(e) or husband/wife before?** ☐ Yes ☐ No If "Yes," give name of alien, place and date of filing and result.	**Arrival/Departure Record (I-94) Number** ☐☐☐☐ — ☐☐☐☐☐☐☐☐ **Date of Arrival** *(mm/dd/yyyy)* **Date authorized stay expired, or will expire as shown on I-94 or I-95**

INITIAL RECEIPT _____ RESUBMITTED _____ RELOCATED: Rec'd. _____ Sent _____ COMPLETED: Appv'd. _____ Denied _____ Ret'd. _____

Form I-129F(Rev. 04/16/04) Y

B. Information about your alien fiancé(e). *(Continued)*

13. List all children of your alien fiancé(e) *(if any)*

Name *(First/Middle/Last)*	Dateo f Birth	Country of Birth	Present Address

14. Address in the United States where your fiancé(e) intends to live.

(Number and Street)	(Town or City)	(State)

15. Your fiancé(e)'s address abroad.

(Number and Street)	(Town or City)	(State or Province)

(Country)	(Phone Number)

16. If your fiancé(e)'s native alphabet uses other than Roman letters, write his or her name and address abroad in the native alphabet.

(Name)	(Number and Street)

(Town or City)	(State or Province)	(Country)

17. Is your fiancé(e) related to you? ☐ Yes ☐ No

If you are related, state the nature and degree of relationship, e.g., third cousin or maternal uncle, etc.

18. Has your fiancé(e) met and seen you? ☐ Yes ☐ No

Describe the circumstances under which you met. If you have not personally met each other, explain how the relationship was established, and explain in detail any reasons you may have for requesting that the requirement that you and your fiancé(e) must have met should not apply to you.

19. Your fiancé(e) will apply for a visa abroad at the American embassy or consulate in:

(City)	(Country)

(Designation of a U.S. embassy or consulate outside the country of your fiancé(e)'s last residence does not guarantee acceptance for processing by that foreign post. Acceptance is at the discretion of the designated embassy or consulate.)

C. Other information.

If you are serving overseas in the Armed Forces of the United States, please answer the following:

I presently reside or am stationed overseas and my current mailing address is: | I plan to return to the United States on or about:

PENALTIES: You may by law be imprisoned for not more than five years, or fined $250,000, or both, for entering into a marriage contract for the purpose of evading any provision of the immigration laws, and you may be fined up to $10,000 or imprisoned up to five years, or both, for knowingly and willfully falsifying or concealing a material fact or using any false document in submitting this petition.

YOUR CERTIFICATION: I am legally able to and intend to marry my alien fiancé(e) within 90 days of his or her arrival in the United States. I certify, under penalty of perjury under the laws of the United States of America, that the foregoing is true and correct. Furthermore, I authorize the release of any information from my records which the Bureau of Citizenship and Immigration Services needs to determine eligibility for the benefit that I am seeking.

Signature	**Date** *(mm/dd/yyyy)*	**Daytime Telephone Number** *(with area code)*

D. Signature of person preparing form, if other than above. *(Sign below.)*

I declare that I prepared this application at the request of the applicant and it is based on all information of which I have knowledge.

Signature	Print or Type Your Name	G-28 ID Number	Date *(mm/dd/yyyy)*

Firm Name and Address	Daytime Telephone Number *(with area code)*

Form I-129F(Rev. 04/16/04) Y Page 2

OMB No. 1615-0010; Exp. 9/30/05

U.S. Department of Homeland Security
Bureau of Citizenship and Immigration Services

I-129S, Nonimmigrant Petition
Based on Blanket L Petition

Purpose of This Form.

This form is for an employer to classify employees as L-1 nonimmigrant interacompany transferees under a blanket L petiton approval.

Who May File.

An employer who has already obtained approval of a blanket L-1 petition may file this form to classify employees outside the United States as executives, managers or specialized knowledge professionals. If the employee is in the United States and you are requesting a change of status or extension of stay for that employee, use Form I-129, Petition for a Nonimmigrant Worker.

General Filing Instructions.

Please answer all questions by typing or clearly printing in black ink. Indicate that an item is not applicable with "N/A." If the answer is "none," write "none." If you need extra space to ansert any tiem, attach a sheet of paper with your name and alien registration number (A#), if any, and indicate the number of the item to which the answer related. You must file your petition with the required **Initial Evidence**. Your petition must be properly signed. Retain a copy of the form and supporting documents for your records.

Translations. Any foreign language document must be accompanied by a full English translation that a translator has certified as complete and correct. The translator must also certify that he or she is competent to translate the foreign language into English.

Copies. If these instructions state that a copy of a document may be filed with this petition, and you choose to send us the original, we may keep that original for our records.

Initial Evidence.

You must file your petition with:

- a copy of the approval notice for the blanket petition;

- a letter from the alien's foreign qualifying employer detailing his or her dates of employment, job duties, qualifications and salary; the letter must also show that the alien worked for the employer for at least one continuous year in the three-year period preceeding the filing of the petition in an executive, managerial or specialized knowledge professional capacity; and

- if the alien is a specialized knowledge professiona, a copy of a U.S. degree, a foreign degree equivalent to a U.S. degree, or evidence establishing that the combination of the beneficiary's education and experience is the equivalent of a U.S. degree.

Where to File.

If the alien requires a visa, he or she should present the completed petition at a U.S. embassy or consulate abroad.

If the alien is not required to obtain a visa, he or she should file this petition at the Service Center of the Bureau of Citizenship and Immigraton Services (BCIS) that approved the blanket petition. The BCIS is comprised of offices of the former Immigration and Naturalization Service.

Fee.

There is no fee for this petition.

Processing Information.

Acceptance. A petiton that is not signed will be rejected with a notice that the petition is deficient. You may correct the deficiency and resubmit the petition. However, a petition is not considered properly filed until it is accepted by the BCIS.

Initial processing. Once the petition has been accepted, it will be checked for completeness, including submission of the required initial evidence. If you do not completely fill out the form or file it without required initial evidence, you will not establish a basis for eligibility and we may deny your petition.

Requests for mor information or interview. We may request more information or evidence or we may request that you appear at a BCIS office for an interview. We may also request that you submit the original of any copy. We will return these originals when they are not longer required.

Decision. You will be notified in writing of the decision on your petition. If you filed the petition at a BCIS service center and it is approved, the approval notice will be sent to you so you can send it to the beneficiary to present at a port of entry when he or she enters the United States.

Penalties.

If you knowingly and willfully falsify or conceal a material fact or submit a false document with this request, we will deny the benefit you are seeking and may deny any other immigration benefit. In addition, you will face severe penalties provided by law and you may be subject to criminal prosecution.

Privacy Act Notice.

We ask for the information on this form and associated evidence to determine if you have established eligibility for the immigration benefit you are seeking. Our legal right to ask for this information is in 8 USC 1154. We may provide this information to other government agencies. Failure to provide this information and any requested evidence may delay a final decision or result in denial of

Information and BCIS Forms.

For information on immigration laws, regulations and procedures and to order BCIS forms, call our **National Customer Service Center** toll-free at **1-800-375-5283** or visit our internet web site at **www.bcis.gov**.

Paperwork Reduction Act Notice.

A person is not required to respond to a collection of information unless it displays a currently valid OMB control number. We try to create forms and instructions that are accurate, can be easily understood and that impose the least possible burden on you to provide us with information. Often this is difficult because some immigration laws are very complex. The estimated average time to complete and file this application is as follows: (1) 10 minutes to learn about the law and form; (2) 10 minutes to complete the form; and (3) 15 minutes to assemble and file the petition; for a total estimated average of 35 minutes per petition. If you have comments regarding the accuracy of this estimate or suggestions for making this form simpler, you can write to: Bureau of Citizenship and Immigration Services, HQRFS, 425 I Street, N.W., Room 4034, Washington, DC 20536; OMB No. 1615-0010. **DO NOT MAIL YOUR COMPLETED APPLICATION TO THIS ADDRESS.**

Form I-129S Instruction (Rev. 04/23/03)N (Prior versions may be used until 09/30/03)

OMB No. 1615-0010; Exp. 9/30/05

U.S. Department of Homeland Security
Bureau of Citizehsip and Immigration Services

I-129S, Nonimmigrant Petition Based on Blanket L Petition

START HERE - Please Type or Print

FOR BCIS USE ONLY

Part 1.   Information about employer.

Sponsoring Company of Organization's Name

Address - ATTN:

Street Number and Name   Room/Suite #

City or Town   State or Province   Country   Zip/Postal Code

Returned	Receipt
Date	
Date	
Resubmitted	
Date	
Date	
Reloc Sent	
Date	

Part 2.   Information about employment.

This alien will be a:

a. ☐ manager/executive

b. ☐ specialized knowledge professional

Blanket petition approval number:

| Date |
| Date |
| Reloc Rec'd |
| Date |
| Date |
| ☐ Petitioner Interviewed on _____ |
| ☐ Beneficiary Interviewed on _____ |

Part 3.   Information about employee.

Family Name   Given Name   Middle Name

Foreign Address: Street Number and Name   Apt. #

City or Town   State or Province   Country   Zip/Postal Code

Date of Birth *(mm/dd/yyyy)*   Country of Birth   Country of Citizenship

Approved as:
☐ manager/executive
☐ specialized knowledge

Validity Dates:
From: _____
To: _____

Part 4.   Additional information about the employment.

Address: Street Number and Name   Room/Suite #

City or Town   State or Province   Country   Zip/Postal Code

Date of intended employment *(mm/dd/yyyy):*

From: To:

Weekly Wage   Hours Per Week

$ $

Title and detailed description of duties to be performed

Denied (give reason)

Action Block

To Be Completed By
Attorney or Representative, if any.
☐ Fill in box if G-28 is attached to represent the petition.

ATTY State License #

Form I-129S Form (Rev. 04/23/03)N (Prior versions may be used until 09/30/03)

Part 4.   Information about employer.   *(Continued)*

Give the alien's dates of prior periods of stay in the United States in a work authorized capacity and the type of visa.

Give the alien's dates of employment and job duties for the immediate prior three years.

Summarize the alien's education and other work experience.

Part 8. Signature. *Read the information on penalties in the instructions before completing this section.*

I certify, under penalty of perjury under the laws of the United States of America, that this petition and the evidence submitted with it are all true and correct. I am filing this on behalf of an organization, and I certify that I am empowered to do so by that organization. If this petition is to extend a prior petition, I certify that the proposed employment is under the same terms and conditions as in the prior approved petition. I authorize the release of any information from my records, or from the petitioning organizations recordes that the Bureau of Citizenship and Immigration Services needs to determine eligibility for the benefit being sought.

Signature	Date *(mm/dd/yyyy)*	Daytime Telephone Number *(with area code)*

Please Note: If you do not completely fill out this form or fail to submit required documents listed in the instructions, the person(s) petitioned for may not be found eligible for the requested benefit and this petition may be denied.

Part 9. Signature of person preparing form if other than above. *(Sign below.)*

I declare that I prepared this application at the request of the applicant and it is based on all information of which I have knowledge.

Signature	Print or Type Your Name	Fax Number *(if any)*	Date *(mm/dd/yyyy)*

Firm Name and Address	Daytime Telephone Number *(with area code)*

Form I-129S (Rev. 04/23/03)N (Prior versions may be used until 09/30/03) Page 2

Department of Homeland Security
U.S. Citizenship and Immigration Services

OMB #1615-0012; Expires 01/31/07

I-130, Petition for Alien Relative

Instructions

Read the instructions carefully. If you do not follow the instructions, the U.S. Citizenship and Immigration Services (USCIS) may have to return your petition, which may delay final action. NOTE: USCIS is comprised of offices of the former Immigration and Naturalization Service.

1. Who May File?

A citizen or lawful permanent resident of the United States may file this form with the U.S. Citizenship and Immigration Services (USCIS) to establish a relationship to certain alien relatives who wish to immigrate to the United States.

You must file a separate form for each eligible relative.

2. For Whom May You File?

A. If you are a citizen, you may file this form for:

1) Your husband, wife or unmarried child under 21 years old;
2) Your parent if you are at least 21 years old;
3) Your unmarried son or daughter over 21 years old;
4) Your married son or daughter of any age;
5) Your brother or sister if you are at least 21 years old.

B. If you are a lawful permanent resident, you may file this form for:

1) Your husband or wife;
2) Your unmarried child under 21 years of age;
3) Your unmarried son or daughter over 21 years of age.

NOTE:

- If your relative qualifies under paragraph **A(3)**, **A(4)** or **A(5)** above, separate petitions are not required for his or her husband or wife or unmarried children under 21 years of age.

- If your relative qualifies under paragraph **B(2)** or **B(3)** above, separate petitions are not required for his or her unmarried children under 21 years of age.

- The persons described above under this **NOTE** will be able to apply for an immigrant visa along with your relative.

3. For Whom May You Not File?

You may not file for a person in the following categories:

A. An adoptive parent or adopted child, if the adoption took place after the child's 16th birthday, or if the child has not been in the legal custody and living with the parent(s) for at least two years.

B. A natural parent, if the United States citizen son or daughter gained permanent residence through adoption.

C. A stepparent or stepchild, if the marriage that created the relationship took place after the child's 18th birthday.

D. A husband or wife, if you and your spouse were not both physically present at the marriage ceremony, and the marriage was not consummated.

E. A husband or wife, if you gained lawful permanent resident status by virtue of a prior marriage to a United States citizen or lawful permanent resident, unless:

1) A period of five years has elapsed since you became a lawful permanent resident; or

2) You can establish by clear and covincing evidence that the prior marriage through which you gained your immigrant status was not entered into for the purpose of evading any provision of the immigration laws; or

3) Your prior marriage through which you gained your immigrant status was terminated by the death of your former spouse.

F. A husband or wife, if he or she was in exclusion, deportation, removal, rescission or judicial proceedings regarding his or her right to remain in the United States when the marriage took place, unless such spouse has resided outside the United States for a two-year period after the date of the marriage.

G. A husband or wife, if it has been legally determined that such an alien has attempted or conspired to enter into a marriage for the purpose of evading the immigration laws.

H. A grandparent, grandchild, nephew, niece, uncle, aunt, cousin or in-law.

4. What Are the General Filing Instructions?

A. Type or print legibly in black ink.

B. If extra space is needed to complete any item, attach a continuation sheet, indicate the item number, and date and sign each sheet.

C. Answer all questions fully and accurately. If any item does not apply, write "N/A."

D. **Translations.** Any foreign language document must be accompanied by a full English translation that the translator has certified as complete and correct, and by the translator's certification that he or she is competent to translate the foreign language into English.

E. **Copies.** If these instructions state that a copy of a document may be filed with this petition, submit a copy. If you choose to send the original, USCIS may keep that original for our records. If USCIS requires the original, it will be requested.

5. What Documents Do You Need to Show That You Are a United States Citizen?

A. If you were born in the United States, a copy of your birth certificate, issued by the civil registrar, vital statistics office, or other civil authority. If a birth certificate is not available, see **Section 9** on **Page 3** titled, **"What If a Document Is Not Avaliable?"**

B. A copy of your naturalization certificate or certificate of citizenship issued by USCIS or the former INS.

C. A copy of Form FS-240, Report of Birth Abroad of a Citizen of the United States, issued by an American embassy or consulate.

D. A copy of your unexpired U.S. passport; or

E. An original statement from a U.S. consular officer verifying that you are a U.S. citizen with a valid passport.

F. If you do not have any of the above documents and you were born in the United States, see instructions under **Section 9 on Page 3**, **"What If a Document Is Not Available?"**

6. What Documents Do You Need to Show That You Are a Permanent Resident?

If you are a permanent resident, you must file your petition with a copy of the front and back of your permanent resident card. If you have not yet received your card, submit copies of your passport biographic page and the page showing admission as a permanent resident, or other evidence of permanent resident status issued by USCIS or the former INS.

7. What Documents Do You Need to Prove a Family Relationship?

You have to prove that there is a family relationship between you and your relative. If you are filing for:

A. A husband or wife, submit the following documentation:

1) A copy of your marriage certificate.

2) If either you or your spouse were previously married, submit copies of documents showing that all prior marriages were legally terminated.

3) A passport-style color photo of yourself and a passport-style color photo of your husband or wife, taken within 30 days of the date of this petition. The photos must have a white background and be glossy, unretouched and not mounted. The dimensions of the full frontal facial image should be about 1 inch from the chin to top of the hair. Using pencil or felt pen, lightly print the name (and Alien Registration Number, if known) on the back of each photograph.

4) A completed and signed Form G-325A, Biographic Information, for you and a Form G-325A for your husband or wife. Except for your name and signature, you do not have to repeat on the Form G-325A the information given on your Form I-130 petition.

B. A child and you are the mother: Submit a copy of the child's birth certificate showing your name and the name of your child.

C. A child and you are the father: Submit a copy of the child's birth certificate showing both parents' names and your marriage certificate.

D. A child born out of wedlock and you are the father: If the child was not legitimated before reaching 18 years old, you must file your petition with copies of evidence that a bona fide parent-child relationship existed between the father and the child before the child reached 21 years. This may include evidence that the father lived with the child, supported him or her, or otherwise showed continuing parental interest in the child's welfare.

E. A brother or sister: Submit a copy of your birth certificate and a copy of your brother's or sister's birth certificate showing that you have at least one common parent. If you and your brother or sister have a common father but different mothers, submit copies of the marriage certificates of the father to each mother and copies of documents showing that any prior marriages of either your father or mothers were legally terminated. If you and your brother or sister are related through adoption or through a stepparent, or if you have a common father and either of you were not legitimated before your 18th birthday, see also **H** and **I** below.

F. A mother: Submit a copy of your birth certificate showing your name and your mother's name.

G. A father: Submit a copy of your birth certificate showing the names of both parents. Also give a copy of your parents' marriage certificate establishing that your father was married to your mother before you were born, and copies of documents showing that any prior marriages of either your father or mother were legally terminated. If you are filing for a stepparent or adoptive parent, or if you are filing for your father and were not legitimated before your 18th birthday, also see **D, H** and **I**.

H. Stepparent/stepchild: If your petition is based on a stepparent-stepchild relationship, you must file your petition with a copy of the marriage certificate of the stepparent to the child's natural parent showing that the marriage occurred before the child's 18th birthday, and copies of documents showing that any prior marriages were legally terminated.

I. Adoptive parent or adopted child: If you and the person you are filing for are related by adoption, you must submit a copy of the adoption decree(s) showing that the adoption took place before the child became 16 years old. If you adopted the sibling of a child you already adopted, you must submit a copy of the adoption decree(s) showing that the adoption of the sibling occured before that child's 18th birthday. In either case, you must also submit copies of evidence that each child was in the legal custody of and resided with the parent(s) who adopted him or her for at least two years before or after the adoption. Legal custody may only be granted by a court or recognized government entity and is usually granted at the time the adoption is finalized. However, if legal custody is granted by a court or recognized government agency prior to the adoption, that time may count to fulfill the two-year legal custody requirement.

8. What If Your Name Has Changed?

If either you or the person you are filing for is using a name other than shown on the relevant documents, you must file your petition with copies of the legal documents that effected the change, such as a marriage certificate, adoption decree or court order.

9. What If a Document Is Not Available?

In such situation, submit a statement from the appropriate civil authority certifying that the document or documents are not available. You must also submit secondary evidence, including:

A. Church record: A copy of a document bearing the seal of the church, showing the baptism, dedication or comparable rite occurred within two months after birth, and showing the date and place of the child's birth, date of the religious ceremony and the names of the child's parents.

B. School record: A letter from the authority (preferably the first school attended) showing the date of admission to the school, the child's date of birth or age at that time, place of birth, and names of the parents.

C. Census record: State or Federal census record showing the names, place of birth, date of birth or the age of the person listed.

D. Affidavits: Written statements sworn to or affirmed by two persons who were living at the time and who have personal knowledge of the event you are trying to prove. For example, the date and place of birth, marriage or death. The person making the affidavit does not have to be a U.S. citizen. Each affidavit should contain the following information regarding the person making the affidavit: his or her full name, address, date and place of birth and his or her relationship to you, if any, full information concerning the event, and complete details explaining how the person acquired knowledge of the event.

10. Where Should You File This Form?

If you reside in the United States, file this form at the USCIS Service Center having jurisdiction over your place of residence.

If you live in Connecticut, Delaware, District of Columbia, Maine, Maryland, Massachusetts, New Hampshire, New Jersey, New York, Pennsylvania, Puerto Rico, Rhode Island, Vermont, U.S. Virgin Islands, Virginia or West Virginia, mail this petition to:

USCIS Vermont Service Center
75 Lower Welden Street
St. Albans, VT 05479-0001

If you live in Alaska, Colorado, Idaho, Illinois, Indiana, Iowa, Kansas, Michigan, Minnesota, Missouri, Montana, Nebraska, North Dakota, Ohio, Oregon, South Dakota, Utah, Washington, Wisconsin or Wyoming, mail this petition to:

USCIS Nebraska Service Center
P.O. Box 87130,
Lincoln, NE 68501-7130

If you live in Alabama, Arkansas, Florida, Georgia, Kentucky, Louisiana, Mississippi, New Mexico, North Carolina, Oklahoma, South Carolina, Tennessee or Texas, mail this petition to:

USCIS Texas Service Center
P.O. Box 850919
Mesquite, TX 75185-0919

If you live in Arizona, California, Guam, Hawaii or Nevada, mail this petition to:

USCIS California Service Center
P.O. Box 10130,
Laguna Niguel, CA 92607-0130

NOTE: If the Form I-130 petition is being filed concurrently with Form I-485, Application to Register Permanent Residence or Adjust Status, submit both forms at the local USCIS office having jurisdiction over the place where the Form I-485 applicant resides.

Applicants who reside in the jurisdiction of the Baltimore, MD, USCIS District Office should submit the Form I-130 petition and the Form I-485 concurrently to:

USCIS Vermont Service Center
75 Lower Welden Street
St. Albans, VT 05479-0001

Petitioners residing abroad: If you live in Canada, file your petition at the Vermont Service Center. **Exception**: If you are a U.S. citizen residing in Canada, and you are petitioning for your spouse, child, or parent, you may file the petition at the nearest American Embassy or Consulate, except for those in Quebec City. If you reside elsewhere outside the United States, file your relative petition at the USCIS office overseas or the U.S. Embassy or Consulate having jurisdiction over the area where you live. For further information, contact the nearest American Embassy or Consulate.

11. What Is the Fee?

You must pay **$190.00** to file this form. **The fee will not be refunded, whether the petition is approved or not. Do not mail cash.** All checks or money orders, whether U.S. or foreign, must be payable in U.S. currency at a financial institution in the United States. When a check is drawn on the account of a person other than yourself, write your name on the face of the check. If the check is not honored, USCIS will charge you $30.00.

Pay by check or money order in the exact amount. Make the check or money order payable to the **Department of Homeland Security**, unless:

A. You live in Guam and are filing your petition there, make the check or money order payable to the "Treasurer, Guam" or

B. You live in the U.S. Virgin Islands and you are filing your petition there, make your check or money order payable to the "Commissioner of Finance of the Virgin Islands."

12. When Will a Visa Become Available?

When a petition is approved for the husband, wife, parent or unmarried minor child of a United States citizen, these persons are classified as immmediate relatives. They do not have to wait for a visa number because immediate relatives are not subject to the immigrant visa limit.

For alien relatives in preference categories, a limited number of immigrant visas are issued each year. The visas are processed in the order in which the petitions are properly filed and accepted by the USCIS. To be considered properly filed, a petition must be fully completed and signed, and the fee must be paid.

For a monthly report on the dates when immigrant visas are available, call the **U.S. Department of State** at **(202) 647-0508.**

13. Notice to Persons Filing for Spouses, If Married Less Than Two Years.

Pursuant to section 216 of the Immigration and Nationality Act, your alien spouse may be granted conditional permanent resident status in the United States as of the date he or she is admitted or adjusted to conditional status by a USCIS officer. Both you and your conditional resident spouse are required to file Form I-751, Joint Petition to Remove Conditional Basis of Alien's Permanent Resident Status, during the 90-day period immediately before the second anniversary of the date your alien spouse was granted conditional permanent resident status.

Otherwise, the rights, privileges, responsibilites and duties that apply to all other permanent residents apply equally to a conditional permanent resident. A conditional permanent resident is not limited to the right to apply for naturalization, file petitions on behalf of qualifying relatives or reside permanently in the United States as an immigrant in accordance with our nation's immigration laws.

NOTE: Failure to file the Form I-751 joint petition to remove the conditional basis of the alien spouse's permanent resident status will result in the termination of his or her permanent resident status and initiation of removal proceedings.

14. What Are the Penalties for Marriage Fraud or Submitting False Information?

Title 8, United States Code, Section 1325, states that any individual who knowingly enters into a marriage contract for the purpose of evading any provision of the immigration laws shall be imprisoned for not more than five years, or fined not more than $250,000, or both.

Title 18, United States Code, Section 1001, states that whoever willfully and knowingly falsifies a material fact, makes a false statement or makes use of a false document will be fined up to $10,000, imprisoned for up to five years, or both.

15. What Is Our Authority for Collecting This Information?

We request the information on this form to carry out the immigration laws contained in Title 8, United States Code, Section 1154(a). We need this information to determine whether a person is eligible for immigration benefits. The information you provide may also be disclosed to other Federal, state, local and foreign law enforcement and regulatory agencies during the course of the investigation required by the USCIS. You do not have to give this information. However, if you refuse to give some or all of it, your petition may be denied.

16. Paperwork Reduction Act Notice.

A person is not required to respond to a collection of information unless it displays a currently valid OMB control number. The public reporting burden for this collection of information is estimated to average 30 minutes per response, including the time for reviewing instructions, searching existing data sources, gathering and maintaining the data needed, and completing and reviewing the collection of information. Send comments regarding this burden estimate or any other aspect of this collection of information, including suggestions for reducing this burden to the: U.S. Citizenship and Immigration Services, Regulatory Management Division, 111 Massachutts, Avenue N.W., Washington, D.C. 20529; OMB No.1615-0012. **Do not mail your completed petition to this address.**

Checklist.

- Did you answer each question on the Form I-130 petition?
- Did you sign and date the petition?
- Did you enclose the correct filing fee for each petition?
- Did you submit proof of your U.S. citizenship or lawful permanent residence?
- Did you submit other required supporting evidence?

If you are filing for your husband or wife, did you include:
- Your photograph?
- His or her photograph?
- Your completed Form G-325A?
- His or her Form G-325A?

Information and Forms: For information on immigration laws, regulations and procedures or to order USCIS forms, call our toll-free forms line at I-800-870-3676, our National Customer Service Center at 1-800-375-5283 or visit the USCIS website at **www.uscis.gov.**

Form I-130 Instructions (Rev. 10/26/05)Y Page 4

■ *150*

Department of Homeland Security
U.S. Citizenship and Immigration Services

OMB #1615-0012; Expires 01/31/07
I-130, Petition for Alien Relative

DO NOT WRITE IN THIS BLOCK - FOR USCIS OFFICE ONLY		
A#	Action Stamp	Fee Stamp

Section of Law/Visa Category
- ☐ 201(b) Spouse - IR-1/CR-1
- ☐ 201(b) Child - IR-2/CR-2
- ☐ 201(b) Parent - IR-5
- ☐ 203(a)(1) Unm. S or D - F1-1
- ☐ 203(a)(2)(A)Spouse - F2-1
- ☐ 203(a)(2)(A) Child - F2-2
- ☐ 203(a)(2)(B) Unm. S or D - F2-4
- ☐ 203(a)(3) Married S or D - F3-1
- ☐ 203(a)(4) Brother/Sister - F4-1

Petition was filed on: _____ (priority date)
- ☐ Personal Interview   ☐ Previously Forwarded
- ☐ Pet. ☐ Ben. " A" File Reviewed   ☐ I-485 Filed Simultaneously
- ☐ Field Investigation   ☐ 204(g) Resolved
- ☐ 203(a)(2)(A) Resolved   ☐ 203(g) Resolved

Remarks:

A. Relationship   You are the petitioner.   Your relative is the beneficiary.

1. I am filing this petition for my:	2. Are you related by adoption?	3. Did you gain permanent residence through adoption?
☐ Husband/Wife ☐ Parent ☐ Brother/Sister ☐ Child	☐ Yes ☐ No	☐ Yes ☐ No

B. Information about you

1. **Name** (Family name in CAPS)   (First)   (Middle)

2. **Address** (Number and Street)   (Apt.No.)

(Town or City)   (State/Country)   (Zip/Postal Code)

3. **Place of Birth** (Town or City)   (State/Country)

4. **Date of Birth** (mm/dd/yyyy)

5. **Gender** ☐ Male ☐ Female

6. **Marital Status** ☐ Married ☐ Single ☐ Widowed ☐ Divorced

7. **Other Names Used** (including maiden name)

8. **Date and Place of Present Marriage** (if married)

9. **U.S. Social Security Number** (if any)

10. **Alien Registration Number**

11. **Name(s) of Prior Husband(s)/Wive(s)**

12. **Date(s) Marriage(s) Ended**

13. **If you are a U.S. citizen, complete the following:**
My citizenship was acquired through (check one):
- ☐ Birth in the U.S.
- ☐ Naturalization. Give certificate number and date and place of issuance.

☐ Parents. Have you obtained a certificate of citizenship in your own name?
- ☐ Yes. Give certificate number, date and place of issuance. ☐ No

14a. **If you are a lawful permanent resident alien, complete the following:** Date and place of admission for or adjustment to lawful permanent residence and class of admission.

14b. **Did you gain permanent resident status through marriage to a U.S. citizen or lawful permanent resident?**
☐ Yes ☐ No

C. Information about your relative

1. **Name** (Family name in CAPS)   (First)   (Middle)

2. **Address** (Number and Street)   (Apt. No.)

(Town or City)   (State/Country)   (Zip/Postal Code)

3. **Place of Birth** (Town or City)   (State/Country)

4. **Date of Birth** (mm/dd/yyyy)

5. **Gender** ☐ Male ☐ Female

6. **Marital Status** ☐ Married ☐ Single ☐ Widowed ☐ Divorced

7. **Other Names Used** (including maiden name)

8. **Date and Place of Present Marriage** (if married)

9. **U. S. Social Security Number** (if any)

10. **Alien Registration Number**

11. **Name(s) of Prior Husband(s)/Wive(s)**

12. **Date(s) Marriage(s) Ended**

13. **Has your relative ever been in the U.S.?** ☐ Yes ☐ No

14. **If your relative is currently in the U.S., complete the following:**
He or she arrived as a::
(visitor, student, stowaway, without inspection, etc.)

Arrival/Departure Record (I-94)   Date arrived (mm/dd/yyyy)

Date authorized stay expired, or will expire, as shown on Form I-94 or I-95

15. **Name and address of present employer** (if any)

Date this employment began (mm/dd/yyyy)

16. **Has your relative ever been under immigration proceedings?**
☐ No ☐ Yes Where _____ When _____
☐ Removal ☐ Exclusion/Deportation ☐ Recission ☐ Judicial Proceedings

INITIAL RECEIPT   RESUBMITTED   RELOCATED: Rec'd ____ Sent ____   COMPLETED: Appv'd ____ Denied ____ Ret'd ____

Form I-130 (Rev. 10/26/05)Y

C. Information about your alien relative (continued)

17. List husband/wife and all children of your relative.

(Name)	(Relationship)	(Date of Birth)	(Country of Birth)

18. Address in the United States where your relative intends to live.

(Street Address)	(Town or City)	(State)

19. Your relative's address abroad. (Include street, city, province and country)

Phone Number (if any)

20. If your relative's native alphabet is other than Roman letters, write his or her name and foreign address in the native alphabet.

(Name)   Address (Include street, city, province and country):

21. If filing for your husband/wife, give last address at which you lived together. (Include street, city, province, if any, and country):

From: To:
(Month) (Year)   (Month) (Year)

22. Complete the information below if your relative is in the United States and will apply for adjustment of status.

Your relative is in the United States and will apply for adjustment of status to that of a lawful permanent resident at the USCIS office in:

_____ . If your relative is not eligible for adjustment of status, he or she

(City)   (State)

will apply for a visa abroad at the American consular post in _____

(City)   (Country)

NOTE: Designation of an American embassy or consulate outside the country of your relative's last residence does not guarantee acceptance for processing by that post. Acceptance is at the discretion of the designated embassy or consulate.

D. Other information

1. If separate petitions are also being submitted for other relatives, give names of each and relationship.

2. Have you ever before filed a petition for this or any other alien? ☐ Yes ☐ No

If "Yes," give name, place and date of filing and result.

WARNING: USCIS investigates claimed relationships and verifies the validity of documents. USCIS seeks criminal prosecutions when family relationships are falsified to obtain visas.

PENALTIES: By law, you may be imprisoned for not more than five years or fined $250,000, or both, for entering into a marriage contract for the purpose of evading any provision of the immigration laws. In addition, you may be fined up to $10,000 and imprisoned for up to five years, or both, for knowingly and willfully falsifying or concealing a material fact or using any false document in submitting this petition.

YOUR CERTIFICATION: I certify, under penalty of perjury under the laws of the United States of America, that the foregoing is true and correct. Furthermore, I authorize the release of any information from my records that the U.S. Citizenship and Immigration Services needs to determine eligibility for the benefit that I am seeking.

E. Signature of petitioner.

Date _____   Phone Number (___)

F. Signature of person preparing this form, if other than the petitioner.

I declare that I prepared this document at the request of the person above and that it is based on all information of which I have any knowledge.

Print Name _____   Signature _____   Date _____

Address _____   **G-28 ID or VOLAG Number, if any.** _____

Form I-130 (Rev. 10/26/05)Y Page 2

Department of Homeland Security
U. S. Citizenship and Immigration Services

OMB No. 1615-0013; Expires 11/30/07

I-131, Application for Travel Document

INSTRUCTIONS

What Is the Purpose of This Form?

This form is used to apply to the U.S. Citizenship and Immigration Services (USCIS), comprised of offices of the former Immigration and Naturalization Service (INS), for the following travel documents:

- **Reentry Permit** - A reentry permit allows a permanent resident or conditional resident to apply for admission to the United States upon return from abroad during the permit's validity, without having to obtain a returning resident visa from a U.S. embassy or consulate.

- **Refugee Travel Document** - A refugee travel document is issued to a person classified as a refugee or asylee, or to a permanent resident who obtained such status as a result of being a refugee or asylee in the United States. Persons who hold such status must have a refugee travel document to return to the United States after temporary travel abroad unless he or she is in possession of a valid advance parole document. A refugee travel document is issued by the USCIS to implement Article 28 of the United Nations Convention of July 28, 1951.

- **Advance Parole Document** - An advance parole document is issued solely to authorize the temporary parole of a person into the United States. The document may be accepted by a transportation company in lieu of a visa as an authorization for the holder to travel to the United States. An advance parole document is not issued to serve in place of any required passport.

Advance parole is an extraordinary measure used sparingly to bring an otherwise inadmissible alien to the United States for a temporary period of time due to a compelling emergency. Advance parole cannot be used to circumvent the normal visa issuing procedures and is not a means to bypass delays in visa issuance.

NOTE: If you are in the United States and wish to travel abroad, you do not need to apply for advance parole if both conditions described below in numbers **1** and **2** are met:

1. You are in one of the following nonimmigrant categories:

    a. An H-1, temporary worker, or H-4, spouse or child of an H-1; **or**

    b. An L-1, intracompany transferee, or L-2, spouse or child of an L-1; **or**

    c. A K-3, spouse, or K-4, child of a U.S. citizen; **or**

    d. A V-2, spouse, or V-3, child of a lawful permanent resident; **and**

2. A Form I-485, Application to Register Permanent Residence or Adjust Status, was filed on your behalf and is pending with the USCIS.

However, upon returning to the United States, you must present your valid H, L, K or V nonimmigrant visa and continue to remain eligible for that status.

Who May File This Form?

Each applicant must file a separate application for a travel document.

I. Reentry Permit.

A. ***If you are in the United States*** as a permanent resident or conditional permanent resident, you may apply for a reentry permit.

Departure from the United States before a decision is made on an application for a reentry permit does not affect the application.

You must be physically present in the United States when you file the application. However, a reentry permit may be sent to a U.S. embassy or consulate or Department of Homeland Security (DHS) office abroad for you to pick up, if you request it when you file your application.

With the exception of having to obtain a returning resident visa abroad, a reentry permit does not relieve you of any of the requirements of the United States immigration laws.

If you stay outside the United States for less than one year, you are not required to apply for a reentry permit. You may reenter the United States on your Permanent Resident Card (Form I-551).

If you intend to apply in the future for naturalization, absences from the United States for one year or more will generally break the continuity of your required continuous residence in the United States. If you intend to remain outside the United States for one year or more, you should file a Form N-470, Application to Preserve Residence for Naturalization Purposes. For further information, contact your local USCIS office.

B. *Validity of reentry permit.*

1. Generally, a reentry permit issued to a permanent resident shall be valid for two years from the date of issuance. However, if since becoming a permanent resident you have been outside the United States for more than four of the last five years, the permit will be limited to one year, except that a permit with a validity of two years may be issued to the following:

    a. A permanent resident whose travel is on the order of the United States government, other than an exclusion, deportation, removal or recission order.

    b. A permanent resident employed by a public international organization of which the United States is a member by treaty or statute.

Form I-131 Instructions (Rev. 10/26/05) Y

c. A permanent resident who is a professional athlete and regularly competes in the United States and worldwide.

2. A reentry permit issued to a conditional resident shall be valid for two years from the date of issuance, or to the date the conditional resident must apply for removal of the conditions on his or her status, whichever date comes first.

3. A reentry permit may not be extended.

C. *A reentry permit may not be issued to you if:*

1. You have already been issued such a document and it is still valid, unless the prior document has been returned to the USCIS, or you can demonstrate that it was lost; **or**

2. A notice was published in the Federal Register that precludes the issuance of such a document for travel to the area where you intend to go.

NOTICE to permanent or conditional residents who remain outside the United States for more than one year: If you do not obtain a reentry permit and remain outside the United States for one year or more, it may be determined that you have abandoned your permanent or conditional resident status.

II. Refugee Travel Document.

A. *If you are in the United States* in valid refugee or asylee status, or if you are a permanent resident as a direct result of your refugee or asylee status in the United States, you may apply for a refugee travel document. Generally, you must have a refugee travel document to return to the United States after temporary travel abroad.

You must be physically present in the United States when you file the application. However, a refugee travel document may be sent to a United States embassy or consulate or DHS office abroad for you to pick up, if you request it when you file your application.

B. *Validity of refugee travel document.*

1. A refugee travel document shall be valid for one year.

2. A refugee travel document may not be extended.

C. *A refugee travel document may not be issued to you if:*

1. You have already been issued such a document and it is still valid, unless the prior document has been returned to the USCIS, or you can demonstrate that it was lost; **or**

2. A notice was published in the Federal Register that precludes the issuance of such a document for travel to the area where you intend to go.

NOTICE to permanent residents who obtain permanent residence as a result of their refugee or asylee status: If you do not obtain a reentry permit and remain outside the United States for one year or more, it may be determined that you have abandoned your permanent resident status.

III. Advance Parole Document.

Travel Warning

Before you apply for an advance parole document, read this travel warning carefully.

- If you have been unlawfully present in the United States for more than 180 days but less than one year and you leave before removal proceedings are started against you, you may be inadmissible for three years from the date of departure.

- If you have been unlawfully present in the United States for one year or more, you may be inadmissible for ten years from the date of departure regardless of whether you left before, during or after removal proceedings.

- Unlawful presence is defined as being in the United States without having been inspected and admitted or paroled (illegal entry), or after the period of authorized stay has expired.

- However, certain immigration benefits and time spent in the United States while certain applications are pending may place you in a period of authorized stay. These include, but are not limited to, a properly filed adjustment of status application, Temporary Protected Status (TPS), deferred enforced departure (DED), asylum and withholding of removal.

- Although advance parole may allow you to return to the United States, your departure may trigger the three-or ten-year bar, if you accrued more than 180 days of unlawful presence **BEFORE** the date you were considered to be in a period of authorized stay.

- Therefore, if you apply for adjustment of status after you return to the United States, resume an adjustment application that was pending before you left, or return to a status that requires you to establish that you are not inadmissible, you will need to apply for and receive a waiver of inadmissibility before your adjustment application may be approved or your status continued.

- Generally, only those persons who can establish extreme hardship to their U. S. citizen or lawful permanent resident spouse or parent may apply for the waiver for humanitarian reasons, to assure family unity or when it is otherwise in the public interest. (See sections 209(c), 212(a)(9) and 244(c) of the Immigration and Nationality Act for more information on unlawful presence and the available waivers.)

A. *If you are outside the United States and need to visit the United States temporarily for emergent humanitarian reasons:*

1. You may apply for an advance parole document. However, your application must be based on the fact that you cannot obtain the necessary visa and any required waiver of inadmissibility. Parole under these conditions is granted on a case-by-case basis for temporary entry, according to such conditions as prescribed.

2. A person in the United States may file this application on your behalf. In so doing, he or she should complete **Part 1** of the form with information about him or herself.

B. *If you are in the United States and seek advance parole:*

1. You may apply if you have an adjustment of status application pending and you seek to travel abroad for emergent personal or bona fide business reasons; or

2. You may apply if you are classified as a refugee or asylee and you seek to travel abroad for emergent personal or bona fide business reasons, or you are traveling to Canada to apply for a U.S. immigrant visa. (See **Part II, Refugee Travel Document on Page of 2 of these instructions,** for additional information on refugee/asylee travel); or

3. You may apply if you have been granted Temporary Protected Status or another immigration status that allows you to return to that status after a brief, casual and innocent absence (as defined in 8 CFR 244.1) from the United States.

C. *An advance parole document may not be issued to you if:*

1. You held J-1 nonimmigrant status and are subject to the two-year foreign residence requirement as a result of that status; or

2. You are in exclusion, deportation, removal or recission proceedings.

D. *If you travel before the advance parole document is issued, your application will be deemed abandoned if:*

1. You depart from the United States; or

2. The person seeking advance parole attempts to enter the United States before a decision is made on the application.

General Filing Instructions.

Every application must be properly signed and filed with the correct fee. If you are under 14 years of age, your parent or guardian may sign the application on your behalf.

Any applicaton that is not signed or accompanied by the correct fee will be rejected and returned to you. You may correct the deficiency and resubmit the application. However, an application is not considered properly filed until it is accepted by the USCIS.

Please answer all questions by typing or clearly printing in black ink. If an item is not applicable to you, write "N/A." If the answer is none, please write "None." If you need extra space to answer a question, attach a separate sheet of paper with your name and A #, if any, written at the top and indicate the number of the question.

Initial Evidence.

I. Evidence of Eligibility.

We may request additional information or evidence, or we may request that you appear at a USCIS office for an interview. You must file your application with all the required evidence. If you do not submit the required evidence, it will delay the issuance of the document you are requesting.

All applications must include **a copy of an official photo identity document showing your photo, name and date of birth.** (Example: a valid government issued driver's license, passport identity page, Form I-551, Permanent Resident Card or any other official identity document.) The copy must **clearly** show the photo and identity information. **A Form I-94, Arrival/Departure Document, is not acceptable as a photo identity document.**

If you are applying for a:

A. Reentry Permit.

You **must** attach:

1. A copy of the front and back of your Form I-551, Permanent Resident Card; or

2. If you have not yet received your Form I-551, a copy of the biographic page(s) of your passport and a copy of the visa page showing your initial admission as a permanent resident, or other evidence that you are a permanent resident; or

3. A copy of the Form I-797, Notice of Action, approval notice of an application for replacement of your Permanent Resident Card or temporary evidence of permanent resident status.

B. *Refugee Travel Document.*

You **must** attach a copy of the document issued to you by the USCIS or former INS showing your refugee or asylee status and the expiration date of such status.

C. *Advance Parole Document.*

1. *If you are in the United States,* you **must** attach:

   a. A copy of any document issued to you by the USCIS or former INS showing your present status in the United States; and

   b. An explanation or other evidence showing the circumstances that warrant issuance of an advance parole document; or

c. If you are an applicant for adjustment of status, a copy of the USCIS or former INS receipt as evidence that you filed the adjustment application;

d. If you are traveling to Canada to apply for an immigrant visa, a copy of the U.S. consular appointment letter.

2. *If you are applying for a person who is outside the United States,* you **must** attach:

a. A statement of how and by whom medical care, transportation, housing, and other expenses and subsistence needs will be met; and

b. An Affidavit of Support (Form I-134), with evidence of the sponsor's occupation and ability to provide necessary support; and

c. A statement explaining why a U.S. visa cannot be obtained, including when and where attempts were made to obtain a visa; and

d. A statement explaining why a waiver of inadmissability cannot be obtained to allow issuance of a visa, including when and where attempts were made to obtain a waiver, and a copy of any USCIS or former INS decision on your waiver request; and

e. A copy of any decision on an immigrant petition filed for the person, and evidence regarding any pending immigrant petition; and

f. A complete description of the emergent reasons explaining why advance parole should be authorized and including copies of any evidence you wish considered, and indicating the length of time for which the parole is requested.

II. Photographs.

A. *If you are filing for a reentry permit or a refugee travel document, or if you are in the United States and filing for an advance parole document:*

You **must** submit two identical color photographs of yourself taken within 30 days of the filing of this application. The photos must have a white background, be printed on thin paper with a glossy finish, and be unmounted and unretouched. **NOTE: Digital photos are not acceptable**.

The photos should show a full frontal position of your face, with your head bare (unless you are wearing a headress as required by a religious order of which you are a member).

The photos should be no larger than 2 by 2 inches. From the top of the head to just below the chin, the image of your head should be about 1 and 1/4 inches. Using a pencil, lightly print your Alien Registration Number (A#), if any, on the back of each photo.

B. *If the person seeking advance parole is outside the United States:*

1. If you are applying for an advance parole document and you are outside the United States, do not submit the photographs with your application. Prior to issuing the parole document, the U.S. embassy or consulate or DHS office abroad will provide you with information regarding the photograph requirements.

2. If you are filing this application for an advance parole document for another person, submit the required photographs of the person to be paroled.

III. Copies.

If these instructions state that a copy of a document may be filed with this application and you choose to send us the original document, we may keep that original for our records. If we request that you submit original documents of any copies, we will return the originals when they are no longer required.

Invalidation of Travel Document.

Any travel document obtained by making a material false representation or concealment in this application will be invalid.

A travel document will also be invalid if you are ordered removed or deported from the United States.

In addition, a refugee travel document will be invalid if the United Nations Convention of July 28, 1951, shall cease to apply or shall not apply to you as provided in Article 1C, D, E or F of the Convention.

Processing Information.

We may request additional information or evidence or we may request that you appear at a USCIS office for an interview. You must file your application with all the required evidence. If you do not submit the required evidence, it will delay the issuance of the document you are requesting. If you do not establish a basis for eligibility, we may deny your application.

Where to File.

A. **If you are applying for a reentry permit or refugee travel document,** mail the application to:

USCIS Nebraska Service Center
P.O. Box 87131
Lincoln, NE 68501-7131

B. **If you are in the United States and filing for an advance parole document:**

1. If you filed at a USCIS field office to adjust your status as a permanent resident, submit or mail this application to that office according to its filing procedures.

2. If you filed at a USCIS service center to adjust your status as a permanent resident, mail this application to that service center. The service center address is noted on the USCIS or former INS receipt related to the filing of your adjustment application. You can also obtain the service center address by visiting the USCIS website at **www.uscis.gov** or calling our National Customer Service Center at **1-800-375-5283.**

3. If you were granted Temporary Protected Status, file this application at the local USCIS office having jurisdiction over your place of residence.

C. If you are requesting an advance parole document, and are in removal proceedings or are the beneficiary of a Private Bill, mail this application to:

Immigration and Customs Enforcement
Parole and Humanitarian Assistance Branch
425 "I" Street, N.W.
Attn.: 800 North Capitol, 3rd Floor
Washington, DC 20536

For Overnight Delivery:
Immigration and Customs Enforcement
Parole and Humantarian Assistance Branch
800 North Capitol, 3rd Floor
Washington, DC 20002

D. If you are outside the United States and applying for an advance parole document on humanitarian grounds, or if such a request is being filed on your behalf, mail this application to:

Immigration and Customs Enforcement
Parole and Humanitarian Assistance Branch
425 "I" Street, N.W.
Attn.: 800 North Capitol, 3rd Floor
Washington, DC 20536

E. Haitian Refugee Immigrant Fairness Act (HRIFA) dependent spouse or child outside the United States: If you are the spouse or child of a principal HRIFA applicant and are seeking advance parole to enter the United States to file for adjustment of status as a permanent resident, mail this application to:

USCIS Nebraska Service Center
P.O. Box 87131
Lincoln, NE 68501-7131

F. If you are a refugee or asylee who has filed an adjustment of status application and are now requesting an advance parole document, mail this application to:

USCIS Nebraska Service Center
P.O. Box 87131
Lincoln, NE 68501-7131

NOTE: If you are a refugee or asylee and have not filed an adjustment of status application, you cannot apply for advance parole. You must request a refugee travel document before departing from the United States. (See instructions on **Page 4, "Where to File," item A.**)

What Is the Fee?

The fee for this application is $170.00. The fee must be submitted in the exact amount. It cannot be refunded. **Do not mail cash.** All checks and money orders must be drawn on a bank or other financial institution located in the United States and must be payable in U.S. currency. The check or money order should be made payable to the **U.S. Department of Homeland Security** or, **U.S. Citizenship and Immigration Services** except:

A. If you live in Guam and are filing this application there, make your check or money order payable to the "Treasurer, Guam."

B. If you live in the U.S. Virgin Islands and are filing this application there, make your check or money order payable to the "Commissioner of Finance of the Virgin Islands."

Checks are accepted subject to collection. An uncollected check will render the application and any document issued invalid. A charge of $30.00 will be imposed if a check in payment of a fee is not honored by the bank on which it is drawn.

When making out your check or money order, spell out U.S. Department of Homeland Security. Do not use the initials "USDHS" or "DHS."

What If You Claim Nonresident Alien Status on Your Federal Income Tax Return?

If you are an alien who has established residence in the United States after having been admitted as an immigrant or adjusted status to that of an immigrant, and are considering the filing of a nonresident alien tax return or the non-filing of a tax return on the ground that you are a nonresident alien, you should carefully review the consequences of such actions under the Immigration and Nationality Act.

If you file a nonresident alien tax return or fail to file a tax return, you may be regarded as having abandoned residence in the United States and as having lost your permanent resident status under the Act. As a consequence, you may be ineligible for a visa or other document for which permanent resident aliens are eligible.

You may also be inadmissible to the United States if you seek admission as a returning resident, and you may become ineligible for adjustment of status as a permanent resident or naturalization on the basis of your original entry.

Form I-131 Instructions (Rev. 10/26/05) Y Page 5

What Are the Penalties for Providing False Information?

If you knowingly and willfully falsify or conceal a material fact or submit a false document with this request, we will deny the benefit you are seeking and may deny any other immigration benefit. In addition, you will face severe penalties provided by law and may be subject to criminal prosecution and/or removal from the United States.

What Is Our Authority for Collecting This Information?

We ask for the information on this form and associated evidence to determine if you have established eligibility for the immigration benefit you are seeking. Our legal right to ask for this information is in 8 U.S.C. 1203 and 1225. We may provide this information to other government agencies. Failure to provide this information and any requested evidence may delay a final decision or result in denial of your request.

USCIS Forms and Information.

To order USCIS forms, call our toll-free forms line at **1-800-870-3676**. You can get USCIS forms and information on immigration laws, regulations and procedures by calling our **National Customer Service Center** toll-free at **1-800-375-5283** or visiting our internet web site at **www.uscis.gov**.

Use InfoPass for Appointment.

As an alternative to waiting in line for assistance at your local USCIS office, you can now schedule an appointment through our internet-based system, **InfoPass**. To access the system, visit our website at **www.uscis.gov**. Use the **InfoPass** appointment scheduler and follow the screen prompts to set up your appointment. **InfoPass** generates an electronic appointment notice that appears on the screen. Print the notice and take it with you to your appointment. The notice gives the time and date of your appointment, along with the address of the USCIS office.

Paperwork Reduction Act Notice.

An agency may not conduct or sponsor an information collection and a person is not required to respond to a collection of information unless it contains a currently valid OMB control number. We try to create forms and instructions that are accurate, can be easily understood and impose the least possible burden on you to provide us with information. Often this is difficult because some immigration laws are very complex. The estimated average time to complete and file this application is as follows: (1) 10 minutes to learn about the law and form; (2) 10 minutes to complete the form; (3) 35 minutes to assemble and file the application; for a total estimated average of 55 minutes per application. If you have comments regarding the accuracy of this estimate or suggestions for making this form simpler, write to the U.S. Citizenship and Immigration Services, Regulatory Management Division, 111 Massachusetts Ave., N.W., Washington DC 20529; OMB No. 1615-0013. **Do not mail your completed application to this address.**

Department of Homeland Security
U. S. Citizenship and Immigration Services

OMB No. 1615-0013; Expires 11/30/07

I-131, Application for Travel Document

DO NOT WRITE IN THIS BLOCK	FOR USCIS USE ONLY (except G-28 block below)

Document Issued
☐ Reentry Permit
☐ Refugee Travel Document
☐ Single Advance Parole
☐ Multiple Advance Parole
   Valid to: _____
If Reentry Permit or Refugee Travel Document, mail to:
☐ Address in Part 1
☐ American embassy/consulate
   at: _____
☐ Overseas DHS office
   at: _____

Action Block

Receipt

☐ Document Hand Delivered
   On _____ By _____

To be completed by Attorney/Representative, if any.
Attorney State License # _____
☐ Check box if G-28 is attached.

Part 1. Information about you. *(Please type or print in black ink.)*

1. A #

2. Date of Birth *(mm/dd/yyyy)*

3. Class of Admission

4. Gender
   Male ☐   Female ☐

5. Name *(Family name in capital letters)*   *(First)*   *(Middle)*

6. Address *(Number and Street)*   Apt. #

City   State or Province   Zip/Postal Code   Country

7. Country of Birth

8. Country of Citizenship

9. Social Security # *(if any.)*

Part 2. Application type *(check one).*

a. ☐ I am a permanent resident or conditional resident of the United States and I am applying for a reentry permit.

b. ☐ I now hold U.S. refugee or asylee status and I am applying for a refugee travel document.

c. ☐ I am a permanent resident as a direct result of refugee or asylee status and I am applying for a refugee travel document.

d. ☐ I am applying for an advance parole document to allow me to return to the United States after temporary foreign travel.

e. ☐ I am outside the United States and I am applying for an advance parole document.

f. ☐ I am applying for an advance parole document for a person who is outside the United States. *If you checked box "f", provide the following information about that person:*

1. Name *(Family name in capital letters)*   *(First)*   *(Middle)*

2. Date of Birth *(mm/dd/yyyy)*

3. Country of Birth

4. Country of Citizenship

5. Address *(Number and Street)*   Apt. #   Daytime Telephone # *(area/country code)*

City   State or Province   Zip/Postal Code   Country

INITIAL RECEIPT _____ RESUBMITTED _____ RELOCATED: Rec'd. _____ Sent _____ COMPLETED: Appv'd. _____ Denied _____ Ret'd. _____

f

Form I-131 (Rev. 10/26/05) Y

Part 3. Processing information.

1. Date of Intended Departure *(mm/dd/yyyy)*

2. Expected Length of Trip

3. Are you, or any person included in this application, now in exclusion, deportation, removal or recission proceedings? ☐ No ☐ Yes *(Name of DHS office)*:

If you are applying for an Advance Parole Document, skip to Part 7.

4. Have you ever before been issued a reentry permit or refugee travel *for the last document issued to you)*: ☐ No ☐ Yes *(Give the following information*

Date Issued *(mm/dd/yyyy)*:   Disposition *(attached, lost, etc.)*:

5. Where do you want this travel document sent? *(Check one)*

a. ☐ To the U.S. address shown in **Part 1** on the first page of this form.

b. ☐ To an American embassy or consulate at: City: Country:

c. ☐ To a DHS office overseas at: City: Country:

d. If you checked "b" or "c", where should the notice to pick up the travel document be sent?

☐ To the address shown in **Part 2** on the first page of this form.

☐ To the address shown below:

Address *(Number and Street)*   Apt. #   Daytime Telephone # *(area/country code)*

City   State or Province   Zip/Postal Code   Country

Part 4. Information about your proposed travel.

Purpose of trip. *If you need more room, continue on a separate sheet(s) of paper.*   List the countries you intend to visit.

Part 5. Complete only if applying for a reentry permit.

Since becoming a permanent resident of the United States (or during the past five years, whichever is less) how much total time have you spent outside the United States?

☐ less than six months ☐ two to three years
☐ six months to one year ☐ three to four years
☐ one to two years ☐ more than four years

Since you became a permanent resident of the United States, have you ever filed a federal income tax return as a nonresident, or failed to file a federal income tax return because you considered yourself to be a nonresident? *(If "Yes," give details on a separate sheet(s) of paper.)* ☐ Yes ☐ No

Part 6. Complete only if applying for a refugee travel document.

1. Country from which you are a refugee or asylee:

If you answer "Yes" to any of the following questions, you must explain on a separate sheet(s) of paper.

2. Do you plan to travel to the above named country? ☐ Yes ☐ No

3. Since you were accorded refugee/asylee status, have you ever:

a. returned to the above named country? ☐ Yes ☐ No

b. applied for and/or obtained a national passport, passport renewal or entry permit of that country? ☐ Yes ☐ No

c. applied for and/or received any benefit from such country (for example, health insurance benefits)? ☐ Yes ☐ No

4. Since you were accorded refugee/asylee status, have you, by any legal procedure or voluntary act:

a. reacquired the nationality of the above named country? ☐ Yes ☐ No

b. acquired a new nationality? ☐ Yes ☐ No

c. been granted refugee or asylee status in any other country? ☐ Yes ☐ No

Form I-131 (Rev. 10/26/05) Y Page 2

Part 7. Complete only if applying for advance parole.

On a separate sheet(s) of paper, please explain how you qualify for an advance parole document and what circumstances warrant issuance of advance parole. Include copies of any documents you wish considered. *(See instructions.)*

1. For how many trips do you intend to use this document?   ☐ One trip   ☐ More than one trip

2. If the person intended to receive an advance parole document is outside the United States, provide the location (city and country) of the American embassy or consulate or the DHS overseas office that you want us to notify.

City

Country

3. If the travel document will be delivered to an overseas office, where should the notice to pick up the document be sent?

☐ To the address shown in **Part 2** on the first page of this form.

☐ To the address shown below:

Address *(Number and Street)*   Apt. #   Daytime Telephone # *(area/country code)*

City   State or Province   Zip/Postal Code   Country

Part 8. Signature. *Read the information on penalties in the instructions before completing this section. If you are filing for a reentry permit or refugee travel document, you must be in the United States to file this application.*

I certify, under penalty of perjury under the laws of the United States of America, that this application and the evidence submitted with it are all true and correct. I authorize the release of any information from my records that the U.S. Citizenship and Immigration Services needs to determine eligibility for the benefit I am seeking.

Signature   Date *(mm/dd/yyyy)*   **Daytime Telephone Number** *(with area code)*

Please Note: If you do not completely fill out this form or fail to submit required documents listed in the instructions, you may not be found eligible for the requested document and this application may be denied.

Part 9. Signature of person preparing form, if other than the applicant. *(Sign below.)*

I declare that I prepared this application at the request of the applicant and it is based on all information of which I have knowledge.

Signature   Print or Type Your Name

Firm Name and Address   Daytime Telephone Number *(with area code)*

Fax Number *(if any.)*   Date *(mm/dd/yyyy)*

U.S. Department of Homeland Security
Bureau of Citizenship and Immigration Services

OMB No. 1615-0014; Exp. 04-30-07

I-134, Affidavit of Support

Instructions

I. Execution of Affidavit.

A separate affidavit must be submitted for each person. As the sponsor, you must sign the affidavit in your full, true and correct name and affirm or make it under oath.

- If you are **in the United States**, the affidavit may be sworn to or affirmed before an officer of the Bureau of Citizenship and Immigration Services (CIS) without the payment of fee, or before a notary public or other officers authorized to administer oaths for general purposes, in which case the official seal or certificate of authority to administer oaths must be affixed.

- If you are **outside the United States,** the affidavit must be sworn to or affirmed before a U.S. consular or immigration officer.

II. Supporting Evidence.

As the sponsor, you must show you have sufficient income and/or financial resources to assure that the alien you are sponsoring will not become a public charge while in the United States.

Evidence should consist of copies of any or all of the following documentation listed below that are applicable to your situation.

Failure to provide evidence of sufficient income and/or financial resources may result in the denial of the alien's application for a visa or his or her removal from the United States.

The sponsor must submit in duplicate evidence of income and resources, as appropriate:

A. Statement from an officer of the bank or other financial institution where you have deposits, giving the following details regarding your account:
   1. Date account opened;
   2. Total amount deposited for the past year;
   3. Present balance.

B. Statement of your employer on business stationery, showing:
   1. Date and nature of employment;
   2. Salary paid;
   3. Whether the position is temporary or permanent.

C. If self-employed:
   1. Copy of last income tax return filed; or
   2. Report of commercial rating concern.

D. List containing serial numbers and denominations of bonds and name of record owner(s).

III. Sponsor and Alien Liability.

Effective October 1, 1980, amendments to section 1614(f) of the Social Security Act and Part A of Title XVI of the Social Security Act establish certain requirements for determining the eligibility of aliens who apply for the first time for Supplemental Security Income (SSI) benefits.

Effective October 1, 1981, amendments to section 415 of the Social Security Act establish similar requirements for determining the eligibility of aliens who apply for the first time for Aid to Families with Dependent Children (AFDC), currently administered under Temporary Assistance for Needy Families (TANF). Effective December 22, 1981, amendments to the Food Stamp Act of 1977 affect the eligibility of alien participation in the Food Stamp Program.

These amendments require that the income and resources of any person, who as the sponsor of an alien's entry into the United States, executes an affidavit of support or similar agreement on behalf of the alien, and the income and resources of the sponsor's spouse (if living with the sponsor) shall be deemed to be the income and resources of the alien under formulas for determining eligibility for SSI, TANF and Food Stamp benefits during the three years following the alien's entry into the United States.

Documentation on Income and Resources.

An alien applying for SSI must make available to the Social Security Administration documentation concerning his or her income and resources and those of the sponsor, including information that was provided in support of the application for an immigrant visa or adjustment of status.

An alien applying for TANF or Food Stamps must make similar information available to the State public assistance agency.

The Secretary of Health and Human Services and the Secretary of Agriculture are authorized to obtain copies of any such documentation submitted to the CIS or the U.S. Department of State and to release such documentation to a State public assistance agency.

Joint and Several Liability Issues.

Sections 1621(e) and 415(d) of the Social Security Act and subsection 5(i) of the Food Stamp Act also provide that an alien and his or her sponsor shall be jointly and severally liable to repay any SSI, TANF or Food Stamp benefits that are incorrectly paid because of misinformation provided by a sponsor or because of a sponsor's failure to provide information.

Incorrect payments that are not repaid will be withheld from any subsequent payments for which the alien or sponsor are otherwise eligible under the Social Security Act or Food Stamp Act, except that the sponsor was without fault or where good cause existed.

Form I-134 (Rev. 06/17/04)N (Prior versions may be used until 09/30/04)

These provisions do not apply to the SSI, TANF or Food Stamp eligibility of aliens admitted as refugees, granted asylum or Cuban/ Haitian entrants as defined in section 501(e) of P.L. 96-422, and to dependent children of the sponsor or sponsor's spouse.

The provisions also do not apply to the SSI or Food Stamp eligibility of an alien who becomes blind or disabled after admission to the United States for permanent residency.

IV. Authority, Use and Penalties.

Authority for the collection of the information requested on this form is contained in 8 U.S.C. 1182(a)(15),1184(a) and 1258.

The information will be used principally by the CIS, or by any consular officer to whom it may be furnished, to support an alien's application for benefits under the Immigration and Nationality Act and specifically the assertion that he or she has adequate means of financial support and will not become a public charge. Submission of the information is voluntary.

It may also, as a matter of routine use, be disclosed to other federal, state, local and foreign law enforcement and regulatory agencies, including the Department of Health and Human Services, Department of Agriculture, Department of State, Department of Defense and any component thereof (if the deponent has served or is serving in the armed forces of the United States), Central Intelligence Agency, and individuals and organizations during the course of any investigation to elicit further information required to carry out CIS functions.

Failure to provide the information may result in the denial of the alien's application for a visa or his or her removal from the United States.

V. Information and CIS Forms.

For information on immigration laws, regulations and procedures or to order CIS forms, call our National Customer Service Center at **1-800-375-5283** or visit our website at **www.uscis.gov**.

VI. Privacy Act Notice.

We ask for the information on this form and associated evidence to determine if you have established eligibility for the immigration benefit you are seeking. Our legal right to ask for this information is in 8 U.S.C. 1203 and 1225. We may provide this information to other government agencies. Failure to provide this information and any requested evidence may delay a final decision or result in denial of your request.

VII. Paperwork Reduction Act Notice.

An agency may not conduct or sponsor a collection of information and a person is not required to respond to a collection of information unless it displays a currently valid OMB control number. We try to create forms and instructions that are accurate, can be easily understood and that impose the least possible burden on you to provide us with information. Often this is difficult because some immigration laws are very complex. The estimated average time to complete and file this application is 30 minutes per application, including the time to learn about the law and the form, complete the form, and assemble and submit the Affidavit. If you have comments regarding the accuracy of this estimate or suggestions for making this form simpler, write to the Bureau of Citizenship and Immigration Services, Regulations and Forms Services Division (HQRFS), 425 I Street, N.W., Room 4034, Washington, D.C. 20529; OMB No. 1615-0014. **Do not mail your completed application to this address.**

OMB No. 1615-0014; Exp. 04-30-07

U.S. Department of Homeland Security
Bureau of Citizenship and Immigration Services

I-134, Affidavit of Support

(Answer All Items: Type or Print in Black Ink.)

I, _____ residing at _____
(Name)   (Street and Number)

_____
(City)   (State)   (Zip Code if in U.S.)   (Country)

BEING DULY SWORN DEPOSE AND SAY:

1. I was born on _____ at _____
(Date-mm/dd/yyyy)   (City)   (Country)

If you are **not** a native born United States citizen, answer the following as appropriate:

a. If a United States citizen through naturalization, give certificate of naturalization number _____

b. If a United States citizen through parent(s) or marriage, give citizenship certificate number _____

c. If United States citizenship was derived by some other method, attach a statement of explanation.

d. If a lawfully admitted permanent resident of the United States, give "A" number _____

2. That I am _____ years of age and have resided in the United States since (date) _____

3. That this affidavit is executed on behalf of the following person:

Name (Family Name)	(First Name)	(Middle Name)	Gender	Age
Citizen of (Country)		Marital Status	Relationship to Sponsor	
Presently resides at (Street and Number)	(City)	(State)	(Country)	

Name of spouse and children accompanying or following to join person:

Spouse	Gender	Age	Child		Gender	Age
Child	Gender	Age	Child		Gender	Age
Child	Gender	Age	Child		Gender	Age

4. That this affidavit is made by me for the purpose of assuring the United States Government that the person(s) named in item **3** will not become a public charge in the United States.

5. That I am willing and able to receive, maintain and support the person(s) named in item **3**. That I am ready and willing to deposit a bond, if necessary, to guarantee that such person(s) will not become a public charge during his or her stay in the United States, or to guarantee that the above named person(s) will maintain his or her nonimmigrant status, if admitted temporarily and will depart prior to the expiration of his or her authorized stay in the United States.

6. That I understand this affidavit will be binding upon me for a period of three (3) years after entry of the person(s) named in item **3** and that the information and documentation provided by me may be made available to the Secretary of Health and Human Services and the Secretary of Agriculture, who may make it available to a public assistance agency.

7. That I am employed as or engaged in the business of _____ with _____
(Type of Business)   (Name of Concern)

at _____
(Street and Number)   (City)   (State)   (Zip Code)

I derive an annual income of *(if self-employed, I have attached a copy of my last income tax return or report of commercial rating concern which I certify to be true and correct to the best of my knowledge and belief. See instructions for nature of evidence of net worth to be submitted.)* $ _____

I have on deposit in savings banks in the United States $ _____

I have other personal property, the reasonable value which is $ _____

Form I-134 (Rev. 06/17/04)N (Prior versions may be used until 09/30/04)

I have stocks and bonds with the following market value, as indicated on the attached list, which I certify to be true and correct to the best of my knowledge and belief. $_____

I have life insurance in the sum of $_____

With a cash surrender value of $_____

I own real estate valued at $_____

With mortgage(s) or other encumbrance(s) thereon amounting to $ _____

Which is located at _____

| (Street and Number) | (City) | (State) | (Zip Code) |

8. That the following persons are dependent upon me for support: *(Place an "x" in the appropriate column to indicate whether the person named is **wholly** or **partially** dependent upon you for support.)*

Name of Person	Wholly Dependent	Partially Dependent	Age	Relationship to Me

9. That I have previously submitted affidavit(s) of support for the following person(s). If none, state *"None."*

Name	Date submitted

10. That I have submitted visa petition(s) to the Bureau of Citizenship and Immigration Services (CIS) on behalf of the following person(s). If none, state none.

Name	Relationship	Date submitted

11. That I ☐ intend ☐ do not intend to make specific contributions to the support of the person(s) named in item **3**. *(If you check "intend," indicate the exact nature and duration of the contributions. For example, if you intend to furnish room and board, state for how long and, if money, state the amount in United States dollars and state whether it is to be given in a lump sum, weekly or monthly, or for how long.)*

_____
_____
_____

Oath or Affirmation of Sponsor

I acknowledge that I have read Part III of the Instructions, Sponsor and Alien Liability, and am aware of my responsibilities as an immigrant sponsor under the Social Security Act, as amended, and the Food Stamp Act, as amended.

I swear (affirm) that I know the contents of this affidavit signed by me and that the statements are true and correct.

Signature of sponsor _____

Subscribed and sworn to (affirmed) before me this _____ day of _____, _____

at _____. My commission expires on _____

Signature of Officer Administering Oath _____ Title _____

If the affidavit is prepared by someone other than the sponsor, please complete the following: I declare that this document was prepared by me at the request of the sponsor and is based on all information of which I have knowledge.

| (Signature) | (Address) | (Date) |

Form I-134 (Rev. 06/17/04)N (Prior versions may be used until 09/30/04) Page 2

OMB No. 1615-0015; Exp. 06-30-06

Department of Homeland Security
U.S.Citizenship and Immigration Services

I-140, Immigrant Petition for Alien Worker

Purpose of This Form.

This form is used to petition to the U.S. Citizenship and Immigration Services (USCIS) for an immigrant visa based on employment. The USCIS is comprised of offices of the former Immigration and Naturalization Service (INS).

Who May File?

A U.S. employer may file this petition for:

- An outstanding professor or researcher, with at least three years of experience in teaching or research in the academic area, who is recognized internationally as outstanding:

  -- In a tenured or tenure-track position at a university or institution of higher education to teach in the academic area; or

  -- In a comparable position at a university or institution of higher education to conduct research in the area; or

  -- In a comparable position to conduct research for a private employer that employs at least three persons in full-time research activities and which achieved documented accomplishments in an academic field.

- An alien who, in the three years preceding the filing of this petition, has been employed for at least one year by a firm or corporation or other legal entity and who seeks to enter the United States to continue to render services to the same employer, or to a subsidiary or affiliate, in a capacity that is managerial or executive.

- A member of the professions holding an advanced degree or an alien with exceptional ability in the sciences, arts, or business who will substantially benefit the national economy, cultural or educational interests, or welfare of the United States.

- A skilled worker (requiring at least two years of specialized training or experience in the skill) to perform labor for which qualified workers are not available in the United States.

- A member of the professions with a baccalaureate degree.

- An unskilled worker (requiring less than two years of specialized training or experience) to perform labor for which qualified workers are not available in the United States.

In addition, a person may file this petition on his or her own behalf if he or she:

- has extraordinary ability in the sciences, arts, education, business, or athletics demonstrated by sustained national or international acclaim, whose achievements have been recognized in the field; or

- is a member of the profession holding an advanced degree or is claiming exceptional ability in the sciences, arts, or business, and is seeking an exemption of the requirement of a job offer in the national interest (NIW).

General Filing Instructions.

Please answer all questions by typing or clearly printing in black ink. Indicate that an item is not applicable with "N/A." If an answer to a question is "none," write "none." If you need extra space to answer any item, attach a sheet of paper with your name and your A#, if any, and indicate the number of the item to which the answer refers. You must file your petition with the required initial evidence. Your petition must be properly signed and filed with the correct fee.

Initial Evidence.

If you are filing for an alien of extraordinary ability in the sciences, arts, education, business, or athletics, you must file your petition with evidence that the alien has sustained national or international acclaim and that the achievements have been recognized in the field of expertise.

- Evidence of a one-time achievement (i.e., a major, internationally recognized award); or

- At least three of the following:

  -- Receipt of lesser nationally or internationally recognized prizes or awards for excellence in the field of endeavor,

  -- Membership in associations in the field which require outstanding achievements as judged by recognized national or international experts,

  -- Published material about the alien in professional or major trade publications or other major media,

  -- Participation on a panel or individually as a judge of the work of others in the field or an allied field,

  -- Original scientific, scholarly, artistic, athletic, or business-related contributions of major significance in the field,

  -- Authorship of scholarly articles in the field, in professional or major trade publications or other major media,

  -- Display of the alien's work at artistic exhibitions or showcases,

  -- Evidence that the alien has performed in a leading or critical role for organizations or establishments that have distinguished reputations,

  -- Evidence that the alien has commanded a high salary or other high remuneration for services,

  -- Evidence of commercial successes in the performing arts, as shown by box office receipts or record, casette, compact disk, or video sales.

- If the above standards do not readily apply to the alien's occupation, you may submit comparable evidence to establish the alien's eligibility; and

- Evidence that the alien is coming to the United States to continue work in the area of expertise. Such evidence may include letter(s) from prospective employer(s), evidence of prearranged commitments such as contracts, or a statement from the alien detailing plans on how he or she intends to continue work in the United States.

A U.S. employer filing for an outstanding professor or researcher must file the petition with:

- Evidence that the professor or researcher is recognized internationally as outstanding in the academic field specified in the petition. Such evidence shall consist of at least two of the following:

  -- Receipt of major prizes or awards for outstanding achievement in the academic field,

  -- Membership in associations in the academic field, which require outstanding achievements of their members,

  -- Published material in professional publications written by others about the alien's work in the academic field,

  -- Participation on a panel, or individually, as the judge of the work of others in the same or an allied academic field,

  -- Original scientific or scholarly research contributions to the academic field, or

  -- Authorship of scholarly books or articles, in scholarly journals with international circulation, in the academic field.

- Evidence the beneficiary has at least three years of experience in teaching and/or research in the academic field; and

- If you are a university or other institution of higher education, a letter indicating that you intend to employ the beneficiary in a tenured or tenure-track position as a teacher or in a permanent position as a researcher in the academic field; or

- If you are a private employer, a letter indicating that you intend to employ the beneficiary in a permanent research position in the academic field, and evidence that you employ at least three full-time researchers and have achieved documented accomplishments in the field.

A U.S. employer filing for a multinational executive or manager must file the petition with a statement which demonstrates that:

- If the worker is now employed outside the United States, that he or she has been employed outside the United States for at least one year in the past three years in an executive or managerial capacity by the petitioner or by its parent, branch, subsidiary or affiliate; or, if the worker is already employed in the United States, that he or she was employed outside the United States for at least one year in the three years preceding admission as a nonimmigrant in an executive or managerial capacity by the petitioner or by its parent, branch, subsidiary or affiliate;

- The prospective employer in the United States is the same employer or a subsidiary or affiliate of the firm or corporation or other legal entity by which the alien was employed abroad;

- The prospective United States employer has been doing business for at least one year; and

- The alien is to be employed in the United States in a managerial or executive capacity. A description of the duties to be performed should be included.

A U.S. employer filing for a member of the professions with an advanced degree or a person with exceptional ability in the sciences, arts or business must file the petition with:

- A labor certification (see **General Evidence**), or a request for a waiver of a job offer because the employment is deemed to be in the national interest, with documentation provided to show that the beneficiary's presence in the United States would be in the national interest; and either:

  -- An official academic record showing that the alien has a U.S. advanced degree or an equivalent foreign degree, or an official academic record showing that the alien has a U.S. baccalaureate degree or an equivalent foreign degree and letters from current or former employers showing that the alien has at least five years of progressive post-baccalaureate experience in the specialty; or

  -- At least three of the following:

  - An official academic record showing that the alien has a degree, diploma, certificate, or similar award from an institution of learning relating to the area of exceptional ability;

  - Letters from current or former employers showing that the alien has at least ten years of full-time experience in the occupation for which he or she is being sought;

  - A license to practice the profession or certification for a particular profession or occupation;

  - Evidence that the alien has commanded a salary, or other remuneration for services, which demonstrates exceptional ability;

  - Evidence of membership in professional associations; or

  - Evidence of recognition for achievements and significant contributions to the industry or field by peers, governmental entities, or professional or business organizations.

- If the above standards do not readily apply to the alien's occupation, you may submit comparable evidence to establish the alien's eligibility.

A U.S. employer filing for a skilled worker must file the petition with:

- A labor certification (see **General Evidence**);

- Evidence that the alien meets the educational, training, or experience and any other requirements of the labor certification (the minimum requirement is two years of training or experience).

A U.S. employer filing for a professional must file the petition with:

- A labor certification (see **General Evidence**);

- Evidence that the alien holds a U.S. baccalaureate degree or equivalent foreign degree; and

- Evidence that a baccalaureate degree is required for entry into the occupation.

A U.S. employer filing for an unskilled worker must file the petition with:

- A labor certification (see **General Evidence**); and

- Evidence that the beneficiary meets any education, training, or experience requirements required in the labor certification.

General Evidence.

Labor certification. Petitions for certain classifications must be filed with a certification from the U.S. Department of Labor or with documentation to establish that the alien qualifies for one of the shortage occupations in the Department of Labor's Labor Market Information Pilot Program or for an occupation in Group I or II of the Department of Labor's Schedule A.

A certification establishes that there are not sufficient workers who are able, willing, qualified, and available at the time and place where the alien is to be employed and that employment of the alien, if qualified, will not adversely affect the wages and working conditions of similarly employed U.S. workers. Application for certification is made on Form ETA-750 and is filed at the local office of the State Employment Service. If the alien is in a shortage occupation, or for a Schedule A/Group I or II occupation, you may file a fully completed, uncertified Form ETA-750 in duplicate with your petition for determination by the USCIS that the alien belongs to the shortage occupation.

NOTE: When filing for a Schedule A/Group I or II occupation, the petitioner must include evidence of having complied with the Department of Labor regulations at 20 CFR 656.222(b)(2), which require that the position or positions be properly posted for a minimum of ten consecutive days.

Ability to pay wage. Petitions which require job offers must be accompanied by evidence that the prospective U.S. employer has the ability to pay the proffered wage. Such evidence shall be in the form of copies of annual reports, federal tax returns, or audited financial statements.

In a case where the prospective U.S. employer employs 100 or more workers, a statement from a financial officer of the organization which establishes ability to pay the wage may be submitted. In appropriate cases, additional evidence, such as profit/loss statements, bank account records, or personnel records, may be submitted.

Translations. Any foreign language document must be accompanied by a full English translation, which the translator has certified as complete and correct, and by the translator's certification that he or she is competent to translate the foreign language into English.

Copies. If these instructions state that a copy of a document may be filed with this petition and you choose to send us the original, we may keep that original for our records. Copies may be submitted of all documentation with the exception of the Labor Certification which **must** be submitted in the original.

Where to File.

File this petition at the USCIS service center with jurisdiction over the place where the alien will be employed.

If the alien's employment will be in Alabama, Arkansas, Florida, Georgia, Kentucky, Louisiana, Mississippi, New Mexico, North Carolina, South Carolina, Oklahoma, Tennessee or Texas, mail the petition to:

USCIS Texas Service Center
P.O. Box 852135
Mesquite, TX 75185-2135

If the alien's employment will be in Connecticut, Delaware, District of Columbia, Maine, Maryland, Massachusetts, New Hampshire, New Jersey, New York, Pennsylvania, Puerto Rico, Rhode Island, Vermont, the U.S. Virgin Islands, Virginia or West Virginia, mail the petition to:

USCIS Vermont Service Center
75 Lower Welden Street
St. Albans, VT 05479-0001

If the alien's employment will be in Arizona, California, Guam, Hawaii or Nevada, mail the petition to:

USCIS California Service Center
P.O. Box 10140
Laguna Niguel, CA 92607-1014

If the alien's employment will be in Alaska, Colorado, Idaho, Illinois, Indiana, Iowa, Kansas, Michigan, Minnesota, Missouri, Montana, Nebraska, North Dakota, Ohio, Oregon, South Dakota, Utah, Washington, Wisconsin or Wyoming, mail the petition to:

USCIS Nebraska Service Center
P.O. Box 87140
Lincoln, NE 68501-7140

What Is the Fee?

The fee for this petition is $195.00.

The fee must be submitted in the exact amount. It cannot be refunded. **Do not mail cash.**

All checks and money orders must be drawn on a bank or other financial institution located in the United States and must be payable in United States currency. The check or money order should be made payable to the **Department of Homeland Security**, unless:

- If you live in Guam, make your check or money order payable to the "Treasurer, Guam."

- If you live in the U.S. Virgin Islands , make your check or money order payable to the "Commissioner of Finance of the Virgin Islands."

Checks are accepted subject to collection. An uncollected check will render the petition and any document issued invalid. A charge of $30.00 will be imposed if a check in payment of a fee is not honored by the bank on which it is drawn.

How to Check If the Fee Is Correct.

The fee on this form is current as of the edition date appearing in the lower right corner of this page. However, because USCIS fees change periodically, you can verify if the fee is correct by following one of the steps below:

- Visit our website at **www.uscis.gov** and scroll down to "Forms and E-Filing" to check the appropriate fee, or

- Review the Fee Schedule included in your form package, if you called us to request the form, or

- Telephone our National Customer Service Center at **1-800-375-5283** and ask for the fee information.

Processing Information.

Acceptance. Any petition that is not signed or is not accompanied by the correct fee will be rejected with a notice that it is deficient. You may correct the deficiency and resubmit the petition. However, a petition is not considered properly filed until accepted by the USCIS. A priority date will not be assigned until the petition is properly filed.

Initial processing. Once the petition has been accepted, it will be checked for completeness, including submission of the required initial evidence. If you do not completely fill out the form, or file it without the required initial evidence, you will not establish a basis for eligibility, and we may deny your petition.

Requests for more information or interview. We may request more information or evidence, or we may request that you appear at a USCIS office for an interview. We may also request that you submit the originals of any copy. We will return these originals when they are no longer required.

Decision. If you have established eligibility for the benefit requested, your petition will be approved. If you have not established eligibility, your petition will be denied. You will be notified in writing of the decision on your petition.

Meaning of petition approval. Approval of a petition means you have established that the person you are filling for is eligible for the requested classification.

This is the first step towards permanent residence. However, this does not in itself grant permanent residence or employment authorization. You will be given information about the requirements for the person to receive an immigrant visa or to adjust status after your petition is approved.

Instructions for Industry and Occupation Codes.

NAICS Code. The North American Industry Classification System (NAICS) code can be obtained from the U.S. Department of Commerce, U.S. Census Bureau at (www.census.gov/epcd/www/naics.html). Enter the code from left to right, one digit in each of the six boxes. If you use a code which is less than six digits, enter the code left to right and then add zeros in the remaining unoccupied boxes.

The code sequence 33466 would be entered as:

| 3 | 3 | 4 | 6 | 6 | 0 |

The code sequence 5133 would be entered as:

| 5 | 1 | 3 | 3 | 0 | 0 |

SOC Code. The Standard Occupational Classification (SOC) System codes can be obtained from the Department of Labor, U.S. Bureau of Labor Statistics (http://stats.bls.gov/soc/socguide.htm). Enter the code from left to right, one digit in each of the six boxes. If you use a code which is less than six digits, enter the code left to right and then add zeros in the remaining unoccupied boxes.

The code sequence 19-1021 would be entered as:

| 1 | 9 | — | 1 | 0 | 2 | 1 |

The code sequence 15-100 would be entered as:

| 1 | 5 | — | 1 | 0 | 0 | 0 |

Penalties.

If you knowingly and willfully falsify or conceal a material fact or submit a false document with this petition, we will deny the benefit your are seeking and may deny any other immigration benefit. In addition, you will face severe penalties provided by law and may be subject to criminal prosecution.

Privacy Act Notice.

We ask for the information on this form and associated evidence to determine if you have established eligibility for the immigration benefit you are seeking. Our legal right to ask for this information is in 8 U.S.C. 1154. We may provide this information to other government agencies. Failure to provide this information and any requested evidence may delay a final decision or result in denial of your request.

USCIS Forms and Information.

To order USCIS forms, call our toll-free forms line at 1-800-870-3676. You can also obtain USCIS forms and information on immigration laws, regulations or procedures by calling our National Customer Service Center at 1-800-375-5283 or visiting our internet website at www.uscis.gov.

Use InfoPass to Make an Appointment.

As an alternative to waiting in line for assistance at your local USCIS office, you can now schedule an appointment through our internet-based system, InfoPass. To access the system, visit our website at www.uscis.gov. Use the InfoPass appointment scheduler and follow the screen prompts to set up your appointment. InfoPass generates an electronic appointment notice that appears on the screen. Print the notice and take it with you to your appointment. The notice gives the time and date of your appointment, along with the address of the USCIS office.

Paperwork Reduction Act Notice.

An agency may not conduct or sponsor an information collection and a person is not required to respond to a collection of information unless it displays a currently valid OMB control number. We try to create forms and instructions that are accurate, can easily be understood, and which impose the least possible burden on you to provide us with information. Often this is difficult because some immigration laws are very complex. The estimate average time to complete and file this application is as follows: (1) 20 minutes to learn about the law and form; (2) 15 minutes to complete the form; and (3) 25 minutes to assemble and file the petition; for a total estimated average of 1 hour per petition. If you have comments regarding the accuracy of this estimate, or suggestions for making this form simpler, you can write to the U.S. Citizenship and Immigration Services, Regulatory Management Division, 111 Massachusetts Avenue, N.W., Washington, D.C. 20529; OMB No. 1615-0015. **Do not mail your completed petition to this address.**

OMB No. 1615-0015; Exp. 06-30-06

Department of Homeland Security
U.S. Citizenship and Immigration Services

I-140, Immigrant Petition
for Alien Worker

START HERE - Please type or print in black ink.

For USCIS Use Only

Part 1. **Information about the person or organization filing this petition.** If an individual is filing, use the top name line. Organizations should use the second line.

Family Name (Last Name) | Given Name (First Name) | Full Middle Name

Company or Organization Name

Address: (Street Number and Name) | Suite #

Attn:

City | State/Province

Country | Zip/Postal Code

IRS Tax # | U.S. Social Security # *(if any)* | E-Mail Address *(if any)*

For USCIS Use Only

Returned | Receipt

Date

Date

Resubmitted

Date

Date

Reloc Sent

Date

Date

Reloc Rec'd

Date

Date

Part 2. Petition type.

This petition is being filed for: *(Check one)*

a. ☐ An alien of extraordinary ability.

b. ☐ An outstanding professor or researcher.

c. ☐ A multinational executive or manager.

d. ☐ A member of the professions holding an advanced degree or an alien of exceptional ability (who is NOT seeking a National Interest Waiver.)

e. ☐ A professional (at a minimum, possessing a bachelor's degree or a foreign degree equivalent to a U.S. bachelor's degree) or a skilled worker (requiring at least two years of specialized training or experience).

f. ☐ (Reserved.)

g. ☐ Any other worker (requiring less than two years of training or experience).

h. ☐ Soviet Scientist.

i. ☐ An alien applying for a National Interest Waiver (who IS a member of the professions holding an advanced degree or an alien of exceptional ability).

Classification:

☐ 203(b)(1)(A) Alien of Extraordinary Ability

☐ 203(b)(1)(B) Outstanding Professor or Researcher

☑ 203(b)(1)(C) Multi-National Executive or Manager

☐ 203(b)(2) Member of Professions w/Adv. Degree or Exceptional Ability

☐ 203(b)(3)(A)(i) Skilled Worker

☐ 203(b)(3)(A)(ii) Professional

☐ 203(b)(3)(A)(iii) Other Worker

Certification:

☐ National Interest Waiver (NIW)

☐ Schedule A, Group I

☐ Schedule A, Group II

Part 3. Information about the person you are filing for.

Family Name (Last Name) | Given Name (First Name) | Full Middle Name

Address: (Street Number and Name) | Apt. #

C/O: (In Care Of)

City | State/Province

Country | Zip/Postal Code | E-Mail Address *(if any)*

Daytime Phone # *(with area/country codes)* | Date of Birth *(mm/dd/yyyy)*

City/Town/Village of Birth | State/Province of Birth | Country of Birth

Country of Nationality/Citizenship | A # *(if any)* | U.S. Social Security # *(if any)*

If in the U.S.

Date of Arrival *(mm/dd/yyyy)* | I-94 # *(Arrival/Departure Document)*

Current Nonimmigrant Status | Date Status Expires *(mm/dd/yyyy)*

Priority Date | **Consulate**

Concurrent Filing:

☐ **I-485 filed concurrently.**

Remarks

Action Block

To Be Completed by
Attorney or Representative, if any.

☐ Fill in box if G-28 is attached to represent the applicant.

ATTY State License #

f

Form I-140 (Rev. 10/26/05)Y

Part 4. Processing Information.

1. Please complete the following for the person named in **Part 3**: *(Check one)*

☐ Alien will apply for a visa abroad at the American Embassy or Consulate at:

City	Foreign Country

☐ Alien is in the United States and will apply for adjustment of status to that of lawful permanent resident.

Alien's country of current residence or, if now in the U.S., last permanent residence abroad.

2. If you provided a U.S. address in **Part 3**, print the person's foreign address:

3. If the person's native alphabet is other than Roman letters, write the person's foreign name and address in the native alphabet:

4. Are any other petition(s) or application(s) being filed with this Form I-140?

☐ No   ☐ Yes-(check all that apply)   ☐ Form I-485   ☐ Form I-765

☐ Form I-131   ☐ Other - attach an explanation.

5. Is the person you are filing for in removal proceedings?   ☐ No   ☐ Yes-attach an explanation.

6. Has any immigrant visa petition ever been filed by or on behalf of this person?   ☐ No   ☐ Yes-attach an explanation.

If you answered yes to any of these questions, please provide the case number, office location, date of decision and disposition of the decision on a separate sheet(s) of paper.

Part 5. Additional information about the petitioner.

1. Type of petitioner *(Check one)*.

☐ Employer   ☐ Self   ☐ Other (Explain, e.g., Permanent Resident, U.S. citizen or any other person filing on behalf of the alien.)

2. If a company, give the following:

Type of Business	Date Established *(mm/dd/yyyy)*	Current Number of Employees

Gross Annual Income	Net Annual Income	NAICS Code

DOL/ETA Case Number

3. If an individual, give the following:

Occupation	Annual Income

Part 6. Basic information about the proposed employment.

1. Job Title	**2.** SOC Code
	☐☐☐ — ☐☐☐☐

3. Nontechnical Description of Job

4. Address where the person will work if different from address in **Part 1**.

5. Is this a full-time position?   **6.** If the answer to **Number 5** is "No," how many hours per week for the position?

☐ Yes ☐ No

7. Is this a permanent position?   **8.** Is this a new position?   **9.** Wages per week

☐ Yes ☐ No   ☐ Yes ☐ No $ _____

Part 7. **Information on spouse and all children of the person for whom you are filing.**

List husband/wife and all children related to the individual for whom the petition is being filed. Provide an attachment of additional family members, if needed.

Name *(First/Middle/Last)*	Relationship	Date of Birth *(mm/dd/yyyy)*	Country of Birth

Part 8. Signature. *Read the information on penalties in the instructions before completing this section. If someone helped you prepare this petition, he or she must complete **Part 9**.*

I certify, under penalty of perjury under the laws of the United States of America, that this petition and the evidence submitted with it are all true and correct. I authorize the U.S. Citizenship and Immigration Services to release to other government agencies any information from my USCIS (or former INS) records, if the USCIS determines that such action is necessary to determine eligibility for the benefit sought.

Petitioner's Signature   **Daytime Phone Number** *(Area/Country Codes)*   **E-Mail Address**

Print Name   **Date** *(mm/dd/yyyy)*

NOTE: *If you do not fully complete this form or fail to submit the required documents listed in the instructions, a final decision on your petition may be delayed or the petition may be denied.*

Part 9. **Signature of person preparing form, if other than above.**   *(Sign below.)*

I declare that I prepared this petition at the request of the above person and it is based on all information of which I have knowledge.

Attorney or Representative: In the event of a Request for Evidence (RFE), may the USCIS contact you by Fax or E-mail? ☐ Yes ☐ No

Signature   **Print Name**   **Date** *(mm/dd/yyyy)*

Firm Name and Address

Daytime Phone Number *(Area/Country Codes)*   **Fax Number** *(Area/Country Codes)*   **E-Mail Address**

OMB No. 1615-0023 (Expires 05-31-05)

Department of Homeland Security
U.S. Citizenship and Immigration Services

I-485, Application to Register
Permanent Residence or Adjust Status

What Is the Purpose of This Form?

This form is used by a person who is in the United States to apply to the U.S. Citizenship and Immigration Services (USCIS), to adjust to permanent resident status or register for permanent residence.

This form may also be used by certain Cuban nationals to request a change in the date that their permanent residence began.

NOTE: USCIS is comprised of offices of the former Immigration and Naturalization Service (INS).

Who May File?

Based on an immigrant petition.

You may apply to adjust your status if:

- An immigrant visa number is immediately available to you based on an approved immigrant petition; or

- You are filing this application with a completed relative petition, special immigrant juvenile petition or special immigrant military petition which if approved would make an immigrant visa number immediately available to you.

Based on being the spouse or child (derivative) at the time another adjustment applicant (principal) files to adjust status or at the time a person is granted permanent resident status in an immigrant category that allows derivative status for spouses and children.

- **If the spouse or child is in the United States, the** individual derivatives may file their Form I-485 adjustment of status applications concurrently with the Form I-485 for the principal applicant, or file the Form I-485 at anytime after the principal is approved, if a visa number is available.

- **If the spouse or child is residing abroad,** the person adjusting status in the United States should file the **Form I-824, Application for Action on an Approved Application or Petition, concurrently** with the principal's adjustment of status application to allow the derivatives to immigrate to the United States without delay if the principal's adjustment of status application is approved. **The fee submitted with the Form I-824 will not be refunded if the principal's adjustment is not granted.**

Based on admission as the fiancé(e) of a U. S. citizen and subsequent marriage to that citizen.

You may apply to adjust status if you were admitted to the United States as the K-1 fiancé(e) of a United States citizen and you married that citizen within 90 days of your entry. If you were admitted as the K-2 child of such a fiancé(e), you may apply to adjust status based on your parent's adjustment application.

Based on asylum status.

You may apply to adjust status after you have been granted asylum in the United States if you have been physically present in the United States for one year after the grant of asylum, provided you still qualify as an asylee or as the spouse or child of a refugee.

Based on Cuban citizenship or nationality.

You may apply to adjust status if:

- You are a native or citizen of Cuba, were admitted or paroled into the United States after January 1, 1959, and thereafter have been physically present in the United States for at least one year; or

- You are the spouse or unmarried child of a Cuban described above and regardless of your nationality, you were admitted or paroled after January 1, 1959, and thereafter have been physically present in the United States for at least one year.

Applying to change the date on which your permanent residence began.

If you were granted permanent residence in the United States prior to November 6, 1966, and are a native or citizen of Cuba, his or her spouse or unmarried minor child, you may ask to change the date your lawful permanent residence began to your date of arrival in the United States or May 2, 1964, whichever date is later.

Based on continuous residence since before January 1, 1972.

You may apply for permanent residence if you have continuously resided in the United States since before January 1, 1972.

Other basis of eligibility.

If you are not included in the above categories, but believe you may be eligible for adjustment or creation of record of permanent residence, contact our National Customer Service Center at **1-800-375-5283** for information on how to use **InfoPass** on our internet website (**www.uscis.gov**). InfoPass can help you make an appointment at your local USCIS office concerning your possible eligibltiy.

Persons Who Are Not Eligible to Adjust Status.

Unless you are applying for creation of record based on continuous residence since before January 1, 1972, or adjustment of status under a category in which special rules apply (such as 245(i) adjustment, asylum adjustment, Cuban adjustment, special immigrant juvenile adjustment, or special immigrant military personnel adjustment), **you are not eligible for adjustment of status if any of the following apply to you:**

- You entered the United States in transit without a visa;
- You entered the United States as a nonimmigrant crewman;
- You were not admitted or paroled following inspection by an immigration officer;
- Your authorized stay expired before you filed this application;
- You were employed in the United States, without USCIS authorization, prior to filing this application;
- You failed to maintain your nonimmigrant status, through no fault of your own or for technical reasons; unless you are applying because you are:
  -- An immediate relative of a United States citizen (parent, spouse, widow, widower or unmarried child under 21 years old);
  -- A K-1 fiancé(e) or a K-2 fiancé(e) dependent who married the United States petitioner within 90 days of admission; or

-- An H or I nonimmigrant or special immigrant (foreign medical graduates, international organization employees or their derivative family members);

- You were admitted as a K-1 fiancé(e), but did not marry the U.S. citizen who filed the petition for you, or you were admitted as the K-2 child of a fiancé(e) and your parent did not marry the U.S. citizen who filed the petition;

- You are or were a J-1 or J-2 exchange visitor and are subject to the two-year foreign residence requirement and you have not complied with or been granted a waiver of the requirement;

- You have A, E or G nonimmigrant status or have an occupation that would allow you to have this status, unless you complete Form I-508 (I-508F for French nationals) to wave diplomatic rights, privileges and immunities and, if you are an A or G nonimmigrant, unless you submit a completed Form I-566;

- You were admitted to Guam as a visitor under the Guam visa waiver program;

- You were admitted to the United States as a visitor under the Visa Waiver Program, unless you are applying because you are an immediate relative of a U.S. citizen (parent, spouse, widow, widower or unmarried child under 21 years old); or

- You are already a conditional permanent resident.

General Filing Instructions.

Please answer all questions by typing or clearly printing in black ink. Indicate that an item is not applicable with "N/A." If the answer is "none," write "none." If you need extra space to answer any item, attach a sheet of paper with your name and your alien registration number (A#), if any, and indicate the number of the item to which the answer refers. You must file your application with the required **Initial Evidence** described below. Your application must be properly signed and filed with the correct fee. If you are under 14 years of age, your parent or guardian may sign your application.

Translations.

Any foreign language document must be accompanied by a full English translation that the translator has certified as complete and correct and by the translator's certification that he or she is competent to translate the foreign language into English.

Copies.

If these instructions state that a copy of a document may be filed with this application, and you choose to send us the original, we may keep the original for our records.

Initial Evidence.

You must file your application with the following evidence:

- *Birth certificate.*
  Submit a copy of your foreign birth certificate or other record of your birth that meets the provisions of secondary evidence found in Title 8, Code of Federal Regulations (CFR), 103.2(b)(2).

- *Copy of passport page with nonimmigrant visa.*
  If you have obtained a nonimmigrant visa(s) from an American embassy or consulate abroad within the last year, submit a photocopy(ies) of the page(s) of your passport containing the visa(s).

- *Photos.*
  Submit two identical natural color passport-style photographs of yourself, taken within 30 days of the application. The photos must have a white background, be unmounted, printed on thin paper, and be glossy and unretouched. The photos must show your full-frontal facial position with your head bare. You may wear a headdress, if required by a religious order of which you are a member. The photos must be no larger than 2 x 2 inches, with the distance from the top of the head to just below the chin about 1 and 1/4 inches. Using a pencil, lightly print your Alien Registration Number (A#), or your name, if you do not have an A#, on the back of each photo.

- *Biometric services.*
  If you are between the ages of 14 and 79, you must be fingerprinted as part of the USCIS biometric services requirement. After you have filed this application, the USCIS will notify you in writing of the time and location where you must go to be fingerprinted. If necessary, USCIS may also take your photograph and signature. Failure to appear to be fingerprinted or for other biometric services may result in a denial of your application.

- *Police clearances.*
  If you are filing for adjustment of status as a member of a special class described in an I-485 supplement form, please read the instructions on the supplement form to see if you need to obtain and submit police clearances, in addition to the required fingerprints, with your application.

- *Medical examination (Section 232 of the Immigraton and Nationality Act (INA)).*
  When required, submit a medical examination report on the form you have obtained from USCIS.

-- **A. Individuals applying for adjustment of status through a USCIS service center.**

   1) General:
   If you are filing your adjustment of status application with a USCIS service center, include your medical examination report with the application, unless you are a refugee or asylee.

   2) Refugees:
   If you are applying for adjustment of status one year after you were admitted as a refugee, you only need to submit a vaccination supplement with your adjustment of status application, not the entire medical report, **unless** there were medical grounds of inadmissibility that arose during the initial examination that you had overseas.

-- **B. Individuals applying for adjustment of status through a local USCIS office and asylees applying for adjustment of status through a service center.**

   If you are filing your adjustment of status application with a local USCIS office, or if you are an asylee filing an adjustment of status application with a service center one year after you were granted asylum, do not submit a medical report with your adjustment of status application. Wait for further instructions from USCIS about how and where to take and submit medical examination report.

-- **Fiancé(e)s.**

If you are a K-1 fiancé(e) or K-2 dependent who had a medical examination within the past year as required for the nonimmigrant fiancé(e) visa, you only need to submit a vaccination supplement, not the entire medical report. You may include the vaccination supplement with your adjustment of status application.

-- **Persons not required to have a medical examination.**

The medical report is not required if you are applying for creation of a record for admission as a lawful permanent resident under section 249 of the INA as someone who has continuously resided in the United States since January 1, 1972 (registry applicant).

- *Form G-325A, Biographic Information Sheet.*

You must submit a completed Form G-325A if you are between 14 and 79 years of age.

- *Evidence of status.*

Submit a copy of your Form I-94, Nonimmigrant Arrival/Departure Record, showing your admission to the United States and current status, or other evidence of your status.

- *Affidavit of Support/Employment Letter.*

-- **Affidavit of Support.**

Submit an Affidavit of Support (Form I-864) if your adjustment of status application is based on your entry as a fiancé(e), a relative visa petition (Form I-130) filed by your relative, or an employment based visa petition (Form I-140) related to a business that is five percent or more owned by your family.

-- **Employment Letter.**

If your adjustment of status application is related to an employment based visa petition (Form I-140), you must submit a letter on the letterhead of the petitioning employer which confirms that the job on which the visa petition is based is still available to you. The letter must also state the salary that will be paid.

NOTE: The affidavit of support and/or employment letter are not required if you applying for creation of record based on continuous residence since before January 1, 1972, asylum adjustment, or a Cuban citizen or a spouse or unmarried child of a Cuban citizen who was admitted after January 1, 1959.)

- *Evidence of eligibility.*

--**Based on an immigrant petition.**

Attach a copy of the approval notice for an immigrant petition that makes a visa number immediately available to you, or submit a complete relative, special immigrant juvenile, or special immigrant military petition which, if approved, will make a visa number immediately available to you.

--**Based on admission as the K-1 fiancé(e) of a United States citizen and subsequent marriage to that citizen.**

Attach a copy of the fiancé(e) petition approval notice, a copy of your marriage certificate and your Form I-94.

-- **Based on asylum status.**

Attach a copy of the letter or Form I-94 that shows the date you were granted asylum.

-- **Based on continuous residence in the United States since before January 1, 1972.**

Attach copies of evidence that shows continuous residence since before January 1, 1972.

-- **Based on Cuban citizenship or nationality.**

Attach evidence of your citizenship or nationality, such as a copy of your passport, birth certificate or travel document.

-- **Based on derivative status as the spouse or child of another adjustment applicant or person granted permanent residence based on issuance of an immigrant visa.**

File your application with the application of the other applicant, or with evidence that the application is pending with USCIS or was approved, or with evidence that your spouse or parent was granted permanent residence based on an immigrant visa, and:

If you are applying as the spouse of that person, also attach a copy of your marriage certificate and copies of documents showing the legal termination of all other marriages by you and your spouse;

If you are applying as the child of that person, also attach a copy of your birth certificate and, if the other person is not your natural mother, copies of evidence (such as a marriage certificate and documents showing the legal termination of all other marriages and an adoption decree) to demonstrate that you qualify as his or her child.

- *Other basis for eligibility.*

Attach copies of documents proving that you are eligible for the classification.

Where to File.

File this application at the USCIS Service Center or local office that has jurisdiction over your place of residence or submit the form to the USCIS Lockbox Facility. For details on where to file your application, read the additional instructions that may be attached to this form, call our National Customer Service Center at **1-800-375-5283,** or visit our website at **www.uscis.gov.**

Fee.

The fee for this application is **$315.00,** or **$215.00** if you are less than 14 years old. There is no application fee if you are filing as a refugee under section 209(a) of the INA.

If you are between the ages of 14 and 79, there is a **$70.00** biometric services fee for USCIS to take your fingerprints and, if necessary, also your photograph and signature. The biometric services fee is in addition to the application fee.

For example, if your application fee is $315.00 and you are between the ages of 14 and 79 years and require fingerprints, the total fee you must pay is $385.00.

You may submit one check or money order for both the application and biometric services fees, including fingerprinting fees. Fees must be submitted in the exact amount. **Do not mail cash.** Fees cannot be refunded. All checks and money orders must be drawn on a bank or other institution located in the United States and must be payable in United States currency. The check or money order should be made payable to the **Department of Homeland Security except:**

-- If you live in Guam and are filing this application there, make your check or money order payable to the "Treasurer, Guam."

-- If you live in the U.S. Virgin Islands and are filing this application freely, make your check or money order payable to the "Commissioner of Finance of the Virgin Islands."

Checks are accepted subject to collection. An uncollected check in payment of an application fee will render the application and any document issued invalid. A charge of $30.00 will be imposed if a check for payment of a fee is not honored by the bank on which it is drawn.

Processing Information.

Acceptance.

Any application that is not signed or is not accompanied by the correct application fee will be rejected with a notice that the application is deficient. You may correct the deficiency and resubmit the application. An application is not considered properly filed until accepted by USCIS.

Initial Processing.

Once an application has been accepted, it will be checked for completeness, including submission of the required initial evidence. If you do not completely fill out the form or file it without required initial evidence, you will not establish a basis for eligibility and we may deny your application.

Requests for More Information.

We may request more information or evidence. We may also request that you submit the originals of any copy. **Originals may be returned to you, if requested.**

Interview.

After you file your application, you may be notified to appear at a USCIS office to answer questions about the application. You will be required to answer these questions under oath or affirmation. You must bring your Arrival-Departure Record (Form I-94) and any passport you have to the interview.

Decision.

You will be notified in writing of the decision on your application.

Selective Service Registration.

If you are a male at least 18 years old, but not yet 26 years old, and required according to the Military Selective Service Act to register with the Selective Service System, USCIS will help you register.

When your signed application is filed and accepted by the USCIS, we will transmit to the Selective Service System your name, current address, Social Security number, date of birth and the date you filed the application. This action will enable the Selective Service System to record your registration as of the filing date of your application. If USCIS does not accept your application and, if still so required, you are responsible to register with the Selective Service System by using other means, provided you are under 26 years of age. If you have already registered, the Selective Service System will check its records to avoid any duplication.

(NOTE: Men 18 through 25 years old who are applying for student financial aid, government employment or job training benefits should register directly with the Selective Service System or such benefits may be denied. Men can register at a local post office or on the Internet at http://www.sss.gov).

Travel Outside the United States for Adjustment of Status Applicants Under Sections 209 and 245 of the Act and Registry Applicants Under Section 249 of the Act.

Your departure from the United States (including brief visits to Canada or Mexico) constitutes an abandonment of your adjustment of status application, unless you are granted permission to depart and you are inspected upon your return to the United States. Such permission to travel is called "advance parole." To request advance parole, you must file Form I-131, Application for Travel Document, with the appropriate fee at the USCIS office where you applied for adjustment of status.

-- **Exceptions:**

1) H, L, V or K3/K4 nonimmigrants:

If you are an H, L,V, or K3/K4 nonimmigrant who continues to maintain his or her status, you may travel on a valid H, L, V or K3/K4 visa without obtaining advance parole.

2) Refugees and Asylees:

If you are applying for adjustment of status one year after you were admitted as a refugee or one year after you were granted asylum, you may travel outside the United States on your valid refugee travel document, if you have one, without the need to obtain advance parole.

-- **WARNING:**

Travel outside of the United States may trigger the 3-and 10-year bar to admission under section 212(a)(9)(B)(i) of the Act for adjustment applicants, but not registry applicants. This ground of inadmissibility is triggered if you were unlawfully present in the United States (i.e., you remained in the United States beyond the period of authorized stay) for more than 180 days before you applied for adjustment of status and you travel outside of the United States while your adjustment of status application is pending.

(NOTE: Only unlawful presence that was accrued on or after April 1, 1997, counts towards the 3-and 10-year bar under section 212 (a)(9) (B)(i) of the Act.)

If you become inadmissible under section 212(a)(9)(B)(i) of the Act while your adjustment of status application is pending, you will need a waiver of inadmissibility under section 212(a)(9)(B)(v) of the Act before your adjustment of status application can be approved. This waiver, however, is granted on a case-by-case basis and in the exercise of discretion. It requires a showing of extreme hardship to your United States citizen or lawful permanent resident spouse or parent, unless you are a refugee or asylee. For refugees and asylees, the waiver may be granted for humanitarian reasons, to assure family unity or if it is otherwise in the public interest.

Penalties.

If you knowingly and willfully falsify or conceal a material fact or submit a false document with this request, we will deny the benefit you are seeking and may deny any other immigration benefit. In addition, you will face severe penalties provided by law and may be subject to criminal prosecution.

Privacy Act Notice.

We ask for the information on this form and associated evidence to determine if you have established eligibility for the immigration benefit you are seeking. Our legal right to ask for this information is in 8 U.S.C. 1255 and 1259. We may provide this information to other government agencies, including the Selective Service System. Your failure to provide information on this form and any requested evidence may delay a final decision or result in denial of your application.

USCIS Forms and Information.

To order USCIS forms call our toll-free forms line at **1-800-870-3676.** You can also get USCIS forms and information on immigration laws, regulations and procedures by telephoning our National Customer Service Center at **1-800-375-5283** or visiting our internet website at **www.uscis.gov.**

Use InfoPass for Appointments.

As an alternative to waiting in line for assistance at your local USCIS office, you can now schedule an appointment through our internet-based system, **Infor Pass.** To access the system, visit our website at www.uscis.gov. Use the **InfoPass** appointment scheduler and follow the screen prompts to set up your appointment. **InfoPass** generates an electronic appointment notice that appears on the screen. Print the notice and take it with you to your appointment. The notice gives the time and date of your appointment, along with the address of the USCIS office.

Paperwork Reduction Act Notice.

An agency may not conduct or sponsor an information collection and a person is not required to respond to a collection of information unless it displays a current valid OMB number. We try to create forms and instructions that are accurate, can be easily understood and that impose the least possible burden on you to provide us with information. Often this is difficult because some immigration laws are very complex. The estimated average time to complete and file this application is computed as follows: (1) 20 minutes to learn about the law and form; (2) 25 minutes to complete the form and (3) 270 minutes to assemble and file the application, including the required interview and travel time, for a total estimated average of 5 hours and 15 minutes per application. If you have comments regarding the accuracy of this estimate or suggestions to make this form simpler, you should write to the U.S. Citizenship and Immigration Services, Regulatory Management Division, 111 Masschuetts Avenue, N.W., Washington, DC 20529; OMB No. 1615-0023. **Do not mail your completed application to this address.**

OMB No. 1615-0023 (Expires 05-31-05)

Department of Homeland Security
U.S. Citizenship and Immigration Services

I-485, Application to Register
Permanent Residence or Adjust Status

START HERE - Please type or print in black ink.

Part 1. Information about you.

Family Name	Given Name	Middle Name

Address- C/O

Street Number and Name	Apt. #

City

State	Zip Code

Date of Birth *(mm/dd/yyyy)*	Country of Birth:
	Country of Citizenship/Nationality:

U.S. Social Security #	A # *(if any)*
Date of Last Arrival *(mm/dd/yyyy)*	I-94 #
Current USCIS Status	Expires on *(mm/dd/yyyy)*

Part 2. Application type. *(check one)*

I am applying for an adjustment to permanent resident status because:

a. ☐ an immigrant petition giving me an immediately available immigrant visa number has been approved. (Attach a copy of the approval notice, or a relative, special immigrant juvenile or special immigrant military visa petition filed with this application that will give you an immediately available visa number, if approved.)

b. ☐ my spouse or parent applied for adjustment of status or was granted lawful permanent residence in an immigrant visa category that allows derivative status for spouses and children.

c. ☐ I entered as a K-1 fiancé(e) of a United States citizen whom I married within 90 days of entry, or I am the K-2 child of such a fiancé(e). (Attach a copy of the fiancé(e) petition approval notice and the marriage certificate).

d. ☐ I was granted asylum or derivative asylum status as the spouse or child of a person granted asylum and am eligible for adjustment.

e. ☐ I am a native or citizen of Cuba admitted or paroled into the United States after January 1, 1959, and thereafter have been physically present in the United States for at least one year.

f. ☐ I am the husband, wife or minor unmarried child of a Cuban described above in (e) and am residing with that person, and was admitted or paroled into the United States after January 1, 1959, and thereafter have been physically present in the United States for at least one year.

g. ☐ I have continuously resided in the United States since before January 1, 1972.

h. ☐ Other basis of eligibility. Explain. (If additional space is needed, use a separate piece of paper.)

_____

_____

I am already a permanent resident and am applying to have the date I was granted permanent residence adjusted to the date I originally arrived in the United States as a nonimmigrant or parolee, or as of May 2, 1964, whichever date is later, and: *(Check one)*

i. ☐ I am a native or citizen of Cuba and meet the description in (e) above.

j. ☐ I am the husband, wife or minor unmarried child of a Cuban, and meet the description in (f) above.

For USCIS Use Only

Returned	Receipt

Resubmitted

Reloc Sent

Reloc Rec'd

Applicant Interviewed

Section of Law
- ☐ Sec. 209(b), INA
- ☐ Sec. 13, Act of 9/11/57
- ☐ Sec. 245, INA
- ☐ Sec. 249, INA
- ☐ Sec. 2 Act of 11/2/66
- ☐ Sec. 2 Act of 11/2/66
- ☐ Other _____

Country Chargeable

Eligibility Under Sec. 245
- ☐ Approved Visa Petition
- ☐ Dependent of Principal Alien
- ☐ Special Immigrant
- ☐ Other _____

Preference

Action Block

To be Completed by *Attorney or Representative,* if any
☐ Fill in box if G-28 is attached to represent the applicant.
VOLAG #
ATTY State License #

Form I-485 (Rev. 04/22/05)N (Prior editions may be used until 9/30/05)

Part 3.   Processing information.

A. City/Town/Village of Birth	Current Occupation
Your Mother's First Name	Your Father's First Name

Give your name exactly how it appears on your Arrival/Departure Record (Form I-94)

Place of Last Entry Into the United States *(City/State)*	In what status did you last enter? *(Visitor, student, exchange alien, crewman, temporary worker, without inspection, etc.)*
Were you inspected by a U.S. Immigration Officer? ☐ Yes ☐ No	
Nonimmigrant Visa Number	Consulate Where Visa Was Issued
Date Visa Was Issued (mm/dd/yyyy)	Gender: ☐ Male ☐ Female	Marital Status: ☐ Married ☐ Single ☐ Divorced ☐ Widowed

Have you ever before applied for permanent resident status in the U.S.?   ☐ No   ☐ Yes. If you checked "Yes," give date and place of filing and final disposition.

B. List your present husband/wife, all of your sons and daughters (If you have none, write "none." If additional space is needed, use separate paper).

Family Name	Given Name	Middle Initial	Date of Birth *(mm/dd/yyyy)*
Country of Birth	Relationship	A #	Applying with you? ☐ Yes ☐ No
Family Name	Given Name	Middle Initial	Date of Birth *(mm/dd/yyyy)*
Country of Birth	Relationship	A #	Applying with you? ☐ Yes ☐ No
Family Name	Given Name	Middle Initial	Date of Birth *(mm/dd/yyyy)*
Country of Birth	Relationship	A #	Applying with you? ☐ Yes ☐ No
Family Name	Given Name	Middle Initial	Date of Birth *(mm/dd/yyyy)*
Country of Birth	Relationship	A #	Applying with you? ☐ Yes ☐ No
Family Name	Given Name	Middle Initial	Date of Birth *(mm/dd/yyyy)*
Country of Birth	Relationship	A #	Applying with you? ☐ Yes ☐ No

C. List your present and past membership in or affiliation with every political organization, association, fund, foundation, party, club, society or similar group in the United States or in other places since your 16th birthday. Include any foreign military service in this part. If none, write "none." Include the name(s) of organization(s), location(s), dates of membership from and to, and the nature of the organization(s). If additional space is needed, use a separate piece of paper.

_____

_____

_____

_____

_____

_____

Form I-485 (Rev. 04/22/05)N (Prior editons may be used 9/30/05) Page 2

Part 3. Processing information. *(Continued)*

Please answer the following questions. (If your answer is **"Yes"** on any one of these questions, explain on a separate piece of paper. Answering **"Yes"** does not necessarily mean that you are not entitled to adjust status or register for permanent residence.)

1. Have you ever, in or outside the United States:

    a. knowingly committed any crime of moral turpitude or a drug-related offense for which you have not been arrested? ☐ Yes ☐ No

    b. been arrested, cited, charged, indicted, fined or imprisoned for breaking or violating any law or ordinance, excluding traffic violations? ☐ Yes ☐ No

    c. been the beneficiary of a pardon, amnesty, rehabilitation decree, other act of clemency or similar action? ☐ Yes ☐ No

    d. exercised diplomatic immunity to avoid prosecution for a criminal offense in the United States? ☐ Yes ☐ No

2. Have you received public assistance in the United States from any source, including the United States government or any state, county, city or municipality (other than emergency medical treatment), or are you likely to receive public assistance in the future? ☐ Yes ☐ No

3. Have you ever:

    a. within the past ten years been a prostitute or procured anyone for prostitution, or intend to engage in such activities in the future? ☐ Yes ☐ No

    b. engaged in any unlawful commercialized vice, including, but not limited to, illegal gambling? ☐ Yes ☐ No

    c. knowingly encouraged, induced, assisted, abetted or aided any alien to try to enter the United States illegally? ☐ Yes ☐ No

    d. illicitly trafficked in any controlled substance, or knowingly assisted, abetted or colluded in the illicit trafficking of any controlled substance? ☐ Yes ☐ No

4. Have you ever engaged in, conspired to engage in, or do you intend to engage in, or have you ever solicited membership or funds for, or have you through any means ever assisted or provided any type of material support to any person or organization that has ever engaged or conspired to engage in sabotage, kidnapping, political assassination, hijacking or any other form of terrorist activity? ☐ Yes ☐ No

5. Do you intend to engage in the United States in:

    a. espionage? ☐ Yes ☐ No

    b. any activity a purpose of which is opposition to, or the control or overthrow of, the government of the United States, by force, violence or other unlawful means? ☐ Yes ☐ No

    c. any activity to violate or evade any law prohibiting the export from the United States of goods, technology or sensitive information? ☐ Yes ☐ No

6. Have you ever been a member of, or in any way affiliated with, the Communist Party or any other totalitarian party? ☐ Yes ☐ No

7. Did you, during the period from March 23, 1933 to May 8, 1945, in association with either the Nazi Government of Germany or any organization or government associated or allied with the Nazi Government of Germany, ever order, incite, assist or otherwise participate in the persecution of any person because of race, religion, national orgin or political opinion? ☐ Yes ☐ No

8. Have you ever engaged in genocide, or otherwise ordered, incited, assisted or otherwise participated in the killing of any person because of race, religion, nationality, ethnic origin or political opinion? ☐ Yes ☐ No

9. Have you ever been deported from the United States, or removed from the United States at government expense, excluded within the past year, or are you now in exclusion, deportation, removal or recission proceedings? ☐ Yes ☐ No

10. Are you under a final order of civil penalty for violating section 274C of the Immigration and Nationality Act for use of fraudulent documents or have you, by fraud or willful misrepresentation of a material fact, ever sought to procure, or procured, a visa, other documentation, entry into the United States or any immigration benefit? ☐ Yes ☐ No

11. Have you ever left the United States to avoid being drafted into the U.S. Armed Forces? ☐ Yes ☐ No

12. Have you ever been a J nonimmigrant exchange visitor who was subject to the two-year foreign residence requirement and have not yet complied with that requirement or obtained a waiver? ☐ Yes ☐ No

13. Are you now withholding custody of a U.S. citizen child outside the United States from a person granted custody of the child? ☐ Yes ☐ No

14. Do you plan to practice polygamy in the United States? ☐ Yes ☐ No

Form I-485 (Rev. 04/22/05)N (Prior editions may be used until 09/30/05) Page 3

Part 4.   Signature. *(Read the information on penalties in the instructions before completing this section. You must file this application while in the United States.)*

YOUR REGISTRATION WITH THE U.S. CITIZENSHIP AND IMMIGRATION SERVICES. "I understand and acknowledge that, under section 262 of the Immigration and Nationality Act (Act), as an alien who has been or will be in the United States for more than 30 days, I am required to register with the U.S. Citizenship and Immigration Services. I understand and acknowledge that, under section 265 of the Act, I am required to provide USCIS with my current address and written notice of any change of address within **ten** days of the change. I understand and acknowledge that USCIS will use the most recent address that I provide to USCIS, on any form containing these acknowledgements, for all purposes, including the service of a Notice to Appear should it be necessary for USCIS to initiate removal proceedings against me. I understand and acknowledge that if I change my address without providing written notice to USCIS, I will be held responsible for any communications sent to me at the most recent address that I provided to USCIS. I further understand and acknowledge that, if removal proceedings are initiated against me and I fail to attend any hearing, including an initial hearing based on service of the Notice to Appear at the most recent address that I provided to USCIS or as otherwise provided by law, I may be ordered removed in my absence, arrested by USCIS and removed from the United States."

SELECTIVE SERVICE REGISTRATION. The following applies to you if you are a male at least 18 years old, but not yet 26 years old, who is required to register with the Selective Service System: "I understand that my filing this adjustment of status application with the U.S. Citizenship and Immigration Services authorizes USCIS to provide certain registration information to the Selective Service System in accordance with the Military Selective Service Act. Upon USCIS acceptance of my application, I authorize USCIS to transmit to the Selective Service System my name, current address, Social Security Number, date of birth and the date I filed the application for the purpose of recording my Selective Service registration as of the filing date. If, however, USCIS does not accept my application, I further understand that, if so required, I am responsible for registering with the Selective Service by other means, provided I have not yet reached age 26."

 APPLICANT'S CERTIFICATION. I certify, under penalty of perjury under the laws of the United States of America, that this application and the evidence submitted with it is all true and correct. I authorize the release of any information from my records that the U.S. Citizenship and Immigration Services (USCIS) needs to determine eligibility for the benefit I am seeking.

Signature	*Print Your Name*	*Date*	*Daytime Phone Number*
			( )

NOTE: *If you do not completely fill out this form or fail to submit required documents listed in the instructions, you may not be found eligible for the requested document and this application may be denied.*

Part 5.   Signature of person preparing form, if other than above. (sign below)

I declare that I prepared this application at the request of the above person and it is based on all information of which I have knowledge.

Signature	*Print Your Name*	*Date*	*Daytime Phone Number*
			( )
Firm Name and Address			*E-mail Address (if any)*

OMB No. 1615-0026; Exp. 06/30/06

Department of Homeland Security
U.S. Citizenship and Immigration Services

**I-526, Immigrant Petition
by Alien Entrepreneur**

Instructions

Purpose of This Form.

This form is for use by an entrepreneur to petition the U.S. Citizenship and Immigration Services (USCIS) for status as an immigrant to the United States pursuant to section 203(b)(5) of the Immigration and Nationality Act, as amended. That section of the law pertains to immigrant visas for an investor in a new commercial enterprise. USCIS is comprised of offices of the former Immigration and Naturalization Service (INS).

Who May File.

You may file this petition for yourself if you have established a new commercial enterprise:

- In which you will engage in a managerial or policy-making capacity, and

- In which you have invested or are actively in the process of investing the amount required for the area in which the enterprise is located, and

- Which will benefit the U.S. ecomony, and

- Which will create full-time employment in the United States for at least ten U.S. citizens, permanent residents, or other immigrants authorized to be employed, other than yourself, your spouse, your sons or daughters, or any nonimmigrant aliens.

The establishment of a new commercial enterprise may include:

- Creation of a new business;

- The purchase of an existing business with simultaneous or subsequent restructuring or reorganization resulting in a new commercial enterprise; or

- The expansion of an existing business through investment of the amount required, so that a substantial change (at least 40 percent) in either the net worth, number of employees, or both, results.

The amount of investment required in a particular area is set by regulation. Unless adjusted downward for targeted areas or upward for areas of high employment, the amount of investment shall be **$1,000,000 (one million dollars)**. You may obtain additional information from our website at **www.uscis.gov,** or an American embassy or consulate abroad.

General Filing Instructions.

Please answer all questions by typing or clearly printing in black ink. Indicate that an item is not applicable with "N/A." If an answer to a question is "none," please write "none." If you need extra space to answer any item, attach a sheet of paper with your name and your A#, if any, and indicate the number of the item. Your petition must be properly signed and filed with the correct fee.

Initial Evidence Requirements.

The following evidence must be filed with your petition:

- Evidence that you have established a lawful business entity under the laws of the jurisdiction in the United States in which it is located, or, if you have made an investment in an existing business, evidence that your investment has caused a substantial (at least 40 percent) increase in the net worth of the business, the number of employees, or both.

  Such evidence shall consist of copies of articles of incorporation, certificate of merger or consolidation, partnership agreement, certificate of limited partnership, joint venture agreement, business trust agreement, or other similar organizational document; a certificate evidencing authority to do business in a state or municipality, or if such is not required, a statement to that effect; or evidence that the required amount of capital was transferred to an existing business resulting in a substantial increase in the net worth or number of employees, or both.

  This evidence must be in the form of stock purchase agreements, investment agreements, certified financial reports, payroll records or other similar instruments, agreements or documents evidencing the investment and the resulting substantial change.

- Evidence, if applicable, that your enterprise has been established in a targeted employment area. A targeted employment area is defined as a rural area or an area which has experienced high unemployment of at least 150 percent of the national average rate. A rural area is an area not within a metropolitan statistical area or not within the outer boundary of any city or town having a population of 20,000 or more.

- Evidence that you have invested or are actively in the process of investing the amount required for the area in which the business is located.

  Such evidence may include, but need not be limited to, copies of bank statements, evidence of assets that have been purchased for use in the enterprise, evidence of property transferred from abroad for use in the enterprise, evidence of monies transferred or committed to be transferred to the new commercial enterprise in exchange for shares of stock, any loan or mortgage, promissory note, security agreement, or other evidence of borrowing that is secured by assets of the petitioner.

- Evidence that capital is obtained through lawful means. The petition must be accompanied, as applicable, by: foreign business registration records, tax returns of any kind filed within the last five years in or outside the United States, evidence of other sources of capital, or certified copies of any judgment, pending governmental civil or criminal actions, or private civil actions against the petitioner from any court in or outside the United States within the past 15 years.

Form I-526 (Rev. 10/26/05)Y

- Evidence that the enterprise will create at least ten full-time positions for U.S. citizens, permanent residents, or aliens lawfully authorized to be employed (except yourself, your spouse, sons, or daughters, and any nonimmigrant aliens). Such evidence may consist of copies of relevant tax records, Forms I-9, or other similar documents, if the employees have already been hired, or a business plan showing when such employees will be hired within the next two years.

- Evidence that you are or will be engaged in the management of the enterprise, either through the exercise of day-to-day managerial control or through policy formulation. Such evidence may include a statement of your position title and a complete description of your duties, evidence that you are a corporate officer or hold a seat on the board of directors, or, if the new enterprise is a partnership, evidence that you are engaged in either direct management or policy-making activities.

Processing Information.

Acceptance.
Any petition that is not signed or accompanied by the correct fee will be rejected with a notice that it is deficient. You may correct the deficiency and resubmit the petition. However, a petition is not considered properly filed until accepted by USCIS.

Initial processing.
Once the petition has been accepted, it will be checked for completeness, including submission of the required initial evidence. If you do not completely fill out the form or file it without required initial evidence, you will not establish a basis for eligibility and we may deny your petition.

Requests for more information or interview.
We may request more information or evidence or we may request that you appear at a USCIS office for an interview. We may also request that you submit the originals of any copy. We will return these originals when they are no longer required.

Approval.
If you have established that you qualify for investor status, the petition will be approved. If you have requested that the petition be forwarded to an American embassy or consulate abroad, the petition will be sent there unless that consulate does not issue immigrant visas. If you are in the United States and state that you will apply for adjustment of status, and the evidence indicates you are not eligible for adjustment, the petition will be sent to an American embassy or consulate abroad. You will be notified in writing of the approval of the petition and where it has been sent, and the reason for sending it to a place other than the one requested, if applicable.

Meaning of petition approval.
Approval of a petition shows only that you have established that you have made a qualifying investment. It does not guarantee that the American embassy or consulate will issue the immigrant visa. There are other requirements that must be met before a visa can be issued. The American embassy or consulate will notify you of those requirements. Immigrant status granted based on this petition will be conditional. Two years after entry, the conditional investor will have to apply for the removal of conditions based on the ongoing nature of the investment.

Denial.
If you have not established that you qualify for the benefit sought, the petition will be denied. You will be notified in writing of the reasons for the denial.

Copies.

If these instructions state that a copy of a document may be filed with this application and you choose to send us the original, we may keep that original for our records.

Where to File.

If the new commercial enterprise is located, or will principally be doing business in: Alabama, Arkansas, Connecticut, Delaware, District of Columbia, Florida, Georgia, Kentucky, Louisiana, Mississippi, Maine, Maryland, Massachusetts, New Hampshire, New Jersey, New Mexico, New York, North Carolina, South Carolina, Oklahoma, Pennsylvania, Puerto Rico, Rhode Island, Tennessee, or Texas, Vermont, the U.S. Virgin Islands, Virginia or West Virginia, mail the petition to:

USCIS Texas Service Center
P.O. Box 852135
Mesquite, TX 75185-2135

If the new commercial enterprise is located, or will principally be doing business in: Alaska, Arizona, California, Colorado, Guam, Hawaii, Idaho, Illinois, Indiana, Iowa, Kansas, Michigan, Minnesota, Missouri, Montana, Nebraska, Nevada, North Dakota, Ohio, Oregon, South Dakota, Utah, Washington, Wisconsin or Wyoming, mail the petition to:

USCIS California Service Center
P.O. Box 10140
Laguna Niguel, CA 92607-0526

What Is the Fee?

The fee for this petition is **$480.00**.

The fee must be submitted in the exact amount. It cannot be refunded. **Do not mail cash.** All checks and money orders must be drawn on a bank or other institution located in the United States and must be payable in United States currency. The check or money order should be made payable to the **Department of Homeland Security**, unless:

- If you live in Guam and are filing this application there, make your check or money order payable to the "Treasurer, Guam."

- If you live in the U.S. Virgin Islands and are filing this application there, make your check or money order payable to the "Commissioner of Finance of the Virgin Islands."

Form I-526 (Rev. 10/26/05)Y Page 2

Checks are accepted subject to collection. A check returned due to insufficient funds will render the application and any document issued invalid. A charge of $30.00 will be imposed if a check in payment of a fee is not honored by the bank on which it is drawn.

When making out your check or money order, spell out Department of Homeland Security. Do not use the initials "USDHS" or "DHS."

How to Check If the Fee Is Correct.

The fee on this form is current as of the edition date appearing in the lower right corner of this page. However, because USCIS fees change periodically, you can verify if the fee is correct by following one of the steps below:

- Visit our website at **www.uscis.gov** and scroll down to "Forms and E-Filing" to check the appropriate fee, or

- Review the Fee Schedule included in your form package, if you called us to request the form, or

- Telephone our National Customer Service Center at **1-800-375-5283** and ask for the fee information.

USCIS Forms and Information.

To order USCIS forms, call our toll-free forms line at **1-800-870-3676**. You can also obtain information on immigration laws, regulations or procedures by telephoning our National Customer Service Center at **1-800-375-5283** or visiting our internet website at **www.uscis.gov.**

Use InfoPass for Appointments.

As an alternative to waiting in line for assistance at your local USCIS office, you can now schedule an appointment through our internet-based system, **InfoPass.** To access the system, visit our website at **www.uscis.gov.** Use the **InfoPass** appointment scheduler and follow the screen prompts to set up your appointment. **InfoPass** generates an electronic appointment notice that appears on the screen. Print the notice and take it with you to your appointment. The notice gives the time and date of your appointment, along with the address of the USCIS office.

Penalties.

If you knowingly and willfully falsify or conceal a material fact or submit a false document with this request, we will deny the benefit you are seeking and may deny any other immigration benefit. In addition, you will face severe penalties provided by law and may be subject to criminal prosecution.

Privacy Act Notice.

We ask for the information on this form and associated evidence to determine if you have established eligibility for the immigration benefit you are seeking. Our legal right to ask for this information is in 8 USC 1184, 1255 and 1258. We may provide this information to other government agencies. Failure to provide this information and any requested evidence may delay a final decision or result in denial of your petition.

Paperwork Reduction Act Notice.

A person is not required to respond to a collection of information unless it displays a currently valid OMB control number. We try to create forms and instructions that are accurate, can be easily understood and that impose the least possible burden on you to provide us with information. Often this is difficult because some immigration laws are very complex. Accordingly, the reporting burden for this collection of information is computed as follows: (1) learning about the law and form, 15 minutes; (2) completing the form, 25 minutes; and (3) assembling and filing the application, 35 minutes, for an estimated average of 1 hour and 15 minutes per response. If you have comments regarding the accuracy of this estimate or suggestions for making this form simpler, you may write to the U.S. Citizenship and Immigration Services, Regulatory Management Division, 111 Massachuetts Avenue, N.W., Washington, DC 20529; OMB No.1615-0026. **Do not mail your completed petition to this address.**

OMB No. 1615-0026; Exp. 06/30/06

Department of Homeland Security
U.S. Citizenship and Immigration Services

**I-526, Immigrant Petition
by Alien Entrepreneur**

Do Not Write in This Block - For USCIS Use Only (Except G-28 Block Below)		
Classification _____	**Action Block**	Fee Receipt
Priority Date _____		**To be completed by Attorney or Representative, if any** ☐ G-28 is attached Attorney's State License No. _____
Remarks:		

START HERE - Type or print in black ink.

Part 1.   Information about you.

Family Name | Given Name | Middle Name

Address:
In care of

Number and Street   Apt. #

City   State or Province   Country   Zip/Postal Code

Date of Birth (mm/dd/yyyy)   Country of Birth   Social Security # (if any)   A # (if any)

If you are in the United States, provide the following information: Date of Arrival (mm/dd/yyyy)   I-94 #

Current Nonimmigrant Status   Date Current Status Expires (mm/dd/yyyy)   Daytime Phone # with Area Code

Part 2.   Application type. (Check one)

a. ☐ This petition is based on an investment in a commercial enterprise in a targeted employment area for which the required amount of capital invested has been adjusted downward.

b. ☐ This petition is based on an investment in a commercial enterprise in an area for which the required amount of capital invested has been adjusted upward.

c. ☐ This petition is based on an investment in a commercial enterprise that is not in either a targeted area or in an upward adjustment area.

Part 3.   Information about your investment.

Name of commercial enterprise in which funds are invested

Street Address

Phone # with Area Code   Business organized as (corporation, partnership, etc.)

Kind of business (e.g. furniture manfacturer)   Date established (mm/dd/yyyy)   IRS Tax #

RECEIVED: _____   RESUBMITTED: _____   RELOCATED: SENT _____   REC'D _____

f

Part 3. Information about your investment. (Continued.)

Date of your initial investment (mm/dd/yyyy)		Amount of your initial investment	$
Your total capital investment in the enterprise to date	$	Percentage of the enterprise you own	

If you are not the sole investor in the new commercial enterprise, list on separate paper the names of all other parties (natural and non-natural) who hold a percentage share of ownership of the new enterprise and indicate whether any of these parties is seeking classification as an alien entrepreneur. Include the name, percentage of ownership and whether or not the person is seeking classification under section 203(b)(5). **NOTE:** A "natural" party would be an individual person and a "non-natural" party would be an entity such as a corporation, consortium, investment group, partnership, etc.

If you indicated in **Part 2** that the enterprise is in a targeted employment area or in an upward adjustment area, name the county and state: County State

Part 4. Additional information about the enterprise.

Type of Enterprise (check one):

☐ New commercial enterprise resulting from the creation of a new business.

☐ New commercial enterprise resulting from the purchase of an existing business.

☐ New commercial enterprise resulting from a capital investment in an existing business.

Composition of the Petitioner's Investment:

Total amount in U.S. bank account .... $

Total value of all assets purchased for use in the enterprise .... $

Total value of all property transferred from abroad to the new enterprise .... $

Total of all debt financing .... $

Total stock purchases .... $

Other (explain on separate paper) .... $

Total $

Income:

When you made the investment.........	Gross	$	Net	$	
Now..................................	Gross	$	Net	$	

Net worth:

When you made investment..............	Gross	$	Now	$	

Part 5. Employment creation information.

Number of full-time employees in the enterprise in U.S. (excluding you, your spouse, sons and daughters)

When you made your initial investment? [   ]   Now [   ]   Difference [   ]

How many of these new jobs were created by your investment? [   ]   How many additional new jobs will be created by your additional investment? [   ]

What is your position, office or title with the new commercial enterprise?

[   ]

Briefly describe your duties, activities and responsibilities.

[   ]

What is your salary? $ [   ]   What is the cost of your benefits? $ [   ]

Part 6. Processing information.

Check One:

☐ The person named in **Part 1** is now in the United States and an application to adjust status to permanent resident will be filed if this petition is approved.

☐ If the petition is approved and the person named in **Part 1** wishes to apply for an immigrant visa abroad, complete the following for that person:

Country of nationality: [   ]

Country of current residence or, if now in the United States, last permanent residence abroad: [   ]

If you provided a United States address in Part 1, print the person's foreign address:

[   ]

If the person's native alphabet is other than Roman letters, write the foreign address in the native alphabet:

[   ]

Is a Form I-485, Application for Adjustment of Status, attached to this petition?   ☐ Yes   ☐ No

Are you in deportation or removal proceedings?   ☐ Yes (Explain on separate paper)   ☐ No

Have you ever worked in the United States without permission?   ☐ Yes (Explain on separate paper)   ☐ No

Part 7. Signature. *Read the information on penalties in the instrucitons before completing this section.*

I certify, under penalty of perjury under the laws of the United States of America, that this petition and the evidence submitted with it is all true and correct. I authorize the release of any information from my records that the U.S. Citizenship and Immigration Services needs to determine eligibility for the benefit I am seeking.

Signature [   ]   Date [   ]

NOTE: *If you do not completely fill out this form or fail to the submit the required documents listed in the instructions, you may not be found eligible for the immigration benefit you are seeking and this petition may be denied.*

Part 8. Signature of person preparing form, if other than above. (Sign below)

I declare that I prepared this application at the request of the above person and it is based on all information of which I have knowledge.

Signature [   ]   Print Your Name [   ]   Date [   ]

Firm Name [   ]

Address [   ]   Daytime phone # with area code [   ]

U.S. Department of Justice
Immigration and Naturalization Service

OMB Approval No. 1115-0060

Certification by Designated School

SECTION A. This section must be completed by the student, as appropriate. *(Please print or type):*

1. Name:	*(Family in CAPS)*	*(First)*	*(Middle)*	2. Date of birth:

3. Student admission number:	4. Date first granted F-1 or M-1 status:

5. Level of education being sought:	6. Student's major field of study:

7. Describe the proposed employment for practical training:

Beginning date: _____ Ending date: _____ Number of hours per week: _____

8. List all periods of previously authorized employment for practical training:

A. Curricular or work/study:	B. Post completion of studies

Signature of student: _____ Date: _____

SECTION B.   This section must be completed by the designated school official (DSO) of the school the student is attending or was last authorized to attend:

9. I hereby certify that:

The student named above:

☐ Is taking a full course of study at this school, and the expected date of completion is: _____

☐ Is taking less than a full course of study at this school because: _____

☐ Completed the course of study at this school on (date): _____

☐ Did not complete the course of study. Terminated attendance on (date): _____

Check one:

☐ A. The employment is for practical training in the student's field of study. The student has been in the educational program for at least nine (9) months, is in good academic standing, and is eligible for the requested practical training in accordance with INS regulations at 8 CFR 214.2(f)(10). The training that the student will participate in is an integral part of an established curriculum.

☐ B. The employment is for an internship with a recognized international organization and is within the scope of the organization's sponsorship. The student is in good academic standing.

10. Name and title of DSO:	Signature:	Date:

11. Name of school:	School file number:	Telephone Number:

For Official Use Only
Microfilm Index Number:

(See instructions on reverse)

Form I-538 (Rev. 08/12/02)Y

Instructions

A student seeking authorization for off-campus employment (F-1 only) or practical training (F-1 and M-1) must submit as supporting documentation to Form I-765, Application for Employment Authorization, a certification by the designated school official (DSO) of the school the student is attending or was last authorized to attend.

Certification by the DSO is required of all students (F-1 and M-1) seeking authorization for employment off campus or practical training, including required or optional curricular practical training.

The DSO must certify on Form I-538 that the proposed employment is directly related to the student's field of study.

Where to Submit Certification.
A copy of the DSO's certification must be mailed to: ACS Students/Schools (STSC) Section, P.O. Box 170, London, KY 40741. Overnight carrier deliveries must be sent to: ACS - INS, INS Students/Schools (STSC) Section, 1084 South Laurel Road, London, KY 40744.

All students requesting school certification must complete questions 1 through 6. Students requesting a recommendation for practical training must complete questions 7 and 8. Answers to questions 7 through 9 may be continued on this page, if needed.

Since the I-538 is used by the DSO for certification purposes, no fee is required for the submission of this form.

NOTE: M-1 students seeking extensions of stay must file a completed Form I-539, Application to Extend/Change Nonimmigrant Status, supported by a current Form I-20M-N, as appropriate. The I-539 application must be submitted to the INS service center that has jurisdiction over the student's residence.

Reporting Burden.
An agency may not conduct or sponsor an information collection and a person is not required to respond to an information collection unless it contains a currently valid OMB control number. The public reporting burden for this collection of information is estimated to average 4 minutes per response, including the time for reviewing instructions, searching existing data sources, gathering and maintaining the data needed, and completing and reviewing the collection of information. Send comments regarding this burden estimate or any other aspect of this collection of information, including suggestions for reducing this burden, to: U.S. Department of Justice, Immigration and Naturalization Service, HQPDI, 425 I Street N.W., Room 4034, Washington, DC 20536; OMB No. 1115-0060. **DO NOT MAIL YOUR COMPLETED CERTIFICATION TO THIS ADDRESS.**

Comments: _____

_____

_____

_____

_____

_____

_____

_____

_____

_____

OMB No. 1615-0003; Expires 11/30/07

Department of Homeland Security
U.S. Citizenship and Immigration Service

I-539, Application to Extend/ Change Nonimmigrant Status

Instructions

NOTE: You have the option of submitting this paper version of Form I-539 according to form's instructions or you may file the application electronically. To file electronically, visit our internet website at **www. uscis.gov** and follow the instructions on e-filing. Whether you submit this paper form or e-file, the U.S. Citizenship and Immigration Services (USCIS) recomends that you retain a copy of your application and supporting documents for your records. USCIS is comprised of offices of the former Immigration and Naturalization Service (INS).

Purpose of This Form.

You should use this form if you are one of the nonimmigrants listed below and wish to apply to the U.S. Citizenship and Immigration Services (USCIS) for an extension of stay or a change to another nonimmigrant status.

In certain situations, you may use this form to apply for an initial nonimmigrant status.

You may also use this form if you are a nonimmigrant F-1 or M-1 student applying for reinstatement.

Who May File/Initial Evidence.

Extension of Stay or Change of Status:

Nonimmigrants in the United States may apply for an extension of stay or a change of status on this form, except as noted in these instructions under the heading, "Who May Not File."

Multiple Applicants.

You may include your spouse and your unmarried children under age 21 years as co-applicants in your application for the same extension or change of status, if you are all now in the same status or they are all in derivative status.

Required Documentation - Form I-94, Nonimmigrant Arrival/Departure Record.

You are required to submit with your Form I-539 application the original or copy, front and back, of Form I-94 of each person included in your application. If the original Form I-94 or required copy cannot be submitted with this application, include a Form I-102, Application for Replacement/Initial Nonimmigrant Arrival/Departure Document, with the required fee.

Valid Passport.

If you were required to have a passport to be admitted into the United States, you must maintain the validity of your passport during your nonimmigrant stay. If a required passport is not valid when you file the Form I-539 application, submit an explanation with your form.

Additional Evidence.

You may be required to submit additional evidence noted in these instructions.

Nonimmigrant Categories.

This form may be used by the following nonimmigrants listed in alphabetical order:

- **An A, Ambassador, Public Minister, or Career Diplomatic or Consular Officer and their immediate family members.**

  You must submit a copy, front and back, of the Form I-94 of each person included in the application and a Form I-566, Interagency Record of Individual Requesting Change, Adjustment to, or from, A to G Status; or Requesting A, G or NATO Dependent Employment Authorization, certified by the U.S. Department of State to indicate your accredited status.

  NOTE: An A-1 or A-2 nonimmigrant is not required to pay a fee with the Form I-539 application.

- **An A-3, Attendant or Servant of an A nonimmigrant and the A-3's immediate family members.**

  You must submit a copy, front and back, of the Form I-94 of each person included in the application.

  The application must be filed with:

  -- A copy of your employer's Form I-94 or approval notice demonstrating A status;

  -- An original letter from your employer describing your duties and stating that he or she intends to personally employ you; and arrangements you have made to depart from the United States; and

  -- An original Form I-566, certified by the Department of State, indicating your employer's continuing accredited status.

- **A B-1, Visitor for Business or B-2, Visitor for Pleasure.**

  If you are filing for an extension/change, you must file your application with the original Form I-94 of each person included in your application. In addition, you must submit a written statement explaining in detail:

  -- The reasons for your request;

  -- Why your extended stay would be temporary, including what arrangements you have made to depart from the United States; and

  -- Any effect the extended stay may have on your foreign employment or residency.

- **Dependents of an E, Treaty Trader or Investor.**

  If you are filing for an extension/change of status as the dependent of an E, this application must be submitted with:

-- The Form I-129, Petition for Alien Worker, filed for that E or a copy of the filing receipt noting that the petition is pending with USCIS;

-- A copy of the E's Form I-94 or approval notice showing that he or she has already been granted status to the period requested on your application; and

-- Evidence of relationship (example: birth or marriage certificate).

- **NOTE:** An employer or investor should file Form I-129 to request an extension/change to E status for an employee, prospective employee, or the investor. Dependents of E employees should file for an extension/change of status on this form, not Form I-129.

- **An F-1, Academic Student.**

  To request a change to F-1 status or to apply for reinstatement as an F-1 student, you must submit your original Form I-94, as well as the original Form I-94 of each person included in the application.

  Your application must include your original Form I-20 (Certificate of Eligibility for Nonimmigrant Student) issued by the school where you will study. To request either a change or reinstatement, you must submit documentation that demonstrates your ability to pay for your studies and support yourself while you are in the United States.

  F-1 Extensions:

  Do not use this form to request an extension. For information concerning extensions, contact your designated school official at your institution.

  F-1 Reinstatement:

  You will only be considered for reinstatement as an F-1 student if you establish:

  -- That the violation of status was due solely to circumstances beyond your control or that failure to reinstate you would result in extreme hardship;

  -- You are pursuing or will pursue a full course of study;

  -- You have not been employed without authorization; and

  -- You are not in removal proceedings.

- **A G, Designated Principal Resident Representative of a Foreign Government and his or her immediate family members.**

  You must submit a copy, front and back, of the Form I-94, of each person included in the application, and a Form I-566, certified by the Department of State to indicate your accredited status.

  NOTE: A G-1 through G-4 nonimmigrant is not required to pay a fee with the I-539 application.

- **A G-5, Attendant or Servant of a G nonimmigrant and the G-5's immediate family members.**

  You must submit a copy, front and back, of the Form I-94 of each person included in the application.

  The application must also be filed with:

  -- A copy of your employer's Form I-94 or approval notice demonstrating G status;

  -- An original letter from your employer describing your duties and stating that he or she intends to personally employ you; and arrangements you have made to depart from the United States; and

  -- An original Form I-566, certified by the Department of State, indicating your employer's continuing accredited status.

- **Dependents of an H, Temporary Worker.**

  If you are filing for an extension/change of status as the dependent of an employee who is an H temporary worker, this application must be submitted with:

  -- The Form I-129 filed for that employee or a copy of the filing receipt noting that the petition is pending with the USCIS;

  -- A copy of the employee's Form I-94 or approval notice showing that he or she has already been granted status to the period requested on your application; and

  -- Evidence of relationship (example: birth or marriage certificate).

  NOTE: An employer should file Form I-129 to request an extension/change to H status for an employee or prospective employee. Dependents of such employees should file for an extension/change of status on this form, not on Form I-129.

- **A J-1, Exchange Visitor.**

  If you are requesting a change of status to J-1, your application must be filed with an original Form IAP-66, Certificate of Eligibility for Exchange Visitor Status, issued by your program sponsor. You must also submit your original Form I-94, as well as the original Form I-94 of each person included in the application.

  NOTE: A J-1 exchange visitor whose status is for the purpose of receiving graduate medical education or training, who has not received the appropriate waiver, is ineligible for any change of status. Also, a J-1 subject to the foreign residence requirement, who has not received a waiver of that requirement, is only eligible for a change of status to A or G.

J-1 Extensions:

If you are seeking an extension, contact the responsible officer of your program for information about this procedure.

J-1 Reinstatement:

If you are a J-1 exchange visitor seeking reinstatement, you may need to apply for such approval by the Department of State's Office of Education and Cultural Affairs. Contact the responsible officer at your sponsoring program for information on the reinstatement filing procedure.

● **Dependents of an L, Intracompany Transferee.**

If you are filing for an extension/change of status as the dependent of an employee who is an L intracompany transferee, this application must be submitted with:

-- The Form I-129 filed for that employee or a copy of the filing receipt noting that the petition is pending with USCIS;

-- A copy of the employee's Form I-94 or approval notice showing that he or she has already been granted status to the period requested on your application; and

-- Evidence of relationship (example: birth or marriage certificate).

NOTE: An employer should file Form I-129 to request an extension/change to L status for an employee or prospective employee. Dependents of such employees should file for an extension/change of status on this form, not on Form I-129.

● **An M-1, Vocational or Non-Academic Student.**

To request a change to or extension of M-1 status, or apply for reinstatement as an M-1 student, you must submit your original Form I-94, as well as the original Form I-94 of each person included in the application.

Your application must include your original Form I-20 issued by the school where you will study. To request either extension/change or reinstatement, you must submit documentation that demonstrates your ability to pay for your studies and support yourself while you are in the United States.

M-1 Reinstatement:

You will only be considered for reinstatement as an M-1 student if you establish:

-- That the violation of status was due solely to circumstances beyond your control or that failure to reinstate you would result in extreme hardship;

-- You are pursuing or will pursue a full course of study;

-- You have not been employed without authorization; and

-- You are not in removal proceedings.

NOTE: If you are an M-1 student, you are not eligible for a change to F-1 status and you are not eligible for a change to any H status, if the training you received as an M-1 helps you qualify for the H status. Also, you may not be granted a change to M-1 status for training to qualify for H status.

● **An N-1 or N-2, Parent or Child of an Alien Admitted as a Special Immigrant under section 101(a)(27)(I) of the INA.**

You must file the application with a copy, front and back, of your Form I-94 and a copy of the special immigrant's permanent resident card and proof of the relationship (example: birth or marriage certificate).

● **Dependents of an O, Alien of Extraordinary Ability or Achievement.**

If you are filing for an extension/change of status as the dependent of an employee who is classified as an O nonimmigrant, this application must be submitted with:

-- The Form I-129 filed for that employee or a copy of the filing receipt noting that the petition is pending with USCIS;

-- A copy of the employee's Form I-94 or approval notice showing that he or she has already been granted status to the period requested on your application; and

-- Evidence of relationship (example: birth or marriage certificate).

NOTE: An employer should file Form I-129 to request an extension/change to an O status for an employee or prospective employee. Dependents of such employees should file for an extension/change of status on this form, not on Form I-129.

● **Dependents of a P, Artists, Athletes and Entertainers.**

If you are filing for an extension/change of status as the dependent of an employee who is classified as a P nonimmigrant, this application must be submitted with:

-- The Form I-129 filed for that employee or a copy of the filing receipt noting that the petition is pending with the USCIS;

-- A copy of the employee's Form I-94 or approval notice showing that he or she has already been granted status to the period requested on your application; and

-- Evidence of relationship (example: birth or marriage certificate).

NOTE: An employer should file Form I-129 to request an extension/change to P status for an employee or prospective employee. Dependents of such employees should file for an extension/change of status on this form, not on Form I-129.

- **Dependents of an R, Religious Worker.**

If you are filing for an extension/change of status as the dependent of an employee who is classified as an R nonimmigrant, this application must be submitted with:

-- The Form I-129 filed for that employee or a copy of the filing receipt noting that the petition is pending with USCIS;

-- A copy of the employee's Form I-94 or approval notice showing that he or she has already been granted status to the period requested on your application; and

-- Evidence of relationship (example: birth or marriage certificate).

- **TD Dependents of TN Nonimmigrants.**

TN nonimmigrants are citizens of Canada or Mexico who are coming as business persons to the United States to engage in business activities at a professional level, pursuant to the North American Free Trade Agreement (NAFTA). The dependents (spouse or unmarried minor children) of a TN nonimmigrant are designated as TD nonimmigrants. A TD nonimmigrant may accompany or follow to join the TN professional. TD nonimmigrants may not work in the United States.

The Form I-539 shall be used by a TD nonimmigrant to request an extension of stay or by an applicant to request a change of nonimmigrant status to TD classification.

If you are filing for an extension/change of status as the dependent of an employee who is classified as a TN nonimmigrant, this application must be submitted with:

-- The Form I-129 filed for that employee or a copy of the filing receipt noting that the petition is pending with USCIS;

-- A copy of the employee's Form I-94 or approval notice showing that he or she has already been granted status to the period requested on your application; and

-- Evidence of relationship (example: birth or marriage certificate).

- **A V, Spouse or Child of a Lawful Permanent Resident.**

Use this Form I-539 if you are physically present in the United States and wish to request initial status or change status to a V nonimmigrant, or to request an extension of your current V nonimmigrant status.

Applicants should follow the instructions on this form and the attached instructions to Supplement A to Form I-539, Filing Instructions for V Nonimmigrants. The supplement contains additional information and the location where V applicants must file their applications.

NOTE: In addition to the **$200.00** application fee required to file Form I-539, V applicants are required to pay a **$70.00** biometric services fee for USCIS to take their fingerprints.

If necessary USCIS may also take the V applicants photograph and signature as part of the biometric services.

Notice to V Nonimmigrants.

The Legal Immigration Family Equity Act (LIFE), signed into law on December 21, 2000, created a new V visa. This nonimmigrant status allows certain persons to reside legally in the United States and to travel to and from the United States while they wait to obtain lawful permanent residence.

In order to be eligible for a V visa, all of the following conditions must be met:

- You must be the spouse or the unmarried child of a lawful permanent resident;

- A Form I-130, Petition for Alien Relative, must have been filed for you by your permanent resident spouse on or before December 21, 2000; and

- You must have been waiting for at least three years after the Form I-130 was filed for you;

Or you must be the unmarried child (under 21 years of age) of a person who meets the three requirements listed above.

V visa holders will be eligible to adjust to lawful permanent resident status once an immigrant visa becomes available to them. While they are waiting, V visa holders may be authorized to work following their submission and USCIS approval of their Form I-765, Application for Employment Authorization.

WARNING: Be advised that persons in V status who have been in the United States illegally for more than 180 days may trigger the grounds of inadmissibility regarding unlawful presence (for the applicable 3-year or 10-year bar to admission) if they leave the United States. Their departure may prevent them from adjusting status as a permanent resident.

Who May Not File.

You may not be granted an extension or change of status if you were admitted under the Visa Waiver Program or if your current status is:

- An alien in transit (C) or in transit without a visa (TWOV);

- A crewman (D); or

- A fiance'(e) or dependent of a fiance'(e) (K)(1) or (K)(2).

A spouse (K-3) of a U.S. citizen and their children (K-4), accorded such status pursuant to the LIFE Act, may not change to another nonimmigrant status.

EXCEPTION: A K-3 and K-4 are eligible to apply for an extension of status. They should file for an extension during the processing of the Form I-130 filed on their behalf and up to completion of their adjustment of status application.

NOTE: Any nonimmigrant (A to V) may not change their status to K-3 or K-4.

General Filing Instructions.

Please answer all questions by typing or clearly printing in black ink. Indicate that an item is not applicable with "N/A." If the answer is "none," please so state. If you need extra space to answer any item, attach a sheet of paper with your name and your alien registration number (A#), if any, and indicate the number of the item to which the answer refers. Your application must be filed with the required initial evidence. Your application must be properly signed and filed with the correct fee. If you are under 14 years of age, your parent or guardian may sign your application.

Original and Copies.

If these instructions state that a copy of a document may be filed with this application and you choose to send us the original, we will keep that original document in our records.

Translations.

Any foreign language document must be accompanied by a full English translation that the translator has certified as complete and correct, and by the translator's certification that he or she is competent to translate the foreign language into English.

When and Where to File.

You must submit an application for extension of stay or change of status before your current authorized stay expires. We suggest you file at least 45 days before your stay expires, or as soon as you determine your need to change status. Failure to file before the expiration date may be excused if you demonstrate when you file the application that:

- The delay was due to extraordinary circumstances beyond your control;
- The length of the delay was reasonable;
- You have not otherwise violated your status;
- You are still a bona fide nonimmigrant; and
- You are not in removal proceedings.

If you are filing as a V applicant, follow the instructions on the Supplement A to Form I-539, Filing Instructions for V Nonimmigrants, on where to file your application.

If you are filing for reinstatement as an F-1 or M-1 student, submit this application at your local USCIS office. For information on how to use our InfoPass system to make an appointment at your local USCIS office, visit our website at **www.uscis.gov.**

If you are a TD filing for an extension of stay or requesting a change to a nonimmigrant TD status, mail your application to:

> **USCIS Nebraska Service Center**
> **P.O. Box 87539**
> **Lincoln, NE 68501-7539**

If you are an E dependent filing for an extension of stay and you live in Alabama, Arkansas, Connecticut, Delaware, District of Columbia, Florida, Georgia, Kentucky, Louisiana, Maine, Maryland, Massachusetts, Mississippi, New Hampshire, New Jersey, New Mexico, New York, North Carolina, Oklahoma, Pennsylvania, Puerto Rico, Rhode Island, South Carolina, Tennessee, Texas, the U.S. Virgin Islands, Vermont, Virginia or West Virginia, mail your application to:

> **USCIS Texas Service Center**
> **P.O. Box 851182**
> **Mesquite, TX 75185-1182**

If you are an E dependent filing for an extension of stay and you live anywhere else in the United States, mail your application to:

> **USCIS California Service Center**
> **P.O. Box 10539**
> **Laguna Niguel, CA 92607-1053**

In all other instances, mail your application to the USCIS Service Center listed below having jurisdiction over where you live in the United States.

If you live in Connecticut, Delaware, District of Columbia, Maine, Maryland, Massachusetts, New Hampshire, New Jersey, New York, Pennsylvania, Puerto Rico, Rhode Island, the U.S. Virgin Islands, Vermont, Virginia or West Virginia, mail your application to:

> **USCIS Vermont Service Center**
> **75 Lower Welden Street**
> **St. Albans, VT 05479-0001**

If you live in Alabama, Arkansas, Florida, Georgia, Kentucky, Louisiana, Mississippi, New Mexico, North Carolina, Oklahoma, South Carolina, Tennessee or Texas, mail your application to:

> **USCIS Texas Service Center**
> **P.O. Box 851182**
> **Mesquite, TX 75185-1182**

If you live in Arizona, California, Guam, Hawaii or Nevada, mail your application to:

> **USCIS California Service Center,**
> **P.O. Box 10539**
> **Laguna Niguel, CA 92607-1053**

If you live elsewhere in the United States, mail your application to:

> **USCIS Nebraska Service Center**
> **P.O. Box 87539**
> **Lincoln, NE 68501-7539**

What Is the Fee?

The fee for this application is **$200.00**, except for certain A and G nonimmigrants who are not required to pay a fee, as noted in these instructions.

The fee must be submitted in the exact amount. It cannot be refunded. **Do not mail cash.**

All checks and money orders must be drawn on a bank or other institution located in the United States and must be payable in U.S. currency.

The check or money order should be made payable to the **Department of Homeland Security**, except that:

-- If you live in Guam, make your check or money order payable to the "Treasurer, Guam."

-- If you live in the U.S. Virgin Islands, make your check or money order payable to the "Commissioner of Finance of the Virgin Islands."

Checks are accepted subject to collection. An uncollected check will render the application and any document issued invalid. A charge of $30.00 will be imposed if a check in payment of a fee is not honored by the bank on which it is drawn.

How to Check If the Fee Is Correct.

The fee on this form is current as of the edition date appearing in the lower right corner of this page. However, because USCIS fees change periodically, you can verify if the fee is correct by following one of the steps below:

- Visit our website at **www.uscis.gov** and scroll down to "Forms and E-Filing" to check the appropriate fee, or

- Review the Fee Schedule included in your form package, if you called us to request the form, or

- Telephone our National Customer Service Center at **1-800-375-5283** and ask for the fee information.

NOTE: If your petition or application requires a biometric services fee for USCIS to take your fingerprints, photograph or signature, use the same procedure above to confirm the biometrics fee.

Processing Information.

Acceptance.

Any application that is not signed or is not accompanied by the correct fee will be rejected with a notice that the application is deficient. You may correct the deficiency and resubmit the application. An application is not considered properly filed until accepted by USCIS.

Initial Processing.

Once the application has been accepted, it will be checked for completeness. If you do not completely fill out the form, or file it without the required initial evidence, you will not establish a basis for eligibility and we may deny your application.

Requests for More Information or Interview.

We may request more information or evidence or we may request that you appear at a USCIS office for an interview. We may also request that you submit the originals of any copy. We will return these originals when they are no longer required.

Decision.

An application for extension of stay, change of status, initial status or reinstatement, may be approved at the discretion of USCIS. You will be notified in writing of the decision on your application.

Penalties.

If you knowingly and willfully falsify or conceal a material fact or submit a false document with this application, we will deny the benefit you are seeking and may deny any other immigration benefit. In addition, you will face severe penalties provided by law and may be subject to criminal prosecution.

Privacy Act Notice.

We ask for the information on this form and associated evidence to determine if you have established eligibility for the immigration benefit you are seeking. Our legal right to ask for this information is in 8 U.S.C. 1184 and 1258. We may provide this information to other government agencies. Failure to provide this information and any requested evidence may delay a final decision or result in denial of your request.

USCIS Forms and Information.

To order USCIS forms, call our toll-free forms line at **1-800-870-3676**. If you need information on immigration laws, regulations or procedures call our National Customer Service Center at **1-800-375-5283** or visit our internet website at **www.uscis.gov**.

Department of Homeland Security
U.S. Citizenship and Immigration Services

OMB No. 1115-0093; Expires 11/30/07
**I-539, Application to Extend/
Change Nonimmigrant Status**

START HERE - Please type or print in black ink.

For USCIS Use Only

Part 1.   Information about you.

Family Name	Given Name	Middle Name

Address -
In care of -

Street Number and Name		Apt. #

City	State	Zip Code	Daytime Phone #

Country of Birth	Country of Citizenship

Date of Birth (mm/dd/yyyy)	U. S. Social Security # (if any)	A # (if any)

Date of Last Arrival Into the U.S.	I-94 #

Current Nonimmigrant Status	Expires on (mm/dd/yyyy)

USCIS Use Only column:

Returned

Date

Resubmitted

Date

Reloc Sent

Date

Reloc Rec'd

Date

Part 2.   Application type. *(See instructions for fee.)*

1. I am applying for: *(Check one.)*
   a. ☐ An extension of stay in my current status.
   b. ☐ A change of status. The new status I am requesting is:
   c. ☐ Other: *(Describe grounds of eligibility.)*

2. Number of people included in this application: *(Check one.)*
   a. ☐ I am the only applicant.
   b. ☐ Members of my family are filing this application with me.
      The total number of people (including me) in the application is:
      (Complete the supplement for each co-applicant.)

☐ Applicant Interviewed on

Date

☐ *Extension Granted to (Date):*

Change of Status/Extension Granted
   New Class: From *(Date)*: _____
      _____   To *(Date)*: _____

Part 3.   Processing information.

1. I/We request that my/our current or requested status be extended until (mm/dd/yyyy):
2. Is this application based on an extension or change of status already granted to your spouse, child or parent?
   ☐ No ☐ Yes. USCIS Receipt #
3. Is this application based on a separate petition or application to give your spouse, child or parent an extension or change of status? ☐ No ☐ Yes, filed with this I-539.
   ☐ Yes, filed previously and pending with USCIS. Receipt #:
4. If you answered "Yes" to Question 3, give the name of the petitioner or applicant:

If the petition or application is pending with USCIS, also give the following data:

Office filed at	Filed on (mm/dd/yyyy)

If Denied:
☐ Still within period of stay
☐ S/D to: _____
☐ Place under docket control

Remarks:

Action Block

Part 4.   Additional information.

1. For applicant #1, provide passport information: Valid to: (mm/dd/yyyy)
   Country of Issuance
2. Foreign Address: Street Number and Name   Apt. #

City or Town	State or Province

Country	Zip/Postal Code

To Be Completed by
***Attorney or Representative**, if any*

☐ Fill in box if G-28 is attached to represent the applicant.

ATTY State License #

f

Form I-539 (Rev. 10/26/05)Y

Part 4. Additional information.

3. Answer the following questions. If you answer "Yes" to any question, explain on separate sheet of paper.	Yes	No
a. Are you, or any other person included on the application, an applicant for an immigrant visa?	☐	☐
b. Has an immigrant petition ever been filed for you or for any other person included in this application?	☐	☐
c. Has a Form I-485, Application to Register Permanent Residence or Adjust Status, ever been filed by you or by any other person included in this application?	☐	☐
d. Have you, or any other person included in this application, ever been arrested or convicted of any criminal offense since last entering the U.S.?	☐	☐
e. Have you, or any other person included in this application, done anything that violated the terms of the nonimmigrant status you now hold?	☐	☐
f. Are you, or any other person included in this application, now in removal proceedings?	☐	☐
g. Have you, or any other person included in this application, been employed in the U.S. since last admitted or granted an extension or change of status?	☐	☐

- If you answered "Yes" to Question 3f, give the following information concerning the removal proceedings on the attached page entitled "**Part 4. Additional information. Page for answers to 3f and 3g.**" Include the name of the person in removal proceedings and information on jurisdiction, date proceedings began and status of proceedings.

- If you answered "No" to Question 3g, fully describe how you are supporting yourself on the attached page entitled "**Part 4. Additional information. Page for answers to 3f and 3g.**" Include the source, amount and basis for any income.

- If you answered "Yes" to Question 3g, fully describe the employment on the attached page entitled "**Part 4. Additional information. Page for answers to 3f and 3g.**" Include the name of the person employed, name and address of the employer, weekly income and whether the employment was specifically authorized by USCIS.

Part 5. Signature. (*Read the information on penalties in the instructions before completing this section. You must file this application while in the United States.*)

I certify, under penalty of perjury under the laws of the United States of America, that this application and the evidence submitted with it is all true and correct. I authorize the release of any information from my records that the U.S. Citizenship and Immigration Services needs to determine eligibility for the benefit I am seeking.

Signature	Print your Name	Date
Daytime Telephone Number	E-Mail Address	

NOTE: *If you do not completely fill out this form or fail to submit required documents listed in the instructions, you may not be found eligible for the requested benefit and this application may be denied.*

Part 6. Signature of person preparing form, if other than above. (*Sign below.*)

I declare that I prepared this application at the request of the above person and it is based on all information of which I have knowledge.

Signature	Print your Name	Date
Firm Name and Address	Daytime Telephone Number (*Area Code and Number*)	
	Fax Number (*Area Code and Number*)	E-Mail Address

Form I-539 (Rev. 10/26/05)Y Page 2

Part 4. Additional information. Page for answers to 3f and 3g.

If you answered "Yes" to Question 3f in Part 4 on page 3 of this form, give the following information concerning the removal proceedings. Include the name of the person in removal proceedings and information on jurisdiction, date proceedings began and status of procedings.

If you answered "No" to Question 3g in Part 4 on page 3 of this form, fully describe how you are supporting yourself. Include the source, amount and basis for any income.

If you answered "Yes" to Question 3g in Part 4 on page 3 of this form, fully describe the employment. Include the name of the person employed, name and address of the employer, weekly income and whether the employment was specifically authorized by USCIS.

Supplement -1
Attach to Form I-539 when more than one person is included in the petition or application.
(List each person separately. Do not include the person named in the form.)

Family Name	Given Name	Middle Name	Date of Birth (mm/dd/yyyy)
Country of Birth	County of Citizenship	U.S. Social Security # (if any)	A # (if any)

Date of Arrival (mm/dd/yyyy)		I-94 #	

Current Nonimmigrant Status:		Expires on (mm/dd/yyyy)	

Country Where Passport Issued		Expiration Date (mm/dd/yyyy)	

Family Name	Given Name	Middle Name	Date of Birth (mm/dd/yyyy)
Country of Birth	Country of Citizenship	U.S. Social Security # (if any)	A # (if any)

Date of Arrival (mm/dd/yyyy)		I-94 #	

Current Nonimmigrant Status:		Expires on (mm/dd/yyyy)	

Country Where Passport Issued		Expiration Date (mm/dd/yyyy)	

Family Name	Given Name	Middle Name	Date of Birth (mm/dd/yyyy)
Country of Birth	Country of Citizenship	U.S. Social Security # (if any)	A # (if any)

Date of Arrival (mm/dd/yyyy)		I-94 #	

Current Nonimmigrant Status:		Expires on (mm/dd/yyyy)	

Country Where Passport Issued		Expiration Date (mm/dd/yyyy)	

Family Name	Given Name	Middle Name	Date of Birth (mm/dd/yyyy)
Country of Birth	Country of Citizenship	U.S. Social Security # (if any)	A # (if any)

Date of Arrival (mm/dd/yyyy)		I-94 #	

Current Nonimmigrant Status:		Expires on (mm/dd/yyyy)	

Country Where Passport Issued		Expiration Date (mm/dd/yyyy)	

Family Name	Given Name	Middle Name	Date of Birth (mm/dd/yyyy)
Country of Birth	Country of Citizenship	U.S. Social Security # (if any)	A # (if any)

Date of Arrival (mm/dd/yyyy)		I-94 #	

Current Nonimmigrant Status:		Expires on (mm/dd/yyyy)	

Country Where Passport Issued		Expiration Date (mm/dd/yyyy)	

If you need additional space, attach a separate sheet(s) of paper.
Place your name, A #, if any, date of birth, form number and application date at the top of the sheet(s) of paper.

Form I-539 (Rev. 10/26/05)Y Page 4

OMB No. 1615-0028; Expires 08/31/08

Department of Homeland Security
U.S. Citizenship and Immigration Services

**I-600A, Application for Advance
Processing of Orphan Petition**

Instructions

What Is the Purpose of This Form?

This form is used by a U.S. citizen who plans to adopt a foreign-born orphan but does not have a specific child in mind. "Advance Processing" enables USCIS to first adjudicate the application that relates to the qualifications of the applicant(s) as a prospective adoptive parent(s).

Additionally, this form may be used in cases where the child is known and the prospective adoptive parent(s) are traveling to the country where the child is located. However, it is important that prospective adoptive parent(s) be aware that the child must remain in the foreign country where he or she is located until the processing is completed.

NOTE: This Form I-600A application is not a petition to classify an orphan as an immediate relative. Form I-600, Petition to Classify Orphan as an Immediate Relative, is used for that purpose.

1. What Are the Eligibility Requirements?

A. Eligibility for advance processing application (Form I-600A).

An application for advance processing may be filed by a married U.S. citizen and spouse. The spouse of the applicant does not need to be a U.S. citizen; however, he or she must be in a lawful immigration status. An application for advance processing may also be filed by an unmarried U.S citizen who is at least 24 years of age, provided that he or she will be at least 25 at the time of adoption and the filing of an orphan petition on behalf of a child.

B. Eligibility for orphan petition (Form I-600).

In addition to the requirements concerning the citizenship and age of the applicant described above in Instruction **1. A.** when a child is located and identified the following eligibility requirements will apply:

(1) Child.

Under U.S. immigration law, an orphan is an alien child who has no parents because of the death or disappearance of, abandonment or desertion by, or separation or loss from both parents.

An orphan is also a child who has only one parent who is not capable of taking care of the orphan and who has, in writing, irrevocably released the orphan for emigration and adoption.

A petition to classify an alien as an orphan (Form I-600) may not be filed on behalf of a child who is present in the United States, unless that child is in parole status and has not been adopted in the United States.

The petition must be filed before the child's 16th birthday.

(2) Adoption abroad.

If the orphan was adopted abroad, it must be established that both the married applicant and spouse or the unmarried applicant personally saw and observed the child prior to or during the adoption proceedings. The adoption decree must show that a married prospective adoptive parent and spouse adopted the child jointly or that an unmarried prospective parent was at least 25 years of age at the time of the adoption and filing of Form I-600.

(3) Proxy adoption abroad.

If both the applicant and spouse or the unmarried applicant did not personally see and observe the child prior to or during the adoption proceedings abroad, the applicant (and spouse, if married) must submit a statement indicating the applicant's (and, if married, the spouse's) willingness and intent to readopt the child in the United States. If requested, the applicant must submit a statement by an official of the state in which the child will reside that readoption is permissible in that State. In addition, evidence must be submitted to show compliance with the preadoption requirements, if any, of that State.

(4) Preadoption requirements.

If the orphan has not been adopted abroad, the applicant and spouse or the unmarried applicant must establish that the child will be adopted in the United States by the prospective applicant and spouse jointly or by the unmarried prospective applicant, and that the preadoption requirements, if any, of the State of the orphan's proposed residence have been met.

2. What Are the Requirements to File?

A. Proof of U. S. citizenship of the prospective adoptive parent(s).

(1) If a U.S. citizen by birth in the United States, submit a copy of the birth certificate issued by the civil registrar, vital statistics office or other civil authority. If a birth certificate is not available, submit a statement from the appropriate civil authority certifying that a birth certificate is not available. In such a situation, secondary evidence must be submitted, including:

- **Church records** bearing the seal of the church showing the baptism, dedication or comparable rite occurred within two months after birth and showing the date and place of the prospective adoptive parent's birth, date of the religious ceremony and the names of the parents;

- School Records issued by the authority (perferably the first school attended) showing the date of admission to the school, prospective adoptive parent's date of birth or age at the time, the place of birth and the names of the parents;

Form I-600A Instructions (Rev. 10/26/05) Y

- **Census records** (state or federal) showing the name, place of birth, date of birth or age of the prospective adoptive parent listed;

- **Affidavits** sworn to or affirmed by two persons who were living at the time and who have personal knowledge of the date and place of birth in the United States of the prospective adoptive parent. Each affidavit should contain the following information regarding the person making the affidavit: his or her full name, address, date and place of birth and relationship to the prospective adoptive parent, if any, and full information concerning the event and complete details of how the affiant acquired knowledge of the birth; or

- An unexpired **U.S. passport**, initially issued for ten years, may also be submitted as proof of U.S. citizenship.

(2) If the prospective adoptive parent was born outside the United States, submit a copy of one of the following:

- Certificate of Naturalization or Certificate of Citizenship issued the by U.S. Citizenship and Immigration Services (USCIS) or the former Immigration and Naturalization Service (INS);

- Form FS-240, Report of Birth Abroad of a Citizen of the United States, issued by an American embassy;

- An unexpired U.S. passport initally issued for ten years; or

- An original statement from a U.S. consular officer verifying the applicant's U.S. citizenship with a valid passport.

  NOTE: Proof of the lawful immigration status of the applicant's spouse, if applicable, must be submitted. If the spouse is not a U.S. citizen, proof of her or his lawful immigration status, such as Form I-551, Permanent Resident Card; Form I-94, Arrival-Departure Record; or a copy of the biographic pages of the spouse's passport and the nonimmigrant visa pages showing an admission stamp may be submitted.

B. Proof of marriage of applicant and spouse.

The married applicant must submit a copy of the certificate of marriage and proof of termination of all prior marriages of himself or herself and spouse. In the case of an unmarried applicant who was previously married, submit proof of termination of all prior marriages.

NOTE: If any change occurs in the applicant'(s) marital status while the application is pending, immediately notify the USCIS office where the application was filed.

C. Home Study.

The home study must include a statement or attachment recommending or approving the adoption or proposed adoption, and be signed by an official of the responsible State agency in the State of the proposed residence or of an agency authorized by that State.

In the case of a child adopted abroad, the statement or attachment must be signed by an official of an appropriate public or private adoption agency which is licensed in the U.S.

The home study must be prepared by an entity (individual or organization) licensed or otherwise authorized under the laws of the State of the orphan's proposed residence to conduct research and preparation for a home study, including the required personal interviews.

If the recommending agency is licensed, the recommendation must specify that it is licensed, the State in which it is licensed, its license number, if any, and the period of validity of the license.

However, the research, including the interview and the preparation of the home study may be done by an individual or group in the United States or abroad that is satisfactory to the recommending entity.

A responsible State agency or licensed agency may accept a home study made by an unlicensed or foreign agency and use that home study as a basis for a favorable recommendation.

The home study must provide an assessment of the capabilities of the prospective adoptive parent(s) to properly parent the orphan and must include a discussion of the following areas:

(1) An assessment of the financial ability of the adoptive or prospective adoptive parents or parent.

(2) A detailed description of the living accommodations where the adoptive or prospective adoptive parents or parent currently reside(s).

(3) If the prospective adoptive parent or parents are residing abroad at the time of the home study, a description of the living accommmodations where the child will reside in the United States, with the prospective adoptive parent or parents, if known.

(4) An assessment of the physical, mental and emotional capabilities of the adoptive or prospective adoptive parent or parents in relation to rearing and educating the child.

(5) An explanation regarding any history of abuse or violence or any complaints, charges, arrests, citations, convictions, prison terms, pardons, rehabilitation decrees for breaking or violating any law or ordinance by the prospective adoptive parent(s) or any additional adult member of the household over age 18 years.

NOTE: Having committed any crime of moral turpitude or a drug-related offense does not necessarily mean that the prospective adoptive parent(s) will be found not qualified to adopt an orphan. However, failure to disclose such information may result in denial of this application and/or any subsequent petition for an orphan.

D. Biometric services.

As part of the USCIS biometric services requirement, the following persons must be fingerprinted in connection with this application:

- The married prospective adoptive parent and spouse, if applicable, and

- Each additional adult member 18 years of age or older, of the prospective adoptive parent(s)' household. **NOTE:** Submit a copy of the birth certificate of each qualifying household member over 18.

If necessary, USCIS may also take each person's photograph and signature as part of the biometric services.

(1) Petitioners residing in the United States. After filing this petition, USCIS will notify each person in writing of the time and location where they must go to be fingerprinted. Failure to appear to be fingerprinted or for other biometric services may result in denial of this application.

(2) Petitioners residing abroad. Completed fingerprint cards (Forms FD-258) must be submitted with this application. Do not bend, fold or crease the completed fingerprint cards. The fingerprint cards must be prepared by a U.S. embassy or consulate, USCIS office or U.S. military installation.

3. General Filing Instructions.

A. Type or print legibly in black ink.

B. If extra space is needed to complete any item, attach a continuation sheet, indicate the item number, and date and sign each sheet.

C. Translations.

Any foreign language document must be accompanied by a full English translation that the translator has certified as complete and correct. The translator must also certify that he or she is competent to translate the foreign language into English.

D. Copies.

If these instructions tell you to submit a copy of a particular document, you do not have to send the original document. However, if there are stamps, remarks, notations, etc., on the back of the original documents, also submit copies of the back of each document(s). You will not have to submit the original document unless USCIS requests it.

There are times when USCIS must request an original copy of a document. In that case, the original document is generally returned after it has been reviewed.

E. Certification.

The "Certification of Prospective Adoptive Parent" block of Form I-600A must be executed by the prospective adoptive parent. The spouse, if applicable, must execute the **"Certification of Married Prospective Adoptive Parent Spouse"** block on **Page 2** of the form. Failure to do so will result in the rejection of the Form I-600A.

F. Submission of the Application.

A prospective adoptive parent residing in the United States should send the completed application to the USCIS office having jurisdiction over his or her place of residence. A prospective adoptive parent residing outside the United States should consult the nearest American consulate for the overseas or stateside USCIS office designated to act on the application.

4. What Is the Fee.

A fee of **$545.00** must be submitted for filing this application.

In addition to the fee for the application, there is a **$70.00** biometric services fee for fingerprinting every adult person living in the household in the United States where the child will reside.

For example, if an application is filed by a married couple residing in the United States with one additional adult member in their household, the total fees that must be submitted would be **$755.00** (**$545.00** for the petition and **$210.00** for the biometric services fees for fingerprinting the three adults).

NOTE: If the prospective adoptive parent(s) and any other adult members of the household are residing abroad at the time of filing, they are exempt from paying the biometric services fee for fingerprinting. However, they may have to pay fingerprinting fees charged by the U.S. Department of State or military installation.

The fee will not be refunded, whether the application is approved or not. Do not mail cash. All checks or money orders, whether U.S. or foreign, must be payable in U.S. currency at a financial institution in the United States. When a check is drawn on the account of a person other than yourself, write your name on the face of the check. If the check is not honored, USCIS will charge you $30.00.

Pay by check or money order in the exact amount. Make the check or money order payable to the **Department of Homeland Security**, unless:

A. You live in Guam, make the check or money order payable to the "Treasurer, Guam" or

B. You live in the U.S. Virgin Islands, make your check or money order payable to the "Commissioner of Finance of the Virgin Islands."

How to Check If the Fee Is Correct.

The fee on this form is current as of the edition date appearing in the lower right corner of this page. However, because USCIS fees change periodically, you can verify if the fee is correct by following one of the steps below:

- Visit our website at **www.uscis.gov** and scroll down to "Forms and E-Filing" to check the appropriate fee, or

- Review the Fee Schedule included in your form package, if you called us to request the form, or

- Telephone our National Customer Service Center at **1-800-375-5283** and ask for the fee information.

NOTE: If your petition or application requires a biometric services fee for USCIS to take your fingerprints, photograph or signature, you can use the same procedure above to confirm the biometrics fee.

5. What Should You Do After Locating and/or Identifying a Child or Children?

Form I-600, Petition to Classify Orphan as an Immediate Relative, is filed when a child has been located and/or identified for the prospective adoptive parent(s). A new fee is not required if Form I-600 is filed within 18 months from the approval date of the Form I-600A application. If approved in the home study for more than one orphan, the prospective adoptive parent(s) may file a petition for each of the additional children to the maximum number approved. If the orphans are siblings, no additional filing fee is required. However, if the orphans are not siblings, an additional filing fee is required for each orphan beyond the first orphan.

NOTE: Approval of an advance processing application does not guarantee that the orphan petition(s) will be approved.

Form I-600 must be accompanied by all the evidence required by the instructions of that form, except where provided previously with Form I-600A.

Generally, Form I-600 should be submitted at the USCIS office where the advance processing application, Form I-600A, was filed. Prospective adoptive parent(s) going abroad to adopt or locate a child may file Form I-600 with either the USCIS office or American consulate or embassy having jurisdiction over the place where the child is residing or will be located, unless the case is being retained at the USCIS office stateside.

USCIS has offices in the following countries: Austria, China, Cuba, the Dominican Republic, El Salvador, Germany, Ghana, Great Britain, Greece, Guatemala, Haiti, Honduras, India, Italy, Jamaica, Kenya, Korea, Mexico, Pakistan, Panama, Peru, the Philippines, Russia, South Africa, Thailand and Vietnam.

6. Penalties.

Willful false statements on this form or supporting documents may be punished by fine or imprisonment. U.S. Code, Title 18, Sec. 1001 (Formerly Sec. 80.)

7. Authority for Collecting Information.

8 U.S.C 1154 (a). Routine uses for disclosure under the Privacy Act of 1974 have been published in the Federal Register and are available upon request. USCIS will use the information to determine immigrant eligibility. Submission of the information is voluntary, but failure to provide any or all of the information may result in denial of the application.

8. USCIS Forms and Information.

To order USCIS forms, call our toll-free number at **1-800-870-3676**. You can also get USCIS forms and information on laws, regulations and procedures by telephoning our **National Customer Service Center** at **1-800-375-5283** or visiting our internet website at **www.uscis.gov.**

9. Use InfoPass for Appointments.

As an alternative to waiting in line for assistance at your local USCIS office, you can now schedule an appointment through our internet-based system, **InfoPass**. To access the system, visit our website at **www.uscis.gov**. Use the **InfoPass** appointment scheduler and follow the screen prompts to set up your appointment. **InfoPass** generates an electronic appointment notice that appears on the screen. Print the notice and take it with you to your appointment. The notice gives the time and date of your appointment, along with the address of the USCIS office.

10. Reporting Burden.

A person is not required to respond to a collection of information unless it displays a currently valid OMB control number. Public reporting burden for this collection of information is estimated to average 30 minutes per response, including the time for reviewing instructions, searching existing data sources, gathering and maintaining the data needed, and completing and reviewing the collection of information. Send comments regarding this burden estimate or any other aspect of this collection of information, including suggestions for reducing this burden, to U.S. Citizenship and Immigration Services, Regulatory Management Division, 111 Massachusetts Avenue, N.W., Washington, DC 20529; OMB No. 1615-0028. **Do not mail your completed application to this address.**

OMB No. 1615-0028; Expires 08/31/08

Department of Homeland Security
U.S. Citizenship and Immigration Services

I-600A, Application for Advance
Processing of Orphan Petition

Do not write in this block.   **For USCIS Use Only.**

It has been determined that the:

☐ Married   ☐ Unmarried

prospective adoptive parent will furnish proper care to
a beneficiary orphan if admitted to the United States.
There:

☐ are   ☐ are not

preadoptive requirements in the State of the child's proposed
residence.

The following is a description of the preadoption requirements, if any,
of the State of the child's proposed residence:

_____

_____

The preadoption requirements, if any,:

☐ have been met.   ☐ have not been met.

Fee Stamp

DATE OF FAVORABLE
DETERMINATION

DD

DISTRICT

File number of applicant, if applicable.

Please type or print legibly in black ink.

This application is made by the named prospective adoptive parent for advance processing of an orphan petition.

BLOCK I - Information about the prospective adoptive parent.

1. My name is: (Last)   (First)   (Middle)

2. Other names used (including maiden name if appropriate):

3. I reside in the U.S. at: (C/O if appropriate)   (Apt. No.)

(Number and Street)   (Town or City)   (State)   (Zip Code)

4. Address abroad (If any):   (Number and Street)   (Apt. No.)

(Town or City)   (Province)   (Country)

5. I was born on: *(mm/dd/yyyy)*

In: (Town or City)   (State or Province)   (Country)

6. My telephone number is: (Include Area Code)

7. My marital status is:
☐ Married
☐ Widowed
☐ Divorced
☐ Single
  ☐ I have never been married.
  ☐ I have been previously married _____ time(s).

8. If you are now married, give the following information:

Date and place of present marriage *(mm/dd/yyyy)*

Name of present spouse (include maiden name of wife)

Date of birth of spouse *(mm/dd/yyyy)*   Place of birth of spouse

Number of prior marriages of spouse

My spouse resides   ☐ With me   ☐ Apart from me
                                              (provide address below)

(Apt. No.)   (No. and Street)   (City)   (State)   (Country)

9. I am a citizen of the United States through:
☐ Birth   ☐ Parents   ☐ Naturalization

If acquired through naturalization, give name under which naturalized,
number of naturalization certificate, and date and place of naturalization.

If not, submit evidence of citizenship. See Instruction 2.a(2).

If acquired through parentage, have you obtained a certificate in your
own name based on that acquisition?
☐ No   ☐ Yes

Have you or any person through whom you claimed citizenship ever lost
United States citizenship?
☐ No   ☐ Yes (If Yes, attach detailed explanation.)

Received	Trans. In	Ret'd Trans. Out	Completed

f

Form I-600A (Rev. 10/26/05) Y

BLOCK II - General information.

10. Name and address of organization or individual assisting you in locating or identifying an orphan

(Name)

_____

(Address)

11. Do you plan to travel abroad to locate or adopt a child?

☐ Yes   ☐ No

12. Does your spouse, if any, plan to travel abroad to locate or adopt a child?

☐ Yes   ☐ No

13. If the answer to Question **11** or **12** is "Yes," give the following information:

a. Your date of intended departure _____

b. Your spouse's date of intended departure _____

c. City, province _____

14. Will the child come to the United States for adoption after compliance with the preadoption requirements, if any, of the State of proposed residence?

☐ Yes   ☐ No

15. If the answer to Question **14** is "No," will the child be adopted abroad after having been personally seen and observed by you and your spouse, if married?

☐ Yes   ☐ No

16. Where do you wish to file your orphan petition?

The USCIS office located at

_____

The American Embassy or Consulate at

_____

17. Do you plan to adopt more than one child?

☐ Yes   ☐ No

If "Yes," how many children do you plan to adopt?

Certification of prospective adoptive parent.

I certify, under penalty of perjury under the laws of the United States of America, that the foregoing is true and correct and that I will care for an orphan/orphans properly if admitted to the United States.

_____
(Signature of Prospective Adoptive Parent)

Executed on (Date)

Certification of married prospective adoptive parent spouse.

I certify, under penalty of perjury under the laws of the United States of America, that the foregoing is true and correct and that my spouse and I will care for an orphan/orphans properly if admitted to the United States.

_____
(Signature of Prospective Adoptive Parent Spouse)

Executed on (Date)

Signature of person preparing form, if other than petitioner.

I declare that this document was prepared by me at the request of the petitioner and is based entirely on information of which I have knowledge.

_____
(Signature)

Street Address and Room or Suite No./City/State/Zip Code

Executed on (Date)

OMB No. 1615-0028; Expires 08/31/08

Department of Homeland Security
U.S. Citizenship and Immigration Services

**I-600, Petition to Classify Orphan
as an Immediate Relative**

Instructions

1. Eligibility.

A. Child.

Under immigration law, an orphan is an alien child who has no parents because of the death or disappearance of, abandonment or desertion by, or separation or loss from both parents.

An orphan is also an alien child who has only one parent who is not capable of taking care of the orphan and who has in writing irrevocably released the alien for emigration and adoption.

A petition to classify an alien as an orphan may not be filed on behalf of a child in the United States, unless that child is in parole status and has not been adopted in the United States.

The petition must be filed before the child's 16th birthday.

B. Parent(s).

The petition may be filed by a married U.S. citizen and spouse or unmarried U.S. citizen at least 25 years of age. The spouse does not need to be a U.S. citizen, but must be in lawful immigration status.

C. Adoption abroad.

If the orphan was adopted abroad, it must be established that both the married petitioner and spouse or the unmarried petitioner personally saw and observed the child prior to or during the adoption proceedings. The adoption decree must show that a married petitioner and spouse adopted the child jointly or that an unmarried petitioner was at least 25 years of age at the time of the adoption

D. Proxy adoption abroad.

If both the petitioner and spouse or the unmarried petitioner did not personally see and observe the child prior to or during the adoption proceedings abroad, the petitioner (and spouse, if married) must submit a statement indicating the petitioner's (and, if married, the spouse's) willingness and intent to readopt the child in the United States.

If requested by USCIS, the petitioner must submit a statement by an official of the State in which the child will reside that readoption is permissible in that State. In addition, evidence of compliance with the preadoption requirements, if any, of that State must be submitted.

E. Preadoption requirements.

If the orphan has not been adopted abroad, the petitioner and spouse or the unmarried petitioner must establish that:

- The child will be adopted in the United States by the petitioner and spouse jointly or by the unmarried petitioner, and that

- The preadoption requirements, if any, of the State of the orphan's proposed residence have been met.

2. Filing Petition for Known Child.

An orphan petition for a child who has been identified must be submitted on a completed Form I-600 with the certification of the petitioner executed and required fee. If the petitioner is married, the Form I-600 must also be signed by the petitioner's spouse.

The petition must be accompanied by the following:

A. Proof of U.S. citizenship of the petitioner.

If a U.S. citizen by birth in the United States, submit a copy of the birth certificate, issued by the civil registrar, vital statistics office or other civil authority. If a birth certificate is not available, submit a statement from the appropriate civil authority certifying that a birth certificate is not available. In such a situation, secondary evidence must be submitted, including:

- **Church records** bearing the seal of the church showing the baptism, dedication or comparable rite occurred within two months after birth and showing the date and place of the petitioner's birth, date of the religious ceremony and the names of the parents;

- **School records** issued by the authority (perferably the first school attended) showing the date of admission to the school, the petitioner's birth date or age at the time, the place of birth and the names of the parents;

- **Census records** (state or federal) showing the name, place of birth, date of birth or age of the petitioner listed;

- **Affidavits** sworn to or affirmed by two persons who were living at the time and who have personal knowledge of the date and place of birth in the United States of the petitioner. Each affidavit should contain the following information regarding the person making the affidavit: his or her full name, address, date and place of birth and relationship to the petitioner, if any, and full information concerning the event and complete details of how the affiant acquired knowledge of petitioner's birth; or

- An unexpired **U.S. passport**, initially issued for ten years may also be submitted as proof of U.S. citizenship.

If the petitioner was born outside the United States, submit a copy of one of the following:

- Certificate of Naturalization or Certificate of Citizenship issued by the U.S. Citizenship and Immigration Services (USCIS) or former Immigration and Naturalization Service (INS);

- Form FS-240, Report of Birth Abroad of a Citizen of the United States, issued by an American embassy;

- An unexpired U.S. passport initally issued for ten years, or

- An original statement from a U.S. consular officer verifying the applicant's U.S. citizenship with a valid passport.

NOTE: Proof of the lawful immigration status of the petitioner's spouse, if applicable, must be submitted. If the spouse is not a U.S. citizen, proof of the spouse's lawful immigration status, such as Form I-551, Permanent Resident Card; Form I-94, Arrival-Departure Record; or a copy of the biographic pages of the spouse's passport and the nonimmigrant visa pages showing an admission stamp may be submitted.

B. Proof of marriage of petitioner and spouse.

The married petitioner must submit a copy of the certificate of marriage and proof of termination of all prior marriages of himself or herself and spouse. In the case of an unmarried petitioner who was previously married, submit proof of termination of all prior marriages.

NOTE: If any change occurs in the petitioner's marital status while the case is pending, immediately notify the USCIS office where the petition was filed.

C. Proof of age of orphan.

The petitioner should submit a copy of the orphan's birth certificate if obtainable; if not obtainable, submit an explanation together with the best available evidence of birth.

D. Copies of the death certificate(s) of the child's parent(s), if applicable.

E. A certified copy of adoption decree together with certified translation, if the orphan has been lawfully adopted abroad.

F. Evidence that the sole or surviving parent is incapable of providing for the orphan's care and has in writing irrevocably released the orphan for imigration and adoption, if the orphan has only one parent.

G. Evidence that the orphan has been unconditionally abandoned to an orphanage, if the orphan has been placed in an orphanage by his or her parent or parents.

H. Evidence that the preadoption requirements, if any, of the state of the orphan's proposed residence have been met, if the child is to be adopted in the United States.

If is not possible to submit this evidence upon initial filing of the petition under the laws of the State of proposed residence, it may be submitted later. The petition, however, will not be approved without it.

I. Home Study.

The home study must include a statement or attachment recommending or approving the adoption or proposed adoption and be signed by an official of the responsible State agency in the State of the proposed residence or of an agency authorized by that State. In the case of a child adopted abroad, the statement or attachment must be signed by an official of an appropriate public or private adoption agency that is licensed in the United States.

The home study must be prepared by an entity (individual or organization) licensed or otherwise authorized under the law of the State of the orphan's proposed residence to conduct research and preparation for a home study, including the required personal interviews.

If the recommending entity is licensed, the recommendation must state that it is licensed, where it is licensed, its license number, if any, and the period of validity of the license.

However, the research, including the interview and the preparation of the home study, may be done by an individual or group in the United States or abroad that is satisfactory to the recommending entity.

A responsible State agency or licensed agency may accept a home study made by an unlicensed or foreign agency and use that home study as a basis for a favorable recommendation.

The home study must provide an assessment of the capabilities of the prospective adoptive parent(s) to properly parent the orphan and must include a discussion of the following areas:

- An explanation regarding any history of abuse or violence or any complaints, charges, citations, arrests, convictions, prison terms, pardons rehabilitation decrees for breaking or violating any law or ordinance by the petitioner (s) or any additional adult member of the household over age 18.

NOTE: Having committed any crime of moral turpitude or a drug-related offense does not necessarily mean that a petitioner or petitioner's spouse will be found ineligible to adopt an orphan. However, failure to disclose such information may result in denial of this application and/or any subsequent petition for an orphan.

- An assessment of the financial ability of the petitioner and petitioner's spouse, if applicable.

- A detailed description of the living accommodations where the petitioner and petitioner's spouse currently reside(s).

- If the petitioner and petitioner's spouse are residing abroad at the time of the home study, a description of the living accommmodations where the child will reside in the United States with the petitioner and petitioner's spouse, if known.

- An assessment of the physical, mental and emotional capabilities of the petitioner and petitioner's spouse in relation to rearing and educating the child.

J. Biometric services.

As part of the USCIS biometric services requirements, the following persons must be fingerprinted in connection with this petition:

- The petitioner and petitioner's spouse, if applicable, and

- Each additional adult member the petitioner's household, 18 years of age or older. **NOTE:** Submit a copy of the birth certificate of each household member over 18.

If necessary, USCIS may also take a photograph and signature of those named above as part of the biometric services.

Petitioners residing in the United States. After filing this petition, USCIS will notify each person in writing of the time and location where they must go to be fingerprinted. Failure to appear to be fingerprinted or for other biometric services may result in denial of the petition.

Petitioners residing abroad. Completed fingerprint cards (Forms FD-258) must be submitted with the petition. Do not bend, fold or crease completed fingerprint cards. Fingerprint cards must be prepared by a U.S. embassy or consulate, USCIS office or military installation.

3. Filing Petition for Known Child Without Full Documentation on Child or Home Study.

When a child has been identified but the documentary evidence relating to the child or the home study is not yet available, an orphan petition may be filed without that evidence or home study.

The evidence outlined in Instructions **2A** and **2B** (proof of petitioner's U.S. citizenship and documentation of marriage of petitioner and spouse), however, must be submitted.

If the necessary evidence relating to the child or the home study is not submitted within one year from the date of submission of the petition, the petition will be considered abandoned and the fee will not be refunded. Any further proceeding will require the filing of a new petition.

4. Submitting Advance Processing Application for Orphan Child Not Yet Identified.

A prospective petitioner may request advance processing when the child has not been identified or when the prospective petitioner and/or spouse is or are going abroad to locate or adopt a child.

If unmarried, the prospective petitioner must be at least 24 years of age, provided that he or she will be at least 25 at the time of the adoption and the completed petition on behalf of a child is filed.

The request must be on Form I-600A, Application for Advance Processing of Orphan Petition, and accompanied by the evidence requested on that form.

After a child or children are located and/or identified, a separate Form I-600 must be filed for each child. If only one Form I-600 is filed, a new fee is not required, provided the form is filed while the advance processing application (Form I-600A) application is pending or within 18 months of the approval of the advance processing application.

5. When Child/Children Are Located and/or Identified.

A separate Form I-600, Petition to Classify Orphan as an Immediate Relative, must be filed for each child.

Generally, Form I-600 should be submitted at the USCIS office where the advance processing application was filed.

If a prospective petitioner goes abroad to adopt or locate a child in one of the countries noted below, he or she should file Form I-600 at the USCIS office having jurisdiction over the place where the child is residing or will be located, unless the case is retained at the stateside office.

USCIS has offices in the following countries: Austria, China, Cuba, the Dominican Republic, El Salvador, Germany, Ghana, Great Britain, Greece, Guatemala, Haiti, Honduras, India, Italy, Jamaica, Kenya, Korea, Mexico, Pakistan, Panama, Peru, the Philippines, Russia, South Africa, Thailand and Vietnam.

If a prospective petitioner goes abroad to any country not listed above to adopt or locate a child he or she should file Form I-600 at the American embassy or consulate having jurisdiction over the place where the child is residing or will be located, unless the case is retained at the Stateside office.

6. General Filing Instructions.

A. Type or print legibly in black ink.

B. If extra space is needed to complete any item, attach a continuation sheet, indicate the item number, and date and sign each sheet.

C. **Translations.**

Any foreign language document must be accompanied by a full English translation, that the translator has certified as complete and correct, and by the translator's certification that he or she is competent to translate the foreign language.

D. **Copies.**

If these instructions tell you to submit a copy of a particular document, you do not have to send the original document. However, if there are stamps, remarks, notations, etc., on the back of the original documents, also submit copies of the back of the document(s). You do not have to submit the original document unless USCIS requests it.

There are times when USCIS must request an original copy of a document. In that case, the original is generally returned after it has been reviewed.

7. Filing the Petition.

A petitioner residing in the United States should send the completed petition to the USCIS office having jurisdiction over his or her place of residence. A petitioner residing outside the United States should consult the nearest American embassy or consulate designated to act on the petition.

8. What Is the Fee?

A fee of **$545.00** must be submitted for filing this petition. However, a fee is not required for this petition if you filed an advance processing application (Form I-600A) within the previous 18 months and it was approved or is still pending.

In addition to the fee for the application, there is a **$70.00** biometric services fee for fingerprinting every adult person living in the household in the United States where the child will reside.

For example, if a petition is filed by a married people residing in the United States with one additional adult member in their household, the total fee that must be submitted would be **$755.00** (**$545.00** for the petition and **$210.00** for biometric services for fingerprinting the three adults).

NOTE: If the prospective adoptive parents and any other adult members of the household reside abroad at the time of filing, they are exempt from paying the USCIS biometric services fee. However, they may have to pay the fingerprinting fee charged by the U.S. consular office or military installation.

When more than one petition is submitted by the same petitioner on behalf of orphans who are siblings, only one Form I-600 petition and fee for biometric services is required, unless re-fingerprinting is ordered. If the orphans are not siblings, a separate filing fee must be submitted for each additional Form I-600 petition.

The fee will not be refunded, whether the petition is approved or not. **Do not mail cash.** All checks or money orders, whether U.S. or foreign, must be payable in U.S. currency at a financial institution in the United States. When a check is drawn on the account of a person other than yourself, write your name on the face of the check. If the check is not honored, USCIS will charge you $30.00.

Pay by check or money order in the exact amount. Make the check or money order payable to the **Department of Homeland Security**, unless:

A. You live in Guam, make the check or money order payable to the "Treasurer, Guam" or ;

B. You live in the U.S. Virgin Islands, make your check or money order payable to the "Commissioner of Finance of the Virgin Islands."

How to Check If the Fee Is Correct.

The fee on this form is current as of the edition date appearing in the lower right corner of this page. However, because USCIS fees change periodically, you can verify if the fee is correct by following one of the steps below:

- Visit our website at **www.uscis.gov** and scroll down to "Forms and E-Filing" to check the appropriate fee, or

- Review the Fee Schedule included in your form package, if you called us to request the form, or

- Telephone our National Customer Service Center at **1-800-375-5283** and ask for the fee information.

NOTE: If your petition or application requires a biometric services fee for USCIS to take your fingerprints, photograph or signature, you can use the same procedure above to confirm the biometrics fee.

9. Penalties.

Willful false statements on this form or supporting documents may be punished by fine or imprisonment. U.S. Code, Title 18, Sec. 1001 (formerly Sec. 80.)

10. Authority to Collect Information.

8 USC 1154(a). Routine uses for disclosure under the Privacy Act of 1974 have been published in the Federal Register and are available upon request. USCIS will use the information to determine immigrant eligibility. Submission of the information is voluntary, but failure to provide any or all of the information may result in denial of the petition.

11. USCIS Forms and Information.

To order USCIS forms, call our toll-free number at 1-800-870-3676. You can also get USCIS forms and information on laws, regulations and procedures by telephoning our National Customer Service Center at 1-800-375-5283 or visiting our internet website at www.uscis.gov.

12. Use InfoPass for Appointments.

As an alternative to waiting in line for assistance at your local USCIS office, you can now schedule an appointment through our internet-based system, **InfoPass**. To access the system, visit our website at **www.uscis.gov**. Use the **InfoPass** appointment scheduler and follow the screen prompts to set up your appointment. **InfoPass** generates an electronic appointment notice that appears on the screen. Print the notice and take it with you to your appointment. The notice gives the time and date of your appointment, along with the address of the USCIS office.

13. Reporting Burden.

A person is not required to respond to a collection of information unless it displays a currently valid OMB control number.

Public reporting burden for this collection of information is estimated to average 30 minutes per response, including the time for reviewing instructions, searching existing data sources, gathering and maintaining the data needed, and completing and reviewing the collection of information.

Send comments regarding this burden estimate or any other aspect of this collection of information, including suggestions for reducing this burden, to the: U.S. Citizenship and Immigration Services, Regulatory Management Division, 111 Massachusetts Avenue, N.W., Washington, DC 20529; OMB No. 1615-0028. **Do not mail your completed petition.**

OMB No. 1615-0028; Expires 08/31/08

I-600, Petition to Classify Orphan as an Immediate Relative

Department of Homeland Security
U.S. Citizenship and Immigration Services

Do not write in this block.   **(For USCIS Use Only.)**

TO THE SECRETARY OF STATE:

The petition was filed by:

☐ Married petitioner   ☐ Unmarried petitioner

The petition is approved for orphan:

☐ Adopted abroad   ☐ Coming to U.S. for adoption. Preadoption requirements have been met.

Remarks:

Fee Stamp

File number

DATE OF ACTION
DD
DISTRICT

Type or print legibly in black ink. Complete a separate petition for each child.
Petition is being made to classify the named orphan as an immediate relative

Block I - Information about petitioner.

1. My name is: (Last)   (First)   (Middle)

2. Other names used (including maiden name if appropriate):

3. I reside in the U.S. at: (C/O if appropriate)   (Apt. No.)

   (Number and Street)   (Town or City)   (State) (Zip Code)

4. Address Abroad (if any):   (Number and Street)   (Apt. No.)

   (Town or city)   (Province)   (Country)

5. I was born on: *(mm/dd/yyyy)*

   In: (Town or City)   (State or Province)   (Country)

6. My telephone number is: (Include Area Code)

7. My marital status is:

   ☐ Married
   ☐ Widowed
   ☐ Divorced
   ☐ Single
     ☐ I have never been married.
     ☐ I have been previously married _____ time(s).

8. If you are now married, give the following information:

   Date and place of present marriage *(mm/dd/yyyy)*

   Name of present spouse (include maiden name of wife)

   Date of birth of spouse *(mm/dd/yyyy)* Place of birth of spouse

   Number of prior marriages of spouse

   My spouse resides ☐ With me ☐ Apart from me (provide address below)

   (Apt. No.) (No. and Street)   (City)   (State) (Country)

9. I am a citizen of the United States through:

   ☐ Birth ☐ Parents ☐ Naturalization

   If acquired through naturalization, give name under which naturalized, number of naturalization certificate, and date and place of naturalization:

   If not, submit evidence of citizenship. See Instruction **2.a(2)**.

   If acquired through parentage, have you obtained a certificate in your own name based on that acquisition?

   ☐ No ☐ Yes

   Have you or any person through whom you claimed citizenship ever lost U.S. citizenship?

   ☐ No ☐ Yes (If Yes, attach detailed explanation.)

Received	Trans. In	Ret'd Trans. Out	Completed

f

Form I-600 (Rev. 10/26/05)Y

Block II - Information about orphan beneficiary.

10. Name at Birth (First) (Middle) (Last)

11. Name at Present (First) (Middle) (Last)

12. Any other names by which orphan is or was known.

13. Gender ☐ Male   **14.** Date of birth *(mm/dd/yyyy)*
☐ Female

15. Place of Birth (City) (State or Province) (Country)

16. The beneficiary is an orphan because (check one):
☐ He or she has no parents.
☐ He or she has only one parent who is the sole or surviving parent.

17. If the orphan has only one parent, answer the following:
a. State what has become of the other parent:

b. Is the remaining parent capable of providing for the orphan's support?   ☐ Yes   ☐ No
c. Has the remaining parent in writing irrevocably released the orphan for emigration and adoption?   ☐ Yes   ☐ No

18. Has the orphan been adopted abroad by the petitioner and spouse jointly or the unmarried petitioner?   ☐ Yes   ☐ No

If yes, did the petitioner and spouse or unmarried petitioner personally see and observe the child prior to or during the adoption proceedings?   ☐ Yes   ☐ No

Date of adoption *(mm/dd/yyyy)*

Place of adoption

19. If either answer in Question **18** is "No," answer the following:
a. Do petitioner and spouse jointly or does the unmarried petitioner intend to adopt the orphan in the United States?   ☐ Yes   ☐ No
b. Have the preadoption requirements, if any, of the orphan's proposed State of residence been met?   ☐ Yes   ☐ No
c. If **b** is answered "No," will they be met later?   ☐ Yes   ☐ No

20. To petitioner's knowledge, does the orphan have any physical or mental affliction?   ☐ Yes   ☐ No
If "Yes," name the affliction.

21. Who has legal custody of the child?

22. Name of child welfare agency, if any, assisting in this case:

23. Name of attorney abroad, if any, representing petitioner in this case.
Address of above.

24. Address in the United States where orphan will reside.

25. Present address of orphan.

25. If orphan is residing in an institution, give full name of institution.

26. If orphan is not residing in an institution, give full name of person with whom orphan is residing.

27. Give any additional information necessary to locate orphan, such as name of district, section, zone or locality in which orphan resides.

28. Location of American embassy or consulate where application for visa will be made.
(City in Foreign Country) (Foreign Country)

Certification of petitioner.
I certify, under penalty of perjury under the laws of the United States of America, that the foregoing is true and correct and that I will care for an orphan or orphans properly if admitted to the United States.

(Signature of Petitioner)

Executed on (Date)

Certification of married prospective petitioner's spouse.
I certify, under penalty of perjury under the laws of the United States of America, that the foregoing is true and correct and that my spouse and I will care for an orphan or orphans properly if admitted to the United States.

(Signature of Petitioner)

Executed on (Date)

Signature of person preparing form, if other than petitioner.
I declare that this document was prepared by me at the request of the petitioner and is based entirely on information of which I have knowledge.

(Signature)

Street Address and Room or Suite No./City/State/Zip Code

Executed on (Date)

Form I-600 (Rev. 10/26/05)Y Page 2

OMB No. 1615-0038; Expires 09/30/08

Department of Homeland Security
U.S. Citizenship and Immigration Services

**I-751, Petition to Remove
Conditions on Residence**

Purpose of This Form.

This form is for a conditional resident who obtained such status through marriage to petition to the U.S. Citizenship and Immigration Services (USCIS) to remove the conditions on his or her residence. USCIS is comprised of offices of the former Immigration and Naturalization Service (INS).

Who May File.

If you were granted conditional resident status through marriage to a U.S. citizen or permanent resident, use this form to petition for the removal of those conditions.

If you are still married, the petition should be filed jointly by you and the spouse through whom you obtained conditional status. However, you may apply for a waiver of this joint filing requirement if:

- You entered the marriage in good faith, but your spouse subsequently died;
- You entered the marriage in good faith, but the marriage was later terminated due to divorce or annulment;
- You entered the marriage in good faith and have remained married, but have been battered or subjected to extreme cruelty by your U.S. citizen or permanent resident spouse; or
- The termination of your status and removal would result in extreme hardship.

You may include your conditional resident children in your petition, or they may file separately.

General Filing Instructions.

Please answer all questions by typing or clearly printing in black ink. Indicate that an item is not applicable with "N/A." If an answer is "none," write "none." If you need extra space to answer any item, attach a sheet of paper with your name and your Alien Registration Number (A#), and indicate the number of the item to which the answer refers. You must file your petition with the required initial evidence. Your petition must be properly signed and accompanied by the correct fee. If you are under 14 years of age, your parent or guardian may sign the petition on your behalf.

Translations. Any foreign language document must be accompanied by a full English translation that the translator has certified as complete and correct, and by the translator's certification that he or she is competent to translate the foreign language into English.

Copies. If these instructions state that a copy of a document may be filed with this petition and you choose to send us the original, we may keep that original for our records.

Initial Evidence.

Permanent Resident Card. You must file your petition with a copy of your Permanent Resident Card or Alien Registration Card, and a copy of the Permanent Resident or Alien Registration cards of any of your conditional resident children you are including in your petition. Submit copies of both front and back sides of the card.

Photographs.

The conditional resident filing this petition must submit two standard passport-style photographs of him or herself taken within 30 days of submission of the petition. The photos should be 2x2 inches in size and have a white background. The photos should be glossy and not retouched or mounted. The dimension of the facial image should be about 1 inch to 1 3/8 inches from the chin to the top of the hair in a full frontal view. Using a pencil or felt pen, lightly print your name and Alien Registration Number (A#) on the back of the photographs.

Evidence of the Relationship. Submit copies of documents indicating that the marriage upon which you were granted conditional status was entered in "good faith" and was not for the purpose of circumventing immigration laws. Submit copies of as many documents as you wish to establish this fact and to demonstrate the circumstances of the relationship from the date of the marriage to the present date, and to demonstrate any circumstances surrounding the end of the relationship, if it has ended. The documents should cover the period from the date of your marriage to the filing of this petition. Examples of such documents are:

- Birth certificate(s) of child(ren) born to the marriage.
- Lease or mortgage contracts showing joint occupancy and/or ownership of your communal residence.
- Financial records showing joint ownership of assets and joint responsibility for liabilities, such as joint savings and checking accounts, joint federal and state tax returns, insurance policies that show the other spouse as the beneficiary, joint utility bills, joint installments or other loans.
- Other documents you consider relevant to establish that your marriage was not entered into in order to evade the U.S. immigration laws.
- Affidavits sworn to or affirmed by at least two people who have known both of you since your conditional residence was granted and have personal knowledge of your marriage and relationship. (Such persons may be required to testify before an immigration officer as to the information contained in the affidavit.) The original affidavit must be submitted and also contain the following information regarding the person making the affidavit: his or her full name and address; date and place of birth; relationship to you or your spouse, if any; and full information and complete details explaining how the person acquired his or her knowledge. Affidavits must be supported by other types of evidence listed above.

If you are filing to waive the joint filing requirement due to the death of your spouse, submit also a copy of the death certificate with your petition.

If you are filing to waive the joint filing requirement because your marriage has been terminated, submit also a copy of the divorce decree or other document terminating or annulling the marriage with your petition.

If you are filing to waive the joint filing requirement because you and/or your conditional resident child were battered or subjected to extreme cruelty, also file your petition with the following:

- Evidence of the physical abuse, such as copies of reports or official records issued by police, judges, medical personnel, school officials and representatives of social service agencies, and original affidavits as described under *Evidence of the Relationship*; or

- Evidence of the abuse, such as copies of reports or official records issued by police, courts, medical personnel, school officials, clergy, social workers and other social service agency personnel. You may also submit any legal documents relating to an order of protection against the abuser or relating to any legal steps you may have taken to end the abuse. You may also submit evidence that you sought safe haven in a battered women's shelter or similar refuge, as well as photographs evidencing your injuries.

- A copy of your divorce decree, if your marriage was terminated by divorce on grounds of physical abuse or extreme cruelty.

If you are filing for a waiver of the joint filing requirement because the termination of your status and removal would result in "extreme hardship", you must submit with your petition evidence that your removal would result in hardship significantly greater than the hardship encountered by other aliens who are removed from this country after extended stays. The evidence must relate only to those factors that arose since you became a conditional resident.

If you are a child filing separately from your parent, also submit your petition a full explanation as to why you are filing separately, along with copies of any supporting *documentation*.

When to File.

Filing jointly. If you are filing this petition jointly with your spouse, you must file it during the **90 days** immediately before the second anniversary of the date you were accorded conditional resident status. This is the date your conditional residence expires.

However, if you and your spouse are outside the United States on orders of the U.S. Government during the period in which the petition must be filed, you may file it within **90 days** of your return to the United States.

Filing with a request that the joint filing requirement be waived. You may file this petition at any time after you are granted conditional resident status and before you are removed.

Effect of not filing. If this petition is not filed, you will automatically lose your permanent resident status as of the second anniversary of the date on which you were granted conditional status. You will then become removable from the United States. If your failure to file was through no fault of your own, you may file your petition late with a written explanation and request that USCIS excuse the late filing. Failure to file before the expiration date may be excused if you demonstrate when you submit the application that the delay was due to extraordinary circumstances beyond your control and that the length of the delay was reasonable.

Where to File.

If you live in Connecticut, Delaware, District of Columbia, Maine, Maryland, Massachusetts, New Hampshire, New Jersey, New York, Pennsylvania, Puerto Rico, Rhode Island, Vermont, Virgin Islands, Virginia or West Virginia, mail your petition to:

USCIS Vermont Service Center
75 Lower Welden Street
St. Albans, VT 05479-0001

If you live in Alabama, Arkansas, Florida, Georgia, Kentucky, Louisiana, Mississippi, New Mexico, North Carolina, Oklahoma, South Carolina, Tennessee or Texas, mail your petition to:

USCIS Texas Service Center
P.O. Box 850965,
Mesquite, TX 75185-0965

If you live in Arizona, California, Guam, Hawaii or Nevada, mail your petition to:

USCIS California Service Center
P.O. Box 10751
Laguna Niguel, CA 92607-0751

If you live elsewhere in the United States mail your petition to:

USCIS Nebraska Service Center
P.O. Box 87751
Lincoln, NE 68501-7751

NOTE: If you or your spouse are currently serving with or employed by the U.S. Government, either in a civilian or military capacity and assigned outside the United States, mail your petition to the USCIS Service Center having jurisdiction over your residence of record in the United States. Include a copy of the U.S. Government orders assigning you and your spouse abroad.

What Is the Fee?

The fee for this petition is **$205.00**.

The fee must be submitted in the exact amount. It cannot be refunded. **Do not mail cash.**

All checks and money orders must be drawn on a bank or other institution located in the United States and must be payable in United States currency. The check or money order should be made payable to the **U.S. Department of Homeland Security**.

Except:

- If you live in Guam, make your check or money order payable to the "Treasurer, Guam."

- If you live in the U.S. Virgin Islands, make your check or money order payable to the "Commissioner of Finance of the Virgin Islands."

Do not use the initials USDHS or DHS on your check or money order.

Checks are accepted subject to collection. An uncollected check will render the petition and any document issued invalid. A charge of $30.00 will be imposed if a check in payment of a fee is not honored by the bank on which it is drawn.

How to Check If the Fee Is Correct.

The fee on this form is current as of the edition date appearing in the lower right corner of this page. However, because USCIS fees change periodically, you can verify if the fee is correct by following one of the steps below:

- Visit our website at **www.uscis.gov** and scroll down to "Forms and E-Filing" to check the appropriate fee, or

- Review the Fee Schedule included in your form package, if you called us to request the form, or

- Telephone our National Customer Service Center at **1-800-375-5283** and ask for the fee information.

Processing Information.

Acceptance. Any petition that is not signed or accompanied by the correct fee will be rejected with a notice that the petition is deficient. You may correct the deficiency and resubmit the petition. A petition is not considered properly filed until accepted by USCIS.

Initial processing. Once a petition has been accepted, it will be checked for completeness, including submission of the required initial evidence. If you do not completely fill out the form or file it without the required initial evidence, you will not establish a basis for eligibility and we may deny your petition.

Requests for more information or interview. We may request more information or evidence, or we may request that you appear at a USCIS office for an interview. We may also request that you submit the originals of any copies. We will return these originals when they are no longer required.

Decision. You will be advised in writing of the decision on your petition.

Penalties.

If you knowingly and willfully falsify or conceal a material fact or submit a false document with this request, we will deny the benefit you are filing for and may deny any other immigration benefit. In addition, you will face severe penalties provided by law and may be subject to criminal prosecution.

Do You Need USCIS Forms or Information?

To order USCIS forms, call our toll-free forms line at **1-800-870-3676**. You can also obtain USCIS forms and information on immigration laws, regulations or procedures by calling our National Customer Service Center at **1-800-375-5283** or visiting our internet website at **www.uscis.gov.**

Use InfoPass to Make an Appointment.

As an alternative to waiting in line for assistance at your local USCIS office, you can now schedule an appointment through our internet-based system, **InfoPass.** To access the system, visit our website at **www.uscis.gov.** Use the **InfoPass** appointment scheduler and follow the screen prompts to set up your appointment. **InfoPass** generates an electronic appointment notice that appears on the screen. Print the notice and take it with you to your appointment. The notice gives the time and date of your appointment, along with the address of the USCIS office.

Privacy Act Notice.

We ask for the information on this form and associated evidence to determine if you have established eligibility for the immigration benefit you are seeking. Our legal right to ask for this information is in 8 USC 1184, 1255 and 1258. Failure to provide this information and any requested evidence may delay a final decision or result in denial of your request.

All the information provided on this form, including addresses, are protected by the Privacy Act and the Freedom of Information Act. This information may be released to other government agencies. However, the information will not be released in any form whatsoever to a third party who requests it without a court order, or without your written consent. In the case of a child, the written consent must be provided by the parent or legal guardian who filed the form on the child's behalf.

Paperwork Reduction Act Notice.

We try to create forms and instructions that are accurate, can be easily understood and that impose the least possible burden on you to provide us with information. Often this is difficult because some immigration laws are very complex. The estimated average time to complete and file this application is as follows: (1) 15 minutes to learn about the law and form; (2) 15 minutes to complete the form; and (3) 50 minutes to assemble and file the petition; for a total estimated average of 1 hour and 20 minutes per petition. If you have comments regarding the accuracy of this estimate, or suggestions for making this form simpler, write to the U.S. Citizenship and Immigration Services, Regulatory Management Division, 111 Massachusetts Ave, N. W., Washington, DC 20529; OMB No. 1615-0038. **Do not mail your completed petition to this address.**

OMB No. 1615-0038; Expires 09/30/05

Department of Homeland Security
U.S. Citizenship and Immigration Services

I-751, Petition to Remove Conditions on Residence

START HERE - Please type or print in black ink.

Part 1. Information about you.

For USCIS Use Only	
Returned	Receipt

Family Name (Last Name)   Given Name (First Name)   Full Middle Name

Date

Address: (Street Number and Name)   Apt. #

Date

Resubmitted

C/O: (In Care Of)

Date

City   State/Province

Date

Reloc Sent

Country   Zip/Postal Code

Date

Mailing Address, if different than above: (Street Number and Name)   Apt. #

Date
Reloc Rec'd

C/O: (In Care Of)

Date

City   State/Province

Date

Country   Zip/Postal Code

☐ Petitioner
Interviewed
on
_____

Remarks

Date of Birth *(mm/dd/yyyy)*   Country of Birth   Country of Citizenship

Alien Registration Number *(#A)*   Social Security # *(if any)*

Conditional Residence Expires on *(mm/dd/yyyy)*   Daytime Phone # *(Area/Country Codes)*

Part 2. Basis for petition. *(Check one.)*

Action Block

a. ☐ My conditional residence is based on my marriage to a U.S. citizen or permanent resident, and we are filing this petition together.

b. ☐ I am a child who entered as a conditional permanent resident and I am unable to be included in a joint petition to remove the conditional basis of are alien's permanent residence (Form 1-751) filed by my parent(s).

OR

My conditional residence is based on my marriage to a U.S. citizen or permanent resident, but I am unable to file a joint petition and I request a waiver because: **(Check one.)**

c. ☐ My spouse is deceased.

d. ☐ I entered into the marriage in good faith but the marriage was terminated through divorce/annulment.

e. ☐ I am a conditional resident spouse who entered a marriage in good faith, and during the marriage I was battered by or was the subject of extreme cruelty by my U.S. citizen or permanent resident spouse or parent.

f. ☐ I am a conditional resident child who was battered by or subjected to extreme cruelty by my U.S. citizen or conditional resident parent(s).

g. ☐ The termination of my status and removal from the United States would result in an extreme hardship.

To Be Completed by
Attorney or Representative, if any.
☐ Fill in box if G-28 is attached to represent the applicant.
ATTY State License #

f   Form I-751 (Rev. 10/26/05) Y

Part 3. Additional information about you.

1. Other Names Used *(including maiden name)*:

2. Date of Marriage *(mm/dd/yyyy)*   3. Place of Marriage   4. If your spouse is deceased, give the date of death *(mm/dd/yyyy)*

5. Are you in removal, deportation or rescission proceedings? ☐ Yes ☐ No

6. Was a fee paid to anyone other than an attorney in connection with this petition? ☐ Yes ☐ No

7. Since becoming a conditional resident, have you ever been arrested, cited, charged, indicted, convicted, fined or imprisoned for breaking or violating any law or ordinance (excluding traffic regulations), or committed any crime for which you were not arrested? ☐ Yes ☐ No

8. If you are married, is this a different marriage than the one through which conditional residence status was obtained? ☐ Yes ☐ No

9. Have you resided at any other address since you became a permanent resident? *(If yes, attach a list of all addresses and dates.)* ☐ Yes ☐ No

10. Is your spouse currently serving with or employed by the U.S. government and serving outside the United States? ☐ Yes ☐ No

If you answered "Yes" to any of the above, provide a detailed explanation on a separate sheet(s) of paper. Place your name and Alien Registration Number (A#) at the top of each sheet and give the number of the item that refers to your response.

Part 4. Information about the spouse or parent through whom you gained your conditional residence.

Family Name   First Name   Middle Name

Address

Date of Birth *(mm/dd/yyyy)*   Social Security # *(if any)*   A# *(if any)*

Part 5. Information about your children. List all your children. *Attach other sheet(s) if necessary.*

Name *(First/Middle/Last)*	Date of Birth *(mm/dd/yyyy)*	A # *(if any)*	If in U.S., give address/immigration status	Living with you?
				☐ Yes ☐ No
				☐ Yes ☐ No
				☐ Yes ☐ No
				☐ Yes ☐ No
				☐ Yes ☐ No

Part 6. Signature   *Read the information on penalties in the instructions before completing this section. If you checked block "a" in Part 2, your spouse must also sign below.*

I certify, under penalty of perjury of the laws of the United States of America, that this petition and the evidence submitted with it is all true and correct. If conditional residence was based on a marriage, I further certify that the marriage was entered in accordance with the laws of the place where the marriage took place and was not for the purpose of procuring an immigration benefit. I also authorize the release of any information from my records that the U.S. Citizenship and Immigration Services needs to determine eligibility for the benefit sought.

Signature   Print Name   Date *(mm/dd/yyyy)*

Signature of Spouse   Print Name   Date *(mm/dd/yyyy)*

NOTE: If you do not completely fill out this form or fail to submit any required documents listed in the instructions, you may not be found eligible for the requested benefit and this petition may be denied.

Part 7. Signature of person preparing form, if other than above.

I declare that I prepared this petition at the request of the above person and it is based on all information of which I have knowledge.

Signature   Print Name   Date *(mm/dd/yyyy)*

Firm Name and Address   Daytime Phone Number *(Area/Country Codes)*

E-Mail Address *(If any)*

Form I-751 (Rev. 10/26/05) Y Page 2

Department of Homeland Security
U.S. Citizenship and Immigration Services

OMB No. 1615-0040; Expires 08/31/08

Application for Employment Authorization

Form I-765 (Rev. 10/26/05)Y

OMB No. 1615-0040; Expires 08/31/08

Department of Homeland Security
U.S. Citizenship and Immigration Services

I-765, Application for
Employment Authorization

Instructions

The U.S. Citizenship and Immigration Services (USCIS) recommends that you retain a copy of your completed application for your records.
NOTE: USCIS is comprised of offices of the former Immigration and Naturalization Service (INS).

Index

Part 1. General.

Purpose of the Application. Certain aliens who are temporarily in the United States may file a Form I-765, Application for Employment Authorization, to request an Employment Authorization Document (EAD). Other aliens who are authorized to work in the United States without restrictions should also use this form to apply to USCIS for a document evidencing such authorization. Please review **Part 2: Eligibility Categories** to determine whether you should use this form.

If you are a Lawful Permanent Resident, a Conditional Resident, or a nonimmigrant authorized to be employed with a specific employer under 8 CFR 274a.12(b), please do **not** use this form.

Definitions

Employment Authorization Document (EAD): Form I-688, Form I-688A, Form I-688B, Form I-766, or any successor document issued by USCIS as evidence that the holder is authorized to work in the United States.

Renewal EAD: an EAD issued to an eligible applicant at or after the expiration of a previous EAD issued under the same category.

Replacement EAD: an EAD issued to an eligible applicant when the previously issued EAD has been lost, stolen, mutilated, or contains erroneous information, such as a misspelled name.

Interim EAD: an EAD issued to an eligible applicant when USCIS has failed to adjudicate an application within 90 days of receipt of a properly filed EAD application or within 30 days of a properly filed initial EAD application based on an asylum application filed on or after January 4, 1995. The interim EAD will be granted for a period not to exceed 240 days and is subject to the conditions noted on the document.

Part 2. Eligibility Categories.

The USCIS adjudicates a request for employment authorization by determining whether an applicant has submitted the required information and documentation, and whether the applicant is eligible. In order to determine your eligibility, you must identify the category in which you are eligible and fill in that category in **Question 16** on the Form I-765. Enter only **one** of the following category numbers on the application form. For example, if you are a refugee applying for an EAD, you should write "(a)(3)" at Question 16.

For easier reference, the categories are subdivided as follows:

Asylee/Refugee Categories

Refugee--(a)(3). File your EAD application with either a copy of your Form I-590, Registration for Classification as Refugee, approval letter or a copy of a Form I-730, Refugee/Asylee Relative Petition, approval notice.

Paroled as a Refugee--(a)(4). File your EAD application with a copy of your Form I-94, Arrival/Departure Record.

Asylee (granted asylum)--(a)(5). File your EAD application with a copy of the USCIS letter, or judge's decision, granting you asylum. It is not necessary to apply for an EAD as an asylee until 90 days before the expiration of your current EAD.

Asylum Applicant (with a pending asylum application) who Filed for Asylum on or after January 4, 1995--(c)(8). (For specific instructions for applicants with pending asylum claims, see page 5).

Nationality Categories

Citizen of Micronesia, the Marshall Islands or Palau--(a)(8). File your EAD application if you were admitted to the United States as a citizen of the Federated States of Micronesia (CFA/FSM), the Marshall Islands (CFA/MIS), or Palau, pursuant to agreements between the United States and the former trust territories.

Deferred Enforced Departure (DED)/Extended Voluntary Departure--(a)(11). File your EAD application with evidence of your identity and nationality.

Temporary Protected Status (TPS)--(a)(12). File your EAD application with Form I-821, Application for Temporary Protected Status. If you are filing for an initial EAD based on your TPS status, include evidence of identity and nationality as required by the Form I-821 instructions.

Temporary treatment benefits --(c)(19). For an EAD based on 8 CFR 244.5. Include evidence of nationality and identity as required by the Form I-821 instructions.

- Extension of TPS status: include a copy (front and back) of your last available TPS document: EAD, Form I-94 or approval notice.

- Registration for TPS only without employment authorization : file the Form I-765, Form I-821, and a letter indicating that this form is for registration purposes only. No fee is required for the Form I-765 filed as part of TPS registration. (Form I-821 has separate fee requirements.)

NACARA Section 203 Applicants who are eligible to apply for NACARA relief with USCIS --(c)(10). See the instructions to Form I-881, Application for Suspension of Deportation or Special Rule Cancellation of Removal, to determine if you are eligible to apply for NACARA 203 relief with USCIS.

If you are eligible, follow the instructions below and submit your Form I-765 at the same time you file your Form I-881 application with USCIS:

- If you are filing a Form I-881 with USCIS, file your EAD application at the same time and at the same filing location. Your response to **Question 16** on the Form I-765 should be **"(c)(10)."**

- If you have already filed your I-881 application at the service center specified on the Form I-881, and now wish to apply for employment authorization, your response to **Question 16** on Form I-765 should be **"(c)(10)."** You should file your EAD application at the Service Center designated in Part 5 of these instructions.

- If you are a NACARA Section 203 applicant who previously filed a Form I-881 with USCIS, and the application is still pending, you may renew your EAD. Your response to **Question 16** on Form I-765 should be **"(c)(10)."** Submit the required fee and the EAD application to the service center designated in Part 5 of these instructions.

Dependent of TECRO E-1 Nonimmigrant--(c)(2). File your EAD application with the required certification from the American Institute in Taiwan if you are the spouse, or unmarried dependent son or daughter of an E-1 employee of the Taipei Economic and Cultural Representative Office.

Foreign Students

F-1 Student Seeking Optional Practical Training in an Occupation Directly Related to Studies--(c)(3)(i). File your EAD application with a Certificate of Eligibility of Nonimmigrant (F-1) Student Status (Form I-20 A-B/I-20 ID) endorsed by a Designated School Official within the past 30 days.

F-1 Student Offered Off-Campus Employment under the Sponsorship of a Qualifying International Organization-- (c)(3)(ii). File your EAD application with the international organization's letter of certification that the proposed employment is within the scope of its sponsorship, and a Certificate of Eligibility of Nonimmigrant (F-1) Student Status--For Academic and Language Students (Form I-20 A-B/I-20 ID) endorsed by the Designated School Official within the past 30 days.

F-1 Student Seeking Off-Campus Employment Due to Severe Economic Hardship--(c)(3)(iii). File your EAD application with Form I-20 A-B/I-20 ID, Certificate of Eligibility of Nonimmigrant (F-1) Student Status--For Academic and Language Students, and any evidence you wish to submit, such as affidavits, that detail the unforeseen economic circumstances that cause your request, and evidence you have tried to find off-campus employment with an employer who has filed a labor and wage attestation.

J-2 Spouse or Minor Child of an Exchange Visitor--(c)(5). File your EAD application with a copy of your J-1's (principal alien's) Certificate of Eligibility for Exchange Visitor (J-1) Status (Form IAP-66). You must submit a written statement, with any supporting evidence showing, that your employment is not necessary to support the J-1 but is for other purposes.

M-1 Student Seeking Practical Training after Completing Studies--(c)(6). File your EAD application with a completed Form I-539, Application to Change/Extend Nonimmigrant Status. Form I-20 M-N, Certificate of Eligibility for Nonimmigrant (M-1) Student Status--For Vocational Students endorsed by the Designated School Official within the past 30 days.

Eligible Dependents of Employees of Diplomatic Missions, International Organizations, or NATO

Dependent of A-1 or A-2 Foreign Government Officials--(c)(1). Submit your EAD application with Form I-566, Inter-Agency Record of Individual Requesting Change/Adjustment to, or from, A or G Status; or Requesting A, G, or NATO Dependent Employment Authorization, through your diplomatic mission to the Department of State (DOS). The DOS will forward all favorably endorsed applications directly to the Nebraska Service Center for adjudication.

Dependent of G-1, G-3 or G-4 Nonimmigrant--(c)(4). Submit your EAD application with a Form I-566, Inter-Agency Record of Individual Requesting Change/Adjustment to or from A or G Status; or Requesting A, G, or NATO Dependent Employment Authorization, through your international organization to the Department of State (DOS). [In New York City, the United Nations (UN) and UN missions should submit such applications to the United States Mission to the UN (USUN).] The DOS or USUN will forward all favorably endorsed applications directly to the Nebraska Service Center for adjudication.

Dependent of NATO-1 through NATO-6--(c)(7). Submit your EAD application with Form I-566, Inter-Agency Record of Individual Requesting Change/Adjustment to, or from, A or G Status; or Requesting A, G or NATO Dependent Employment Authorization, to NATO/SACLANT, 7857 Blandy Road, C-027, Suite 100, Norfolk, VA 23551-2490. NATO/SACLANT will forward all favorably endorsed applications directly to the Nebraska Service Center for adjudication.

Employment-Based Nonimmigrant Categories

B-1 Nonimmigrant who is the personal or domestic servant of a nonimmigrant employer--(c)(17)(i). File your EAD application with:

- Evidence from your employer that he or she is a B, E, F, H, I, J, L, M, O, P, R, or TN nonimmigrant and you were employed for at least one year by the employer before the employer entered the United States or your employer regularly employs personal and domestic servants and has done so for a period of years before coming to the United States; and

- Evidence that you have either worked for this employer as a personal or domestic servant for at least one year or, evidence that you have at least one year's experience as a personal or domestic servant; and

- Evidence establishing that you have a residence abroad which you have no intention of abandoning.

B-1 Nonimmigrant Domestic Servant of a U.S. Citizen-- (c)(17)ii. File your EAD application with:

- Evidence from your employer that he or she is a U.S. citizen; and

- Evidence that your employer has a permanent home abroad or is stationed outside the United States and is temporarily visiting the United States or the citizen's current assignment in the United States will not be longer than four 4 years; and

- Evidence that he or she has employed you as a domestic servant abroad for at least six 6 months prior to your admission to the United States.

B-1 Nonimmigrant Employed by a Foreign Airline--(c)(17)(iii). File your EAD application with a letter from the airline fully describing your duties and indicating that your position would entitle you to E nonimmigrant status except for the fact that you are not a national of the same country as the airline or because there is no treaty of commerce and navigation in effect between the United States and that country.

Spouse of an E-1/E-2 Treaty Trader or Investor--(a)(17). File your EAD application with evidence of your lawful status and evidence you are a **spouse** of a principal E-1/E-2, such as your I-94. (Other relatives or dependents of E-1/E-2 aliens who are in E status are not eligible for employment authorization and may not file under this category.)

Spouse of an L-1 Intracompany Transferee--(a)(18). File your EAD application with evidence of your lawful status and evidence you are a **spouse** of a principal L-1, such as your I-94. (Other relatives or dependents of L-1 aliens who are in L status are not eligible for employment authorization and may not file under this category.)

Family-Based Nonimmigrant Categories

K-1 Nonimmigrant Fiancé(e) of U.S. Citizen or K-2 Dependent--(a)(6). File your EAD application if you are filing within 90 days from the date of entry. This EAD cannot be renewed. Any EAD application other than for a replacement must be based on your pending application for adjustment under (c)(9).

K-3 Nonimmigrant Spouse of U.S. Citizen or K-4 Dependent--(a)(9). File your EAD application along with evidence of your admission such as copies of your Form I-94, passport, and K visa.

Family Unity Program--(a)(13). File your EAD application with a copy of the approval notice, if you have been granted status under this program. You may choose to file your EAD application concurrently with your Form I-817, Application for Voluntary Departure under the Family Unity Program. USCIS may take up to 90 days from the date upon which you are granted status under the Family Unity Program to adjudicate your EAD application. If you were denied Family Unity status solely because your legalized spouse or parent first applied under the Legalization/SAW programs after May 5, 1988, file your EAD application with a new Form I-817 application and a copy of the original denial. However, if your EAD application is based on continuing eligibility under (c)(12), please refer to **Deportable Alien Granted Voluntary Departure.**

LIFE Family Unity--(a)(14). If you are applying for initial employment authorization pursuant to the Family Unity provisions of section 1504 of the LIFE Act Amendments, or an extension of such authorization, you should not be using this form. Please obtain and complete a Form I-817, Application for Family Unity Benefits. If you are applying for a replacement EAD that was issued pursuant to the LIFE Act Amendments Family Unity provisions, file your EAD application with the required evidence listed in **Part 3**.

V-1, V-2 or V-3 Nonimmigrant--(a)(15). If you have been inspected and admitted to the United States with a valid V visa, file this application along with evidence of your admission, such as copies of your Form I-94, passport, and R visa. If you have been granted V status while in the United States, file this application along with evidence of your V status, such as an approval notice. If you are in the United States but you have not yet filed an application for V status, you may file this application at the same time as you file your application for V status. USCIS will adjudicate this application after adjudicating your application for V status.

EAD Applicants Who Have Filed For Adjustment of Status

Adjustment Applicant--(c)(9). File your EAD application with a copy of the receipt notice or other evidence that your Form I-485, Application for Permanent Residence, is pending. You may file Form I-765 together with your Form I-485.

Adjustment Applicant Based on Continuous Residence Since January 1, 1972--(c)(16). File your EAD application with your Form I-485, Application for Permanent Residence; a copy of your receipt notice; or other evidence that the Form I-485 is pending.

Other

N-8 or N-9 Nonimmigrant--(a)(7). File your EAD application with the required evidence listed in **Part 3**.

Granted Withholding of Deportation or Removal --(a)(10). File your EAD application with a copy of the Immigration Judge's order. It is not necessary to apply for a new EAD until 90 days before the expiration of your current EAD.

Applicant for Suspension/Cancelation--(c)(10). File your EAD application with evidence that your Form I-881 application for suspension of deportation ,cancelation of removal or your EOIR-40 is pending

Paroled in the Public Interest--(c)(11). File your EAD application if you were paroled into the United States for emergent reasons or reasons strictly in the public interest.

Deferred Action--(c)(14). File your EAD application with a copy of the order, notice or document placing you in deferred action and evidence establishing economic necessity for an EAD.

Final Order of Deportation--(c)(18). File your EAD application with a copy of the order of supervision and a request for employment authorization which may be based on, but not limited to, the following:

* Existence of a dependent spouse and/or children in the United States who rely on you for support; and

* Existence of economic necessity to be employed;

* Anticipated length of time before you can be removed from the United States.

LIFE Legalization applicant--(c)(24). We encourage you to file your EAD application together with your Form I-485, Application to Regsiter Permanent Residence or Adjust Status, to facilitate processing. However, you may file Form I-765 at a later date with evidence that you were a CSS, LULAC, or Zambrano class member applicant before October 1, 2000 and with a copy of the receipt notice or other evidence that your Form I-485 is pending.

T-1 Nonimmigrant--(a)(16). If you are applying for initial employment authorization as a T-1 nonimmigrant, file this form only if you did not request an employment authorization document when you applied for T nonimmigrant status. If you have been granted T status and this is a request for a renewal or replacement of an employment authorization document, file this application along with evidence of your T status, such as an approval notice.

T-2, T-3, or T-4 Nonimmigrant--(c)(25). File this form with a copy of your T-1's (principal alien's) approval notice and proof of your relationship to the T-1 principal.

Part 3. Required Documentation

All applications must be filed with the documents required below, in addition to the particular evidence required for the category listed in **Part 2**, **Eligibility Categories**, with fee, if required.

If you are required to show economic necessity for your category (See **Part 2**), submit a list of your assets, income and expenses.

Please assemble the documents in the following order:

Your application with the filing fee. See **Part 4**, **Fee** for details.

If you are mailing your application to the USCIS, you must also submit:

- A copy of Form I-94 Departure Record (front and back), if available.
- A copy of your last EAD (front and back).
- Two passport-style color photos with a white background taken no earlier than 30 days before submission to USCIS. They should be unmounted, glossy and unretouched. The photos should show a full-frontal facial position. Your head should be bare unless you are wearing a headdress as required by a religious order to which you belong. The photo should not be larger than 2 x 2 inches, with the distance from the top of the head to just below the chin about 1 1/4 inches. Lightly print our name and your A#, if known, on the back of each photo with a pencil.

Special filing instructions for those with pending asylum applications ((c)(8))

Asylum Applicant (with a pending asylum application) who Filed for Asylum on or after January 4, 1995. *You must wait at leat 150 days following the filing of your asylum claim before you are eligible to apply for an EAD. If you file your EAD application early, it will be denied. File your EAD application with:*
- A copy of the USCIS acknowledgement mailer which was mailed to you; or
- Other evidence that your Form I-589 was filed with USCIS; or
- Evidence that your Form I-589 was filed with an Immigration Judge at the Executive Office for Immigration Review (EOIR); or
- Evidence that your asylum application remains under administrative or judicial review.

Asylum Applicant (with a pending asylum application) who Filed for Asylum and for Withholding of Deportation Prior to January 4, 1995 and is *NOT* in Exclusion or Deportation Proceedings.
You may file your EAD application at any time; however, it will only be granted if USCIS finds that your asylum application is not frivolous. File your EAD application with:

- A complete copy of your previously filed Form I-589; AND
- A copy of your USCIS receipt notice; or
- A copy of the USCIS acknowledgement mailer; or
- Evidence that your Form I-589 was filed with EOIR; or
- Evidence that your asylum application remains under administrative or judicial review; or
- Other evidence that you filed an asylum application.

Asylum Applicant (with a pending asylum application) who Filed an Initial Request for Asylum Prior to January 4, 1995, and *IS IN* Exclusion or Deportation Proceedings. If you filed your Request for Asylum and Withholding of Deportation (Form I-589) prior to January 4, 1995 and you ARE IN exclusion or deportation proceedings, file your EAD application with:

- A date-stamped copy of your previously filed Form I-589; or
- A copy of Form I-221, Order to Show Cause and Notice of Hearing, or Form I-122, Notice to Applicant for Admission Detained for Hearing Before Immigration Judge; or
- A copy of EOIR-26, Notice of Appeal, date stamped by the Office of the Immigration Judge; or
- A date-stamped copy of a petition for judicial review or for *habeas corpus* issued to the asylum applicant; or
- Other evidence that you filed an asylum application with EOIR.

Asylum Application under the ABC Settlement Agreement--(c)(8). If you are a Salvadoran or Guatemalan national eligible for benefits under the ABC settlement agreement, American Baptist Churches v. Thornburgh , 760 F. Supp. 976 (N.D. Cal. 1991), please follow the instructions contained in this section when filing your Form I-765.

You must have asylum application (Form I-589) on file either with USCIS or with an immigration judge in order to receive work authorization. Therefore, please submit evidence that you have previously filed an asylum application when you submit your EAD application. You are not required to submit this evidence when you apply, but it will help USCIS process your request efficiently.

If you are renewing or replacing your EAD, you must pay the filing fee.

Mark your application as follows:

- Write "ABC" in the top right corner of your EAD application. You must identify yourself as an ABC class member if you are applying for an EAD under the ABC settlement agreement.
- Write "(c)(8)" in **Section 16** of the application.

You are entitled to an EAD without regard to the merits of your asylum claim. Your application for an EAD will be decided within 60 days if: (1) you pay the filing fee, (2) you have a complete, pending asylum application on file, and (3) write "ABC" in the top right corner of your EAD application. If you do not pay the filing fee for an initial EAD request, your request may be denied if USCIS finds that your asylum application is frivolous. However, if you cannot pay the filing fee for an EAD, you may qualify for a fee waiver under 8 CFR 103.7(c). See **Part 4** concerning fee waivers.

Part 4. Fee

What Is the Fee?

Applicants must pay a fee of **$180.00** unless noted below.

If a fee is required, it will not be refunded. Pay the exact amount. Checks and money orders must be payable in U.S. currency. Make check or money order payable to the **"Department of Homeland Security,"** unless:

If you live in Guam make your check or money order payable to **"Treasurer, Guam."** If you live in the U.S. Virgin Islands make your check or money order payable to **"Commissioner of Finance of the Virgin Islands."**

A charge of $30.00 will be imposed if a check in payment of a fee is not honored by the bank on which it is drawn. Please do **not** send cash in the mail.

Initial EAD: If this is your initial application and you are applying under one of the following categories, a filing fee is **not** required:

- (a)(3) Refugee;
- (a)(4) Paroled as Refugee;
- (a)(5) Asylee;
- (a)(7) N-8 or N-9 nonimmigrant;
- (a)(8) Citizen of Micronesia, Marshall Islands or Palau;
- (a)(10) Granted Withholding of Deportation;
- (a)(11) Deferred Enforced Departure;
- (a)(16) Victim of Severe Form of Trafficking (T-1);
- (c)(1), (c)(4), or (c)(7) Dependent of certain foreign government, international organization, or NATO personnel; or
- (c)(8) Applicant for asylum [an applicant filing under the special ABC procedures must pay the fee].

Renewal EAD: If this is a renewal application and you are applying under one of the following categories, a filing fee is **not** required:

- (a)(8) Citizen of Micronesia, Marshall Islands, or Palau;
- (a)(10) Granted Withholding of Deportation;
- (a)(11) Deferred Enforced Departure; or
- (c)(1), (c)(4), or (c)(7) Dependent of certain foreign government, international organization, or NATO personnel.

Replacement EAD: If this is your replacement application and you are applying under one of the following categories, *a* filing fee is **not** required:

- (c)(l), (c)(4), or (c)(7) Dependent of certain foreign government, international organization, or NATO personnel.

You may be eligible for a fee waiver under 8 CFR 103.7(c).

USCIS will use the Poverty Guidelines published annually by the Department of Health and Human Services as the basic criteria in determining the applicant's eligibility when economic necessity is identified as a factor.

The Poverty Guidelines will be used as a guide, but not as a conclusive standard, in adjudicating fee waiver requests for employment authorization applications requiring a fee.

How to Check If the Fee Is Correct.

The fee on this form is current as of the edition date appearing in the lower right corner of this page. However, because USCIS fees change periodically, you can verify if the fee is correct by following one of the steps below:

- Visit our website at www.uscis.gov and scroll down to "Forms and E-Filing" to check the appropriate fee, or
- Review the Fee Schedule included in your form package, if you called us to request the form, or
- Telephone our National Customer Service Center at 1-800-375-5283 and ask for the fee information.

NOTE: If your application requires a biometric services fee for USCIS to take your fingerprints, photograph or signature, you can use the same procedure above to confirm the biometrics fee.

Part 5. Where to File

If your response to **Question 16** is: **(a)(3), (a)(4), (a)(5), (a)(7)** or **(a)(8)** mail your application to:

USCIS Service Center
P.O. Box 87765
Lincoln, NE 68501-7765

If your response to **Question 16** is **(a)(9)**, mail your application to:

USCIS
P.O. Box 7218
Chicago, IL 60680-7218

If your response to **Question 16** is **(a)(15)**, mail your application to:

USCIS
P.O. Box 7216
Chicago, IL 60680-7216

If your response to **Question 16** is **(a)(14)** or **(c)(24)**, mail your application to:

USCIS
P.O. Box 7219
Chicago, IL 60680-7219

If your response to **Question 16** is: **(a)(16)** or **(c)(25)** mail your application to:

USCIS Service Center
75 Lower Welden St.
St. Albans, VT 05479-0001

If your response to **Question 16** is: **(a)(10), (c)(11), (c)(12), (c)(14), (c)(16)** or **(c)(18),** apply at the local USCIS office having jurisdiction over your place of residence.

If your response to **Question 16** is: **(a)(12)** or **(c)(19)**, file your EAD application according to the instructions in the Federal Register notice for your particular country's TPS designation.

If your response to **Question 16** is **(c)(1)**, **(c)(4)** or **(c)(7)**, submit your application through your principal's sponsoring organization . Your application will be reviewed and forwarded by the DOS, USUN or NATO/SACLANT to the Nebraska Service Center following certification of your eligibility for an EAD.

If your response to **Question 16** is **(c)(8)** under the special ABC filing instructions and you are filing your asylum and EAD applications together, mail your application to the office where you are filing your asylum application.

If your response to question 16 is **(c)(9)**, file your application at the same local USCIS office or Service Center where you submitted your adjustment of status application.

If your response to question 16 is: **(a)(6), (a)(11), (a)(13), (a)(17), (a)(18), (c)(2), (c)(3)(i), (c)(3)(ii), (c)(3)(iii), (c)(5), (c)(6), (c)(8),(c)(17)(i), (c)(17)(ii) or (c)(17)(iii):**

mail your application based on your address to the appropriate **Service Center**. The correct **Service Center** is based on the state or territory in which you live.

If you live in:		Mail your application to:
Connecticut D.C. Maryland New Hampshire New York Puerto Rico Vermont West Virginia	Delaware Maine Massachusetts New Jersey Pennsylvania Rhode Island Virginia U.S.V.I.	USCIS Service Center 75 Lower Welden Street St. Albans, VT 05479-0001
Arizona Guam Nevada	California Hawaii	**USCIS Service Center** P.O. Box 10765 Laguna Niguel, CA 92067-1076
Alabama Florida Kentucky Mississippi North Carolina South Carolina Texas	Arkansas Georgia Lousiana New Mexico Oklahoma Tennessee	**USCIS Service Center** P.O. Box 851041 Mesquite, TX 75185-1041
Alaska Idaho Indiana Kansas Minnesota Montana North Dakota Oregon Utah Wisconsin	Colorado Illinois Iowa Michigan Missouri Nebraska Ohio South Dakota Washington Wyoming	**USCIS Service Center** P.O. Box 87765 Lincoln, NE 68501-7765

If your response to question 16 is **(c)(10)**, and you are a NACARA 203 applicant eligible to apply for relief with USCIS, or if your I-881 application is still pending with USCIS and you wish to renew your EAD, mail your EAD application with the required fee to the appropriate USCIS service center below:

* If you live in Alabama, Arkansas, Colorado, Connecticut, Delaware, the District of Columbia, Florida, Georgia, Louisiana, Maine, Maryland, Massachusetts, Mississippi, New Hampshire, New Jersey, New Mexico, New York, North Carolina, Oklahoma, Pennsylvania, Puerto Rico, Rhode Island, South Carolina, Tennessee, Texas, Utah, the U.S. Virgin Islands, Vermont, Virginia, West Virginia or Wyoming, mail your application to:

> **USCIS Service Center**
> 75 Lower Welden St.
> St. Albans, VT 05479-0001

* If you live in Alaska, Arizona, California, the Commonwealth of Guam, Hawaii Idaho, Illinois, Indiana, Iowa, Kansas, Kentucky, Michigan, Minnesota, Missouri, Montana, Nebraska, Nevada, North Dakota, Oregon, Ohio, South Dakota, Washington or Wisconsin, mail your application to:

> **USCIS Service Center**
> P.O. Box 10765
> Laguna Niguel, CA 92067-1076

You should submit the fee for the EAD application on a separate check or money order. Do not combine your check or money order with the fee for the Form I-881.

If your response to **Question 16** is **(c)(10) and you are not eligible to apply for NACARA 203 relief with USCIS,** but you are eligible for other deportation or removal relief, apply at the local USCIS office having jurisdiction over your place of residence.

Part 6. Processing Information

Acceptance. If your application is complete and filed at a USCIS Service Center, you will be mailed a Form I-797 receipt notice. However, an application filed without the required fee, evidence, signature or photographs (if required) will be returned to you as incomplete. You may correct the deficiency and resubmit the application; however, an application is not considered properly filed until USCIS accepts it.

Approval. If approved, your EAD will either be mailed to you or you may be required to appear at your local USCIS office to pick it up.

Request for Evidence. If additional information or documentation is required, a written request will be sent to you, specifying the information required or advising you of an interview.

Denial. If your application cannot be granted, you will receive a written notice explaining the basis of your denial.

Interim EAD. If you have not received a decision within 90 days of receipt by USCIS of a properly filed EAD application or within 30 days of a properly filed initial EAD application based on an asylum application filed on or after January 4, 1995, you may obtain interim work authorization by appearing in person at your local USCIS district office. You must bring proof of identity and any notices that you have received from USCIS in connection with your application for employment authorization.

Part 7. Other Information

Penalties for Perjury. All statements contained in response to questions in this application are declared to be true and correct under penalty of perjury. Title 18, United States Code, Section 1546, provides in part:

... Whoever knowingly makes under oath, or as permitted under penalty of perjury under 1746 of Title 28, United States Code, knowingly subscribes as true, any false statement with respect to a material fact in any application, affidavit, or other document required by the immigration laws or regulations prescribed thereunder, or knowingly presents any such application, affidavit, or other document containing any such false statement-shall be fined in accordance with this title or imprisoned not more than five years, or both.

The knowing placement of false information on this application may subject you and/or the preparer of this application to criminal penalties under Title 18 of the United States Code. The knowing placement of false information on this application may also subject you and/or the preparer to civil penalties under Section 274C of the Immigration and Nationality Act (INA), 8 U.S.C. 1324c. Under 8 U.S.C. 1324c, a person subject to a final order for civil document fraud is deportable from the United States and may be subject to fines.

Authority for Collecting this Information. The authority to require you to file Form I-765, Application for Employment Authorization, when applying for employment authorization is found at sections 103(a) and 274A(h)(3) of the Immigration and Nationality Act. Information you provide on your Form I-765 is used to determine whether you are eligible for employment authorization and for the preparation of your Employment Authorization Document if you are found eligible. Failure to provide all information as requested may result in the denial or rejection of this application. The information you provide may also be disclosed to other federal, state, local and foreign law enforcement and regulatory agencies during the course of the USCIS investigations.

USCIS Forms and Information.

To order USCIS forms, call our toll-free number at **1-800-870-3676.** You can also get USCIS forms and information on immigration laws, regulations and procedures by telephoning our **National Customer Service Center** at **1-800-375-5283** or visiting our internet website at **www.uscis.gov.**

Use InfoPass for Appointments.

As an alternative to waiting in line for assistance at your local USCIS office, you can now schedule an appointment through our internet-based system, **InfoPass.** To access the system, visit our website at **www.uscis.gov.** Use the **InfoPass** appointment scheduler and follow the screen prompts to set up your appointment. **InfoPass** generates an electronic appointment notice that appears on the screen. Print the notice and take it with you to your appointment. The notice gives the time and date or your appointment, along with the address of the USCIS office.

Paperwork Reduction Act. An agency may not conduct or sponsor an information collection and a person is not required to respond to a collection of information unless it displays a currently valid OMB control number.

The U.S. Citizenship and Immigration Servies (USCIS) tries to create forms and instructions which are accurate and easily understood. Often this is difficult because immigration law can be very complex.

The public reporting burden for this form is estimated to average three 3 hours and 25 minutes per response, including the time for reviewing instructions, gathering and maintaining the data needed, and completing and reviewing the collection of information.

The USCIS welcomes your comments regarding this burden estimate or any other aspect of this form, including suggestions for reducing this burden to the U.S. Citizenship and Immigration Services, Regulatory Management Division, 111 Massachusetts Avenue, N.W., Washington DC, 20529; OMB No. 1615-0040. **Do not mail your completed application to this address.**

OMB No. 1615-0040

Department of Homeland Security
U.S. Citizenship and Immigration Services

I-765, Application for
Employment Authorization

Do not write in this block.

Remarks	Action Block	Fee Stamp
A#		
Applicant is filing under §274a.12 _____		

☐ Application Approved. Employment Authorized / Extended *(Circle One)*   until _____ (Date).
_____ (Date).

Subject to the following conditions: _____

☐ Application Denied.
  ☐ Failed to establish eligibility under 8 CFR 274a.12 (a) or (c).
  ☐ Failed to establish economic necessity as required in 8 CFR 274a.12(c)(14), (18) and 8 CFR 214.2(f)

I am applying for: ☐ Permission to accept employment.
  ☐ Replacement *(of lost employment authorization document).*
  ☐ Renewal of my permission to accept employment *(attach previous employment authorization document).*

1. Name (Family Name in CAPS)   (First)   (Middle)

2. Other Names Used (Include Maiden Name)

3. Address in the United States (Number and Street)   (Apt. Number)

(Town or City)   (State/Country)   (ZIP Code)

4. Country of Citizenship/Nationality

5. Place of Birth (Town or City)   (State/Province)   (Country)

6. Date of Birth   (mm/dd/yyyy)   7. Gender
  ☐ Male   ☐ Female

8. Marital Status
  ☐ Married   ☐ Single
  ☐ Widowed   ☐ Divorced

9. Social Security Number (Include all numbers you have ever used) (if any)

10. Alien Registration Number (A-Number) or I-94 Number (if any)

11. Have you ever before applied for employment authorization from USCIS?
  ☐ Yes (If yes, complete below)   ☐ No
  Which USCIS Office?   Date(s)
  Results (Granted or Denied - attach all documentation)

12. Date of Last Entry into the U.S.   (mm/dd/yyyy)

13. Place of Last Entry into the U.S.

14. Manner of Last Entry (Visitor, Student, etc.)

15. Current Immigration Status (Visitor, Student, etc.)

16. Go to **Part 2** of the Instructions, Eligibility Categories. In the space below, place the letter and number of the category you selected from the instructions (For example, (a)(8), (c)(17)(iii), etc.).

Eligibility under 8 CFR 274a.12

(   ) (   ) (   )

SAMPLE

Certification.

Your Certification: I certify, under penalty of perjury under the laws of the United States of America, that the foregoing is true and correct. Furthermore, I authorize the release of any information that the U.S. Citizenship and Immigration Services needs to determine eligibility for the benefit I am seeking. I have read the Instructions in **Part 2** and have identified the appropriate eligibility category in **Block 16**.

Signature   Telephone Number   Date

Signature of Person Preparing Form, If Other Than Above: I declare that this document was prepared by me at the request of the applicant and is based on all information of which I have any knowledge.

Print Name   Address   *Signature*   Date

Remarks	Initial Receipt	Resubmitted	Relocated		Completed		
			Rec'd	Sent	Approved	Denied	Returned

f

U.S. Department of Justice
Immigration and Naturalization Service

OMB No. 1115-0174

Application - Alternative Inspection Services

INSTRUCTIONS

Read carefully -- fee will be not refunded. Failure to follow instructions may require return of your application and delay final action.

1. Preparation of Application. Fill in application in single copy only, by typewriter, or print in block letters using only dark ink. Do not use pencil or red ink. Do not leave any question unanswered. Mark any question which does not apply to you "N/A".

2. Who Can Apply.

Citizens and lawful permanent residents of the United States, citizens of Canada and Landed Canadian immigrants who are citizens of British Commonwealth countries are eligible to apply for all programs. Additional eligibility criteria for each program are indicated below:

   A. *Dedicated Commuter Lane Program ("DCL")* - Certain citizens of Mexico and certain non-immigrants.

   B. *Automated Permit Port Program ("APP")* - Certain non-immigrants.

   C. *INSPASS Airport* - Citizens of Visa Waiver Program countries or any other country approved for participation by the Commissioner, Immigration and Naturalization Service (INS).

Each participant in each program must submit a separate application. Persons under 14 years of age may not enroll in either INSPASS Program.

3. Where to Submit This Application. Applications may be submitted in person or by mail to the U.S. port of entry sponsoring the DCL for which you are applying, or at the port of entry having jurisdiction over the APP for which you request access. INSPASS applicants may apply at any INSPASS port of entry in person or by mail.

4. Submission of Application. Each application must be supported by evidence of citizenship, legal resident status, or other documentation as applicable, including but not limited to proof of employment or residence, vehicle registration and insurance. Original documentation must be presented at the time of the personal interview. Personal identifiers, i.e., voice print or other biometrics, may be required for participation.

5. Final Approval. Your application will be reviewed and an interview may be scheduled prior to acceptance. You will be required to produce your original evidence of eligibility at that time. Approval for participation is valid for one year unless otherwise revoked. The pass may not be used for purposes other than those involved in this application and approved by the INS.

6. Denial. An application for participation in a program may be denied at the discretion of the District Director without appeal. All applicants denied shall be so notified. Applications submitted without the required documentation or which are incomplete will be returned without action.

All applicants who have been denied permission to participate in the DCL or APP programs, or who have had their permission to participate in either program revoked for any reason, must wait 90 days from the date of denial or revocation to reapply.

7. Fees.

   A. Application or Replacement Card Fee.

   (1) The application fee for the DCL program is $25 (U.S)., with a maximum amount payable by a family (husband wife, and any minor children) of $50 (U.S.). If fingerprints are required, an additional fee equal to the amount of the current FBI fee for conducting fingerprints checks will be required at the time of application. The fee for a replacement card for the DCL program is $25.

   (2) Presently, there are no application fees for the APP program, or for either INSPASS program.

   B. System Costs Fee.

   (1) A non-refundable fee of $80 (U.S.) will be assessed on all approved applicants for DCLs located at certain ports of entry, with the maximum payable by family (husband, wife and any minor children) of $160 (U.S.). If an approved participant wishes to register more than one vehicle for use in the lane, he/she may be assessed an additional $42, also non refundable, for each additional vehicle.

   (2) Presently, there is no System Costs Fee for the APP program or for either INSPASS Program.

Payment may be made by check or money order in the exact amount. All checks and money orders must be payable in U.S. currency at a financial institution in the United States. Make check or money order payable to "Immigration and Naturalization Service." A charge of $30.00 will be imposed if a check in payment of a fee is not honored by the bank on which it is drawn. At some port of entries, payment may be made by credit card.

8. Privacy Act Statement. The authority to collect this information is contained in Title 8, United States Code. Furnishing the information on this form is voluntary; however, failure to provide all of the requested information may result in the delay of a final decision or denial of your request. The information collected will be used to make a determination on your application. It may also be provided to other government agencies (Federal, state, local and/or foreign). All applicants are subject to a check of criminal information databases in order to determine eligibility.

9. Penalties for False Statements in Applications. Severe penalties are provided by law for knowingly and willfully falsifying or concealing a material fact or using any false document in the submission of this application. Also, a false representation may result in the denial of this application and any other application you may make for any benefit under the immigration laws of the United States.

Form I-823 Instructions (Rev. 08/25/00)Y

10. Random compliance checks. Periodic random checks will be conducted to ensure compliance with the conditions of each program.

11. Applicant acknowledges and agrees that should he/she violate any condition(s) of this program(s), or any law or regulation of any Federal inspection service, or is otherwise determined to be inadmissible to the U.S., his/her participation in this program may be revoked and he/she may be subject to other applicable sanctions. Such sanctions may include, but are not limited to, criminal prosecution, exclusion or deportation proceedings, imposition of civil monetary penalties, and seizure of merchandise and/or vehicles. Conditions by which the applicant must abide include, but are not limited to, the following.

A) Adherence to all Federal, state, and local laws regarding the importation of alcohol and agricultural products; possession and importation of controlled substances, and all other laws and regulations under the jurisdiction of any federal agency.

B) Adherence to all requirements of the Immigration and Nationality Act, as amended, and all INS regulations, regarding documentary requirements.

12. Reporting Burden. A person is not required to respond to a collection of information unless it displays a currently valid OMB control number. We try to create forms and instructions that are accurate, can be easily understood, and which impose the least possible burden on you to provide us with information. Often this is difficult because some immigration laws are very complex. Accordingly, the reporting burden for this collection of information is computed as follows: 1) learning about the form, and reading and understanding U.S. INS Publications 28 minutes; 2) completing the form, 8 minutes; 3) fingerprinting 30 minutes; and 4) assembling and mailing the application, 4 minutes, for an estimated average of 70 minutes per response. If you have comments regarding the accuracy of this estimate, or suggestions for making this form simpler, you can write to the Immigration and Naturalization Service, HQPDI, 425 I Street, N.W; Room 4034, Washington, DC 20536, OMB No. 1115-0174. **Do not mail your completed application to this address.**

U.S. Department of Justice
Immigration and Naturalization Service

OMB No. 1115-0174

Application - Alternative Inspection Services

START HERE - PLEASE TYPE OR PRINT

Application Type: *(Check one)* ☐ Dedicated Commuter Lane   ☐ Automated Permit Port   ☐ INSPASS Airport

| 1. Name: *(Last)* | *(First)* | *(Middle Name)* | 2. Date of Birth: *(MM/DD/YYYY)* |

3. U.S. Alien Registration No. *(If applicable)*

4. Gender: ☐ Male   ☐ Female

5. Place of Birth: *(City)*   *(State)*   *(Country)*

6. Permanent Address *(Street Number and Name):*

| City: | State/Province/Country: | Zip/Postal Code: | 8. Country of Citizenship: |

7. Usual purpose of Entry:

8. Port of entry where you intend to enter the United States:

9. Have you ever been:

    a. Arrested or convicted of a criminal offense, anywhere?   Yes ☐   No ☐
    b. Granted a conditional discharge or pardon?   Yes ☐   No ☐
    c. Found to be in violation of any immigration law?   Yes ☐   No ☐
    d. Found to be in violation of any customs law?   Yes ☐   No ☐
    e. Refused admission to the United States?   Yes ☐   No ☐
    f. Denied any other immigration benefit, whether you applied for the
       benefit directly, or the benefit was sought on your behalf?   Yes ☐   No ☐

      If yes, please explain:

10. Occupation: ————————————————————

    Employer: ————————————————————

    Employer Address: ————————————————————

    Employer Phone #: ———————————— Employer Point of Contact: ————————————

11. Admission Classification

    ☐ United States Citizen

    ☐ Lawful Permanent Resident

    ☐ Other (specify) ————————————————————

Continue on Back   Form I-823 (Rev. 08/25/00)Y Page 3

12. Citizenship and Admissibility

For completion by U.S. citizens only

Passport #: _____ Expiration Date: _____

Other evidence of U.S. Citizenship:_____

For completion by non-U.S. citizens

Passport #: _____ Expiration Date:_____

Issuing Country:_____

AND

Form I-551, Permanent Resident Card #: _____

OR

Visa Classification:_____ Visa #: _____

Place of Issuance: _____ Expiration Date:_____

OR

Border Crossing Card #:_____

Expiration Date: _____

TRANSPORTING UNDOCUMENTED ALIENS NARCOTICS, UNDECLARED MERCHANDISE, FIREARMS CONTRABAND, OR DECLARED CURRENCY IN EXCESS OF $10,000 ARE VIOLATIONS OF UNITED STATES LAW THAT WILL BE PROSECUTED AND PUNISHABLE BY IMPRISONMENT AND FINE.

For Government Use Only

Identification Document(s) Presented:_____ Expiration Date:_____

Type of Application: ☐ Initial ☐ Renewal ☐ Replacement Card

Remarks: _____
_____
_____

U.S. Department of Justice
Immigration and Naturalization Service

OMB No. 1115-0174

Application - Alternative Inspection Services

AUTOMATED PERMIT PORT APPLICATIONS

1. Applicant acknowledges that (s)he is a citizen or lawful permanent resident of the U.S., or non-immigrant as determined eligible by the Commissioner of the Service. Applicant acknowledges that he or she must be in possession of all documentation required by the Immigration and Nationality Act and implementing regulations at all times when using the Automated Permit Port (APP). When in the U.S., a non-U.S. citizen applicant acknowledges that (s)he must remain otherwise eligible to enter the U.S. at time of each use of the APP.

2. Applicant agrees to a full inspection of each vehicle presented for registration in the APP prior to approval of his/her application, and at any time use of the APP. The applicant acknowledges and agrees to be responsible for all contents of the vehicle s(he) occupies when using the APP, whether or not that vehicle is owned by or registered to the applicant.

3. Applicant acknowledges that vehicle registration and insurance must be current when using the APP, and documentation evidencing same must be made available to the Service upon request. If the vehicle is owned or registered to someone other than the applicant, evidence permitting use of the vehicle in the APP must be made available to the Service upon request.

4. Applicant acknowledges and agrees that by submitting this application, (s)he will be subject to a check of criminal information databases prior to and during each use of the APP.

5. Applicant acknowledges that s(he) may only use the APP when occupying the specific vehicle inspected and authorized by the Service for the applicants use of the APP.

6. Applicant acknowledges and agrees that all devices, decals, or other equipment, methodology, or technology used to identify or inspect persons or vehicles remains the property of the U.S. government, and must be surrendered upon request.

7. If the registered owner is not the applicant, then written proof must be provided that the applicant has authorization to register and use the vehicle in the APP.

    A. Vehicle License Number: _____   A. State/Province: _____
        Vehicle Identification Number: _____   Vehicle Make/Model: _____
        Vehicle Year: _____   Vehicle Color: _____
        Vehicle Insurance Number: _____   Registered Owner: _____

    B. Vehicle License Number: _____   B. State/Province: _____
        Vehicle Identification Number: _____   Vehicle Make/Model: _____
        Vehicle Year: _____   Vehicle Color: _____
        Vehicle Insurance Number: _____   Registered Owner: _____

    C. Vehicle License Number: _____   C. State/Province: _____
        Vehicle Identification Number: _____   Vehicle Make/Model: _____
        Vehicle Year: _____   Vehicle Color: _____
        Vehicle Insurance Number: _____   Registered Owner: _____

8. Driver's License #: _____
    Issuing Country and State/Province: _____
    Expiration Date: _____

9. Will you be the sole occupant of the vehicle? *(All occupants of a vehicle used in the APP must have current participation authorization.)*
    (check one) ☐ YES ☐ NO
    If no, who else might be in the vehicle?_____

10. Contact in the United States *(name, address, and phone number)*:
    _____
    _____
    _____

CERTIFICATION:

I certify that I have read, understood, and agree to abide by all conditions required for use of the APP. I also certify that the information provided is true and complete. I understand that all information provided may be shared with other government agencies.

_____   _____
       (Signature of Applicant)   *(Date)*

OMB No. 1115-0174

U.S. Department of Justice
Immigration and Naturalization Service

Application - Alternative Inspection Services

INSPASS AIRPORT PARTICIPANTS

1. Applicant acknowledges he/she is a citizen or permanent resident of the United States, a citizen of Canada, a Landed Canadian Immigrant who is a citizen of a British Commonwealth country, a citizen of a Visa Waiver Program country, or any other country approved for participation by the Commissioner, Immigration and Naturalization Service.

2. Applicant may not use the INSPASS card when entering the United States for a purpose other than that stated in this application.

3. Applicant will <u>not</u> be exempt from the normal examination process when entering for any other purpose.

CERTIFICATION: *(All applicants must sign)*

I certify that I have read, understood, and agree to abide by all conditions listed above for use of the INSPASS. I also certify that the information is true and complete. I understand that any information may be shared with other government agencies.

_____   _____
(Signature of Applicant)   *(Date)*

VISA WAIVER PARTICIPANTS *(To be completed by Visa Waiver Program Applicants Only)*

	YES	NO
A. Do you have a communicable disease, physical or mental disorder; or are you a drug abuser or addict?	☐	☐
B. Have you ever been arrested or convicted for an offense or crime involving moral turpitude or a violation related to a controlled substance; or been arrested or convicted for two or more offenses for which the aggregate sentence to confinement was five years or more; or been a controlled substance trafficker; or are you seeking entry to engage in criminal or immoral activities?	☐	☐
C. Have you ever been or are you now involved in espionage or sabotage; or in terrorist activities; or genocide; or were you involved, in any way, between 1933 and 1945 in persecutions associated with Nazi Germany or its allies?	☐	☐
D. Are you seeking to work in the United States; or have you ever been excluded and deported or previously removed from the United States; or have you ever procured or attempted to procure a visa or entry into the United States by fraud or misrepresentation?	☐	☐
E. Have you ever detained, retained, or withheld custody of a child from a United States citizen granted custody of the child?	☐	☐
F. Have you ever been denied a United States visa or entry into the United States or had a United States visa cancelled?	☐	☐
If yes, when? _____ Where? _____		
G. Have you ever asserted immunity from prosecution?	☐	☐

I understand that I am not entitled to any review or appeal of an immigration officer's determination as to my admissibility, nor am I entitled to contest any determination of deportability other than on the basis of an application for asylum.

_____   _____
(Signature of Applicant)   *(Date)*

WARNING: You may not accept unauthorized employment; or attend school; or represent the foreign information media during your visit under this program. You are authorized to stay in the United States for 90 days or less. You may not apply for: 1) a change of nonimmigrant status; 2) adjustment of status to temporary or permanent resident, unless eligible under section 201(b) of the Immigration and Nationality Act (Act); or 3) an extension of stay. Violation of these terms will subject you to deportation.

Form I-823 (Rev. 08/25/00)Y Page 6

U.S. Department of Justice
Immigration and Naturalization Service

OMB No. 1115-0174

Application - Alternative Inspection Services

DEDICATED COMMUTER LANE PARTICIPANTS

☐ New Application   ☐ Application for Replacement Card   ☐ Renewal

1. Applicant acknowledges that he/she is a citizen or lawful permanent resident of the U.S., or non-immigrant as determined eligible by the INS. Applicant acknowledges that he/she must be in possession of all documentation required the Immigration and Nationality Act and implementing regulations at all times when using the Dedicated Commuter Lane (DCL). When in the U.S., a non-U.S.citizen applicant acknowledges that he/she must remain otherwise eligible to enter the U.S. at time of each use of the DCL.

2. Applicant agrees to a full inspection of each vehicle presented for registration in the DCL prior to approval of his/her application, and at any time use of the DCL. The applicant acknowledges and agrees to be responsible for all contents of the vehicle he/she occupies when using the APP, whether or not that vehicle is owned by or registered to the applicant.

3. Applicant acknowledges that vehicle registration and insurance must be current when using the DCL, and documentation evidencing same must be made available to the INS upon request. If the vehicle is owned or registered to someone other than the applicant, evidence permitting use of the vehicle in the DCL must be made available to the INS upon request.

4. Applicant acknowledges and agrees that by submitting this application, he/she will be subject to a check of criminal information databases prior to and during each use of the DCL.

5. Applicant acknowledges and agrees that by submitting this application, he/she may only use the DCL when occupying the specific vehicle inspected and authorized by the INS for the applicants, use of the DCL.

6. Applicant acknowledges and agrees that he/she has been made aware of the nature and amount of all fees associated with participating in the DCL, including a fingerprint fee, system costs fee, and additional vehicle fee.

7. Applicant acknowledges and agrees that all devices, decals, or other equipment, methodology, or technology used to identify, inspect persons or vehicles remains the property of the U.S. government, and must be surrendered upon request.

8. If the registered owner of the vehicle is not the applicant, then written proof must be provided that the applicant has authorization to register and use the vehicle in the DCL.

A.	Vehicle License Number: _____	A.	State/Province: _____
	Vehicle Identification Number: _____		Vehicle Make/Model: _____
	Vehicle Year: _____		Vehicle Color: _____
	Vehicle Insurance Number: _____		Registered Owner: _____
B.	Vehicle License Number: _____	B.	State/Province: _____
	Vehicle Identification Number: _____		Vehicle Make/Model: _____
	Vehicle Year: _____		Vehicle Color: _____
	Vehicle Insurance Number: _____		Registered Owner: _____
C.	Vehicle License Number: _____	C.	State/Province: _____
	Vehicle Identification Number: _____		Vehicle Make/Model: _____
	Vehicle Year: _____		Vehicle Color: _____
	Vehicle Insurance Number: _____		Registered Owner: _____

9. Driver's License #: _____

Issuing Country and State/Province: _____

Expiration Date: _____

10. Will you be the sole occupant of the vehicle? *(All occupants of a vehicle used in the DCL must have current participation authorization.)*

(check one)   ☐ YES   ☐ NO

If no, who else might be in the vehicle? _____

11. Contact in the United States *(name, address, and phone number)*:

_____

_____

CERTIFICATION:

I certify that I have read, understood, and agree to abide by all conditions required for use of the DCL. I also certify that the information provided is true and complete. I understand that all information provided may be shared with other government agencies.

_____   _____
(Signature of Applicant)   *(Date)*

Form I-823 (Rev. 08/25/00)Y Page 7

U.S. Department of Justice
Immigration and Naturalization Service

OMB No. 1115-0214
Affidavit of Support Under Section 213A of the Act

INSTRUCTIONS

Purpose of this Form

This form is required to show that an intending immigrant has adequate means of financial support and is not likely to become a public charge.

Sponsor's Obligation

The person completing this affidavit is the sponsor. A sponsor's obligation continues until the sponsored immigrant becomes a U.S. citizen, can be credited with 40 qualifying quarters of work, departs the United States permanently, or dies. Divorce does not terminate the obligation. By signing this form, you, the sponsor, agree to support the intending immigrant and any spouse and/or children immigrating with him or her and to reimburse any government agency or private entity that provides these sponsored immigrants with Federal, State, or local means-tested public benefits.

General Filing Instructions

Please answer all questions by typing or clearly printing in black ink only. Indicate that an item is not applicable with "N/A". If an answer is "none," please so state. If you need extra space to answer any item, attach a sheet of paper with your name and Social Security number, and indicate the number of the item to which the answer refers.

You must submit an affidavit of support for each applicant for immigrant status. You may submit photocopies of this affidavit for any spouse or children immigrating with an immigrant you are sponsoring. For purposes of this form, a spouse or child is immigrating with an immigrant you are sponsoring if he or she is: 1) listed in Part 3 of this affidavit of support, and 2) applies for an immigrant visa or adjustment of status within 6 months of the date this affidavit of support is originally completed and signed. The signature on the affidavit must be notarized by a notary public or signed before an Immigration or a Consular officer.

You should give the completed affidavit of support with all required documentation to the sponsored immigrant for submission to either a Consular Officer with Form OF-230, Application for Immigrant Visa and Alien Registration, or an Immigration Officer with Form I-485, Application to Register Permanent Residence or Adjust Status. You may enclose the affidavit of support and accompanying documents in a sealed envelope to be opened only by the designated Government official. The sponsored immigrant must submit the affidavit of support to the Government within 6 months of its signature.

Who Needs an Affidavit of Support under Section 213A?

This affidavit must be filed at the time an intending immigrant is applying for an immigrant visa or adjustment of status. It is required for:

- All immediate relatives, including orphans, and family-based immigrants. (Self-petitioning widow/ers and battered spouses and children are exempt from this requirement); and

- Employment-based immigrants where a relative filed the immigrant visa petition or has a significant ownership interest (5 percent or more) in the entity that filed the petition.

Who Completes an Affidavit of Support under Section 213A?

- For immediate relatives and family-based immigrants, the family member petitioning for the intending immigrant must be the sponsor.

- For employment-based immigrants, the petitioning relative or a relative with a significant ownership interest (5 percent or more) in the petitioning entity must be the sponsor. The term "relative," for these purposes, is defined as husband, wife, father, mother, child, adult son or daughter, brother, or sister.

- If the petitioner cannot meet the income requirements, a joint sponsor may submit an additional affidavit of support.

A sponsor, or joint sponsor, must also be:

- A citizen or national of the United States or an alien lawfully admitted to the United States for permanent residence;

- At least 18 years of age; and

- Domiciled in the United States or its territories and possessions.

Sponsor's Income Requirement

As a sponsor, your household income must equal or exceed 125 percent of the Federal poverty line for your household size. For the purpose of the affidavit of support, household size includes yourself, all persons related to you by birth, marriage, or adoption living in your residence, your dependents, any immigrants you have previously sponsored using INS Form I-864 if that obligation has not terminated, and the intending immigrant(s) in Part 3 of this affidavit of support. The poverty guidelines are calculated and published annually by the Department of Health and Human Services. Sponsors who are on active duty in the U.S. Armed Forces other than for training need only demonstrate income at 100 percent of the poverty line *if* they are submitting this affidavit for the purpose of sponsoring their spouse or child.

If you are currently employed and have an *individual* income which meets or exceeds 125 percent of the Federal poverty line or (100 percent, if applicable) for your household size, you do not need to list the income of any other person. When determining your income, you may include the income generated by individuals related to you by birth, marriage, or adoption who are living in your residence, if they have lived in your residence for the previous 6 months, or who are listed as dependents on your most recent Federal income tax return whether or not they live in your residence. For their income to be considered, these household members or dependents must be willing to make their income available for the support of the sponsored immigrant(s) if necessary, and to complete and sign Form I-864A, Contract Between Sponsor and Household Member. However, a household member who is the immigrant you are sponsoring only need complete Form I-864A if his or her income will be used to determine your ability to support a spouse and/or children immigrating with him or her.

If in any of the most recent 3 tax years, you and your spouse each reported income on a joint income tax return, but you want to use only your own income to qualify (and your spouse is not submitting a Form I-864A), you may provide a separate breakout of your individual income for these years. Your individual income will be based on the earnings from your W-2 forms, Wage and Tax Statement, submitted to IRS for any such years. If necessary to meet the income requirement, you may also submit evidence of other income listed on your tax returns which can be attributed to you. You must provide documentation of such reported income, including Forms 1099 sent by the payer, which show your name and Social Security number.

You must calculate your household size and total household income as indicated in Parts 4.B. and 4.C. of this form. You must compare your total household income with the minimum income requirement for your household size using the poverty guidelines. For the purposes of the affidavit of support, determination of your ability to meet the income requirements will be based on the most recent poverty guidelines published in the Federal Register at the time the Consular or Immigration Officer makes a decision on the intending immigrant's application for an immigrant visa or adjustment of status. Immigration and Consular Officers will begin to use updated poverty guidelines on the first day of the second month after the date the guidelines are published in the Federal Register.

If your total household income is equal to or higher than the minimum income requirement for your household size, you do not need to provide information on your assets, and you may *not* have a joint sponsor unless you are requested to do so by a Consular or Immigration Officer. If your total household income does not meet the minimum income requirement, the intending immigrant will be ineligible for an immigrant visa or adjustment of status, unless:

- You provide evidence of assets that meet the requirements outlined under "Evidence of Assets" below; and/or

- The immigrant you are sponsoring provides evidence of assets that meet the requirements under "Evidence of Assets" below; or

- A joint sponsor assumes the liability of the intending immigrant with you. A joint sponsor must execute a separate affidavit of support on behalf of the intending

immigrant and any accompanying family members. A joint sponsor must individually meet the minimum requirement of 125 percent of the poverty line based on his or her household size and income and/or assets, including any assets of the sponsored immigrant.

The Government may pursue verification of any information provided on or in support of this form, including employment, income, or assets with the employer, financial or other institutions, the Internal Revenue Service, or the Social Security Administration.

Evidence of Income
In order to complete this form you must submit the following evidence of income:

- A copy of your complete Federal income tax return, as filed with the Internal Revenue Service, for each of the most recent 3 tax years. If you were not required to file a tax return in any of the most recent 3 tax years, you must provide an explanation. If you filed a joint income tax return and are using only your own income to qualify, you must also submit copies of your W-2s for each of the most recent 3 tax years, and if necessary to meet the income requirement, evidence of other income reported on your tax returns, such as Forms 1099.

- If you rely on income of any members of your household or dependents in order to reach the minimum income requirement, copies of their Federal income tax returns for the most recent 3 tax years. These persons must each complete and sign a Form I-864A, Contract Between Sponsor and Household Member.

- Evidence of current employment or self-employment, such as a recent pay statement, or a statement from your employer on business stationery, showing beginning date of employment, type of work performed, and salary or wages paid. You must also provide evidence of current employment for any person whose income is used to qualify.

Evidence of Assets
If you want to use your assets, the assets of your household members or dependents, and/or the assets of the immigrant you are sponsoring to meet the minimum income requirement, you must provide evidence of assets with a cash value that equals at least five times the difference between your total household income and the minimum income requirement. For the assets of a household member, other than the immigrant(s) you are sponsoring, to be considered, the household member must complete and sign Form I-864A, Contract Between Sponsor and Household Member.

All assets must be supported with evidence to verify location, ownership, and value of each asset. Any liens and liabilities relating to the assets must be documented. List only assets that can be readily converted into cash within one year. Evidence of assets includes, but is not limited to the following:

- Bank statements covering the last 12 months, *or* a statement from an officer of the bank or other financial institution in which you have deposits, including deposit/withdrawal history for the last 12 months, and current balance;

- Evidence of ownership and value of stocks, bonds, and certificates of deposit, and date(s) acquired;

- Evidence of ownership and value of other personal property, and date(s) acquired; and

- Evidence of ownership and value of any real estate, and date(s) acquired.

Change of Sponsor's Address

You are required by 8 U.S.C. 1183a(d) and 8 CFR 213a.3 to report every change of address to the Immigration and Naturalization Service and the State(s) in which the sponsored immigrant(s) reside(s). You must report changes of address to INS on Form I-865, Sponsor's Notice of Change of Address, within 30 days of any change of address. You must also report any change in your address to the State(s) in which the sponsored immigrant(s) live.

Penalties

If you include in this affidavit of support any material information that you know to be false, you may be liable for criminal prosecution under the laws of the United States.

If you fail to give notice of your change of address, as required by 8 U.S.C. 1183a(d) and 8 CFR 213a.3, you may be liable for the civil penalty established by 8 U.S.C. 1183a(d)(2). The amount of the civil penalty will depend on whether you failed to give this notice because you were aware that the immigrant(s) you sponsored had received Federal, State, or local means-tested public benefits.

Privacy Act Notice

Authority for the collection of the information requested on this form is contained in 8 U.S.C. 1182(a)(4), 1183a, 1184(a), and 1258. The information will be used principally by the INS or by any Consular Officer to whom it is furnished, to support an alien's application for benefits under the Immigration and Nationality Act and specifically the assertion that he or she has adequate means of financial support and will not become a public charge. Submission of the information is voluntary. Failure to provide the information will result in denial of the application for an immigrant visa or adjustment of status.

The information may also, as a matter of routine use, be disclosed to other Federal, State, and local agencies or private entities providing means-tested public benefits for use in civil action against the sponsor for breach of contract. It may also be disclosed as a matter of routine use to other Federal, State, local, and foreign law enforcement and regulatory agencies to enable these entities to carry out their law enforcement responsibilites.

Reporting Burden

A person is not required to respond to a collection of information unless it displays a currently valid OMB control number. We try to create forms and instructions that are accurate, can be easily understood, and which impose the least

possible burden on you to provide us with information. Often this is difficult because some immigration laws are very complex. The reporting burden for this collection of information on Form I-864 is computed as follows: 1) learning about the form, 63 minutes; 2) completing the form, 105 minutes; and 3) assembling and filing the form, 65 minutes, for an estimated average of 3 hours and 48 minutes minutes per response. The reporting burden for collection of information on Form I-864A is computed as: 1) learning about the form, 20 minutes; 2) completing the form, 55 minutes; 3) assembling and filing the form, 30 minutes, for an estimated average of 1 hour and 45 minutes per response. If you have comments regarding the accuracy of this estimates, or suggestions for making this form simpler, you can write to the Immigration and Naturalization Service, HQPDI, 425 I Street, N.W., Room 4034, Washington, DC 20536. **DO NOT MAIL YOUR COMPLETED AFFIDAVIT OF SUPPORT TO THIS ADDRESS.**

CHECK LIST

The following items must be submitted with Form I-864, Affidavit of Support Under Section 213A:

For *ALL* sponsors:

☐ This form, the **I-864, completed and signed** before a notary public or a Consular or Immigration Officer.

☐ Proof of **current employment** or self employment.

☐ Your individual Federal **income tax returns for the most recent 3 tax years,** or an explanation if fewer are submitted. Your **W-2s** for any of the most recent 3 tax years for which you filed a joint tax return but are using only your own income to qualify. Forms 1099 or evidence of other reported income *if* necessary to qualify.

For *SOME* sponsors:

☐ *If the immigrant you are sponsoring is bringing a spouse or children,* **photocopies of the immigrant's affidavit of support** for each spouse and/or child immigrating with the immigrant you are sponsoring.

☐ *If you are on active duty in the U.S. Armed Forces and are sponsoring a spouse or child using the 100 percent of poverty level exception,* **proof of your active military status.**

*If you are using the income of **persons in your household or dependents** to qualify,*

☐ A separate **Form I-864A** for each person whose income you will use. A sponsored immigrant/household member who is not immigrating with a spouse and/or child **does not need to complete Form I-864A.**

☐ Proof of their **residency and relationship** to you if they are not listed as dependents on your income tax return for the most recent tax year.

☐ Proof of their **current employment** or self-employment.

☐ Copies of their individual Federal **income tax returns for the 3 most recent tax years,** or an explanation if fewer are submitted.

If you use your assets or the assets of the sponsored immigrant to qualify,

☐ **Documentation of assets** establishing location, ownership, date of acquisition, and value. Evidence of any liens or liabilities against these assets.

☐ A separate **Form I-864A** for each household member other than the sponsored immigrant/household member.

If you are a joint sponsor or the relative of an employment-based immigrant requiring an affidavit of support, **proof of your citizenship status.**

☐ For U.S. citizens or nationals, a copy of your birth certificate, passport, or certificate of naturalization or citizenship.

☐ For lawful permanent residents, a copy of both sides of your I-551, Permanent Resident Card.

OMB No. 1115-0214

U.S. Department of Justice
Immigration and Naturalization Service

Affidavit of Support Under Section 213A of the Act

START HERE - Please Type or Print

Part 1.   Information on Sponsor (You)

Last Name	First Name	Middle Name

Mailing Address *(Street Number and Name)*	Apt/Suite Number

City	State or Province

Country	ZIP/Postal Code	Telephone Number

Place of Residence if different from above *(Street Number and Name)* Apt/Suite Number	
City	State or Province
Country	ZIP/Postal Code	Telephone Number

Date of Birth *(Month, Day, Year)*	Place of Birth *(City, State, Country)*	Are you a U.S. Citizen? ☐ Yes ☐ No

Social Security Number	A-Number *(If any)*

FOR AGENCY USE ONLY

This Affidavit	Receipt
[ ] Meets	
[ ] Does not meet	

Requirements of Section 213A

Officer or I.J. Signature

Location

Date

Part 2.   Basis for Filing Affidavit of Support

I am filing this affidavit of support because *(check one)*:

a. ☐   I filed/am filing the alien relative petition.

b. ☐   I filed/am filing an alien worker petition on behalf of the intending

immigrant, who is related to me as my _____ .
(relationship)

c. ☐   I have ownership interest of at least 5% _____ .
(name of entity which filed visa petition)

which filed an alien worker petition on behalf of the intending

immigrant, who is related to me as my _____
(relationship)

d. ☐   I am a joint sponsor willing to accept the legal obligations with any other sponsor(s).

Part 3.   Information on the Immigrant(s) You Are Sponsoring

Last Name	First Name	Middle Name

Date of Birth *(Month, Day, Year)*	Sex ☐ Male ☐ Female	Social Security Number *(If any)*

Country of Citizenship	A-Number *(If any)*

Current Address *(Street Number and Name)*	Apt/Suite Number	City

State/Province	Country	ZIP/Postal Code	Telephone Number

List any spouse and/or children immigrating with the immigrant named above in this Part: *(Use additional sheet of paper if necessary.)*

Name	Relationship to Sponsored Immigrant			Date of Birth			A-Number *(If any)*	Social Security *(If any)*
	Spouse	Son	Daughter	Mo.	Day	Yr.		

Form I-864 (Rev. 11/05/01)Y

Part 4.   Eligibility to Sponsor

To be a sponsor you must be a U.S. citizen or national or a lawful permanent resident. If you are not the petitioning relative, you must provide proof of status. To prove status, U.S. citizens or nationals must attach a copy of a document proving status, such as a U.S. passport, birth certificate, or certificate of naturalization, and lawful permanent residents must attach a copy of both sides of their Permanent Resident Card (Form I-551).

The determination of your eligibility to sponsor an immigrant will be based on an evaluation of your demonstrated ability to maintain an annual income at or above 125 percent of the Federal poverty line (100 percent if you are a petitioner sponsoring your spouse or child and you are on active duty in the U.S. Armed Forces). The assessment of your ability to maintain an adequate income will include your current employment, household size, and household income as shown on the Federal income tax returns for the 3 most recent tax years. Assets that are readily converted to cash and that can be made available for the support of sponsored immigrants if necessary, including any such assets of the immigrant(s) you are sponsoring, may also be considered.

The greatest weight in determining eligibility will be placed on current employment and household income. If a petitioner is unable to demonstrate ability to meet the stated income and asset requirements, a joint sponsor who *can* meet the income and asset requirements is needed. Failure to provide adequate evidence of income and/or assets or an affidavit of support completed by a joint sponsor will result in denial of the immigrant's application for an immigrant visa or adjustment to permanent resident status.

A. Sponsor's Employment

I am: 1 . ☐ Employed by _____ *(Provide evidence of employment)*

Annual salary _____ or hourly wage $ _____ *(for _____ hours per week)*

2. ☐ Self employed _____ *(Name of business)*

Nature of employment or business _____

3. ☐ Unemployed or retired since _____

B. Sponsor's Household Size

Number

1. Number of persons (related to you by birth, marriage, or adoption) living in your residence, including yourself *(Do NOT include persons being sponsored in this affidavit.)* _____

2. Number of immigrants being sponsored in this affidavit *(Include all persons in Part 3.)* _____

3. Number of immigrants **NOT** living in your household whom you are obligated to support under a previously signed Form I-864. _____

4. Number of persons who are otherwise dependent on you, as claimed in your tax return for the most recent tax year. _____

5. Total household size. *(Add lines 1 through 4.)*   **Total** _____

List persons below who are included in lines 1 or 3 for whom you previously have submitted INS Form I-864, *if your support obligation has not terminated.*

(If additional space is needed, use additional paper)

Name	A-Number	Date Affidavit of Support Signed	Relationship

Form I-864 (Rev. 11/05/01)Y Page 2

Part 4.   Eligibility to Sponsor   *(Continued)*

C. Sponsor's Annual Household Income

Enter total unadjusted income from your Federal income tax return for the most recent tax year below. If you last filed a joint income tax return but are using only your *own* income to qualify, list total earnings from your W-2 Forms, or, *if* necessary to reach the required income for your household size, include income from other sources listed on your tax return. If your *individual* income does not meet the income requirement for your household size, you may also list total income for anyone related to you by birth, marriage, or adoption currently living with you in your residence if they have lived in your residence for the previous 6 months, or any person shown as a dependent on your Federal income tax return for the most recent tax year, even if not living in the household. For their income to be considered, household members or dependents must be willing to make their income available for support of the sponsored immigrant(s) and to complete and sign Form I-864A, Contract Between Sponsor and Household Member. A sponsored immigrant/household member only need complete Form I-864A if his or her income will be used to determine your ability to support a spouse and/or children immigrating with him or her.

You must attach evidence of current employment and copies of income tax returns as filed with the IRS for the most recent 3 tax years for yourself and all persons whose income is listed below. See "Required Evidence " in Instructions. Income from all 3 years will be considered in determining your ability to support the immigrant(s) you are sponsoring.

☐ I filed a single/separate tax return for the most recent tax year.
☐ I filed a joint return for the most recent tax year which includes only my own income.
☐ I filed a joint return for the most recent tax year which includes income for my spouse and myself.
 ☐ I am submitting documentation of my individual income (Forms W-2 and 1099).
 ☐ I am qualifying using my spouse's income; my spouse is submitting a Form I-864A.

Indicate most recent tax year _____
                                        (tax year)

Sponsor's individual income $ _____

or

Sponsor and spouse's combined income $ _____
(If spouse's income is to be considered, spouse must submit Form I-864A.)

Income of other qualifying persons.
*(List names; include spouse if applicable.
Each person must complete Form I-864A.)*

_____ $ _____
_____ $ _____
_____ $ _____

Total Household Income $ _____

Explain on separate sheet of paper if you or any of the above listed individuals were not required to file Federal income tax returns for the most recent 3 years, or if other explanation of income, employment, or evidence is necessary.

D. Determination of Eligibility Based on Income

1. ☐ I am subject to the 125 percent of poverty line requirement for sponsors.
    ☐ I am subject to the 100 percent of poverty line requirement for sponsors on active duty in the U.S. Armed
       Forces sponsoring their spouse or child.
2.   Sponsor's total household size, from Part 4.B., line 5   _____ .
3.   Minimum income requirement from the Poverty Guidelines chart for the year of _____ is $ _____
       for this household size.   *(year)*

If you are currently employed and your household income for your household size is equal to or greater than the applicable poverty line requirement (from line D.3.), you do not need to list assets (Parts 4.E. and 5) or have a joint sponsor (Part 6) unless you are requested to do so by a Consular or Immigration Officer. You may skip to Part 7, Use of the Affidavit of Support to Overcome Public Charge Ground of Admissibility. **Otherwise, you should continue with Part 4.E.**

Part 4.   Eligibility to Sponsor   *(Continued)*

E. Sponsor's Assets and Liabilities

Your assets and those of your qualifying household members and dependents may be used to demonstrate ability to maintain an income at or above 125 percent (or 100 percent, if applicable) of the poverty line *if* they are available for the support of the sponsored immigrant(s) and can readily be converted into cash within 1 year. The household member, other than the immigrant(s) you are sponsoring, must complete and sign Form I-864A, Contract Between Sponsor and Household Member. List the cash value of each asset *after* any debts or liens are subtracted. Supporting evidence must be attached to establish location, ownership, date of acquisition, and value of each asset listed, including any liens and liabilities related to each asset listed. See "Evidence of Assets" in Instructions.

Type of Asset	Cash Value of Assets *(Subtract any debts)*
Savings deposits	$
Stocks, bonds, certificates of deposit	$
Life insurance cash value	$
Real estate	$
Other *(specify)*	$
Total Cash Value of Assets	$ _____

Part 5.   Immigrant's Assets and Offsetting Liabilities

The sponsored immigrant's assets may also be used in support of your ability to maintain income at or above 125 percent of the poverty line *if* the assets are or will be available in the United States for the support of the sponsored immigrant(s) and can readily be converted into cash within 1 year.

The sponsored immigrant should provide information on his or her assets in a format similar to part 4.E. above. Supporting evidence must be attached to establish location, ownership and value of each asset listed, including any liens and liabilities for each asset listed. See "Evidence of Assets" in Instructions.

Part 6.   Joint Sponsors

If household income and assets do not meet the appropriate poverty line for your household size, a joint sponsor is required. There may be more than one joint sponsor, but each joint sponsor must individually meet the 125 percent of poverty line requirement based on his or her household income and/or assets, including any assets of the sponsored immigrant. By submitting a separate Affidavit of Support under Section 213A of the Act (Form I-864), a joint sponsor accepts joint responsibility with the petitioner for the sponsored immigrant(s) until they become U.S. citizens, can be credited with 40 quarters of work, leave the United States permanently, or die.

Part 7.   Use of the Affidavit of Support to Overcome Public Charge Ground of Inadmissibility

---

Section 212(a)(4)(C) of the Immigration and Nationality Act provides that an alien seeking permanent residence as an immediate relative (including an orphan), as a family-sponsored immigrant, or as an alien who will accompany or follow to join another alien is considered to be likely to become a public charge and is inadmissible to the United States unless a sponsor submits a legally enforceable affidavit of support on behalf of the alien. Section 212(a)(4)(D) imposes the same requirement on an employment-based immigrant, and those aliens who accompany or follow to join the employment-based immigrant, if the employment-based immigrant will be employed by a relative, or by a firm in which a relative owns a significant interest. Separate affidavits of support are required for family members at the time they immigrate if they are not included on this affidavit of support or do not apply for an immigrant visa or adjustment of status within 6 months of the date this affidavit of support is originally signed. The sponsor must provide the sponsored immigrant(s) whatever support is necessary to maintain them at an income that is at least 125 percent of the Federal poverty guidelines.

I submit this affidavit of support in consideration of the sponsored immigrant(s) not being found inadmissible to the United States under section 212(a)(4)(C) (or 212(a)(4)(D) for an employment-based immigrant) and to enable the sponsored immigrant(s) to overcome this ground of inadmissibility. I agree to provide the sponsored immigrant(s) whatever support is necessary to maintain the sponsored immigrant(s) at an income that is at least 125 percent of the Federal poverty guidelines. I understand that my obligation will continue until my death or the sponsored immigrant(s) have become U.S. citizens, can be credited with 40 quarters of work, depart the United States permanently, or die.

Part 7.   Use of the Affidavit of Support to Overcome Public Charge Grounds   *(Continued)*

Notice of Change of Address.

Sponsors are required to provide written notice of any change of address within 30 days of the change in address until the sponsored immigrant(s) have become U.S. citizens, can be credited with 40 quarters of work, depart the United States permanently, or die. To comply with this requirement, the sponsor must complete INS Form I-865. Failure to give this notice may subject the sponsor to the civil penalty established under section 213A(d)(2) which ranges from $250 to $2,000, unless the failure to report occurred with the knowledge that the sponsored immigrant(s) had received means-tested public benefits, in which case the penalty ranges from $2,000 to $5,000.

> *If my address changes for any reason before my obligations under this affidavit of support terminate, I will complete and file INS Form I-865, Sponsor's Notice of Change of Address, within 30 days of the change of address. I understand that failure to give this notice may subject me to civil penalties.*

Means-tested Public Benefit Prohibitions and Exceptions.

Under section 403(a) of Public Law 104-193 (Welfare Reform Act), aliens lawfully admitted for permanent residence in the United States, with certain exceptions, are ineligible for most Federally-funded means-tested public benefits during their first 5 years in the United States. This provision does not apply to public benefits specified in section 403(c) of the Welfare Reform Act or to State public benefits, including emergency Medicaid; short-term, non-cash emergency relief; services provided under the National School Lunch and Child Nutrition Acts; immunizations and testing and treatment for communicable diseases; student assistance under the Higher Education Act and the Public Health Service Act; certain forms of foster-care or adoption assistance under the Social Security Act; Head Start programs; means-tested programs under the Elementary and Secondary Education Act; and Job Training Partnership Act programs.

Consideration of Sponsor's Income in Determining Eligibility for Benefits.

If a permanent resident alien is no longer statutorily barred from a Federally-funded means-tested public benefit program and applies for such a benefit, the income and resources of the sponsor and the sponsor's spouse will be considered (or deemed) to be the income and resources of the sponsored immigrant in determining the immigrant's eligibility for Federal means-tested public benefits. Any State or local government may also choose to consider (or deem) the income and resources of the sponsor and the sponsor's spouse to be the income and resources of the immigrant for the purposes of determining eligibility for their means-tested public benefits. The attribution of the income and resources of the sponsor and the sponsor's spouse to the immigrant will continue until the immigrant becomes a U.S. citizen or has worked or can be credited with 40 qualifying quarters of work, provided that the immigrant or the worker crediting the quarters to the immigrant has not received any Federal means-tested public benefit during any creditable quarter for any period after December 31, 1996.

> *I understand that, under section 213A of the Immigration and Nationality Act (the Act), as amended, this affidavit of support constitutes a contract between me and the U.S. Government. This contract is designed to protect the United States Government, and State and local government agencies or private entities that provide means-tested public benefits, from having to pay benefits to or on behalf of the sponsored immigrant(s), for as long as I am obligated to support them under this affidavit of support. I understand that the sponsored immigrants, or any Federal, State, local, or private entity that pays any means-tested benefit to or on behalf of the sponsored immigrant(s), are entitled to sue me if I fail to meet my obligations under this affidavit of support, as defined by section 213A and INS regulations.*

Civil Action to Enforce.

If the immigrant on whose behalf this affidavit of support is executed receives any Federal, State, or local means-tested public benefit before this obligation terminates, the Federal, State, or local agency or private entity may request reimbursement from the sponsor who signed this affidavit. If the sponsor fails to honor the request for reimbursement, the agency may sue the sponsor in any U.S. District Court or any State court with jurisdiction of civil actions for breach of contract. INS will provide names, addresses, and Social Security account numbers of sponsors to benefit-providing agencies for this purpose. Sponsors may also be liable for paying the costs of collection, including legal fees.

Part 7. **Use of the Affidavit of Support to Overcome Public Charge Grounds** *(Continued)*

I acknowledge that section 213A(a)(1)(B) of the Act grants the sponsored immigrant(s) and any Federal, State, local, or private agency that pays any means-tested public benefit to or on behalf of the sponsored immigrant(s) standing to sue me for failing to meet my obligations under this affidavit of support. I agree to submit to the personal jurisdiction of any court of the United States or of any State, territory, or possession of the United States if the court has subject matter jurisdiction of a civil lawsuit to enforce this affidavit of support. I agree that no lawsuit to enforce this affidavit of support shall be barred by any statute of limitations that might otherwise apply, so long as the plaintiff initiates the civil lawsuit no later than ten (10) years after the date on which a sponsored immigrant last received any means-tested public benefits.

Collection of Judgment.

I acknowledge that a plaintiff may seek specific performance of my support obligation. Furthermore, any money judgment against me based on this affidavit of support may be collected through the use of a judgment lien under 28 U.S.C 3201, a writ of execution under 28 U.S.C 3203, a judicial installment payment order under 28 U.S.C 3204, garnishment under 28 U.S.C 3205, or through the use of any corresponding remedy under State law. I may also be held liable for costs of collection, including attorney fees.

Concluding Provisions.

I, _____, certify under penalty of perjury under the laws of the United States that:

(a) I know the contents of this affidavit of support signed by me;

(b) All the statements in this affidavit of support are true and correct;

(c) I make this affidavit of support for the consideration stated in Part 7, freely, and without any mental reservation or purpose of evasion;

(d) Income tax returns submitted in support of this affidavit are true copies of the returns filed with the Internal Revenue Service; and

(e) Any other evidence submitted is true and correct.

_____   _____
(Sponsor's Signature)   *(Date)*

Subscribed and sworn to (or affirmed) before me this

_____ day of _____, _____
                                   (Month)   *(Year)*

at _____.

My commission expires on _____.

_____
(Signature of Notary Public or Officer Administering Oath)

_____
(Title)

Part 8. **If someone other than the sponsor prepared this affidavit of support, that person must complete the following:**

I certify under penalty of perjury under the laws of the United States that I prepared this affidavit of support at the sponsor's request, and that this affidavit of support is based on all information of which I have knowledge.

Signature	Print Your Name	Date	Daytime Telephone Number

Firm Name and Address

OMB No. 1615-0052

N-400 Application for Naturalization

Department of Homeland Security
U.S Citizenship and Immigration Services

Print clearly or type your answers using CAPITAL letters. Failure to print clearly may delay your application. Use black ink.

Part 1. Your Name. *(The Person Applying for Naturalization)*

Write your USCIS "A"- number here:
A

A. Your current legal name.

Family Name *(Last Name)*

Given Name *(First Name)*   Full Middle Name *(If applicable)*

B. Your name **exactly** as it appears on your Permanent Resident Card.

Family Name *(Last Name)*

Given Name *(First Name)*   Full Middle Name *(If applicable)*

C. If you have ever used other names, provide them below.

Family Name *(Last Name)*	Given Name *(First Name)*	Middle Name

D. Name change *(optional)*

Please read the Instructions before you decide whether to change your name.

1. Would you like to legally change your name? ☐ Yes ☐ No

2. If "Yes," print the new name you would like to use. Do not use initials or abbreviations when writing your new name.

Family Name *(Last Name)*

Given Name *(First Name)*   Full Middle Name

For USCIS Use Only

Bar Code	Date Stamp
	Remarks

Action Block

Part 2. Information About Your Eligibility. *(Check Only One)*

I am at least 18 years old **AND**

A. ☐ I have been a Lawful Permanent Resident of the United States for at least five years.

B. ☐ I have been a Lawful Permanent Resident of the United States for at least three years, **and** I have been married to and living with the same U.S. citizen for the last three years, **and** my spouse has been a U.S. citizen for the last three years.

C. ☐ I am applying on the basis of qualifying military service.

D. ☐ Other *(Please explain)* _____

_____

Form N-400 (Rev. 10/26/05)Y

Part 3. Information About You.	Write your USCIS "A"- number here: A

A. U.S. Social Security Number   **B.** Date of Birth *(mm/dd/yyyy)*   **C.** Date You Became a Permanent Resident *(mm/dd/yyyy)*

D. Country of Birth   **E.** Country of Nationality

F. Are either of your parents U.S. citizens? *(if yes, see Instructions)* ☐ Yes ☐ No

G. What is your current marital status? ☐ Single, Never Married ☐ Married ☐ Divorced ☐ Widowed

☐ Marriage Annulled or Other *(Explain)* _____

H. Are you requesting a waiver of the English and/or U.S. History and Government requirements based on a disability or impairment and attaching a Form N-648 with your application? ☐ Yes ☐ No

I. Are you requesting an accommodation to the naturalization process because of a disability or impairment? *(See Instructions for some examples of accommodations.)* ☐ Yes ☐ No

If you answered "Yes," check the box below that applies:

☐ I am deaf or hearing impaired and need a sign language interpreter who uses the following language. _____

☐ I use a wheelchair.

☐ I am blind or sight impaired.

☐ I will need another type of accommodation. Please explain: _____

_____

_____

Part 4. Addresses and Telephone Numbers.

A. Home Address - Street Number and Name *(Do **not** write a P.O. Box in this space)*   Apartment Number

City	County	State	ZIP Code	Country

B. Care of   Mailing Address - Street Number and Name *(If different from home address)*   Apartment Number

City	State	ZIP Code	Country

C. Daytime Phone Number *(If any)*   Evening Phone Number *(If any)*   E-mail Address *(If any)*

( )   ( )

Part 5. Information for Criminal Records Search.

Write your USCIS "A"- number here:
A

NOTE: The categories below are those required by the FBI. See Instructions for more information.

A. Gender

☐ Male   ☐ Female

B. Height

Feet   Inches

C. Weight

Pounds

D. Are you Hispanic or Latino?   ☐ Yes   ☐ No

E. Race *(Select one or more.)*

☐ White   ☐ Asian   ☐ Black or African American   ☐ American Indian or Alaskan Native   ☐ Native Hawaiian or Other Pacific Islander

F. Hair color

☐ Black   ☐ Brown   ☐ Blonde   ☐ Gray   ☐ White   ☐ Red   ☐ Sandy   ☐ Bald (No Hair)

G. Eye color

☐ Brown   ☐ Blue   ☐ Green   ☐ Hazel   ☐ Gray   ☐ Black   ☐ Pink   ☐ Maroon   ☐ Other

Part 6. Information About Your Residence and Employment.

A. Where have you lived during the last five years? Begin with where you live now and then list every place you lived for the last five years. If you need more space, use a separate sheet(s) of paper.

Street Number and Name, Apartment Number, City, State, Zip Code and Country	Dates *(mm/dd/yyyy)*	
	From	To
Current Home Address - Same as Part 4.A		Present

B. Where have you worked (or, if you were a student, what schools did you attend) during the last five years? Include military service. Begin with your current or latest employer and then list every place you have worked or studied for the last five years. If you need more space, use a separate sheet of paper.

Employer or School Name	Employer or School Address *(Street, City and State)*	Dates *(mm/dd/yyyy)*		Your Occupation
		From	To	

Form N-400 (Rev. 10/26/05)Y Page 3

Part 7. Time Outside the United States. *(Including Trips to Canada, Mexico and the Caribbean Islands)*	Write your USCIS "A"- number here: A

A. How many total days did you spend outside of the United States during the past five years? [   ] days

B. How many trips of 24 hours or more have you taken outside of the United States during the past five years? [   ] trips

C. List below all the trips of 24 hours or more that you have taken outside of the United States since becoming a Lawful Permanent Resident. Begin with your most recent trip. If you need more space, use a separate sheet(s) of paper.

Date You Left the United States *(mm/dd/yyyy)*	Date You Returned to the United States *(mm/dd/yyyy)*	Did Trip Last Six Months or More?	Countries to Which You Traveled	Total Days Out of the United States
		☐ Yes ☐ No		
		☐ Yes ☐ No		
		☐ Yes ☐ No		
		☐ Yes ☐ No		
		☐ Yes ☐ No		
		☐ Yes ☐ No		
		☐ Yes ☐ No		
		☐ Yes ☐ No		
		☐ Yes ☐ No		
		☐ Yes ☐ No		

Part 8. Information About Your Marital History

A. How many times have you been married (including annulled marriages)? [   ] If you have **never** been married, go to Part 9.

B. If you are now married, give the following information about your spouse:

1. Spouse's Family Name *(Last Name)*   Given Name *(First Name)*   Full Middle Name *(If applicable)*

2. Date of Birth *(mm/dd/yyyy)*   **3.** Date of Marriage *(mm/dd/yyyy)*   **4.** Spouse's U.S. Social Security #

5. Home Address - Street Number and Name   Apartment Number

City   State   Zip Code

Part 8. Information About Your Marital History. *(Continued)*

Write your USCIS "A"- number here:
A

C. Is your spouse a U.S. citizen? ☐ Yes ☐ No

D. If your spouse is a U.S. citizen, give the following information:

    1. When did your spouse become a U.S. citizen? ☐ At Birth ☐ Other

    If "Other," give the following information:

    2. Date your spouse became a U.S. citizen

    3. Place your spouse became a U.S. citizen *(Please see Instructions)*

        City and State

E. If your spouse is **not** a U.S. citizen, give the following information :

    1. Spouse's Country of Citizenship

    2. Spouse's USCIS "A"- Number *(If applicable)*
    A

    3. Spouse's Immigration Status

    ☐ Lawful Permanent Resident ☐ Other _____

F. If you were married before, provide the following information about your prior spouse. If you have more than one previous marriage, use a separate sheet(s) of paper to provide the information requested in Questions 1-5 below.

    1. Prior Spouse's Family Name *(Last Name)*   Given Name *(First Name)*   Full Middle Name *(If applicable)*

    2. Prior Spouse's Immigration Status
    ☐ U.S. Citizen
    ☐ Lawful Permanent Resident
    ☐ Other _____

    3. Date of Marriage *(mm/dd/yyyy)*

    4. Date Marriage Ended *(mm/dd/yyyy)*

    5. How Marriage Ended
    ☐ Divorce ☐ Spouse Died ☐ Other

G. How many times has your current spouse been married (including annulled marriages)? ▢

    If your spouse has **ever** been married before, give the following information about **your spouse's** prior marriage.
    If your spouse has more than one previous marriage, use a separate sheet(s) of paper to provide the information requested in Questions 1 - 5 below.

    1. Prior Spouse's Family Name *(Last Name)*   Given Name *(First Name)*   Full Middle Name *(If applicable)*

    2. Prior Spouse's Immigration Status
    ☐ U.S. Citizen
    ☐ Lawful Permanent Resident
    ☐ Other

    3. Date of Marriage *(mm/dd/yyyy)*

    4. Date Marriage Ended *(mm/dd/yyyy)*

    5. How Marriage Ended
    ☐ Divorce ☐ Spouse Died ☐ Other _____

Part 9. Information About Your Children.	Write your USCIS "A"- number here: A

A. How many sons and daughters have you had? For more information on which sons and daughters you should include and how to complete this section, see the Instructions.

B. Provide the following information about all of your sons and daughters. If you need more space, use a separate sheet(s) of paper.

Full Name of Son or Daughter	Date of Birth *(mm/dd/yyyy)*	USCIS "A"- number *(if child has one)*	Country of Birth	Current Address *(Street, City, State and Country)*
		A		
		A		
		A		
		A		
		A		
		A		
		A		
		A		

Part 10. Additional Questions.

Please answer Questions 1 through 14. If you answer "Yes" to any of these questions, include a written explanation with this form. Your written explanation should (1) explain why your answer was "Yes" and (2) provide any additional information that helps to explain your answer.

A. General Questions.

1. Have you **ever** claimed to be a U.S. citizen *(in writing or any other way)*? ☐ Yes ☐ No

2. Have you **ever** registered to vote in any Federal, state or local election in the United States? ☐ Yes ☐ No

3. Have you **ever** voted in any Federal, state or local election in the United States? ☐ Yes ☐ No

4. Since becoming a Lawful Permanent Resident, have you **ever** failed to file a required Federal, state or local tax return? ☐ Yes ☐ No

5. Do you owe any Federal, state or local taxes that are overdue? ☐ Yes ☐ No

6. Do you have any title of nobility in any foreign country? ☐ Yes ☐ No

7. Have you ever been declared legally incompetent or been confined to a mental institution within the last five years? ☐ Yes ☐ No

Form N-400 (Rev. 10/26/05)Y Page 6

Part 10. Additional Questions. (Continued)	Write your USCIS "A"- number here:
	A

B. Affiliations.

8. a. Have you **ever** been a member of or associated with any organization, association, fund, foundation, party, club, society or similar group in the United States or in any other place? ☐ Yes ☐ No

b. If you answered "Yes," list the name of each group below. If you need more space, attach the names of the other group(s) on a separate sheet(s) of paper.

Name of Group	Name of Group
1.	6.
2.	7.
3.	8.
4.	9.
5.	10.

9. Have you **ever** been a member of or in any way associated *(either directly or indirectly)* with:

a. The Communist Party? ☐ Yes ☐ No

b. Any other totalitarian party? ☐ Yes ☐ No

c. A terrorist organization? ☐ Yes ☐ No

10. Have you **ever** advocated *(either directly or indirectly)* the overthrow of any government by force or violence? ☐ Yes ☐ No

11. Have you **ever** persecuted *(either directly or indirectly)* any person because of race, religion, national origin, membership in a particular social group or political opinion? ☐ Yes ☐ No

12. Between March 23, 1933 and May 8, 1945, did you work for or associate in any way *(either directly or indirectly)* with:

a. The Nazi government of Germany? ☐ Yes ☐ No

b. Any government in any area (1) occupied by, (2) allied with, or (3) established with the help of the Nazi government of Germany? ☐ Yes ☐ No

c. Any German, Nazi, or S.S. military unit, paramilitary unit, self-defense unit, vigilante unit, citizen unit, police unit, government agency or office, extermination camp, concentration camp, prisoner of war camp, prison, labor camp or transit camp? ☐ Yes ☐ No

C. Continuous Residence.

Since becoming a Lawful Permanent Resident of the United States:

13. Have you **ever** called yourself a "nonresident" on a Federal, state or local tax return? ☐ Yes ☐ No

14. Have you **ever** failed to file a Federal, state or local tax return because you considered yourself to be a "nonresident"? ☐ Yes ☐ No

Part 10. Additional Questions. (Continued)	Write your USCIS "A"- number here: A

D. Good Moral Character.

For the purposes of this application, you must answer "Yes" to the following questions, if applicable, even if your records were sealed or otherwise cleared or if anyone, including a judge, law enforcement officer or attorney, told you that you no longer have a record.

15. Have you **ever** committed a crime or offense for which you were **not** arrested? ☐ Yes ☐ No

16. Have you **ever** been arrested, cited or detained by any law enforcement officer (including USCIS or former INS and military officers) for any reason? ☐ Yes ☐ No

17. Have you **ever** been charged with committing any crime or offense? ☐ Yes ☐ No

18. Have you **ever** been convicted of a crime or offense? ☐ Yes ☐ No

19. Have you **ever** been placed in an alternative sentencing or a rehabilitative program (for example: diversion, deferred prosecution, withheld adjudication, deferred adjudication)? ☐ Yes ☐ No

20. Have you **ever** received a suspended sentence, been placed on probation or been paroled? ☐ Yes ☐ No

21. Have you **ever** been in jail or prison? ☐ Yes ☐ No

If you answered "Yes" to any of Questions 15 through 21, complete the following table. If you need more space, use a separate sheet (s) of paper to give the same information.

Why were you arrested, cited, detained or charged?	Date arrested, cited, detained or charged? *(mm/dd/yyyy)*	Where were you arrested, cited, detained or charged? *(City, State, Country)*	Outcome or disposition of the arrest, citation, detention or charge *(No charges filed, charges dismissed, jail, probation, etc.)*

Answer Questions 22 through 33. If you answer "Yes" to any of these questions, attach (1) your written explanation why your answer was "Yes" and (2) any additional information or documentation that helps explain your answer.

22. Have you **ever**:

    a. Been a habitual drunkard? ☐ Yes ☐ No

    b. Been a prostitute, or procured anyone for prostitution? ☐ Yes ☐ No

    c. Sold or smuggled controlled substances, illegal drugs or narcotics? ☐ Yes ☐ No

    d. Been married to more than one person at the same time? ☐ Yes ☐ No

    e. Helped anyone enter or try to enter the United States illegally? ☐ Yes ☐ No

    f. Gambled illegally or received income from illegal gambling? ☐ Yes ☐ No

    g. Failed to support your dependents or to pay alimony? ☐ Yes ☐ No

23. Have you **ever** given false or misleading information to any U.S. government official while applying for any immigration benefit or to prevent deportation, exclusion or removal? ☐ Yes ☐ No

24. Have you **ever** lied to any U.S. government official to gain entry or admission into the United States? ☐ Yes ☐ No

Part 10. Additional Questions. (Continued)	Write your USCIS "A"- number here: A

E. Removal, Exclusion and Deportation Proceedings.

25. Are removal, exclusion, rescission or deportation proceedings pending against you? ☐ Yes ☐ No

26. Have you **ever** been removed, excluded or deported from the United States? ☐ Yes ☐ No

27. Have you **ever** been ordered to be removed, excluded or deported from the United States? ☐ Yes ☐ No

28. Have you **ever** applied for any kind of relief from removal, exclusion or deportation? ☐ Yes ☐ No

F. Military Service.

29. Have you **ever** served in the U.S. Armed Forces? ☐ Yes ☐ No

30. Have you **ever** left the United States to avoid being drafted into the U.S. Armed Forces? ☐ Yes ☐ No

31. Have you **ever** applied for any kind of exemption from military service in the U.S. Armed Forces? ☐ Yes ☐ No

32. Have you **ever** deserted from the U.S. Armed Forces? ☐ Yes ☐ No

G. Selective Service Registration.

33. Are you a male who lived in the United States at any time between your 18th and 26th birthdays in any status except as a lawful nonimmigrant? ☐ Yes ☐ No

   If you answered "NO," go on to question 34.

   If you answered "YES," provide the information below.

   If you answered "YES," but you did not register with the Selective Service System and are still under 26 years of age, you must register before you apply for naturalization, so that you can complete the information below:

   Date Registered (mm/dd/yyyy) [   ]   Selective Service Number [   ]

   If you answered "YES," but you did not register with the Selective Service and you are now 26 years old or older, attach a statement explaining why you did not register.

H. Oath Requirements. *(See Part 14 for the Text of the Oath)*

Answer Questions 34 through 39. If you answer "No" to any of these questions, attach (1) your written explanation why the answer was "No" and (2) any additional information or documentation that helps to explain your answer.

34. Do you support the Constitution and form of government of the United States? ☐ Yes ☐ No

35. Do you understand the full Oath of Allegiance to the United States? ☐ Yes ☐ No

36. Are you willing to take the full Oath of Allegiance to the United States? ☐ Yes ☐ No

37. If the law requires it, are you willing to bear arms on behalf of the United States? ☐ Yes ☐ No

38. If the law requires it, are you willing to perform noncombatant services in the U.S. Armed Forces? ☐ Yes ☐ No

39. If the law requires it, are you willing to perform work of national importance under civilian direction? ☐ Yes ☐ No

Part 11. Your Signature.	Write your USCIS "A"- number here:
	A

I certify, under penalty of perjury under the laws of the United States of America, that this application, and the evidence submitted with it, are all true and correct. I authorize the release of any information that the USCIS needs to determine my eligibility for naturalization.

Your Signature

Date *(mm/dd/yyyy)*

Part 12. Signature of Person Who Prepared This Application for You. *(If Applicable)*

I declare under penalty of perjury that I prepared this application at the request of the above person. The answers provided are based on information of which I have personal knowledge and/or were provided to me by the above named person in response to the *exact questions* contained on this form.

Preparer's Printed Name

Preparer's Signaure

Date *(mm/dd/yyyy)*

Preparer's Firm or Organization Name *(If applicable)*

Preparer's Daytime Phone Number

Preparer's Address - Street Number and Name

City

State

Zip Code

NOTE: Do not complete Parts 13 and 14 until a USCIS Officer instructs you to do so.

Part 13. Signature at Interview.

I swear (affirm) and certify under penalty of perjury under the laws of the United States of America that I know that the contents of this application for naturalization subscribed by me, including corrections numbered 1 through _____ and the evidence submitted by me numbered pages 1 through _____ , are true and correct to the best of my knowledge and belief.

Subscribed to and sworn to (affirmed) before me

Officer's Printed Name or Stamp

Date *(mm/dd/yyyy)*

Complete Signature of Applicant

Officer's Signature

Part 14. Oath of Allegiance.

If your application is approved, you will be scheduled for a public oath ceremony at which time you will be required to take the following oath of allegiance immediately prior to becoming a naturalized citizen. By signing, you acknowledge your willingness and ability to take this oath:

I hereby declare, on oath, that I absolutely and entirely renounce and abjure all allegiance and fidelity to any foreign prince, potentate, state, or sovereignty, of whom or which which I have heretofore been a subject or citizen;

that I will support and defend the Constitution and laws of the United States of America against all enemies, foreign and domestic;

that I will bear true faith and allegiance to the same;

that I will bear arms on behalf of the United States when required by the law;

that I will perform noncombatant service in the Armed Forces of the United States when required by the law;

that I will perform work of national importance under civilian direction when required by the law; and

that I take this obligation freely, without any mental reservation or purpose of evasion; so help me God.

Printed Name of Applicant

Complete Signature of Applicant

PLEASE TYPE OR PRINT YOUR ANSWERS IN THE SPACE PROVIDED BELOW EACH ITEM

1. SURNAMES OR FAMILY NAMES (Exactly as in Passport)	**DO NOT WRITE IN THIS SPACE**

DO NOT WRITE IN THIS SPACE

B-1/B-2 MAX   B-1 MAX   B-2 MAX

OTHER _____ MAX
Visa Classification

MULT OR _____
Number Applications

MONTHS _____
Validity

L.O. CHECKED

ON _____ BY _____

ISSUED/REFUSED

ON _____ BY _____

UNDER SEC.   214(b)   221(g)

OTHER _____ INA

REFUSAL REVIEWED BY

1. SURNAMES OR FAMILY NAMES (Exactly as in Passport)

2. FIRST NAME AND MIDDLE NAME (Exactly as in Passport)

3. OTHER NAMES (Maiden, Religious, Professional, Aliases)

4. DATE OF BIRTH (Day, Month, Year)   8. PASSPORT NUMBER

5. PLACE OF BIRTH
(City, Province)   (Country)   DATE PASSPORT ISSUED (Day, Month, Year)

6. NATIONALITY   7. SEX ☐ MALE ☐ FEMALE   DATE PASSPORT EXPIRES (Day, Month, Year)

9. HOME ADDRESS (include apartment no., street, city, province, and postal zone)

10. NAME AND STREET ADDRESS OF PRESENT EMPLOYER OR SCHOOL
(Postal box number unacceptable)

11. HOME TELEPHONE NO.   12. BUSINESS TELEPHONE NO.

13. MARITAL STATUS
☐ Married ☐ Single ☐ Widowed ☐ Divorced ☐ Separated
If married, give name and nationality of spouse

14. NAMES AND RELATIONSHIPS OF PERSONS TRAVELING WITH YOU
(NOTE: A separate application must be made for a visa for each traveller regardless of age.)

15. HAVE YOU EVER APPLIED FOR A U.S. NONIMMIGRANT VISA?
☐ NO ☐ YES
HAVE YOU EVER APPLIED FOR A U.S. IMMIGRANT VISA?
☐ NO ☐ YES
WHERE? _____
WHEN? _____
VISA WAS ISSUED ☐   VISA WAS REFUSED ☐

16. HAS YOUR U.S. VISA EVER BEEN CANCELLED?
☐ NO ☐ YES
WHERE? _____
WHEN? _____
BY WHOM? _____

17. Bearers of visitors visas generally may not work or study in the U.S.
DO YOU INTEND TO WORK IN THE U.S.
If YES, explain. ☐ NO ☐ YES

18. DO YOU INTEND TO STUDY IN THE U.S.
If YES, explain. ☐ NO ☐ YES

19. PRESENT OCCUPATION
(If retired, state past occupation)

20. WHO WILL FURNISH FINANCIAL SUPPORT, INCLUDING TICKETS?

21. AT WHAT ADDRESS WILL YOU STAY IN THE U.S.A.?

22. WHAT IS THE PURPOSE OF YOUR TRIP?
tourism

23. WHEN DO YOU INTEND TO ARRIVE IN THE U.S.A.?

24. HOW LONG DO YOU PLAN TO STAY IN THE U.S.A.?

25. HAVE YOU EVER BEEN IN THE U.S.A.?
☐ NO ☐ YES
WHEN? _____
FOR HOW LONG? _____

NONIMMIGRANT VISA APPLICATION	**COMPLETE ALL QUESTIONS ON BOTH PAGES OF THIS FORM**
OPTIONAL FORM 156 (Rev. 1-98) PAGE 1 Department of State	50156-108 PREVIOUS EDITIONS OBSOLETE	NSN 7540-00-139--0053

26. HAVE YOU OR ANYONE ACTING FOR YOU EVER INDICATED TO A U.S. CONSULAR OR IMMIGRATION EMPLOYEE A DESIRE TO IMMIGRATE TO THE U.S., OR HAVE YOU ENTERED A U.S. VISA LOTTERY?

☐ NO ☐ YES

HAS ANYONE EVER FILED AN IMMIGRANT VISA PETITION ON YOUR BEHALF?

☐ NO ☐ YES

HAS A LABOR CERTIFICATION FOR EMPLOYMENT IN THE U.S. EVER BEEN REQUESTED BY YOU OR ON YOUR BEHALF? ☐ NO ☐ YES

27. ARE ANY OF THE FOLLOWING IN THE U.S., RESIDE IN THE U.S., OR HAVE U.S. LEGAL PERMANENT RESIDENCE? (Check the boxes that apply and indicate that person's status in the U.S., i.e., studying, working, permanent resident, U.S. citizen, etc.)

☐ SPOUSE _____   ☐ BROTHER/SISTER _____   ☐ FIANCE/E _____

☐ PARENT _____   ☐ SON/DAUGHTER _____   _____

28. WHERE HAVE YOU LIVED FOR THE PAST FIVE YEARS? DO NOT INCLUDE PLACES YOU HAVE VISITED FOR PERIODS OF SIX MONTHS OR LESS.

Countries	Cities	Approximate Dates

29. IMPORTANT: ALL PARTICIPANTS MUST READ AND CHECK THE APPROPRIATE BOX FOR EACH ITEM.
A visa may not be issued to persons who are within specific categories defined by law as inadmissable to the United States (except when a waiver is obtained in advance). Are any of the following applicable to you?

- Have you ever been afflicted with a communicable disease of public health significance, a dangerous physical or mental disorder, or been a drug abuser or addict? [212(a)(1)] ☐ YES ☐ NO

- Have you ever been arrested or convicted for any offense or crime, even though subject of a pardon, amnesty or other similiar legal action? Have you ever distributed or sold a controlled substance (drug), or been a prostitute or procurer for prostitutes? [212(a)(2)] ☐ YES ☐ NO

- Do you seek to enter the United States to engage in export control violations, subversive or terrorist activities, or any other unlawful purpose? Are you a member or representative of a terrorist organization as currently designated by the U.S. Secretary of State? Have you ever participated in persecutions directed by the Nazi government of Germany; or have you ever participated in genocide? [212(a)(3)] ☐ YES ☐ NO

- Have you ever been refused admission to the U.S., or the subject of a deportation hearing, or sought to obtain or assist others to obtain a visa, entry into the U.S., or sought to obtain a visa or any U.S. Immigration benefit by fraud or wilful misrepresentation? Have you attended a U.S. public elementary school on student (F) status, or a public secondary school without reimbursing the school after November 30, 1996? [212(a)(6)] ☐ YES ☐ NO

- Have you ever departed or remained outside the United States to avoid military service? [212(a)(8)] ☐ YES ☐ NO

- Have you ever violated the terms of a U.S. visa, or been unlawfully present in, or deported from, the United States? [212(a)(9)] ☐ YES ☐ NO

- Have you ever withheld custody of a U.S. citizen child outside the United States from a person granted legal custody by a U.S. court, voted in the United States in violation of any law or regulation, or renounced U.S. citizenship for the purpose of avoiding taxation? [212(a)(10)] ☐ YES ☐ NO

A YES answer does not automatically signify ineligibility for a visa, but if you answered YES to any of the above, or if you have any question in this regard, personal appearance at this office is recommended. If appearance is not possible at this time, attach a statement of facts in your case to this application.

30. I certify that I have read and understood all the questions set forth in this application and the answers I have furnished on this form are true and correct to the best of my knowledge and belief. I understand that any false or misleading statement may result in the permant refusal of a visa or denial of entry into the United States. I understand that possession of a visa does not entitle the bearer to enter the United States of America upon arrival at port of entry if he or she is found inadmissible.

APPLICANT'S SIGNATURE _____

DATE OF APPLICATION _____

If this application has been prepared by a travel agency or another person on your behalf, the agent should indicate name and address of agency or person with appropriate signature of individual preparing form.

SIGNATURE OF PERSON PREPARING FORM _____
(If other than applicant)

DO NOT WRITE IN THIS SPACE

37mm x 37mm

──── PHOTO ────

Glue Photo Here

OMB Approval No. 44-R1301

U.S. DEPARTMENT OF LABOR
Employment and Training Administration

APPLICATION
FOR
ALIEN EMPLOYMENT CERTIFICATION

IMPORTANT: READ CAREFULLY BEFORE COMPLETING THIS FORM
PRINT legibly in ink or use a typewriter. If you need more space to answer questions in this form, use a separate sheet. Identify each answer with the number of the corresponding question. SIGN AND DATE each sheet in original signature.

To knowingly furnish any false information in the preparation of this form and any supplement thereto or to aid, abet, or counsel another to do so is a felony punishable by $10,000 fine or 5 years in the penitentiary, or both (18 U.S.C. 1001)

PART A. OFFER OF EMPLOYMENT

1. Name of Alien   (Family name in capital letter, First, Middle, Maiden)

2. Present Address of Alien   (Number, Street, City and Town, State ZIP code or Province, Country)

3. Type of Visa   (If in U.S.)

The following information is submitted as an offer of employment.

4. Name of Employer   (Full name of Organization)

5. Telephone

6. Address   (Number, Street, City and Town, State ZIP code)

7. Address Where Alien Will Work   (if different from item 6)

8. Nature of Employer's Business Activity

9. Name of Job Title

10. Total Hours Per Week
   a. Basic   b. Overtime

11. Work Schedule (Hourly)
   a.m.
   p.m.

12. Rate of Pay
   a. Basic $ per _____   b. Overtime $ per hour

13. Describe Fully the job to be Performed   (Duties)

14. State in detail the MINIMUM education, training, and experience for a worker to perform satisfactorily the job duties described in item 13 above.

15. Other Special Requirements

EDU-CATION (Enter number of years)	Grade School	High School	College	College Degree Required (specify)
				Major Field of Study

TRAIN-ING	No. Yrs.	No. Mos.	Type of Training

EXPERI-ENCE	Job Offered		Related Occupation		Related Occupation (specify)
	Yrs.	Mos.	Yrs.	Mos.	

Number

16. Occupational Title of Person Who Will Be Alien's Immediate Supervisor

17. Number of Employees Alien Will Supervise

◄ ENDORSEMENTS   (Make no entry in section - for Government use only)

Date Forms Received	
L.O.	S.O.
R.O.	N.O.
Ind. Code	Occ. Code
Occ. Title	

Replaces MA 7-50A, B and C (Apr. 1970 edition) which is obsolete.

ETA 750 (Oct. 1979)

18. COMPLETE ITEMS ONLY IF JOB IS TEMPORARY			19. IF JOB IS UNIONIZED (Complete)	
a. No. of Openings To Be Filled By Aliens Under Job Offer	b. Exact Dates You Expect To Employ Alien		a. Number of Local	b. Name of Local
	From	To		
				c. City and State

20. STATEMENT FOR LIVE-AT-WORK JOB OFFERS (Complete for Private Household ONLY)

a. Description of Residence		b. No. Persons residing at Place of Employment			c. Will free board and private room not shared with any-one be provided?	("X" one)
("X" one) ☐ House ☐ Apartment	Number of Rooms	Adults	Children	Ages		☐ YES ☐ NO
		BOYS				
		GIRLS				

21. DESCRIBE EFFORTS TO RECRUIT U.S. WORKERS AND THE RESULTS. (Specify Sources of Recruitment by Name)

22. Applications require various types of documentation. Please read Part II of the instructions to assure that appropriate supporting documentation is included with your application.

23. EMPLOYER CERTIFICATIONS

By virtue of my signature below, I HEREBY CERTIFY the following conditions of employment.

a. I have enough funds available to pay the wage or salary offered the alien.

b. The wage offered equals or exceeds the prevailing wage and I guarantee that, if a labor certification is granted, the wage paid to the alien when the alien begins work will equal or exceed the prevailing wage which is applicable at the time the alien begins work.

c. The wage offered is not based on commissions, bonuses, or other incentives, unless I guarantee a wage paid on a weekly, bi-weekly, or monthly basis.

d. I will be able to place the alien on the payroll on or before the date of the alien's proposed entrance into the United States.

e. The job opportunity does not involve unlawful discrimination by race, creed, color, national origin, age, sex, religion, handicap, or citizenship.

f. The job opportunity is not:

(1) Vacant because the former occupant is on strike or is being locked out in the course of a labor dispute involving a work stoppage.

(2) At issue in a labor dispute involving a work stoppage.

g. The job opportunity's terms, conditions and occupational environment are not contrary to Federal, State or local law.

h. The job opportunity has been and is clearly open to any qualified U.S. worker.

24. DECLARATIONS

DECLARATION OF EMPLOYER ➤ Pursuant to 28 U.S.C. 1746, I declare under penalty of perjury the foregoing is true and correct.

SIGNATURE	DATE
NAME (Type or Print)	TITLE

AUTHORIZATION OF AGENT OF EMPLOYER ➤ I HEREBY DESIGNATE the agent below to represent me for the purposes of labor certification and I TAKE FULL RESPONSIBILITY for accuracy of any representations made by my agent.

SIGNATURE OF EMPLOYER	DATE
NAME OF AGENT (Type or Print)	ADDRESS OF AGENT (Number, Street, City, State, ZIP code)

SAMPLE

PART B. STATEMENT OF QUALIFICATIONS OF ALIEN

FOR ADVICE CONCERNING REQUIREMENTS FOR ALIEN EMPLOYMENT CERTIFICATION: If alien is in the U.S., contact nearest office of Immigration and Naturalization Service. If alien is outside U.S., contact nearest U.S. Consulate.

IMPORTANT: READ ATTACHED INSTRUCTIONS BEFORE COMPLETING THIS FORM.

Print legibly in ink or use a typewriter. If you need more space to fully answer any questions on this form, use a separate sheet. Identify each answer with the number of the corresponding question. Sign and date each sheet.

1. Name of Alien (Family name in capital letters)	First name	Middle name	Maiden name

2. Present Address (No., Street, City or Town, State or Province and ZIP code)	Country	3. Type of Visa (If in U.S.)

4. Alien's Birthdate (Month, Day, Year)	5. Birthplace (City or Town, State or Province)	Country	6. Present Nationality or Citizenship (Country)

7. Address in United States Where Alien Will Reside

8. Name and Address of Prospective Employer if Alien has job offer in U.S.	9. Occupation in which Alien is Seeking Work

10. "X" the appropriate box below and furnish the information required for the box marked

		City in Foreign Country	Foreign Country
a.	☐ Alien will apply for a visa abroad at the American Consulate in		

		City	State
b.	☐ Alien is in the United States and will apply for adjustment of status to that of a lawful permanent resident in the office of the Immigration and Naturalization Service at		

11. Names and Addresses of Schools, Colleges and Universities Attended (Include trade or vocational training facilities)	Field of Study	FROM		TO		Degrees or Certificates Received
		Month	Year	Month	Year	

SPECIAL QUALIFICATIONS AND SKILLS

12. Additional Qualifications and Skills Alien Possesses and Proficiency in the use of Tools, Machines or Equipment Which Would Help Establish if Alien Meets Requirements for Occupation in Item 9.

13. List Licenses (Professional, journeyman, etc.)

14. List Documents Attached Which are Submitted as Evidence that Alien Possesses the Education, Training, Experience, and Abilities Represented

Endorsements	DATE REC. DOL
	O.T. & C.
(Make no entry in this section - FOR Government Agency USE ONLY)	

(Items continued on next page)

15. WORK EXPERIENCE.	List all jobs held during the last three (3) years. Also, list any other jobs related to the occupation for which the alien is seeking certification as indicated in item 9.				

a. NAME AND ADDRESS OF EMPLOYER

NAME OF JOB	DATE STARTED Month	Year	DATE LEFT Month	Year	KIND OF BUSINESS

DESCRIBE IN DETAIL THE DUTIES PERFORMED, INCLUDING THE USE OF TOOLS, MACHINES OR EQUIPMENT	NO. OF HOURS PER WEEK

b. NAME AND ADDRESS OF EMPLOYER

NAME OF JOB	DATE STARTED Month	Year	DATE LEFT Month	Year	KIND OF BUSINESS

DESCRIBE IN DETAIL THE DUTIES PERFORMED, INCLUDING THE USE OF TOOLS, MACHINES OR EQUIPMENT	NO. OF HOURS PER WEEK

c. NAME AND ADDRESS OF EMPLOYER

NAME OF JOB	DATE STARTED Month	Year	DATE LEFT Month	Year	KIND OF BUSINESS

DESCRIBE IN DETAIL THE DUTIES PERFORMED, INCLUDING THE USE OF TOOLS, MACHINES OR EQUIPMENT	NO. OF HOURS PER WEEK

16. DECLARATIONS

DECLARATION OF ALIEN ➤	Pursuant to 28 U.S.C. 1746, I declare under penalty of perjury the foregoing is true and correct.

SIGNATURE OF ALIEN	DATE

AUTHORIZATION OF AGENT OF ALIEN ➤	I hereby designate the agent below to represent me for the purposes of labor certification and I take full responsibility for accuracy of any representations made by my agent.

SIGNATURE OF ALIEN	DATE

NAME OF AGENT (Type or print)	ADDRESS OF AGENT (No., Street, City, State, ZIP code)

SAMPLE

15. WORK EXPERIENCE.		List all jobs held during the last three (3) years. Also, list any other jobs related to the occupation for which the alien is seeking certification as indicated in item 9.				

d. NAME AND ADDRESS OF EMPLOYER

NAME OF JOB	DATE STARTED Month	Year	DATE LEFT Month	Year	KIND OF BUSINESS

DESCRIBE IN DETAIL THE DUTIES PERFORMED, INCLUDING THE USE OF TOOLS, MACHINES OR EQUIPMENT	NO. OF HOURS PER WEEK

e. NAME AND ADDRESS OF EMPLOYER

NAME OF JOB	DATE STARTED Month	Year	DATE LEFT Month	Year	KIND OF BUSINESS

DESCRIBE IN DETAIL THE DUTIES PERFORMED, INCLUDING THE USE OF TOOLS, MACHINES OR EQUIPMENT	NO. OF HOURS PER WEEK

f. NAME AND ADDRESS OF EMPLOYER

NAME OF JOB	DATE STARTED Month	Year	DATE LEFT Month	Year	KIND OF BUSINESS

DESCRIBE IN DETAIL THE DUTIES PERFORMED, INCLUDING THE USE OF TOOLS, MACHINES OR EQUIPMENT	NO. OF HOURS PER WEEK

16. DECLARATIONS

DECLARATION OF ALIEN	➤	Pursuant to 28 U.S.C. 1746, I declare under penalty of perjury the foregoing is true and correct.	

SIGNATURE OF ALIEN	DATE

AUTHORIZATION OF AGENT OF ALIEN	➤	I hereby designate the agent below to represent me for the purposes of labor certification and I take full responsibility for accuracy of any representations made by my agent.	

SIGNATURE OF ALIEN	DATE

NAME OF AGENT (Type or print)	ADDRESS OF AGENT (No., Street, City, State, ZIP code)

Labor Condition Application for H-1B &H-1B1 Nonimmigrants

U.S. Department of Labor
Employment and Training Administration

Form ETA 9035
OMB Approval: 1205-0310
Expiration Date: 09/30/2005

A. Program Designation
You must choose one of the following: ○ H-1B   ○ H-1B1 Chile   ○ H-1B1 Singapore

B. Employer's Information

If you want the application returned by mail, leave the Return Fax Number blank.

1. Return Fax Number
([ ][ ][ ]) [ ][ ][ ] - [ ][ ][ ][ ]

2. Employer's Name

3. Employer's Address (Number and Street)

4. Employer's City   State   Zip/Postal Code

5. Employer's EIN Number   6. Employer's Phone Number   Extension
[ ][ ] - [ ][ ][ ][ ][ ][ ][ ]   ([ ][ ][ ]) [ ][ ][ ] - [ ][ ][ ][ ]

C. Rate of Pay

1. Wage Rate (or Rate From) (Required):
$ [ ][ ][ ][ ][ ] . [ ][ ]

2. Rate Up To (Optional):
$ [ ][ ][ ][ ][ ] . [ ][ ]

3. Rate is Per:
○ Year   ○ Week
○ Month   ○ Hour
○ 2 Weeks

4. Is this position part-time?
○ Yes
○ No

Please Note: Part-time hours worked by nonimmigrant(s) will be in the range of hours stated on the USCIS Form(s) I-129.

D. Period of Employment and Occupation Information *Please Note: The Date Information MUST be in MM/DD/YYYY format*

1. Begin Date
[ ][ ] / [ ][ ] /

2. End Date
[ ][ ] / [ ][ ] /

3. Occupational Code

4. Number of H-1B or H-1B1 Nonimmigrants

5. Job Title

E. Information Relating to Work Location for the H-1B or H-1B1 Nonimmigrants   **This section is REQUIRED**

Do NOT write "Same As Above". This section MUST be filled out.

1. City   State

2. Prevailing Wage
$ [ ][ ][ ][ ][ ] . [ ][ ]

3. Wage is Per:
○ Year   ○ Week
○ Month   ○ Hour
○ 2 Weeks

4. Wage Source
○ SESA
○ Collective Bargaining Agreement
○ Other

If OTHER is chosen as the Wage Source, Numbers 5 and 6 in this section MUST be filled out.

5. Year Source Published

6. Other Wage Source

Page Link
[6][3][1][6][7][5]

If filing the form electronically, the Page Link field will be automatically created for you upon printing. If filing the form manually, please ensure that the Page Link field contains a 6 digit number that is repeated on all 3 pages.

50346

Labor Condition Application for H-1B &H-1B1 Nonimmigrants	U.S. Department of Labor Employment and Training Administration	Form ETA 9035 OMB Approval: 1205-0310 Expiration Date: 09/30/2005

E. Subsection A Information for Additional or Subsequent Work Location
This Section should be completed only if filing for more than 1 work location.

1. City

State

2. Prevailing Wage

$ [   ] . [   ]

3. Wage is Per:
○ Year   ○ Week
○ Month   ○ Hour
○ 2 Weeks

4. Wage Source
○ SESA
○ Collective Bargaining Agreement
○ Other

If OTHER is chosen as the Wage Source, Numbers 5 and 6 in this section MUST be filled out.

5. Year Source Published

6. Other Wage Source

F. Employer Labor Condition Statements

! **Please Note: In order for your application to be processed, you MUST read section E of the Labor Condition Application cover pages under the heading "Employer Labor Condition Statements" and agree to all 4 labor condition statements summarized below:**

(1) Wages: Pay nonimmigrants at least the local prevailing wage or the employer's actual wage, whichever is higher, and pay for non-productive time. Offer nonimmigrants benefits on the same basis as U.S. workers.

(2) Working Conditions: Provide working conditions for nonimmigrants which will not adversely affect the working conditions of workers similarly employed.

(3) Strike, Lockout, or Work Stoppage: No strike or lockout in the occupational classification at the place of employment.

(4) Notice: Notice to union or to workers at the place of employment. A copy of this form to H-1B and H-1B1 workers.

I have read and agree to Employer Labor Condition Statements 1, 2, 3, and 4 as set forth in Section E of the Labor Condition Application Cover Pages.   ○ Yes   ○ No

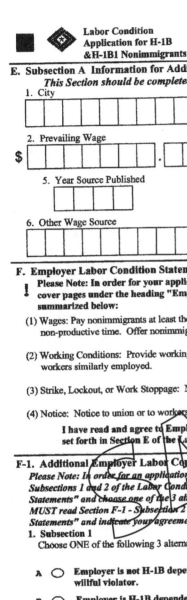

F-1. Additional Employer Labor Condition Statements - H-1B Employers Only

Please Note: In order for an application regarding H-1B nonimmigrants to be processed, you MUST read Section F-1 - Subsections 1 and 2 of the Labor Condition Application cover pages under the heading "Additional Employer Labor Condition Statements" and choose one of the 3 alternatives (A, B, or C) listed below in Subsection 1. If you mark Alternative B, you MUST read Section F-1 - Subsection 2 of the cover pages under the heading "Additional Employer Labor Condition Statements" and indicate your agreement to all 3 additional statements summarized below in Subsection 2.

1. Subsection 1
Choose ONE of the following 3 alternatives:

A ○ Employer is not H-1B dependent and is not a willful violator.

B ○ Employer is H-1B dependent and/or a willful violator.

C ○ Employer is H-1B dependent and/or a willful violator BUT will use this application ONLY to support H-1B petitions for exempt nonimmigrants.

2. Subsection 2
If Alternative B in Subsection 1 is marked, the following Additional Labor Condition Statements are applicable:

A. Displacement: Non-displacement of the U.S. workers in employer's work force;

B. Secondary Displacement: Non-displacement of U.S. workers in another employer's work force; and

C. Recruitment and Hiring: Recruitment of U.S. workers and hiring of U.S. worker applicant(s) who are equally or better qualified than the H-1B nonimmigrant(s).

I have read and agree to Additional Labor Condition Statements 2 A, B, and C.   ○ Yes   ○ No

Page Link							If filing the form electronically, the Page Link field will be automatically created for you upon printing. If filing the form manually, please ensure that the Page Link field contains a 6 digit number that is repeated on all 3 pages.
6	3	1	6	7	5		50346

Form ETA 9035 - Page 2 of 3

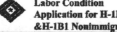

Labor Condition Application for H-1B &H-1B1 Nonimmigrants	U.S. Department of Labor Employment and Training Administration	Form ETA 9035 OMB Approval: 1205-0310 Expiration Date: 09/30/2005

G. Public Disclosure Information
You must choose one of the two options listed in this Section.

1. Public disclosure information will be kept at: ◯ Employer's principal place of business

◯ Place of employment

H. Declaration of Employer

By signing this form, I, on behalf of the employer, attest that the information and labor condition statements provided are true and accurate; that I have read the sections E, F, and F-1 of the cover pages (Form ETA 9035CP), and that I agree to comply with the Labor Condition Statements as set forth in the cover pages and with the Department of Labor regulations (20 CFR part 655, Subparts H and I). I agree to make this application, supporting documentation, and other records available to officials of the Department of Labor upon request during any investigation under the Immigration and Nationality Act.

1. First Name of Hiring or Other Designated Official   MI

2. Last Name of Hiring or Other Designated Official

3. Hiring or Other Designated Official Title

5. Date Signed

4. Signature - Do NOT let signature extend beyond the box

Making fraudulent representations on this Form can lead to civil or criminal action under 18 U.S.C. 1001, 18 U.S.C. 1546, or other provisions of law.

I. Contact Information

1. Contact First Name   MI

2. Contact Last Name

3. Contact Phone Number   Extension

(   )   -

J. U.S. Government Agency Use Only

By virtue of my signature below, I hereby acknowledge this application certified for

Date Starting _____   and Date Ending _____

_____
Signature and Title of Authorized DOL Official   ETA Case Number   Date

The Department of Labor is not the guarantor of the accuracy, truthfulness, or adequacy of a certified labor condition application.

K. Complaints

Complaints alleging misrepresentation of material facts in the labor condition application and/or failure to comply with the terms of the labor condition application may be filed with any office of the Wage and Hour Division, U.S. Department of Labor. Complaints alleging failure to offer employment to an equally or better qualified U.S. worker, or an employer's misrepresentation regarding such offer(s) of employment, may be filed with: U.S Department of Justice * Office of the Special Counsel for Immigration-Related Unfair Employment Practices* 950 Pennsylvania Ave. NW * Washington, DC * 20530.

Page Link						If filing the form electronically, the Page Link field will be automatically created for you upon printing. If filing the form manually, please ensure that the Page Link field contains a 6 digit number that is repeated on all 3 pages.
6	3	1	6	7	5	

50346

Form ETA 9035 - Page 3 of 3

OMB Approval: 1205-0451
Expiration Date: 03/31/2008

Application for Permanent Employment Certification
ETA Form 9089
U.S. Department of Labor

Please read and review the filing instructions before completing this form. A copy of the instructions can be found at http://workforcesecurity.doleta.gov/foreign/.

Employing or continuing to employ an alien unauthorized to work in the United States is illegal and may subject the employer to criminal prosecution, civil money penalties, or both.

A. Refiling Instructions

1. Are you seeking to utilize the filing date from a previously submitted Application for Alien Employment Certification (ETA 750)?	❏ Yes	❏ No
1-A. If Yes, enter the previous filing date		
1-B. Indicate the previous SWA or local office case number OR if not available, specify state where case was originally filed:		

B. Schedule A or Sheepherder Information

1. Is this application in support of a Schedule A or Sheepherder Occupation?	❏ Yes	❏ No
If Yes, do NOT send this application to the Department of Labor. All applications in support of Schedule A or Sheepherder Occupations must be sent directly to the appropriate Department of Homeland Security Office.		

C. Employer Information (Headquarters or Main Office)

1. Employer's name			
2. Address 1			
Address 2			
3. City	State/Province	Country	Postal code
4. Phone number		Extension	
5. Number of employees		6. Year commenced business	
7. FEIN (Federal Employer Identification Number)			8. NAICS code
9. Is the employer a closely held corporation, partnership, or sole proprietorship in which the alien has an ownership interest, or is there a familial relationship between the owners, stockholders, partners, corporate officers, incorporators, and the alien?		❏ Yes	❏ No

D. Employer Contact Information (This section must be filled out. This information must be different from the agent or attorney information listed in Section E).

1. Contact's last name	First name		Middle initial
2. Address 1			
Address 2			
3. City	State/Province	Country	Postal code
4. Phone number		Extension	
5. E-mail address			

ETA Form 9089

OMB Approval: 1205-0451   Application for Permanent Employment Certification
Expiration Date: 03/31/2008   ETA Form 9089
                                      U.S. Department of Labor

E. Agent or Attorney Information (If applicable)

1. Agent or attorney's last name	First name	Middle initial

2. Firm name

3. Firm EIN	4. Phone number	Extension

5. Address 1

   Address 2

6. City	State/Province	Country	Postal code

7. E-mail address

F. Prevailing Wage Information (as provided by the State Workforce Agency)

1. Prevailing wage tracking number (if applicable)	2. SOC/O*NET(OES) code

3. Occupation Title	4. Skill Level

5. Prevailing wage   Per: (Choose only one)
   $ ❑ Hour   ❑ Week   ❑ Bi-Weekly   ❑ Month   ❑ Year

6. Prevailing wage source (Choose only one)
   ❑ OES   ❑ CBA   ❑ Employer Conducted Survey   ❑ DBA   ❑ SCA   ❑ Other

6-A. If Other is indicated in question 6, specify:

7. Determination date	8. Expiration date

G. Wage Offer Information

1. Offered wage
   From: To: (Optional)   Per: (Choose only one)
   $ $ ❑ Hour   ❑ Week   ❑ Bi-Weekly   ❑ Month   ❑ Year

H. Job Opportunity Information (Where work will be performed)

1. Primary worksite (where work is to be performed) address 1

   Address 2

2. City	State	Postal code

3. Job title

4. Education: minimum level required:
❑ None   ❑ High School   ❑ Associate's   ❑ Bachelor's   ❑ Master's   ❑ Doctorate   ❑ Other

4-A. If Other is indicated in question 4, specify the education required:

4-B. Major field of study

5. Is training required in the job opportunity?   5-A. If Yes, number of months of training required:
   ❑ Yes   ❑ No

OMB Approval: 1205-0451
Expiration Date: 03/31/2008

Application for Permanent Employment Certification
ETA Form 9089
U.S. Department of Labor

H. Job Opportunity Information Continued

5-B. Indicate the field of training:
6. Is experience in the job offered required for the job?   6-A. If Yes, number of months experience required: ❑ Yes   ❑ No
7. Is there an alternate field of study that is acceptable?   ❑ Yes   ❑ No
7-A. If Yes, specify the major field of study:
8. Is there an alternate combination of education and experience that is acceptable?   ❑ Yes   ❑ No
8-A. If Yes, specify the alternate level of education required: ❑ None   ❑ High School   ❑ Associate's   ❑ Bachelor's   ❑ Master's   ❑ Doctorate   ❑ Other
8-B. If Other is indicated in question 8-A, indicate the alternate level of education required:
8-C. If applicable, indicate the number of years experience acceptable in question 8:
9. Is a foreign educational equivalent acceptable?   ❑ Yes   ❑ No
10. Is experience in an alternate occupation acceptable?   10-A. If Yes, number of months experience in alternate occupation required: ❑ Yes   ❑ No
10-B. Identify the job title of the acceptable alternate occupation:
11. Job duties – If submitting by mail, add attachment if necessary. Job duties description must begin in this space.
12. Are the job opportunity's requirements normal for the occupation?   ❑ Yes   ❑ No   *If the answer to this question is No, the employer must be prepared to provide documentation demonstrating that the job requirements are supported by business necessity.*
13. Is knowledge of a foreign language required to perform the job duties?   ❑ Yes   ❑ No   *If the answer to this question is Yes, the employer must be prepared to provide documentation demonstrating that the language requirements are supported by business necessity.*
14. Specific skills or other requirements – If submitting by mail, add attachment if necessary. Skills description must begin in this space.

OMB Approval: 1205-0451   Application for Permanent Employment Certification
Expiration Date: 03/31/2008   ETA Form 9089

U.S. Department of Labor

H. Job Opportunity Information Continued

15. Does this application involve a job opportunity that includes a combination of occupations?	❏ Yes ❏ No
16. Is the position identified in this application being offered to the alien identified in Section J?	❏ Yes ❏ No
17. Does the job require the alien to live on the employer's premises?	❏ Yes ❏ No
18. Is the application for a live-in household domestic service worker?	❏ Yes ❏ No
18-A. If Yes, have the employer and the alien executed the required employment contract and has the employer provided a copy of the contract to the alien?	❏ Yes ❏ No ❏ NA

I. Recruitment Information

a. Occupation Type – All must complete this section.

1. Is this application for a **professional occupation**, other than a college or university teacher? Professional occupations are those for which a bachelor's degree (or equivalent) is normally required.	❏ Yes ❏ No
2. Is this application for a college or university teacher? **If Yes, complete questions 2-A and 2-B below.**	❏ Yes ❏ No
2-A. Did you select the candidate using a competitive recruitment and selection process?	❏ Yes ❏ No
2-B. Did you use the basic recruitment process for professional occupations?	❏ Yes ❏ No

b. Special Recruitment and Documentation Procedures for College and University Teachers – Complete only if the answer to question I.a.2-A is Yes.

3. Date alien selected:
4. Name and date of national professional journal in which advertisement was placed:
5. Specify additional recruitment information in this space. Add an attachment if necessary.

c. Professional/Non-Professional Information – **Complete this section unless your answer to question B.1 or I.a.2-A is YES.**

6. Start date for the SWA job order	7. End date for the SWA job order
8. Is there a Sunday edition of the newspaper in the area of intended employment?	❏ Yes ❏ No
9. Name of newspaper (of general circulation) in which the first advertisement was placed:	
10. Date of first advertisement identified in question 9:	
11. Name of newspaper or professional journal (if applicable) in which second advertisement was placed:	
	❏ Newspaper ❏ Journal

ETA Form 9089   Page 4 of 10

OMB Approval: 1205-0451   Application for Permanent Employment Certification
Expiration Date: 03/31/2008   ETA Form 9089
                                    U.S. Department of Labor

I. Recruitment Information Continued

12. Date of second newspaper advertisement or date of publication of journal identified in question 11:

d. Professional Recruitment Information – Complete if the answer to question I.a.1 is YES or if the answer to I.a.2-B is YES.   Complete at least 3 of the items.

13. Dates advertised at job fair From: To:	14. Dates of on-campus recruiting From: To:
15. Dates posted on employer web site From: To:	16. Dates advertised with trade or professional organization From: To:
17. Dates listed with job search web site From: To:	18. Dates listed with private employment firm From: To:
19. Dates advertised with employee referral program From: To:	20. Dates advertised with campus placement office From: To:
21. Dates advertised with local or ethnic newspaper From: To:	22. Dates advertised with radio or TV ads From: To:

e. General Information – All must complete this section.

23. Has the employer received payment of any kind for the submission of this application?	❏ Yes ❏ No		
23-A. If Yes, describe details of the payment including the amount, date and purpose of the payment:			
24. Has the bargaining representative for workers in the occupation in which the alien will be employed been provided with notice of this filing at least 30 days but not more than 180 days before the date the application is filed?	❏ Yes	❏ No	❏ NA
25. If there is no bargaining representative, has a notice of this filing been posted for 10 business days in a conspicuous location at the place of employment, ending at least 30 days before but not more than 180 days before the date the application is filed?	❏ Yes	❏ No	❏ NA
26. Has the employer had a layoff in the area of intended employment in the occupation involved in this application or in a related occupation within the six months immediately preceding the filing of this application?	❏ Yes	❏ No	
26-A. If Yes, were the laid off U.S. workers notified and considered for the job opportunity for which certification is sought?	❏ Yes	❏ No	❏ NA

J. Alien Information (This section must be filled out. This information must be different from the agent or attorney information listed in Section E).

1. Alien's last name	First name	Full middle name
2. Current address 1		
Address 2		

3. City	State/Province	Country	Postal code

4. Phone number of current residence

5. Country of citizenship	6. Country of birth
7. Alien's date of birth	8. Class of admission
9. Alien registration number (A#)	10. Alien admission number (I-94)

11. Education: highest level achieved relevant to the requested occupation: ❏   None   ❏   High School   ❏   Associate's   ❏   Bachelor's   ❏   Master's   ❏   Doctorate   ❏   Other

ETA Form 9089   Page 5 of 10

OMB Approval: 1205-0451
Expiration Date: 03/31/2008

Application for Permanent Employment Certification
ETA Form 9089
U.S. Department of Labor

J. Alien Information Continued

11-A. If Other indicated in question 11, specify	
12. Specify major field(s) of study	
13. Year relevant education completed	
14. Institution where relevant education specified in question 11 was received	
15. Address 1 of conferring institution	
Address 2	

16. City	State/Province	Country	Postal code

17. Did the alien complete the training required for the requested job opportunity, as indicated in question H.5?	❏ Yes ❏ No ❏ NA
18. Does the alien have the experience as required for the requested job opportunity indicated in question H.6?	❏ Yes ❏ No ❏ NA
19. Does the alien possess the alternate combination of education and experience as indicated in question H.8?	❏ Yes ❏ No ❏ NA
20. Does the alien have the experience in an alternate occupation specified in question H.10?	❏ Yes ❏ No ❏ NA
21. Did the alien gain any of the qualifying experience with the employer in a position substantially comparable to the job opportunity requested?	❏ Yes ❏ No ❏ NA
22. Did the employer pay for any of the alien's education or training necessary to satisfy any of the employer's job requirements for this position?	❏ Yes ❏ No
23. Is the alien currently employed by the petitioning employer?	❏ Yes ❏ No

K. Alien Work Experience

List all jobs the alien has held during the past 3 years. Also list any other experience that qualifies the alien for the job opportunity for which the employer is seeking certification.

a. *Job 1*

1. Employer name	
2. Address 1	
Address 2	

3. City	State/Province	Country	Postal code

4. Type of business	5. Job title	
6. Start date	7. End date	8. Number of hours worked per week

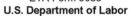

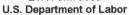

OMB Approval: 1205-0451
Expiration Date: 03/31/2008

Application for Permanent Employment Certification
ETA Form 9089
U.S. Department of Labor

K. Alien Work Experience Continued

9. Job details (duties performed, use of tools, machines, equipment, skills, qualifications, certifications, licenses, etc. Include the phone number of the employer and the name of the alien's supervisor.)

b. Job 2

1. Employer name			
2. Address 1			
Address 2			
3. City	State/Province	Country	Postal code
4. Type of business		5. Job title	
6. Start date	7. End date	8. Number of hours worked per week	

9. Job details (duties performed, use of tools, machines, equipment, skills, qualifications, certifications, licenses, etc. Include the phone number of the employer and the name of the alien's supervisor.)

c. Job 3

1. Employer name			
2. Address 1			
Address 2			
3. City	State/Province	Country	Postal code
4. Type of business		5. Job title	
6. Start date	7. End date	8. Number of hours worked per week	

OMB Approval: 1205-0451
Expiration Date: 03/31/2008

Application for Permanent Employment Certification

ETA Form 9089
U.S. Department of Labor

K. Alien Work Experience Continued

> 9. Job details (duties performed, use of tools, machines, equipment, skills, qualifications, certifications, licenses, etc. Include the phone number of the employer and the name of the alien's supervisor.)

L. Alien Declaration

I declare under penalty of perjury that Sections J and K are true and correct. I understand that to knowingly furnish false information in the preparation of this form and any supplement thereto or to aid, abet, or counsel another to do so is a federal offense punishable by a fine or imprisonment up to five years or both under 18 U.S.C. §§ 2 and 1001. Other penalties apply as well to fraud or misuse of ETA immigration documents and to perjury with respect to such documents under 18 U.S.C. §§ 1546 and 1621.

*In addition, I **further declare** under penalty of perjury that I intend to accept the position offered in Section H of this application if a labor certification is approved and I am granted a visa or an adjustment of status based on this application.*

1. Alien's last name	First name	Full middle name
2. Signature	Date signed	

Note – The signature and date signed do not have to be filled out when electronically submitting to the Department of Labor for processing, but must be complete when submitting by mail. If the application is submitted electronically, any resulting certification MUST be signed *immediately upon receipt* from DOL before it can be submitted to USCIS for final processing.

M. Declaration of Preparer

1. **Was the application completed by the employer?** If No, you must complete this section.	❑ Yes ❑ No

I hereby certify that I have prepared this application at the direct request of the employer listed in Section C and that to the best of my knowledge the information contained herein is true and correct. I understand that to knowingly furnish false information in the preparation of this form and any supplement thereto or to aid, abet, or counsel another to do so is a federal offense punishable by a fine, imprisonment up to five years or both under 18 U.S.C. §§ 2 and 1001. Other penalties apply as well to fraud or misuse of ETA immigration documents and to perjury with respect to such documents under 18 U.S.C. §§ 1546 and 1621.

2. Preparer's last name	First name	Middle initial
3. Title		
4. E-mail address		
5. Signature	Date signed	

Note – The signature and date signed do not have to be filled out when electronically submitting to the Department of Labor for processing, but must be complete when submitting by mail. If the application is submitted electronically, any resulting certification MUST be signed *immediately upon receipt* from DOL before it can be submitted to USCIS for final processing.

ETA Form 9089   Page 8 of 10

OMB Approval: 1205-0451
Expiration Date: 03/31/2008

Application for Permanent Employment Certification
ETA Form 9089
U.S. Department of Labor

N. Employer Declaration

By virtue of my signature below, ***I HEREBY CERTIFY*** *the following conditions of employment:*

1. The offered wage equals or exceeds the prevailing wage and I will pay at least the prevailing wage.
2. The wage is not based on commissions, bonuses or other incentives, unless I guarantees a wage paid on a weekly, bi-weekly, or monthly basis that equals or exceeds the prevailing wage.
3. I have enough funds available to pay the wage or salary offered the alien.
4. I will be able to place the alien on the payroll on or before the date of the alien's proposed entrance into the United States.
5. The job opportunity does not involve unlawful discrimination by race, creed, color, national origin, age, sex, religion, handicap, or citizenship.
6. The job opportunity is not:
    a. Vacant because the former occupant is on strike or is being locked out in the course of a labor dispute involving a work stoppage; or
    b. At issue in a labor dispute involving a work stoppage.
7. The job opportunity's terms, conditions, and occupational environment are not contrary to Federal, state or local law.
8. The job opportunity has been and is clearly open to any U.S. worker.
9. The U.S. workers who applied for the job opportunity were rejected for lawful job-related reasons.
10. The job opportunity is for full-time, permanent employment for an employer other than the alien.

I hereby designate the agent or attorney identified in section E (if any) to represent me for the purpose of labor certification and, by virtue of my signature in Block 3 below, **I take full responsibility** for the accuracy of any representations made by my agent or attorney.

I declare under penalty of perjury that I have read and reviewed this application and that to the best of my knowledge the information contained herein is true and accurate. *I understand that to knowingly furnish false information in the preparation of this form and any supplement thereto or to aid, abet, or counsel another to do so is a federal offense punishable by a fine or imprisonment up to five years or both under 18 U.S.C. §§ 2 and 1001. Other penalties apply as well to fraud or misuse of ETA immigration documents and to perjury with respect to such documents under 18 U.S.C. §§ 1546 and 1621.*

1. Last name	First name	Middle initial
2. Title		
3. Signature	Date signed	

Note – The signature and date signed do not have to be filled out when electronically submitting to the Department of Labor for processing, but must be complete when submitting by mail. If the application is submitted electronically, any resulting certification MUST be signed *immediately upon receipt* from DOL before it can be submitted to USCIS for final processing.

O. U.S. Government Agency Use Only

Pursuant to the provisions of Section 212 (a)(5)(A) of the Immigration and Nationality Act, as amended, I hereby certify that there are not sufficient U.S. workers available and the employment of the above will not adversely affect the wages and working conditions of workers in the U.S. similarly employed.

_____
Signature of Certifying Officer

_____
Date Signed

_____
Case Number

_____
Filing Date

ETA Form 9089

Page 9 of 10

OMB Approval: 1205-0451
Expiration Date: 03/31/2008

Application for Permanent Employment Certification
ETA Form 9089
U.S. Department of Labor

| **P. OMB Information** | *Paperwork Reduction Act Information Control Number 1205-0451* |

Persons are not required to respond to this collection of information unless it displays a currently valid OMB control number.

Respondent's reply to these reporting requirements is required to obtain the benefits of permanent employment certification (Immigration and Nationality Act, Section 212(a)(5)). Public reporting burden for this collection of information is estimated to average 1¼ hours per response, including the time for reviewing instructions, searching existing data sources, gathering and maintaining the data needed, and completing and reviewing the collection of information. Send comments regarding this burden estimate to the Division of Foreign Labor Certification * U.S. Department of Labor * Room C4312 * 200 Constitution Ave., NW * Washington, DC * 20210.
Do NOT send the completed application to this address.

Q. Privacy Statement Information

In accordance with the Privacy Act of 1974, as amended (5 U.S.C. 552a), you are hereby notified that the information provided herein is protected under the Privacy Act. The Department of Labor (Department or DOL) maintains a System of Records titled Employer Application and Attestation File for Permanent and Temporary Alien Workers (DOL/ETA-7) that includes this record.

Under routine uses for this system of records, case files developed in processing labor certification applications, labor condition applications, or labor attestations may be released as follows: in connection with appeals of denials before the DOL Office of Administrative Law Judges and Federal courts, records may be released to the employers that filed such applications, their representatives, to named alien beneficiaries or their representatives, and to the DOL Office of Administrative Law Judges and Federal courts, and in connection with administering and enforcing immigration laws and regulations, records may be released to such agencies as the DOL Office of Inspector General, Employment Standards Administration, the Department of Homeland Security, and the Department of State.

Further relevant disclosures may be made in accordance with the Privacy Act and under the following circumstances: in connection with federal litigation; for law enforcement purposes; to authorized parent locator persons under Pub. L. 93-647; to an information source or public authority in connection with personnel, security clearance, procurement, or benefit-related matters; to a contractor or their employees, grantees or their employees, consultants, or volunteers who have been engaged to assist the agency in the performance of Federal activities; for Federal debt collection purposes; to the Office of Management and Budget in connection with its legislative review, coordination, and clearance activities; to a Member of Congress or their staff in response to an inquiry of the Congressional office made at the written request of the subject of the record; in connection with records management; and to the news media and the public when a matter under investigation becomes public knowledge, the Solicitor of Labor determines the disclosure is necessary to preserve confidence in the integrity of the Department, or the Solicitor of Labor determines that a legitimate public interest exists in the disclosure of information, unless the Solicitor of Labor determines that disclosure would constitute an unwarranted invasion of personal privacy.

ETA Form 9089   Page 10 of 10

U.S. Citizenship and Immigration Services

USCIS Is Making Photos Simpler

**Old Three-Quarter
Style Photo**

**New Passport
Style Photo**

Photos Must Be in Color

Washington, DC — In accordance with language specified in the Border Security Act of 2003, U.S. Citizenship and Immigration Services (USCIS) announced a change in the photo requirements for all applicants from a three-quarter face position to a standard, full-frontal face position to take effect **August 2, 2004**.

USCIS will accept both three-quarter and full-frontal color photographs until **September 1, 2004,** after which only full-frontal color will be accepted.

The application process of customers who have already submitted materials that include color photos with the three-quarter standard **will not** be affected by this change.

All photos must be of just the person. Where more than one photo is required, all photos of the person must be identical. All photos must meet the specifications for full-frontal/passport photos.

For more information on photo standards, visit the Department of State website at http://www.travel.state.gov/passport/pptphotos/index.html, or contact the USCIS National Customer Service Center at 1 800 375 5283.

List of forms that require photos is on the back

M-603 (07/04)

Applications and Petitions That Require Photos, and the Number Required

2 photos are required for the following forms:

I-90 – Renew or replace your Permanent Resident Card (green card)

I-131 – Re-entry permit, refugee travel document, or advance parole

I-485 – Adjust status and become a permanent resident while in the U.S.

I-765 – Employment Authorization/Employment Authorization Document (EAD)

I-777 – Replace Northern Mariana Card

I-821 – Temporary Protected Status (TPS) Program

N-300 – Declaration of Intent (to apply for U.S. citizenship)

N-400 – Naturalization (to become a U.S. citizen)

N-565 – Replace Naturalization/Citizenship Certificate

3 photos are required for the following forms:

I-698 – Temporary Resident's application under the 1987 Legalization Program for permanent resident status — file 1 photo for your application, and bring the other 2 with you to your interview

N-600K – To apply for U.S. citizenship for foreign-born child residing abroad with U.S. citizen parent

4 photos are required for the following forms:

I-817 – To apply for Family Unity Benefits

I-881 – NACARA — suspension of deportation or special rule cancellation

File the following with your photos and of others as shown below:

I-129F – Fiancé(e) Petition — file with 1 photo of you + 1 photo of fiancé(e)

I-130 – Relative petition — if filing for your husband or wife, file with 1 photo of you + 1 photo of your husband or wife

I-589 – Asylum — file with 1 photo of you + 1 photo of each family member listed in Part A. II that you are including in your application

I-730 – Relative petition filed by a person granted Asylum or Refugee status — file with 1 photo of the family member for whom you are filing the I-730

I-914 – 'T' nonimmigrant status — file with 3 photos of you + 3 photos of each immediate family member for which you file an I-914A supplement

All photos must be of just the person. Where more than one photo is required, all photos of the person must be identical. All photos must meet the specifications for full-frontal/passport photos.

For more information, visit our website at www.uscis.gov, or call our customer service at 1 800 375 5283.

20
Directory of Immigrations Lawyers

The next several pages contain names of attorneys who are members of the American Immigration Lawyer's Association. Next Decade, Inc. has no affiliation with these attorneys. However, if you choose to contact them, please let them know that you obtained their name from this book.

CALIFORNIA

Michael W. Schoenleber,
Attorney at Law
Schoenleber & Waltermire,
911 22nd Street
Sacramento, CA 95816
(916) 441-5327
(916) 669-1046 (fax)
info@mwslaw.com

Evelyn G. Zneimer, Esquire
Law Offices of Evelyn G. Zneimer
1930 Wilshire Boulevard, Suite 910
Los Angeles, CA 90057
(213) 484-2106
(213) 484-2037 (fax)
ezneimer@socal.rr.com

CONNECTICUT

Robert A. Maresca, Attorney
Antignani & Maresca, P.C.
275 Congress Street
Bridgeport, CT 06604
(203) 367-8437
(203) 367-4440 (fax)
marescalaw.imm@snet.net

Andrew L. Wizner, Partner
Leete, Kosto & Wizner, LLP
21 Oak Street, Suite 309
Hartford, CT 06106
(860) 249-8100
(860) 727-9184 (fax)
awizner@lkwvisa.com (personal)
lkw@lkwvisa.com (firm-wide general email box)

Elizabeth B. Leete (Partner)
Leete, Kosto & Wizner, LLP
21 Oak Street, Suite 309
Hartford, CT 06106
(860) 249-8100
(860) 727-9184 (fax)
eleete@lkwvisa.com (personal)
lkw@lkwvisa.com (firm-wide general email box)

Gale Kosto (Partner)
Leete, Kosto & Wizner, LLP
21 Oak Street, Suite 309
Hartford, CT 06106
(860) 249-8100
(860) 727-9184 (fax)
gkosto@lkwvisa.com (personal)
lkw@lkwvisa.com (firm-wide general email box)

Eric Fleischmann, Partner
Leete, Kosto & Wizner, LLP
21 Oak Street, Suite 309
Hartford, CT 06106
(860) 249-8100
(860) 727-9184 (fax)
ericf@lkwvisa.com (personal)
lkw@lkwvisa.com (firm-wide general
email box)

FLORIDA

James R. LaVigne, President
LaVigne, Coton & Associates, P.A.
7087 Grand National Drive, Suite 100
Orlando, FL 32819
(407) 316-9988
(407) 316-8820 (fax)
attylavign@aol.com

ILLINOIS

Scott D. Pollock, President
Scott D. Pollock & Associates, P.C.
105 W. Madison Street, Suite 2200
Chicago,IL 60602
(312) 444-1940
(312) 444-1950 (fax)
spollock@lawfirm1.com

Maria Baldini-Potermin
Scott D. Pollock & Associates, P.C.
105 W. Madison Street, Suite 2200
Chicago,IL 60602
(312) 444-1940
(312) 444-1950 (fax)
mbaldini-potermin@lawfirm1.com

Marta Delgado, Associate
Scott D. Pollock & Associates, P.C.
105 W. Madison Street, Suite 2200
Chicago,IL 60602
(312) 444-1940
(312) 444-1950 (fax)
mdelgado@lawfirm1.com

Kathryn Weber, Associate
Scott D. Pollock & Associates, P.C.
105 W. Madison Street, Suite 2200
Chicago,IL 60602
(312) 444-1940
(312) 444-1950 (fax)
kweber@lawfirm1.com

Fatima Mohyuddin, Associate
Scott D. Pollock & Associates, P.C.
105 W. Madison Street, Suite 2200
Chicago,IL 60602
(312) 444-1940
(312) 444-1950 (fax)
fmohyuddin@lawfirm1.com

Anne Relias, Associate
Scott D. Pollock & Associates, P.C.
105 W. Madison Street, Suite 2200
Chicago,IL 60602
(312) 444-1940
(312) 444-1950 (fax)
aralias@lawfirm1.com

Ben H. Kim, Attorney
Law Offices of Ben H. Kim &
Associates
3403 W. Lawrence Ave., Suite 201
Chicago, IL 60625
(773) 583-3558
(773) 583-1022 (fax)

MARYLAND

Michael L. Kabik, Chairman-
Immigration, Nationality and
Consular Practice Group
Shulman, Rogers, Gandal, Pordy &
Ecker, P.A.
11921 Rockville Pike
Rockville, MD 20852
(301) 231-0937
(301) 230-2891 (fax)
mkabik@srgpe.com

MICHIGAN
Michael E. Wooley, Esquire
Braun Kendrick Finkbeiner P.L.C.
4301 Fashion Square Boulevard
Saginaw, MI 48603
(989) 498-2100
(989) 799-4666 (fax)
mikwoo@bkf-law.com

MONTANA
James P. Sites, Attorney
Crowley, Haughey, Hanson, Toole &
Dietrich, P.L.L.P.
500 TransWestern Plaza II
490 N. 31st Street, PO Box 2529
Billings, MT 59103
(406) 252-3441
(406) 256-8526 (fax)
jsites@crowleylaw.com

NEW JERSEY
Alan M. Lubiner, Attorney at Law
Lubiner & Schmidt
216 North Avenue East
Cranford, NJ 07016
(908) 709-0500
(908) 709-9447 (fax)
alubiner@lslawyers.com

Vratislav Pechota, Jr., Esq.
Law Office of Vratislav Pechota, Jr.
100 Overlook Centre (Regus), 2nd Fl
Princeton, NJ 08540
(917) 653-4550
(212) 244-0355 (fax)
immigration@prodigy.net

Susan W. Scheer, Esq.
18 Macculloch Ave.
Morristown, NJ 07960
(973) 984-8400
(973) 984-8490
laurie@susanscheerlaw.com

Anthony F. Siliato, Esq.
Meyner and Landis LLP
One Gateway Center- Suite 2500
Newark, NJ 07102
(973) 624-2800
(973) 624-0356 (fax)
asiliato@meyner.com

Jerard A. Gonzalez, Esq.
Meyner and Landis LLP
One Gateway Center- Suite 2500
Newark, NJ 07102
(973) 624-2800
(973) 624-0356 (fax)
jgonzalez@meyner.com

Jerard A. Gonzalez, Esq.
Meyner and Landis LLP
25 Mian Street-Suite 200
Hackensack, NJ 07601
(201) 489-1351
(201) 489-1353 (fax)
jgonzalez@meyner.comc

NEW YORK
Alan M. Lubiner, Attorney at Law
Lubiner & Schmidt
111 Broadway
New York, NY 10006
(212) 227-4100
(212) 406-3244 (fax)
alubiner@lslawyers.com

Vratislav Pechota, Jr., Esq.
Law Office of Vratislav Pechota, Jr.
14 Penn Plaza, 255 West 34th Street,
Suite 1806
New York, NY 10122
(212) 268-4969
(212) 244-0355
immigration@prodigy.net

OHIO

Farhad Sethna, Attorney
Law Office of Farhad Sethna
17 South Main Street, Suite 201
Akron, OH 44308-1803
(330) 376-6766
(330) 376-7344 (fax)
www.immigration-america.com

Margaret Wong, Managing Partner,
Attorney
Margaret Wong & Assoc. Co., LPA
3150 Chester Avenue
MWW Center, Suite 200
Cleveland, OH 44114
(216) 566-9908
(216) 566-1125 (fax)
wong@imwong.com

Scott Bratton, Partner, Attorney
Margaret Wong & Assoc. Co., LPA
3150 Chester Avenue
MWW Center, Suite 200
Cleveland, OH 44114
(216) 566-9908
(216) 566-1125 (fax)
bratton@imwong.com

Lawrence Hadfield, Attorney
Margaret Wong & Assoc. Co., LPA
3150 Chester Avenue
MWW Center, Suite 200
Cleveland, OH 44114
(216) 566-9908
(216) 566-1125 (fax)
hadfield@imwong.com

Troy Murphy, Attorney
Margaret Wong & Assoc. Co., LPA
3150 Chester Avenue
MWW Center, Suite 200
Cleveland, OH 44114
(216) 566-9908
(216) 566-1125 (fax)
murphy@imwong.com

Lori Pinjuh, Attorney
Margaret Wong & Assoc. Co., LPA
3150 Chester Avenue
MWW Center, Suite 200
Cleveland, OH 44114
(216) 566-9908
(216) 566-1125 (fax)
pinjuh@imwong.com

Susan Saliba, Attorney
Margaret Wong & Assoc. Co., LPA
3150 Chester Avenue
MWW Center, Suite 200
Cleveland, OH 44114
(216) 566-9908
(216) 566-1125 (fax)
saliba@imwong.com

TENNESSEE

Barry L. Frager, Attorney at Law
The Frager Law Firm, P.C.
5100 Poplar Avenue, Suite 2204
Memphis, TN 38137
(901) 763-3188
(901) 763-3475 (fax)
Toll Free: 1-888-889 VISA (8472)
bfrager@fragerlawfirm.com

Ari J. Sauer (Licensed in NY & NJ only)
The Frager Law Firm, P.C.
5100 Poplar Avenue, Suite 2204
Memphis, TN 38137
(901) 763-3188
(901) 763-3475 (fax)
Toll Free: 1-888-889 VISA (8472)
bfrager@fragerlawfirm.com

Barry L. Frager, Attorney at Law
The Frager Law Firm, P.C.
1040 Murfreesboro Pike, Suite 206
Nashville, TN 37217
(615) 366-1000
(615) 366-1444 (fax)
Toll Free: 1-866-421-0900
bfrager@fragerlawfirm.com

VIRGINIA
Kenneth J. Lasky, Attorney
Magee, Foster, Goldstein & Sayers, P.C.
310 First Street, S.W., Suite 1200
Roanoke, VA 24011
(540) 343-9800
(540) 343-9898 (fax)
klasky@mfgs.com

APPENDIX A
Filing Fees for Frequently Used Immigration Forms

FORM		FEE
I-90	Application to Replace Permanent Residence Card	$190
I-102	Application by Nonimmigrant Alien for Replacement of Arrival Document	$160
I-129	Petition for a Nonimmigrant Worker	$190
I-129F	Petition for Alien Fiance	$170
I-130	Petition for Alien Relative	$170
I-131	Application for Travel Document	$165
I-140	Immigrant Petition for Alien Worker	$195
I-360	Petition for Amerasian, Widow(er), or Special Immigrant	$190
I-485	Application to Register Permanent Residence or Adjust Status	$325
	($215.00 under age 14)	
I-526	Immigrant Petition by Alien Entrepreneur	$480
I-539	Application to Extend/Change Nonimmigrant Status	$200
I-751	Petition to Remove Conditions on Residence	$205
I-765	Application for Employment Authorization	$180
N-400	Application for Naturalization	$330
Biometrics fee (for those applications that require fingerprinting)		$70

APPENDIX B
USCIS Service Office Addresses

There are four Regional Service Centers in the U.S. that process most routine non-immigrant and immigrant visa petitions, as well as all naturalization applications.

Vermont Service Center (VSC)

(direct mailing address)
U.S. Department of Homeland Security
75 Lower Welden Street
St. Albans, VT 05479-0001

(this address for N-400 Naturalization applications)
U.S. Department of Homeland Security
75 Lower Welden Street
St. Albans, VT 05479-9400

Service Area: The VSC accepts and processes certain applications and petitions from individuals residing in the following states: Connecticut, Delaware, Maine, Maryland, Massachusetts, New Hampshire, New Jersey, New York, Pennsylvania, Puerto Rico, Rhode Island, Vermont, Virginia, Virgin Islands, West Virginia, and the District of Columbia.

The following applications and petitions must be filed, by mail, at the Service Center:

IAP-66, I-102, I-129F, I-129, I-129S, I-130, I-131, I-140, I-360, I-485, I-526, I-539, I-589, I-690, I-694, I-695, I-698, I-751, I-765, I-817, I-821, I-824, I-829, N-400, G-639, Waivers, Appeals and Motions relating to cases denied at Service Centers.

All forms not listed above should be filed with your local USCIS Office. See addresses listed below.

Nebraska Service Center (NSC)

(this address for general correspondence)
P.O Box 82521
Lincoln, NE 68501-2521

Service Area: The NSC accepts and processes certain applications and petitions from individuals residing in the following states: Alaska, Colorado, Idaho, Illinois, Indiana, Iowa, Kansas, Michigan, Minnesota, Missouri, Montana, Nebraska, North Dakota, Ohio, Oregon, South Dakota, Utah, Washington, Wisconsin and Wyoming.

Texas Service Center (TSC)

(this address for general correspondence)   (courier delivery)
USCIS TSC   USCIS TSC
PO Box 851488   4141 N. St. Augustine Road
Mesquite, TX 75185-1488   Dallas, TX 75227

Service Area: The TSC accepts and processes certain applications and petitions from individuals residing in the following states: Alabama, Arkansas, Florida, Georgia, Kentucky, Louisiana, Mississippi, New Mexico, North Carolina, South Carolina, Oklahoma, Tennessee, and Texas.

California Service Center (CSC)

(this address for mail)
U.S. Department of Homeland Security
USCIS
California Service Center
P.O. Box 30111
Laguna Niguel, CA 92607-0111

Service Area: The CSC accepts and processes certain applications and petitions from people residing in the following states: California, Nevada, Arizona, Hawaii, and the Territory of Guam.

As noted previously, there are some applications, the most common being Form I-90 that are still filed with the local USCIS offices. The addresses are provided below. All telephone inquiries should be made to USCIS Customer Service at 1-800-375-5283.

ALASKA   New Federal Building
                    620 East 10th Ave, Rm. 102
                    Anchorage, AK 99501-3701

ARIZONA   Federal Building   Federal Building
                    2035 North Central Ave.   6431 S. Country Club Rd.
                    Phoenix, AZ 85004   Tucson, AZ 85706

ARKANSAS   4977 Old Greenwood Road
                    Fort Smith, AR 72903

CALIFORNIA

Federal Building
1177 Fulton Mall
Fresno, CA 93721

Federal Building
300 North Los Angeles St.
Los Angeles, CA 90012

650 Capitol Mall
Sacramento, CA 95814

U.S. Federal Building
880 Front St., Rm. 1234
San Diego, CA 92101-8834

Appraisers Building
630 Sansome St.
San Francisco, CA 94111-2280

1887 Monterey Road
San Jose, CA 95112

34 Civic Center Plaza
Santa Ana, CA 92701

655 W. Rialto Avenue
San Bernardino, CA 92410-3327

COLORADO

Albrecht Center
4730 Paris St.
Denver, CO 80239

CONNECTICUT

Abraham Ribicoff Federal Building
450 Main St., 4th Floor
Hartford, CT 06103-3060

DELAWARE

1305 McD Drive
Dover, DE 19901

DISTRICT OF COLUMBIA

Washington District Office
2675 Prosperity Avenue
Fairfax, VA 22031

FLORIDA

4121 Southpoint Blvd.
Jacksonville, FL 32216

7880 Biscayne Blvd.
Miami, FL 33138

9403 Tradeport Drive
Orlando, FL 32827

5524 W. Cypress
Tampa, FL 33607

West Palm Beach Satellite Office
326 Fern St-Suite 200
West Palm Beach, FL 33401

GEORGIA

Dr. Martin Luther King, Jr. Federal Building
77 Forsyth St., SW, Room 111
Atlanta, GA 30303-0253

GUAM	Sirena Plaza, Suite 801 108 Hernan Cortez Ave. Agana, Guam 96910
HAWAII	595 Ala Moana Blvd. Honolulu, HI 96813
IDAHO	1185 South Vinnell Way Boise, ID 83709
ILLINOIS	10 West Jackson Blvd, # 610 Chicago, IL 60604
INDIANA	Gateway Plaza, Suite 400 950 North Meridian St. Indianapolis, IN 46204
IOWA	Des Moines Sub-Office 210 Walnut Street, Room 369 Federal Building Des Moines, IA 50309
KANSAS	271 West 3rd St. North, Suite 1050 Wichita, KS 67202-1212
KENTUCKY	Gene Snyder US Custom House 601 West Broadway, Rm. 601 Louisville, KY 40202
LOUISIANA	Postal Service Building 701 Loyola Ave., Rm. T-8011 New Orleans, LA 70113
MAINE	176 Gannett Drive Portland, ME 04106
MARYLAND	Fallon Federal Building 31 Hopkins Plaza Baltimore, MD 21201
MASSACHUSETTS	John F. Kennedy Federal Office Building Government Center, Rm. 1700 Boston, MA 02203

MICHIGAN	Federal Building 333 Mount Elliott St. Detroit, MI 48207-4381
MINNESOTA	2901 Metro Drive, Suite 100 Bloomington, MN 55425
MISSISSIPPI	Dr. McCoy Federal Building 100 West Capitol Street, Suite 727 Jackson, MS 39269
MISSOURI	9747 Northwest Conant Ave. Kansas City, MO 64153
	1222 Spruce Street St. Louis, MO 63103
MONTANA	2800 Skyway Drive Helena, MT 59602
NEBRASKA	3736 South 132nd St. Omaha, NE 68144

NEVADA

3373 Pepper Lane
Las Vegas, NV 89120

1351 Corporate Boulevard
Reno, NV 89502-7102

NEW HAMPSHIRE

803 Canal Street
Manchester, NH 03101

NEW JERSEY

Federal Building
970 Broad St.
Newark, NJ 07102

1886 Greentree Road
Cherry Hill, NJ 08003

NEW MEXICO

1720 Randolph Rd., SE
PO Box 567
Albuquerque, NM 87106
Tel.# 505 241 0450
Fax: 505 241 0452

NEW YORK	1086 Troy-Schenecdady Rd. Latham, NY 12110 Tel.# 518 220 2100 Fax: 518 220 2171	130 Delaware Ave Buffalo, NY 14202 Tel. # 716 849 6760 Fax: 716 551 3131
	Jacob Javits Federal Bldg. 26 Federal Plaza New York, NY 10278 Tel.# 212 264 5891	711 Stewart Ave. Garden City, NY 11530 Tel.# 516 228 9242 (Citizenship only for Queens, Brooklyn, Nassau and Suffolk)
	Federal Building 100 State Street, Room 418 Rochester, NY 14614 Tel.# 1 800 375 5283 (National Customer Service Center)	412 South Warren Street Syracuse, NY 13202 Tel.# 1 800 375 5283 (National Customer Service Center)
NORTH CAROLINA	210 E. Woodlawn Rd., Bldg. 6, Suite 138 Woodlawn Green Office Complex Charlotte, NC 28217 Tel.# 704 672 6990 Fax: 704 672 6969	
OHIO	J.W. Peck Federal Bldg. 550 Main St., Rm. 4001 Cincinnati, OH 45202	A.J. Celebreeze Federal Office Bldg. 1240 E. 9th St., Rm. 501 Cleveland, OH 44199
	50 W. Broad Street Leveque Tower olumbus, OH 43215	
OKLAHOMA	4400 SW 44th Street, Suite "A" Oklahoma City, OK 73119-2800	
OREGON	Federal Office Building 511 N.W. Broadway Portland, OR 97209	
PENNSYLVANIA	1600 Callowhill St. Philadelphia, PA 19130	3000 Sidney St., Suite 241 Pittsburgh, PA 15203

PUERTO RICO
San Patricio Office Center
7 Tabonuco St., Suite 100
Guaynabo, PR 00968

PO Box 365068
San Juan, PR 00936

RHODE ISLAND
200 Dyer Street
Providence, RI 02903

SOUTH CAROLINA
1 Poston Road, Suite 130
Parkshore Center
Charleston, SC 29407

TENNESSEE
1341 Sycamore View, Suite 100
Memphis, TN 38134

TEXAS
Federal Building
8101 N. Stemmons Freeway
Dallas, TX 75247

1545 Hawkins Blvd., Ste. 167
El Paso, TX 79925

1717 Zoy Street
Harlingen, TX 78552

126 North Point
Houston, TX 77060

US Federal Building
8940 Four Winds Drive
San Antonio, TX 78239

U.S. VIRGIN ISLANDS
Nisky Center
Suite 1A, 1st Floor
Charlotte Amalie, St. Thomas, U.S.V.I. 00802

PO Box 1468
Kingshill, St. Croix, U.S.V.I. 00851

UTAH
5272 S. College Dr., Suite 100
Salt Lake City, UT 84123

VERMONT
64 Gricebrook Rd
St. Albans, VT 05478

VIRGINIA
Norfolk Commerce Park
5280 Henneman Drive
Norfolk, VA 23513

WASHINGTON	12500 Tukwila International Blvd Seattle, WA 98168	U.S. Courthouse 920 W. Riverside, Room 691 Spokane, WA 98201
	415 North 3rd Street Yakima, WA 98901	
WEST VIRGINIA	210 Kanawha Boulevard West Charleston, WV 25302	
WISCONSIN	310 East Knapp Street Milwaukee, WI 53202	

There are no USCIS offices in the following states. Contact the USCIS office in parentheses for further information.

ALABAMA (Atlanta, Georgia)
NORTH DAKOTA (Bloomington, Minnesota)
SOUTH DAKOTA (Bloomington, Minnesota
WYOMING (Denver, Colorado)

**USCIS Headquarters
425 "I" Street, NW
Washington, DC 20536**

Overseas Offices
There are also three overseas District Offices that have jurisdiction for U.S. immigration matters outside the U.S. They are located in Bangkok, Thailand; Mexico City, Mexico; and Rome, Italy. Each of these offices has suboffices as follows:

Bangkok-Beijing, Guangzhou, Ho Chi Minh City, Hong Kong, Manila, Seoul

Mexico City-Ciudad Juarez, Guatemala City, Havana, Kingston, Lima, Monterrey, Panama City, Port-au-Prince, San Salvador, Santo Domingo, Tegucigalpa, Tijuana

Rome-Accra, Athens, Frankfurt, Islamabad, Johannesburg, London, Moscow, Nairobi, New Delhi, Vienna

APPENDIX C
U.S. Department of Labor Office Addresses

Region I.
Labor certification applications processed for jobs in Connecticut, Maine, Massachusetts, New Hampshire, New Jersey, New York, Rhode Island and Vermont, Puerto Rico and the U.S. Virgin Islands

    U.S. Department of Labor
    ETA/Alien Labor Certification
    JFK Federal Building-Rm. E-350
    Boston, MA 02203
    Tel.# 617 788-0170
    Fax: 617 788-0101

Region II.
Labor certification applications processed for jobs in Delaware, District of Columbia, Maryland, Pennsylvania, Virginia and West Virginia.

    U.S. Department of Labor
    ETA
    The Curtis Center
    170 South Independence Mall West, Suite 825 East
    Philadelphia, PA 19106
    Tel.# 215 861 5200

Region III.
Labor certification applications processed for jobs in Alabama, Florida, Georgia, Kentucky, Mississippi, North Carolina, South Carolina and Tennessee.

    U.S. Department of Labor
    ETA
    Atlanta Federal Center, Room 6M12
    61 Forsyth Street
    Atlanta, GA 30303
    Tel.# 404 562 2092
    Fax: 404 562 2149

Region IV.
Labor certification applications processed for jobs in Arkansas, Colorado, Louisiana, Montana, New Mexico, North Dakota, Oklahoma, South Dakota, Texas, Utah and Wyoming.

    U.S. Department of Labor
    ETA
    525 Griffin Street, Suite 317
    Dallas, Texas 75202
    Tel.# 214 767 8263
    Fax: 214 767 5113

Region V.
Labor certification applications processed for jobs in Illinois, Indiana, Iowa, Kansas, Michigan, Minnesota, Missouri, Nebraska, Ohio and Wisconsin.

    U.S. Department of Labor
    ETA
    230 South Dearborn Street, 6th Floor
    Chicago, IL 60604
    Tel.# 312 596 5400

Region VI.
Labor certification applications processed for jobs in Alaska, Arizona, California, Guam, Hawaii, Idaho, Nevada, Oregon and Washington.

    U.S. Department of Labor
    ETA
    71 Stevenson Street, Suite 830
    PO Box 193767
    San Francisco, CA 94119-3767
    Tel.# 415 975 4610
    Fax: 415 975 4612

APPENDIX D
U.S. Passport Agencies

These offices serve customers who are traveling within 2 weeks (14 days), or who need foreign visas to travel.

Most offices open between 8:00 and 9:00 a.m. and close between 3:00 and 4:00 p.m., Monday through Friday, excluding Federal holidays

Boston, Massachusetts
Thomas P. O'Neill Federal Building
10 Causeway Street, Suite 247
Boston, MA 02222-1094
Automated Appointment Number:
(877) 487-2778

Chicago, Illinois
Kluczynski Federal Office Building
230 S. Dearborn, 18th Floor
Chicago, IL 60604-1564
Automated Appointment Number:
(312) 341-6020

Honolulu, Hawaii
Prince Kuhio Federal Building
300 Ala Moana Blvd.-Suite 1-330
Honolulu, HI 96850
Recorded Information: (808) 522-8283

Houston, Texas
Mickey Leland Federal Building
1919 Smith Street, Suite 1400
Houston, TX 77002-8049
Automated Appointment Number:
(713) 751-0294

Norwalk, Connecticut
50 Washington Street
Norwalk, CT 06854
Automated Appointment Number:
(203) 299-5443

Los Angeles, California
Federal Building
11000 Wilshire Blvd.-Suite 1000
Los Angeles, CA 90024-3615
Automated Appointment Number:
(310) 575-5700

Miami, Florida
Claude Pepper Federal Office Building
51 SW First Ave.-3rd Floor
Miami, FL 33130-1680
Automated Appointment Number:
(305) 539-3600

New Orleans, Louisiana
One Canal Place (corner of Canal and North Peters Street)
365 Canal Street, Suite 1300
New Orleans, LA 70130-6508
Automated Appointment Number:
(504) 412-2600

New York City, New York
376 Hudson Street
New York, NY 10014
Automated Appointment Number:
(212) 206-3500
Note: This office is no longer able to accept walk-in customers who do not have an appointment.

Philadelphia, Pennsylvania
U.S. Custom House
200 Chestnut Street, Room 103
Philadelphia, PA 19106-2970
Automated Appointment Number:
(215) 418-5937

San Francisco, California
95 Hawthorne Street, 5th Floor
San Francisco, CA 94105-3901
Automated Appointment Number:
(415) 538-2700

Seattle, Washington
Henry Jackson Federal Building
915 Second Ave.-Suite 992
Seattle, WA 98174-1091
Automated Appointment Number:
(206) 808-5700

Washington, DC
1111 19th Street, N.W.
Washington, DC 20524
Automated Appointment Number: (202) 647-0518

Special Issuance Agency
1111 19th Street, NW, Suite 200
Washington, DC 20036
Note: Applications for Diplomatic, Official, and
No-Fee Passports

INDEX

BOOK ORDER FORM

Two easy ordering methods:

Credit Card Orders
Call the publisher, Next Decade, Inc.
Telephone: 800-595-5440

Check or Money Orders
Complete this form, attach your payment,
and mail to:
Next Decade, Inc.
39 Old Farmstead Road, Chester, NJ 07930

If you have any questions, call us: Telephone: 908-879-6625
Email: info@nextdecade.com   www.nextdecade.com

YOUR NAME AND TITLE: _____

NAME OF ORGANIZATION (if applicable): _____

STREET ADDRESS: _____

CITY: _____ STATE: _____ ZIP: _____

TELEPHONE: _____ FAX: _____

E-MAIL: _____

Please ship _____ copies of **Immigration Made Simple** at $22.95 per copy $ _____

Please ship _____ copies of **Citizenship Made Simple** at $16.95 per copy $ _____

NJ orders ONLY add 6% sales tax if required $ _____

Shipping: Add $5.00 for the first copy and $1.00 for each additional copy $ _____

I HAVE ENCLOSED THE TOTAL $ _____

A check/money order made payable to **Next Decade, Inc.** for $ _____ is enclosed.

Credit Card Payments: ❏ Visa   ❏ Mastercard

Credit Card # (16 digits) _____ Expiration Date: _____

Name as it appears on the card: _____

Signature: _____